ILLAUNLOUGHAN ISLAND:

AN EARLY MEDIEVAL MONASTERY IN COUNTY KERRY

Illaunloughan Island:

an early medieval monastery in County Kerry

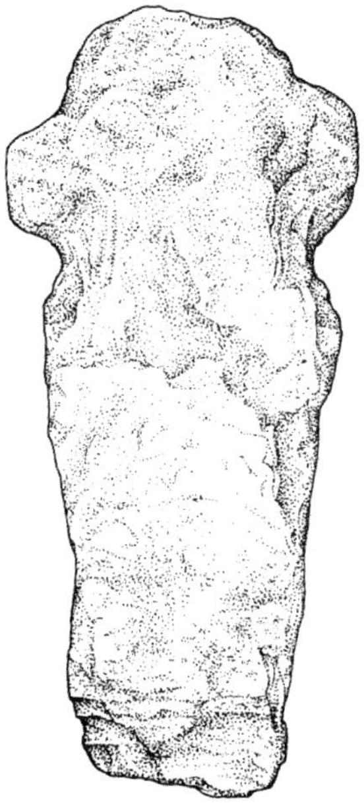

Jenny White Marshall and Claire Walsh

with

G.D. Rourke, E.V. Murray and F. McCormick

Word*well*

First published in 2005 by
Wordwell Ltd
PO Box 69, Bray, Co. Wicklow
www.wordwellbooks.com

Library of Congress Cataloging-in-Publication Data are available for this book.

A CIP catalogue record for this book is available from the British Library.

ISBN 1 869857 79 8

This publication has received support from the Heritage Council under the 2004 Publications Grant Scheme and from the Department of the Environment, Heritage and Local Government.

Cover design: Rachel Dunne

Copy-editing: Aisling Flood and Emer Condit

Typesetting and layout: Wordwell Ltd

Book design: Nick Maxwell

Printed by E.G. Zure S.A., Bilbao

The authors dedicate the book to good friends, now gone,
Rainer Berger and Frank Mitchell.

Contents

Preface

Illaunloughan was a small monastery on the Atlantic edge of Ireland, in use from the late seventh to the ninth century. The extensive and well-dated material evidence obtained through excavation provided a chronological framework for activities and architectural structures that were previously of uncertain age in Ireland; it also revealed the penetration of Christian practice from other parts of the world into a remote Irish monastery.

The evidence supports an eighth-century date for the construction of a drystone oratory and *leacht,* and a large gable shrine and its mound. The complex reliquary structure was built to honour the corporeal relics of the Illaunloughan saints, but the community also used the eastern quadrant of its mound as their graveyard, an indication that the Christian custom of burial near the saints was current in Ireland in this period. The fosterage of young children on island monastic sites was suggested by the discovery of their remains in the monastic graveyard.

Most excavation results are presented in formal archaeological format, but we believed that the evolution of an island monastic site might interest the general public as well as professional archaeologists. We have, therefore, divided the book into four sections.

Part 1 is an overview of the monastery written for the general public. It traces the development of the settlement over two periods, with the extensive use of many illustrations, plans, drawings and photos to make the material more accessible. The significance of Illaunloughan's structures, economy and architecture is analysed and compared with other regional sites.

Emily Murray and Finbar McCormick of Queen's University, Belfast, discuss the excellent preservation of midden remains, which permitted the first detailed quantitative analysis of diet and economy in the region. They found that the community used both wild and domestic resources, including meat, oats, seabirds and fish. They raise questions about the extent of mainland support of the monastery and the possibility that a marginal environment existed in the area at this time.

Grellan D. Rourke, Senior Conservation Architect for the Heritage Service, discusses the nature of drystone corbelled construction on the Iveragh and Dingle peninsulas of County Kerry. He also proposes a typological sequence that has chronological implications for drystone oratories.

Another chapter discusses the possible symbolism of white quartz stones, scallop shells and the shape of the reliquary shrine. The community placed white quartz stones and scallop shells in with the bones of the saints, apparently for symbolic spiritual purposes. White quartz stones are found on many early medieval Irish sites, but the unusual presence of scallop shells may reflect knowledge of a large scallop shell over the entry to the Tomb of Christ in Jerusalem.

Part 2 presents the full archaeological report in the classic format. This is primarily for archaeologists who seek more specific detailed information about the excavation.

Part 3 contains the finds catalogue.

Part 4 records the conservation of the island. Conservation techniques are of increasing importance and concern to the preservation of archaeological sites. The report also states clearly the limits of necessary reconstruction work.

The specialist reports are available online, or may be obtained on CD (see p. 253).

Acknowledgements

The excavation of Illaunloughan took place over four seasons between 1992 and 1995. Archaeological research is a composite of talents in the arts and the sciences; academic archaeology also benefits from substantial infusions of financial aid. It is with pleasure and deep appreciation that we acknowledge the people who assisted us.

Claire Cotter, the original co-director, organised the excavation and spent a couple of weeks with us before she left for the Discovery Programme, leaving the excavation in the capable hands of Claire Walsh. The archaeologists—Helen Kehoe, Franc Myles, Georgina Scally and Brian Hayden—managed to maintain their standards and good humour while dealing with revolving crews of volunteers with no excavation experience. Good friends Lee Snodgrass and Christine Wagnar joined us for part of two seasons. In times of emergency, when schedules fell behind, Alan Hayden whipped down from Dublin to give us a hand for a day or two that often turned into a week or two. He has generously allowed information from the excavations at Bray Head and Church Island to be cited in this report. The archaeologists, all professionals, made a further generous contribution to the project: they all worked at a substantial discount to their normal fees. Annabelle Konig served as both cook and archaeologist. She managed to cope with a variety of odd diet requirements with good grace.

Rainer Berger, former Chairman of Archaeology at the University of California, Los Angeles, worked with the excavation team for several years until ill health forced him to retire.

We were very fortunate to have Finbar McCormick of Queen's University, Belfast, join our group. He and some of his students, Brian Bentley and Catherine McLoughlin, spent several weeks collecting midden samples over the course of two excavation seasons. The subsequent report is skilfully summarised by Dr Emily Murray in Part 1. It is the most detailed quantitative study to date of the environmental remains of an Early Christian monastic site in Ireland. The specialist reports of Sheila Hamilton-Dyer, Tanya O'Sullivan, Laureen Buckley, Aidan O'Sullivan, Mary Deevy, Ellen O'Carroll, Brenda Collins and Gill M. Plunkett added considerably to our knowledge of island life during this period.

Grellan D. Rourke, Senior Conservation Architect of the Heritage Service, advised and aided us during the excavation, sharing his knowledge of early monastic sites and his expertise in conservation. Illaunloughan was in his district and he allows no site under his supervision to languish. He also generously allowed us access to his drawings, plans and results from the unpublished 1987 survey of the island. A true partner in our work, he wrote the chapters on drystone oratories and conservation of the island.

We thank the University of California Research Expedition Program volunteers for their enthusiastic and cheerful work on site. We enjoyed your company and benefited from your efforts in the field as well as from your financial support.

The cover of the book and all the aerial photographs are owed to the superb photography of Con Brogan, Senior Photographer of the Photographic Section of the Department of the Environment, Heritage and Local Government. We are also indebted to Tony Roche of the Photographic Section, who spent hours picking out the best photographs from its extensive collection. The finished plans are the superb work of Conor McHale, as are most of the finds drawings.

Conleth Manning, Ann Lynch and Ed Bourke, archaeologists from the Department of the Environment, Heritage and Local Government, supported, encouraged and advised the Illaunloughan project from its inception to publication. Raghnall Ó Floinn shared his encyclopaedic knowledge of early medieval sites and finds. Conservation of artefacts was undertaken by Adrian Kennedy and Susannah Kelly.

A.W.B. Vincent and Próinséas Ní Chatháin demonstrated remarkable and touching friendship and support for the excavation. Other good friends, Peter Harbison and Frank Mitchell, frequently dropped by the site and freely shared their knowledge with us.

Jerry O'Sullivan and John Sheehan read the text in rough draft and presented us with a detailed, informative critique, always a delicate, difficult chore for busy professionals. We were impressed by their efforts and happily adopted many of their suggestions. Any errors of misinterpretation or of knowledge, of course, are the fault of the authors.

The people of Valentia Island and Portmagee welcomed us, offered us hospitality and rescued us many a time from various predicaments. We owe particular thanks to Ted Kennedy, whose famous bus took us to work, and who helped plan tours around the countryside for our volunteers and kept an eye on our teenagers at discos. Joe O'Connell and his sons made sure we got to work and, better, came early to get us off the island in dismal conditions. Dermot Walsh loaned us a small boat for emergency exits. Brendan and Margaret O'Keefe enthusiastically supported hungry and thirsty archaeologists, who declared their pub, 'The Fisherman' in Portmagee, base camp.

Funding

The authors gratefully acknowledge financial support from:
The University of California Research Expedition Program
The American Ireland Fund
The Heritage Council
The National Monuments Section, Department of the Environment, Heritage and Local Government

PART 1:
OVERVIEW

Jenny White Marshall

and

Claire Walsh

Introduction

The remains of many small early medieval ecclesiastical settlements built in stone are still visible on the western coast of Ireland; many of them are to be found on the Dingle and Iveragh peninsulas of County Kerry. The Kerry sites are coastal, found either on offshore islands in the Atlantic or in rural areas within a few miles of the sea. Their construction in stone and location in sparsely populated areas have helped to identify and to preserve them.

Illaunloughan is the smallest of the island sites and the one closest to shore, situated only 400m west of the village of Portmagee (Fig. 1a, b). The tiny island, *c.* 0.1ha at high tide, is covered in grass and low-lying; most of it is only a few metres above sea level, except for a narrow ridge across the western end (Fig. 2). Its location in the channel shelters the island from the main force of the sea, although it is swept by gales and spray during severe winter storms. Strong winds, generally south-westerlies from the Atlantic, which reach gale strength more than 120 days a year, must have been the major climatic concern for inhabitants of the island. The marine climate, though extremely wet, with almost twice the rainfall of Dublin, is mild and even, with temperatures rarely ranging more than 10 degrees Celsius during the year (Mitchell 1989, 1).

Today, at low tide, it is possible to walk the 200m to the nearest shore, as the water is, at deepest, *c.* 1m; the channel becomes a mudflat during the exceptional low tides of the equinox. Centuries ago, however, before the erosion of mainland and island, the channel would have been deeper. Tidal currents and storms have visibly reduced the size of the island, as excavation revealed that a number of structures have been partially or completely scoured away. At the time of their construction, *c.* 1200–1300 years ago, the island must have been a minimum of 4–5m larger on each side (see below, discussion of domestic cells, enclosure wall etc.).

The underlying rock of the island, the most common throughout the Iveragh Peninsula, was formed in the later part of the Devonian period *c.* 350–400 million

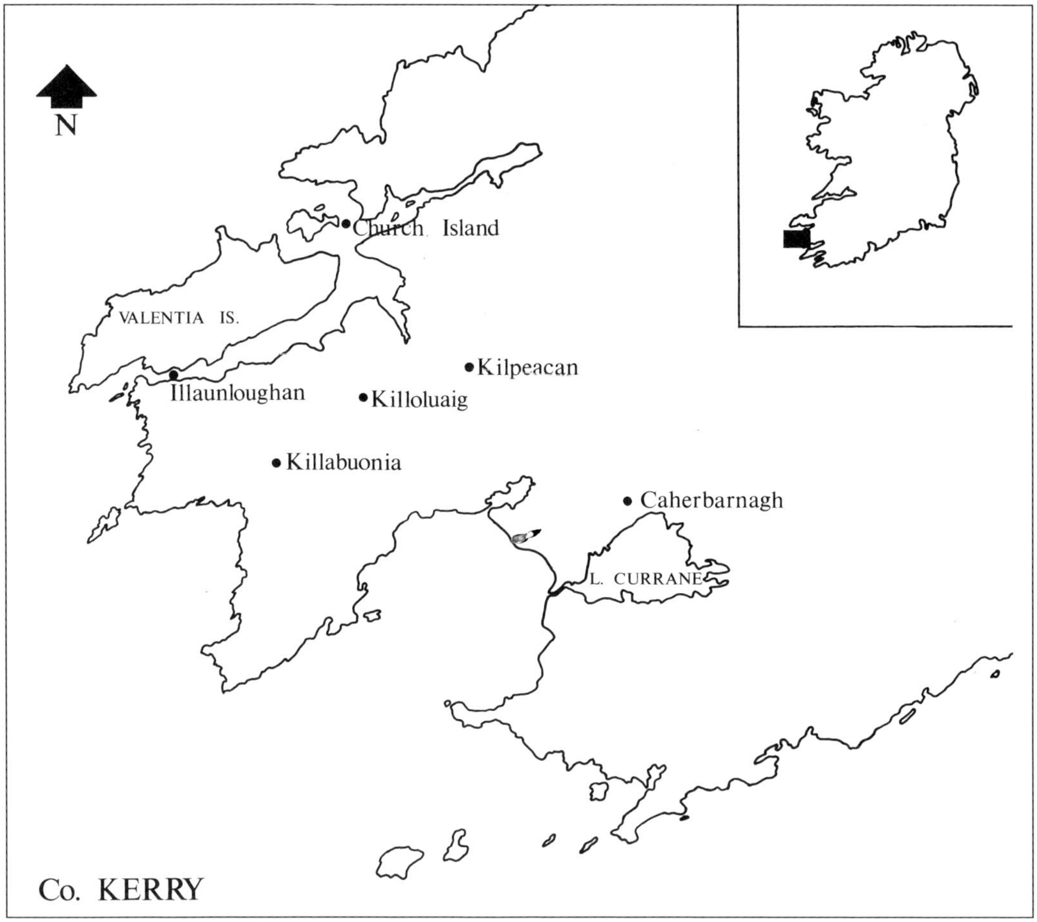

1a—Location map for Illaunloughan, Co. Kerry, showing neighbouring small ecclesiastical sites in south-western Kerry that may have had gable shrines similar to that of Illaunloughan. *(G.D. Rourke)*

years ago. Known as Devonian Old Red Sandstone, it is composed of compressed layers of sedimentary deposits, mixed with silt and gravel. Some 200 million years later, during the Armorican Upheaval, severe compression on Devonian clay deposits produced the fine-grained slate found on Valentia Island and Bolus Head.[1] This handsome stone was used for the oratory on Church Island in Valentia Harbour and for reliquary shrines at the nearby mainland site of Killoluaig and at Illaunloughan.

There are few historical references to the island; even the origin of its name, Loughan, is uncertain. Loughan may have been the name of a saint associated with the island, an assumption supported by the mention of two Lochāns in the *Martyrology of Oengus*, written *c.* AD 830 (Stokes 1905, 255, 263). There is another ecclesiastical site on the Iveragh Peninsula with a similar name, Killoughane (*Cill Lóchāin*), which may give some credence to the veneration of a particular saint in the region (O'Sullivan and Sheehan 1996, 357). Loughan may have a more mundane meaning, however, for Dinneen in his *Irish–English dictionary* defines *lóchān* as

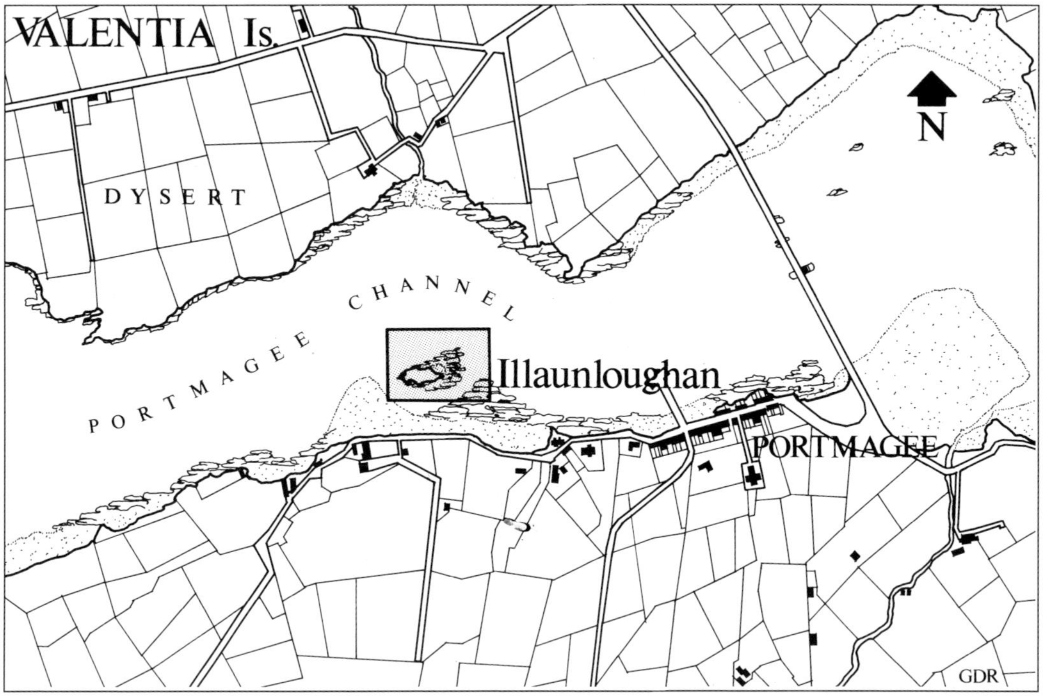

1b—Detailed location map for Illaunloughan, Co. Kerry, showing its position in the Portmagee Channel. *(G.D. Rourke)*

'chaff, light over-dried or withered grass' and further notes 'Oileán an Lócháin, the "Island of broken seaweed", a small island at the southern side of Valentia'.[2]

The foremost specialist on place-names for the Iveragh Peninsula today, Dr Breandán Ó Cíobháin, however, believes that the presence of ecclesiastical remains 'clinch the interpretation of the name as "Island of Lóchán" (a saint) and not Lóchán (an island)'. He adds that although the elements of *oileán, inis* (island) with a following saint's name are not common, there are two other examples of ecclesiastical islands with names of saints in Kerry (Inis Mhic Oileán and Oileán tSeannaigh).[3]

There is no mention of this island in the ecclesiastical annals, and the sole historical reference to it is in the 1841 Ordnance Survey Name Book for Kerry, where O'Connor notes that it was 'a burial place for children and adult strangers' (Killemlagh, 55). In 1957 Françoise Henry described and drew a rough plan of its structures (Fig. 3). In 1987 G.D. Rourke and J.W. Marshall made a detailed survey of the island's drystone structures, which comprised a dwelling cell, an oratory, a well and a gable-shaped structure set inside a large mound bordered by stones, similar to the ones found nearby at Killoluaig and Killabuonia (Fig. 4). A random sample of the exposed midden was analysed and radiocarbon-dated, and the other gable shrines in the area were surveyed.[4] The site had later been reused as a *cillín* (or *ceallúnach*), the burial site mentioned by O'Connor, and numerous plain gravestones marking burials were scattered over the island. All of the visible

2—Illaunloughan from the north before excavation. The circular outline of Hut D is in the upper right of the picture, tucked into the western ridge/enclosure wall. The stones of the gable shrine are visible in the foreground on the lower left, with the outline of the oratory barely visible behind it to the east. *(G.D. Rourke)*

structures on the island, except for the slate gable shrine, were built from the indigenous sandstone.

An extensive section of midden, almost 3m long and exposed for its full depth, was eroding from the southern flank of the island, adjacent to the drystone hut. In 1987 several random samples of bone, charcoal and shell were taken from the erosion-created surface. The bone material was identified as cattle, pig, sheep/goat and a fish vertebra. The shells were molluscs found near the island at low tide today, such as winkles, limpets, oysters and scallops (see Appendix 1). A small sample of charcoal was taken and radiocarbon-dated to the eleventh century.[5]

The dietary range was broad for the small sample taken and, moreover, contradicted most historical records of ascetic monastic diets (see below, Chapter 4). The excellent preservation of the midden remains was a major impetus for excavation, as was the presence of the largest of the extant gable shrines, none of which had previously been excavated. Broader research goals, however, were equally important, such as tracing and dating the evolution of the site during its existence, including its changes in economy, demography and architecture. A close

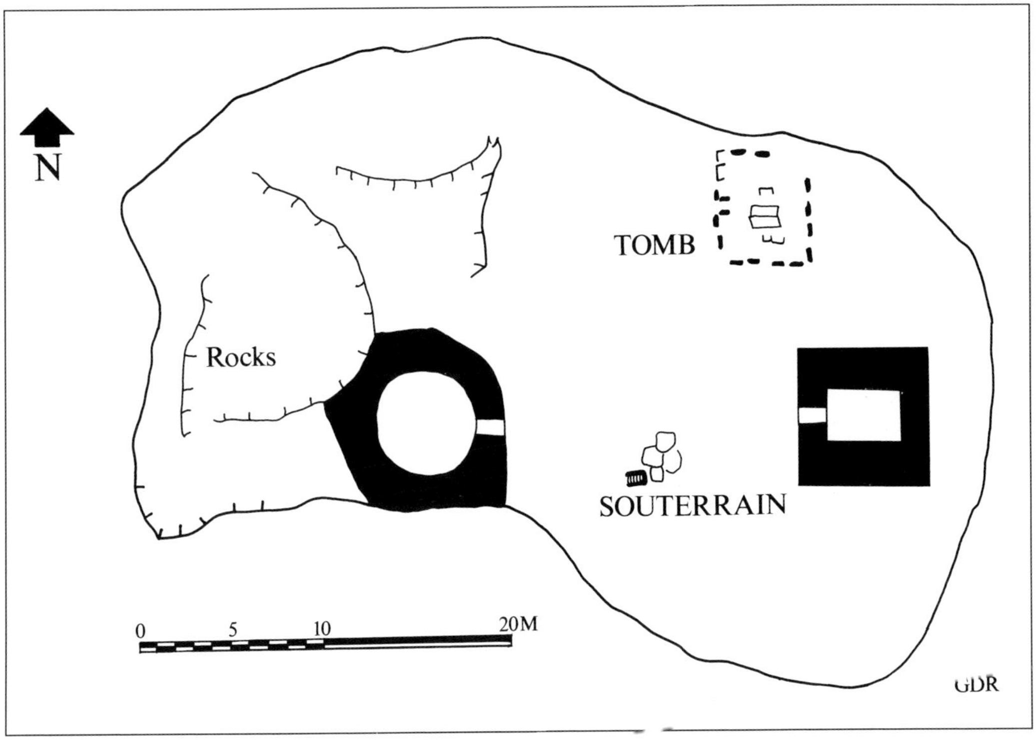

3—Plan of Illaunloughan, with a rough sketch of Hut D, the reliquary shrine (labelled tomb), the oratory and the well, misidentified as a souterrain. *(After Henry 1957, courtesy of the Royal Irish Academy)*

relationship with the mainland, important for all of the island monasteries, was likely here, in view of the small size of the island, its proximity to the mainland and the survey samples of the exposed midden.

In 1996 A. O'Sullivan and J. Sheehan wrote a detailed description of Illaunloughan in *The Iveragh Survey,* based partly on the survey by Rourke and Marshall, the excavation to date and their own observations. They also published the survey map made by Rourke.[6]

Two other Kerry ecclesiastical sites, likely monasteries, had already been almost completely excavated: Church Island, nearby in Valentia Harbour (O'Kelly 1958), and Reask on the Dingle Peninsula (Fanning 1981).[7] Both were significant excavations that added considerably to our knowledge about the early church in Ireland. Church Island, excavated in 1955–6, revealed structures from more than one period, including a well-preserved midden, primary burials and a disturbed reliquary shrine. Although O'Kelly demonstrated the sequence of development of the structures on the site, he was unable to date either sequences or structures as the excavation took place before modern dating techniques were available. A general chronology for the site was attempted, largely by reference to an ogham stone with a cross design carved on it.

Reask, excavated in the 1970s, also revealed evidence of more than one building phase, although little remained of its final architecture and only traces of earlier

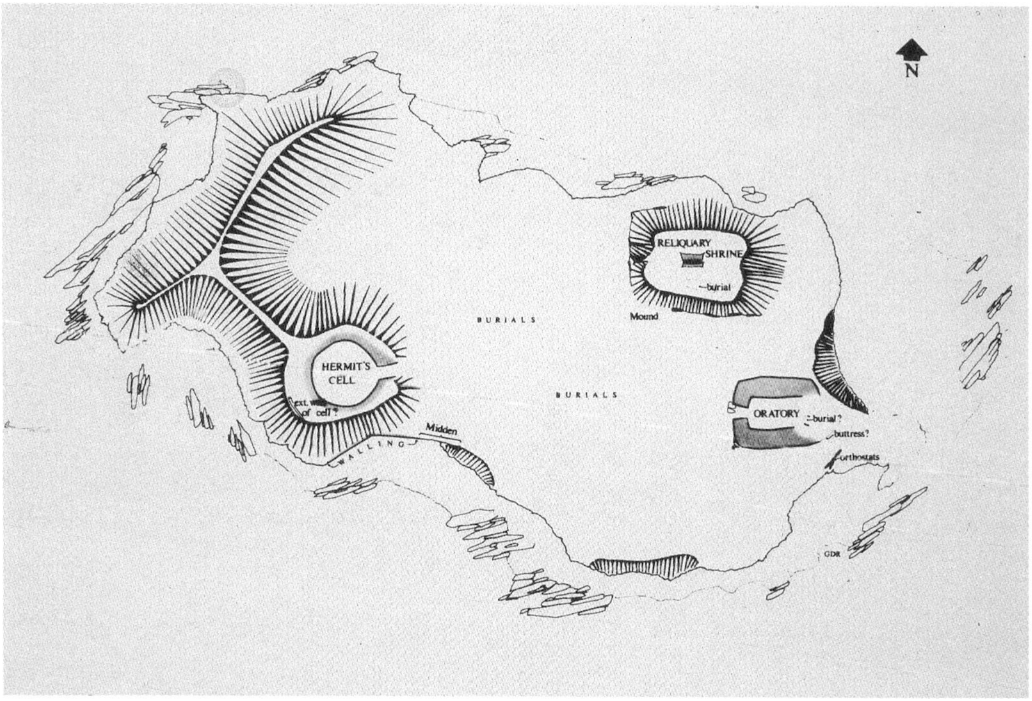

4—Survey plan of Illaunloughan. A more comprehensive survey of the island was made in 1987; it shows the location and size of the structures and includes the midden and burials. *(G.D. Rourke)*

structures could be found. Fanning believed that the first Christian occupation of the site was probably between the mid-fifth and the mid-seventh centuries, based on artefacts of known dates and cross-stone design: a sherd of Bii ware, part of a Roman amphora imported from the Mediterranean found in association with the slab shrine, a blue glass bead found in one of the graves, and the designs inscribed on Cross A (Fanning 1981, 152). He was, unfortunately, unable to date subsequent phases, the stone structures or the time-span of the site because acidic soils had destroyed most of the midden and skeletal remains.

Both the Church Island and Reask excavations uncovered many features similar to those of Illaunloughan, such as a primary phase of construction in timber and earth that was superseded by building in dry stone. One of the objectives of the Illaunloughan excavation was to complement, clarify and extend the information presented by these two important excavations, particularly in the chronological placement of drystone churches and shrines.

Excavation of Illaunloughan began in 1992 and ended after four seasons in 1995, by which time, with some 70 per cent of the island completed, the excavators were satisfied that all relevant areas had been investigated. The original working hypothesis, based on the visible structures, was that Illaunloughan was a small monastic settlement, possibly a hermitage site occupied by one or two men. The main reason for believing that the site was monastic was its island location. Settlement on an island, albeit not very far from shore, showed an intent to be

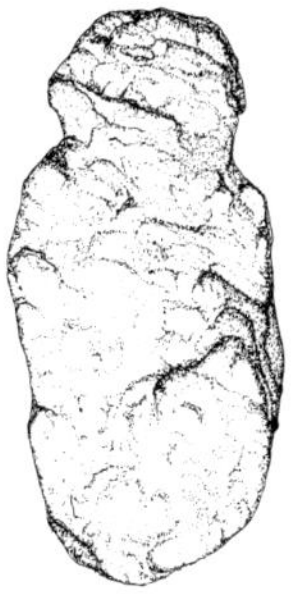

5a—Cross 1. Found during the 1987 survey of the island. Height 0.3m. Width 0.13m. *(G.D. Rourke)*

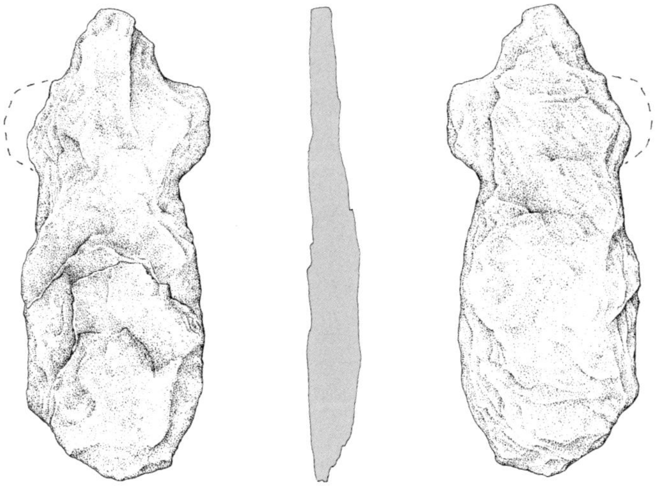

5b—Cross 2. One arm missing but otherwise intact. Height 0.49m. Width 0.18m. *(P. Johnson)*

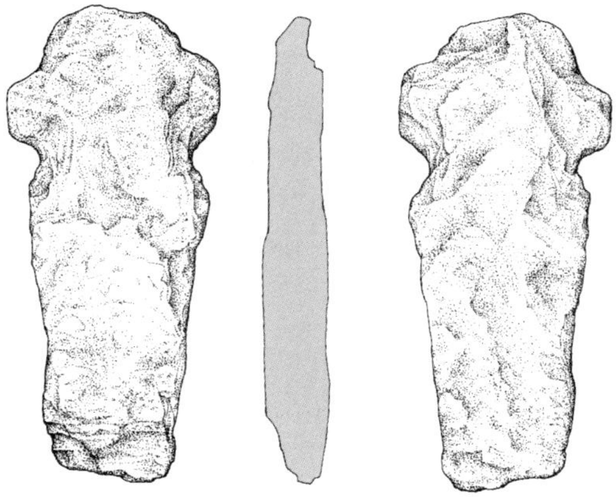

5c—Cross 3. In its original condition. Height 0.4m. Width 0.18m. *(P. Johnson)*

5—Four small cross stones, undecorated but shaped like crosses, a common style found on Valentia Island, Skellig Michael and all along the western coast. They are similar in size and made of sandstone, probably on Illaunloughan. All dimensions were measured at maximum.

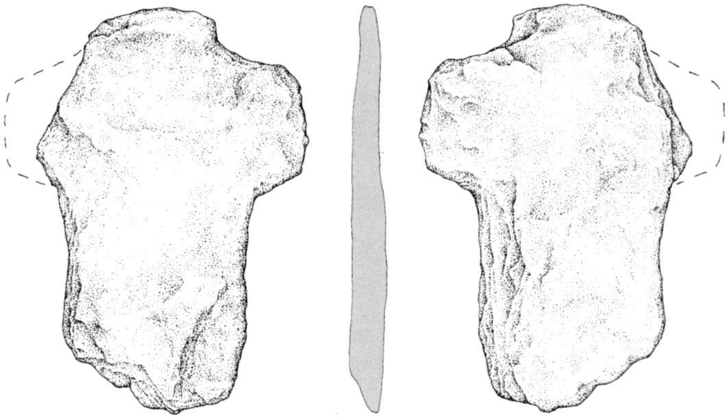

5d—Cross 4. One arm missing; top section is eroded. Height 0.39m. Width 0.26m. *(P. Johnson)*

separate from ordinary life rather than involved with the pastoral care of a community.

Excavation established the religious nature of the community by revealing burials around the rectangular structures, translated bones within the gable shrine and four small cross stones (Figs 5a–e).[8] It also revealed a religious settlement larger than a hermitage.

When, in addition, excavation revealed an absence of female burials among the early graves, this pointed convincingly to a monastic community in the traditional sense of a small group of men, usually not clerics, who withdrew from the ordinary world to live apart, following a religious rule under a leader, usually an abbot.[9]

The details of the excavation are presented by Walsh (Part 2, Stratigraphic Report, and Part 3, Finds Report, below). A more general overview of the excavation is presented here by Marshall and Walsh, as well as an integrated chronological summary with a comparative analysis of other sites in the period.

1

Period 1: Seventh (?) to eighth century. Settlement of the community

There is scant evidence for the use of Illaunloughan before the establishment of the monastery in the form of a sherd of prehistoric pottery of possible Bronze Age date (see Cleary, Appendix 2). No archaeological features from this period were recovered, however, and it is possible that the island was used seasonally, or tidally, as a fishing base and not as a settlement. Bronze Age settlement in the area is attested by the excavation of a hut site and *fulacht fiadh* at Coarhamore, Valentia (Hayden 1994), and by the many field walls and pre-bog deposits on both the south and the north flank of Valentia (Mitchell 1989; O'Sullivan and Sheehan 1996).

The exact date of the foundation of the community on Illaunloughan is uncertain, but radiocarbon dates from the charcoal taken from the hearth of one of the domestic structures indicate it may have been in the seventh century, possibly as early as the mid-seventh century (see n. 5 below). During this active first period, between the mid-seventh and the mid-eighth centuries, three domestic huts and an oratory (a small church) were constructed (Fig. 6). Sod was a primary component of the Period 1 structures, used for the walls of Huts A and B, for the oratory and probably as the principal walling material for Hut C.

The settlement, therefore, did not begin as a hermitage for a solitary monk or two but as a larger community.[10] The community may also have built two shrines at this time: one, south of the oratory, was a small quadrangular structure formed by four upright stones, and the other may have been associated with three graves under the present gable shrine, although the graves are the only remaining evidence of a second shrine here. Evidence for fine metalworking, clay mould fragments and a bone motif-piece were also revealed from Period 1.

Up to twelve members of the community died and were buried before the sod oratory was torn down and replaced by a tiny sod structure (below, pp 32ff). Period 1 clearly lasted long enough for a community that may have had five or six monks to replace its membership twice. The best-dated material for Period 1 is the charcoal from Hut B, the metalworking debris, which dates generally from the

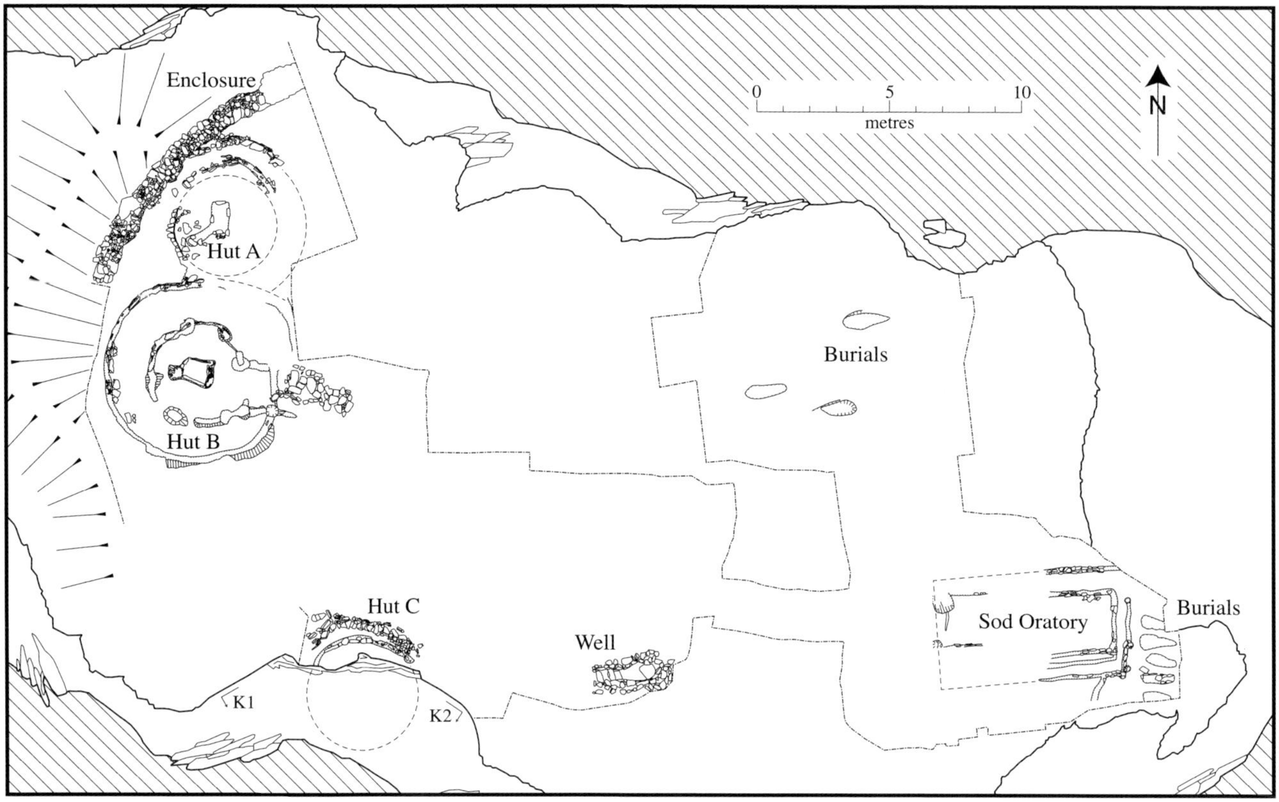

6—Plan of the Period 1 settlement at Illaunloughan, constructed sometime between the mid-seventh and mid-eighth centuries, showing three huts, an oratory, and burials east of the oratory and under the present reliquary shrine. It is probable that most of the burials around the oratory belong to this period. Dotted lines are conjectural. *(C. McHale)*

seventh–eighth century, and the translated bones of three individuals in the reliquary shrine.[11] All of the dates are logically consistent, with an estimated time range between AD 660 and 730–40.

The radiocarbon dates for Period 1 were given to Dr Paula Reimer, at the Center for Accelerator Mass Spectrometry at the Lawrence Livermore National Laboratory in California, to check by Bayesian statistical analysis the mathematical probabilities of Period 1 falling into this time range. The results yielded a time range for Period 1 of between AD 640 and 715 at one-sigma standard deviation and between AD 600 and 760 at two-sigma standard deviations. There is a 68.3 per cent probability, based on the one-sigma range, that the site was founded sometime in the late seventh century (Fig. 7).[12]

Domestic Huts A and B

These two huts were used in the Period 1 settlement because of the close, almost identical, correspondence between the radiocarbon date from Hut B and those of the burials in the cists of the gable shrine. The architecture of the huts, moreover, is similar to that of the Period 1 oratory (see below). Nothing indicates industrial or

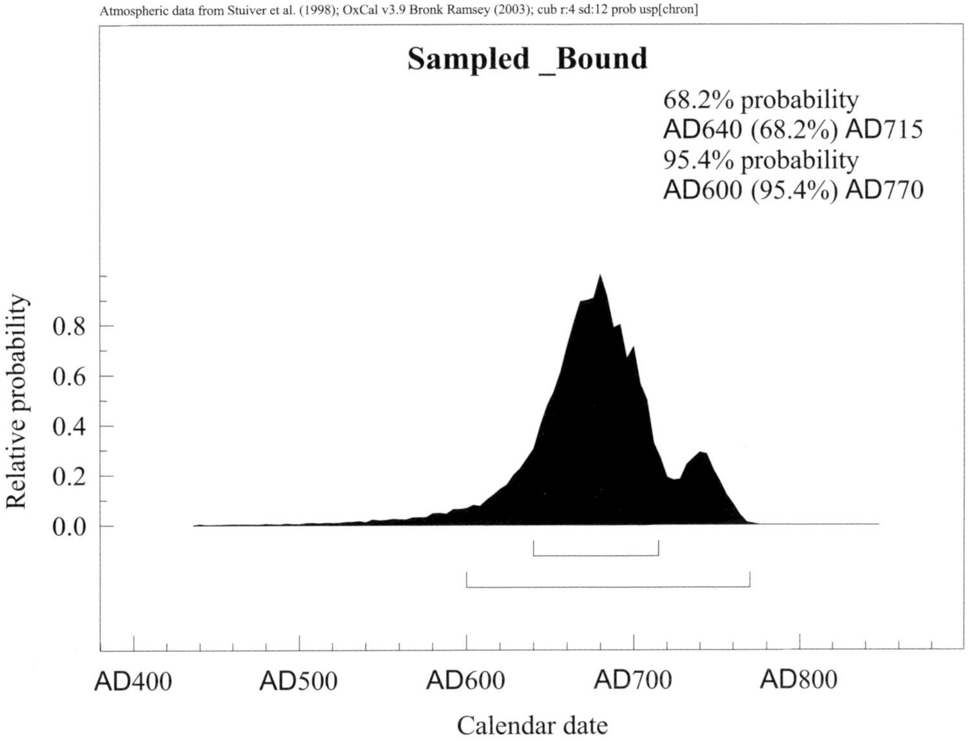

7—The results of Bayesian statistical modelling shown on a graph for the first period of the Illaunloughan monastery. *(P. Reimer, based on C. Bronk Ramsey's OxCal 2003)*

religious activity in or around these huts, but a nearby midden and food refuse around their hearth point to their use as shelter for the original community.

The two conjoined huts A and B in the western section of the island pre-dated the construction of the drystone Hut D (Fig. 8). Huts A and B were built at the same time, and both used sod for their walls, yet their construction varied.

Hut A, 3.7m in internal diameter, only partially remained, but narrow sod walls were contained within two concentric trenches. Three upright stones that remained in the outer trench on the northern side demonstrated that large stones were used to revet the sod wall (Fig. 9a). On the opposite, southern, side a short section of curving drystone wall was all that remained of the inner revetting wall of this cell. There was a stone-defined hearth in the centre of this hut.

The internal diameter of Hut B was approximately the same as that of Hut A, but its external diameter was considerably larger because the walls were thicker. The two shallow parallel trenches of Hut B were cut into bedrock, and post-holes still discernible around the inner trench indicated a post-and-wattle, rather than stone, revetment for the inner sod fill. Hut B also had a stone-kerbed hearth; a charcoal sample from the hearth was radiocarbon-dated to AD 640–751 (Fig. 9b).

A small section of well-set flagstoned path led to the entrance to Hut B, similar to remnants of a path to the doorway of the Period 2 oratory though not as well

8—Illaunloughan in 1995, showing the remains of conjoined huts A and B on the western side of the island with a stone wall running behind them. The wall abuts Hut D and continues north until it abruptly ends north of Huts A and B. *(Con Brogan)*

constructed. Stone paths are commonly found on early medieval ecclesiastical sites. Both Church Island and Reask had such paths, whereas the area between the oratories and the huts at Skellig Michael was completely paved (O'Kelly 1958, 76–7; Fanning 1981, 76, 88; see also Marshall and Rourke 2000) (Fig. 9c).

The huts were built up against the inner face of the stone wall (F91) and were, therefore, later than the wall, although it is probable that both huts and wall were part of the same building programme. The drystone walling, still 0.5m high at the time of excavation, buffered the two huts against the western winds and the sea. This walling extends from the natural rock ridge at the western end of the island, which was heightened by the addition of large flat stones used as capstones (Figs 9 and 10). Stone from the rock ridge may have been quarried out to build it. Much of the rubble and stone on either side of the ridge was collapse from this structure, so the wall was originally higher to enhance shelter. O'Kelly (1958, 75–6) estimated that the enclosure wall at Church Island in Valentia Harbour had probably been 1.5m high.

The wall now ends abruptly on the northern side of the island, where the most extensive damage occurs during winter storms (G.D. Rourke, pers. comm.). O'Kelly (*op. cit.*) estimated that *c.* 57m, over one-third of the enclosure wall on Church Island, had disappeared owing to erosion. Originally this section of walling on Illaunloughan may also have been part of an enclosure wall, a traditional element often found on early medieval Irish sites of high status, secular or ecclesiastical. Monks everywhere had a special need for a spiritual, as well as a physical, boundary

9a—Hut A, Illaunloughan, from the north-east in 1995, showing three upright stones that functioned as external revetting for its sod walls. Directly opposite is a short section of stone walling used as internal revetting for the walls. Hut A was built directly against the stone enclosure wall. *(C. Walsh)*

9b—Hut B, Illaunloughan, from the west in 1995. The remains of this hut consisted of a hearth and post-holes, possibly indicating post-and-wattle revetting for the sod walls of the structure. Remnants of a paved path leading to the hut are visible in the background. *(J.W. Marshall)*

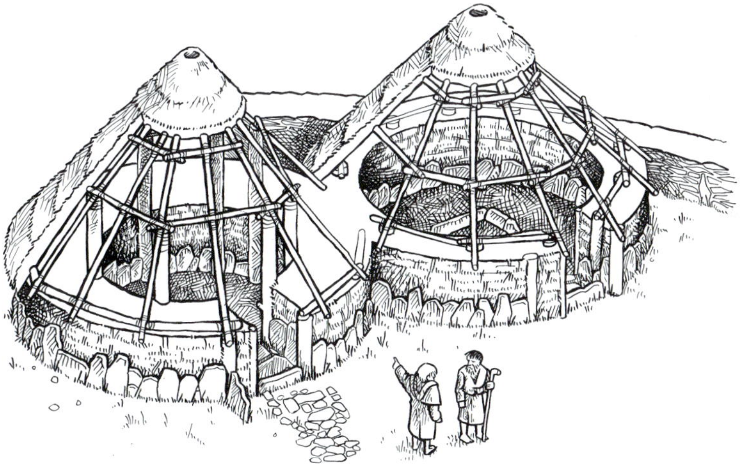

9c—Reconstructed elevation of Huts A and B, Illaunloughan. *(C. McHale)*

10—The enclosure wall running behind Hut B, Illaunloughan. *(J.W. Marshall, 1995)*

to symbolise separation from worldly matters (Bitel 1993, 58–66; Marshall and Rourke 2000, chap. 4). Although the enclosure at Church Island was late, added after the other monastic structures had been built, it is probable that most enclosure walls like that at Illaunloughan were built at the time of the primary structures.

Conjectural estimates of five or six occupants of these huts are based on the size of the two huts, the need for storage space in them for bedding, tools, equipment and other possessions, and the practical limitations on the population imposed by the small size of the island.

Domestic Hut C

Hut C, on the southern edge of the island, also pre-dated Hut D. This hut was the most exposed of the four huts to weather and sea erosion, and consequently most of the hut has disappeared (Fig. 11). A semicircular trench with a single post-hole at the eastern end, possibly part of the entry, was all that remained. All of the Illaunloughan huts had their doors on the eastern side, away from the prevailing winds, as did all of the structures of an early medieval secular settlement excavated on Bray Head, Valentia Island (Hayden 1998). Small, thin slate stones were placed on edge within the trench.[13] Interspersed with these were several white quartz stones, laid deliberately along the surface of the trench. It is possible that these stones braced small posts in a post-and-wattle construction, or they may have supported orthostats in the slot-trench. Hut C is the only structure on the island to

11—Hut C, Illaunloughan, from the north, showing the semicircular trench that was all that remained of the hut. A layer of rubble stone paralleled the arc of the trench and may have been used to retain blocks of sod. A single large post-hole on the eastern end probably marked the entry to the hut. Erosion has removed most of the hut. *(J.W. Marshall, 1993)*

use slate in its construction, apart from the slabs of the principal reliquary shrine. Part of the interior of the hut was covered with thin sheets of slate. The placement of several white quartz stones along the inner slot may also indicate the special status of this hut. Also, a deliberately laid flooring was present, a feature not found anywhere else except in the oratory.

Hut C had an arc of small sandstone blocks, set 0.30–0.40m from the inner trench and aligned with it (Fig. 11). Part of this feature had a central channel, indicating that it probably originally held orthostats, which would have anchored sods. Excavated huts in the immediate area provide parallels. O'Kelly (1958, 70–1) noted the presence of a similar arc of stonework, two to three stones high, almost surrounding the wall of the round stone hut on Church Island at a distance of 0.50m, to retain insulating sods. At the time of the Church Island excavation, sod was still being used this way locally for animal shelters. A similar ring of stones was found at Reask, Co. Kerry, where an arc of stones, still standing to a minimum height of 0.90m, surrounded the conjoined Huts A and B (Fanning 1981, 899–90) (Fig. 12). The stones likely served to anchor blocks of sod used as insulation for the flimsy walls. The closest comparable evidence for the Period 1 structures at Illaunloughan, however, comes from the excavated remains of the farmsteads at Bray Head, on nearby Valentia Island to the east (Walsh 1995; Hayden 1998).

No organic matter was recovered to provide a date for Hut C; however, it lies under midden from Hut D and thus clearly preceded D. The function of Hut C and

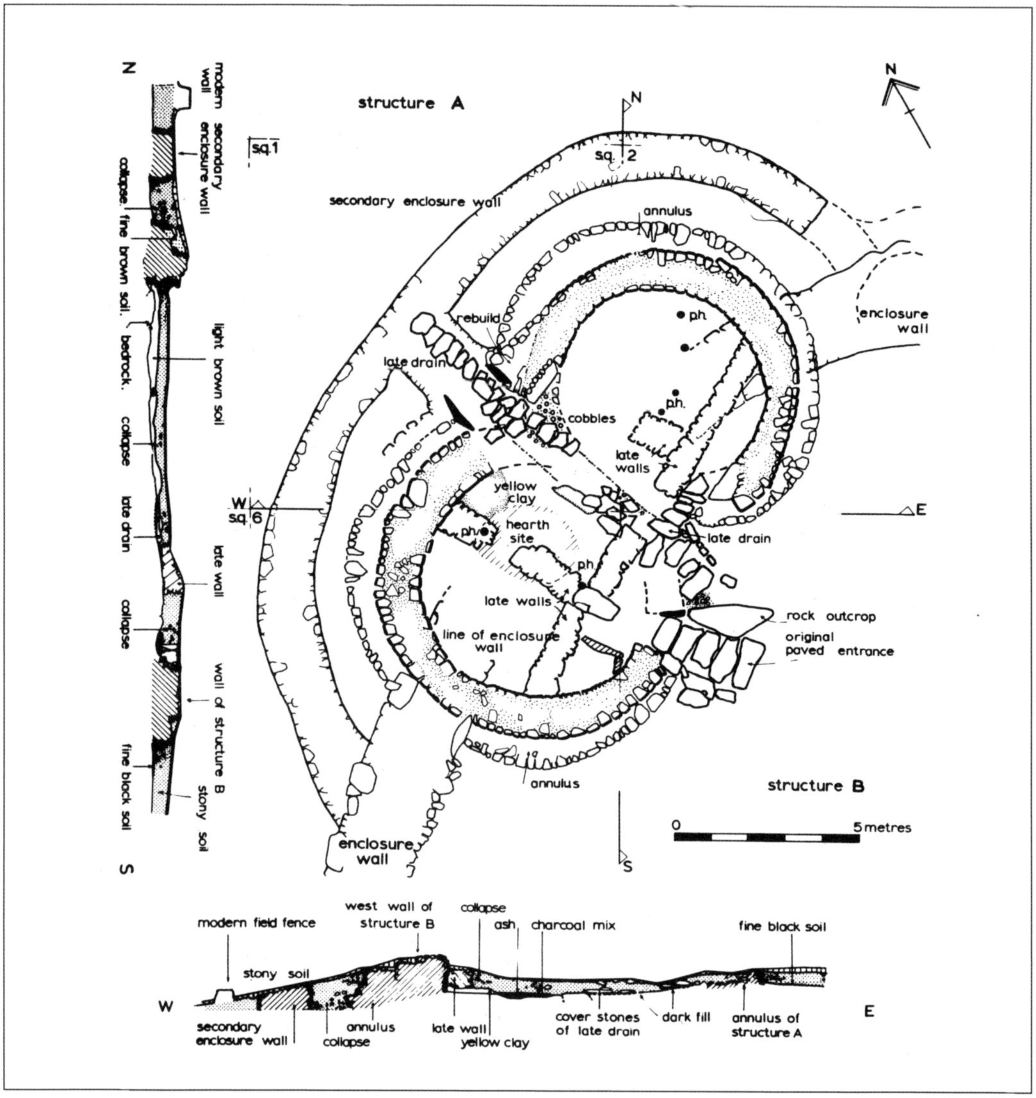

12—Conjoined huts A and B at Reask, Co. Kerry, showing parallel arcs of stone around part of the huts, set at a maximum distance of 0.7m, narrowing as the arc continued. This semicircle of rough stones probably revetted sods placed to protect the huts from wind and water. *(After Fanning 1981, fig. 8, courtesy of the Royal Irish Academy)*

its association with the two conjoined Huts A and B are uncertain; it may have been earlier than or contemporary with them. There was a steady progression of building stronger, better-insulated huts in more protected areas on the island. Hut C, the flimsiest and most exposed of the huts, may have been the earliest hut for habitation, but, proving too exposed, may have been converted fairly quickly to storage and industrial purposes; the metalworking debris associated with Hut C may indicate a late use of the hut contemporary with Huts A and B.

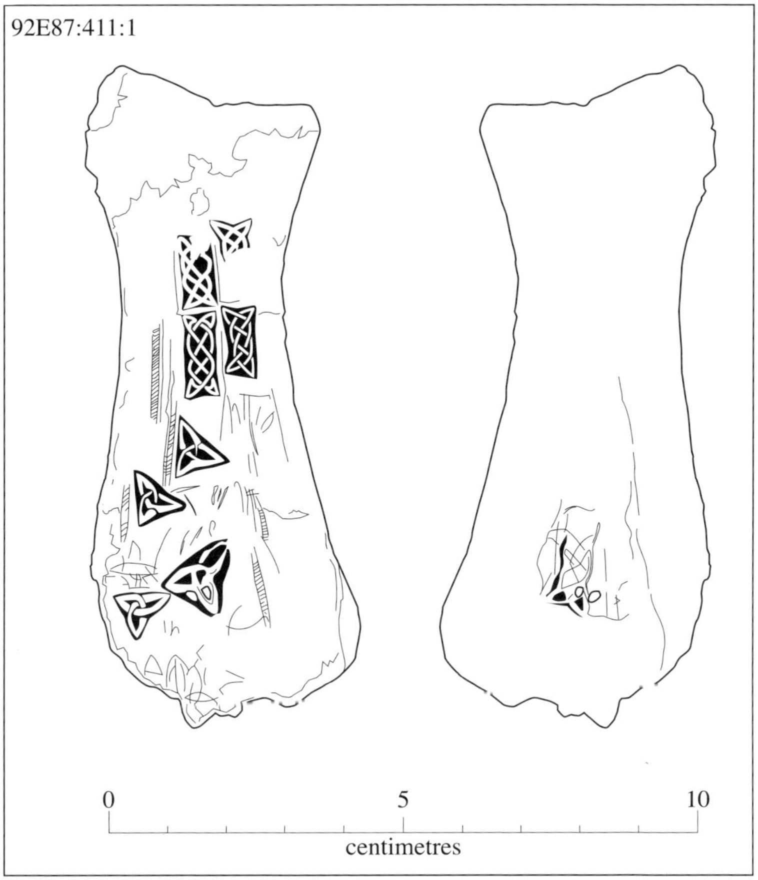

13—Sheep scapula found near metalworking debris near Hut C, Illaunloughan. Motifs carved onto the bone indicated that it was a trial design piece for fine metalworking. The designs on the bone included hatch-marks, triquetra and interlace—all common patterns in the early medieval period. *(C. McHale)*

Metalworking evidence

The early community left behind evidence of fine metalwork, for the designing and casting of copper-alloy brooches. More than 80 fragments of clay moulds were recovered from a localised area in the debris over Hut C. The fragments included two-piece moulds, a crucible and part of a tuyère. More fragments of crucible were recovered from elsewhere on the site, in unstratified or disturbed contexts such as grave fill.

The scarcity of mould fragments from archaeological sites has supported the view that most simple pins were wrought or hammered from already-cast ingots rather than cast in two-piece moulds and that casting was used primarily for more elaborate forms on prestigious sites.[14] Indeed, most of the evidence of mould casting has come from large sites such as Lagore Crannog, Co. Meath (Hencken 1950), Moynagh Lough, Co. Meath (Bradley 1993), Garranes, Co. Cork (Ó Ríordáin 1942), and Whithorn, Galloway, Scotland (Hill 1997).

There was, however, some evidence of bronze-casting at Reask, a more modestly sized site. Fanning believed that the absence of mould evidence even on large sites

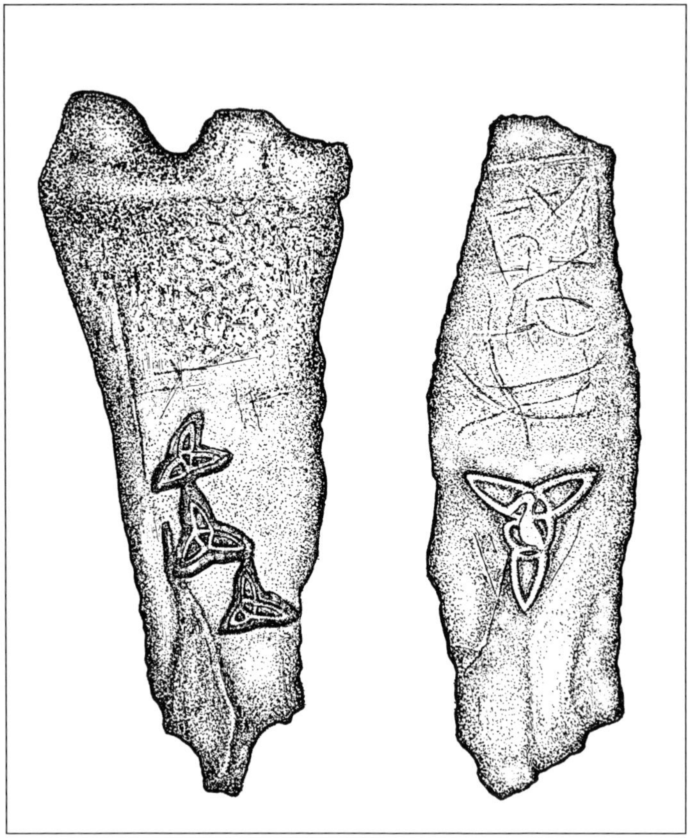

14—Motif-piece from Moynagh Lough, Co. Meath, dated to the seventh/eighth century, showing triquetra designs similar to those on the Illaunloughan piece. *(Courtesy of John Bradley)*

was not surprising because of the fragile, fragmentary nature of clay moulds, which, after being broken open, are apt to disintegrate and disperse quickly, particularly if they were manufactured in the open.[15] The mould fragments preserved at Illaunloughan, however, provided firm evidence that copper-/bronze-alloy casting of rings and brooches in clay moulds was done even on small sites. The fragments of two-piece clay moulds, some with decoration and some plain, demonstrate that a minimum of four objects were made from them: a penannular brooch, a ring-brooch with fret pattern ornamentation, and two pins, one possibly with a decorated square head. No metal objects made from these moulds are represented in the assemblage of artefacts recovered from the occupation and midden levels.

A sheep scapula with carved motifs was found near the mould fragments, suggesting that the metal artefacts manufactured on Illaunloughan were designed on the island (Fig. 13). Small pieces of animal bone were commonly used to carve the design sketch or models for metal casting from the seventh to the eleventh century, but they are usually associated with more prestigious sites that had workshops (Youngs 1989, 179).[16] Incised diagonal hatch-marks and panels of interlace and triquetra knot were carved onto the Illaunloughan bone, all design

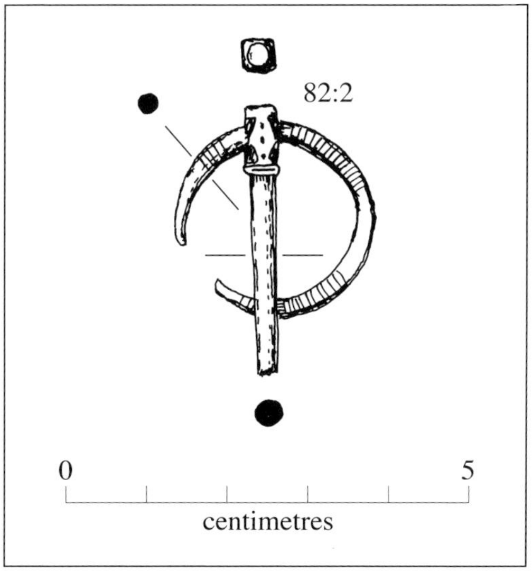

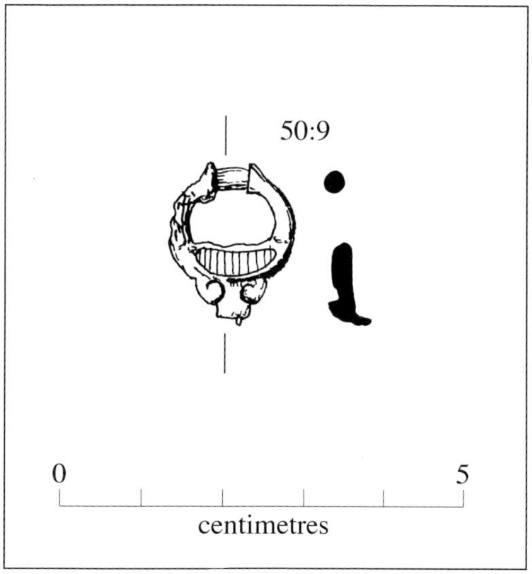

15 (far left)—Penannular ring-brooch of bronze alloy found in the upper levels of the midden on Illaunloughan. Fanning (1994, 5) dated this type of pin to the later eighth–ninth century. *(A. Hayden)*

16 (left)—Annular brooch-pin found in the upper levels of the midden on Illaunloughan, of a type dated by Ó Floinn to the seventh–eighth century. Neither of the pins found in the upper midden levels used the designs found on the bone motif-piece from the lower midden levels. *(A. Hayden)*

elements used throughout this period and that, consequently, have no precise chronological implications. A motif-piece found at Lagore Crannog, Co. Meath, dated to the eighth or the early ninth century (shown in Youngs 1989, 176), displays similar, albeit far more sophisticated, interlace work. Two seventh-/eighth-century pieces from Moynagh Lough also have triquetra designs (Bradley 1989, 179) (Fig. 14).

Four objects of copper/bronze alloy found at higher levels in the midden may be related to this specific evidence of metal-casting. One is a penannular ring-brooch (Fig. 15) with three incised dots on a baluster head. Fanning (1994, 5) dates such ring-brooches to the second half of the eighth to the early ninth century. The second pin is an annular brooch-pin that Ó Floinn dates to the seventh/eighth century (Fig. 16).[17] Neither the fragments of moulds nor the copper/bronze pins found at higher levels in the midden used the decoration found on the bone motif-piece, possibly an indication that considerable evidence has been lost. The precise dating of these simple pins is difficult because the simple styles and the decoration have been used over a long period of time, but there is no reason to doubt that they could fit into a mid-seventh- to ninth-century time-frame.

Although there was no sign of a furnace or metalworking area on Illaunloughan, the concentration of ceramic debris from moulds and crucibles and the bone motif-piece at this undisturbed level suggest that the furnace or metalworking area was nearby. It may have lain a short distance southward, perhaps sheltered by the walls of the timber round house, and been lost to erosion.[18]

Very little is known of the layout of a smith's workshop, despite the number of sites that have provided evidence of metalworking. At Moynagh Lough Crannog metalworking took place in two discrete areas on either side of a timber round house on the periphery of the crannog (Bradley 1993, 76). One work area was a

17—Illaunloughan from the north-east in 1994, showing the parallel trenches that are all that remains of the eastern end of the Period 1 oratory extending from the later stone oratory. *(Con Brogan)*

spread of charcoal that measured 4.2m by 4m and contained mould fragments, crucible sherds, three motif-pieces and an iron tool. The other work area comprised a furnace, two surfaced areas, metalworking debris and charcoal. The furnace was bowl-shaped and small, only 0.35m in diameter and 0.14m deep. A spread of burnt clay close by had probably been sheltered by a screen represented by a fairly random scatter of post-holes (*ibid.*, 79). Another pebbled area may have been a stacking area for the moulds as they cooled.

The 1968 excavations at Cathedral Hill, Armagh, yielded evidence of a hearth used for metalworking (Gaskell Brown and Harper 1984, 157). The structure was in a marginal area, very close to the edge of the infilled ditch of the monastic enclosure. Fanning (1981, 110) excavated crucible fragments, possible tuyère fragments and a hearth for heating them in Structure G at Reask, Co. Kerry.

An early Irish law tract dealing with status, the *Uraicecht Becc*, recorded the honour-price of a coppersmith at seven *sét,* the same status as a silversmith, physician or other skilled craftsman (Kelly 1988, 63).[19] Although sites such as Moynagh Lough (Bradley 1993, 80) offered substantial evidence that there was probably a resident artisan on the site, a travelling artisan is more likely to have worked on Illaunloughan.[20]

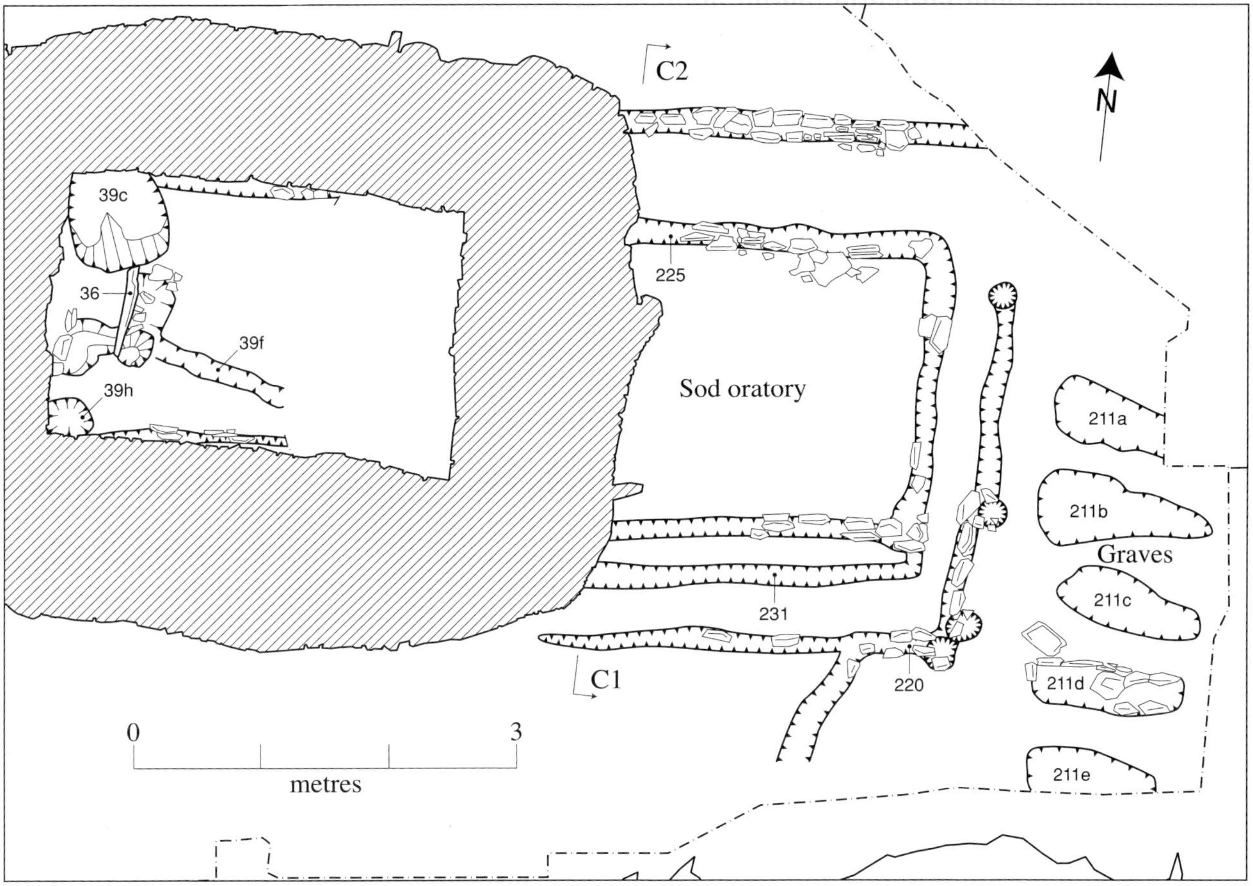

18—Plan of the Period 1 oratory on Illaunloughan, showing three post-holes set in the eastern wall and the graves to the east of the structure. Erosion has probably erased the evidence for a fourth post-hole in the north-eastern corner. *(C. McHale)*

The Period 1 oratory

Excavation revealed the eastern end of a rectangular structure extending a few metres eastward from the drystone oratory, at a lower level (Fig. 17). Two parallel trenches (F220 and F225) defined its eastern end, marking out walls that varied from 0.80m to 1.10m wide. The trenches, *c.* 0.15m deep, still contained a number of thin sandstone slabs (Fig. 18). Parallel trenches, 0.34–0.74m apart, indicated sod construction similar to that in Hut A, using rows of upright stones to brace the sod wall. The sod walls may have collapsed and needed repair or rebuilding a number of times. Evidence of possible subsidence problems may be seen in the extra trench (F231), which may have been the original inner trench for the southern wall of the sod church. The uprights in this shallower and narrower trench may not have been able to hold the sod walls effectively, and it may have been replaced by a more substantial trench (see Walsh, Chapter 9). None of the turf blocks remained, although there was a distinct layer of soil (F224) still present between the trenches and the overlying trench, F231.

The rectangular shape of the structure, its orientation and the presence of five graves to the east of it confirmed that it was an oratory. The sod oratory is earlier than the two successive structures in this area and logically should be contemporary with the building of the round sod huts, but there is no direct dating evidence to confirm this. The lack of direct dating evidence is not critical here, since both the domestic huts and the gable shrine are dated to the same period.

The internal width of the primary oratory is almost identical to that of the later drystone oratory, 2.0m compared to 2.2m, so close that only traces of a stone-lined trench could be discerned beneath the northern walls of the later oratory. A sill stone (F36) found in the interior of the drystone oratory has no association with the threshold of the drystone oratory but appears to have been the threshold of the sod oratory. Based on the sill stone, the internal length of the primary oratory was considerably greater than that of the drystone oratory.

Roof type

Sod walls, because of inherent subsidence and slippage problems, were not built to great heights; for the same reason, they do not make good load-bearing walls. The oratory walls, consequently, were probably not higher than 1.5–2m. The only surviving evidence of a roof is the three post-holes along the eastern border of the oratory (F220 on Fig. 18). The location of the post-holes suggests that the roof structure was carried by post construction, rather than timber framework, and that the post construction supported the wall and carried the roof largely independently of the walls. The spacing of the post-holes indicates that originally there would have been four such posts; one is now eroded away from the north-eastern corner. It is probable that there were other posts in the western, southern and northern walls. The rafters may have rested directly on the posts (Ó Danachair 1957, 63); the narrowness of the building is an indication that this manner of fashioning the roof would have worked.

In 1981 Fred Charles, an architect, proposed an ingenious design for a simple, minimalist structure using earthfast post construction, as opposed to more complex timber-frame construction (Fig. 19a). Essential to his design were materials that were readily available and lightweight and that needed the fewest possible changes: 'The materials had to be the easiest to acquire and handle—straight poles such as birch, willow, alder or a suitable conifer—heavier timbers being used sparingly' (Charles 1981, 12.05, 12.06).[21]

Something very similar to Charles's structure may have been built at Illaunloughan, if allowances are made for a number of possible variations and differences. The structure at Illaunloughan differs from Charles's conjectural one in that the posts were placed on the external rather than the internal side of the structure and there were four rather than three in the eastern end.

Charles's example is presented, in the absence of evidence, as one of a number of hypothetical models only. Nevertheless, there are several elements of his model

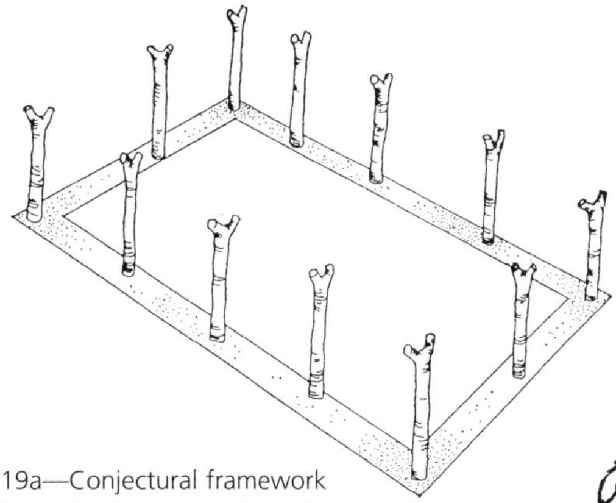

19a—Conjectural framework for a simple construction of a roof for a one-roomed house set upon posts. Charles named this 'post construction' to differentiate it from timber frame construction. *(After Charles 1981, fig. 3, courtesy of the Vernacular Architecture Group)*

19b—Conjectural reconstruction of the Period 1 oratory at Illaunloughan. *(C. McHale)*

that would fit what we know about Illaunloughan. The oratory at Illaunloughan appears to be similar in the use of post construction, and the woods used for Charles's light, economic and effective roof frame are consistent with the local light woodland canopy, consisting of hazel, alder, oak and ash, proposed by O'Carroll based on the contents of the hearth in Hut A (see Appendix 4) for the landscape near Illaunloughan. A low-pitched, hipped roof similar to that of Charles is also likely. Hipped roofs are easy and economical to build, and their roofs slope down so that the roof rafters may extend beyond the ring-beam and/or posts, creating eaves that carry rainwater away from the walls. The presence of posts in the external part of the wall at Illaunloughan suggests a substantial overhang of the rafters (Fig. 19b).

It is also likely that the roof was constructed before the sod walls in order to protect the walls during construction. Ó Danachair (1957, 73) mentions several examples of this custom recorded by the Irish Folklore Commission. A 1997 experiment in reconstructing a Scottish central highlands creel house also mentioned several advantages of constructing the roof before the sod walls (Noble 2000, 86–7).

A thatch roof would have been the most expedient solution for the Period 1 oratory because thatch, of some local material such as oat straw or bent grass, could be quickly and cheaply constructed. In Kerry there is a tradition of thatching using *Molina caerula*, called locally *fionnán*. The mountain slopes behind Portmagee have large quantities of this material.[22] Traditionally, thatch roofs were laid down in three layers. The main supports of the roof were the tie-beams, or couples, and the gables, followed by an interwoven fabric of straw, light rods or wattling, which provided a base for a layer of sods, cut in long, thin strips that overhung the roof. Layers of thatch in *c.* 0.6m strips were then attached to the sod, using straw rope, wooden pins or scallops to fasten them tightly together.[23] The sod protected the structure from wind and cold, and the thatch protected the sod from rain.[24] The duration of such a structure is hard to estimate, but a thatched roof would need repairing or replacing frequently.

Local construction in sod

The three Period 1 Illaunloughan huts used sod as a primary component of their walls, as did the first oratory and possibly the small successive structure in the same location. Sod construction, usually consisting of cut blocks of grassy turf, has long been a common practice in the colder, windier regions of northern Europe in areas where grass grows densely, such as Denmark, Iceland, northern coastal Germany, parts of France, Scotland, the Shetlands, the Orkneys, south-western England and Ireland.[25] Low cost and ease of construction also contributed to its common use. Sod structures could be constructed in a day and were well insulated, with thick walls that were warmer and more watertight than daub-and-wattle structures. The disadvantage was that the walls were weak and apt to slip or subside, even when supported by timber or stone uprights.

Turf-block construction was still being used in Irish dwellings in the late eighteenth century and into the nineteenth century. In 1780 Arthur Young remarked in his book *Tour of Ireland, 1776–1779* that they were the commonest type of one-roomed cabins in Tipperary (Hutton 1970). He estimated that the cost of a sod cabin in County Fermanagh was only £2, as opposed to £15 for a stone-and-thatch cabin; similarly in County Donegal a mud cabin cost £3 and a stone-and-slate house cost £40.[26]

Their perishable nature, and perhaps familiar use, have resulted in few documentary references to and little material evidence of sod or earthen buildings in the early medieval period. In the late seventh century Tirechán casually mentioned earthen churches twice in his Life of Patrick: 'and he [Patrick] made an earthen church in that place'; 'he [Patrick] made there a square earthen church of clay'.[27]

A variety of construction methods exist: sod may be used either as outer insulation material or as the main wall fabric, and in conjunction with wattling, stone, timber or a mixture.[28] The remains of turf in a structure interpreted as an animal shelter were excavated in 1986 at Dunsilly Rath, Co. Antrim (McNeill, in press). At White Fort, Drumaroad, Co. Down, two phases were excavated of a late

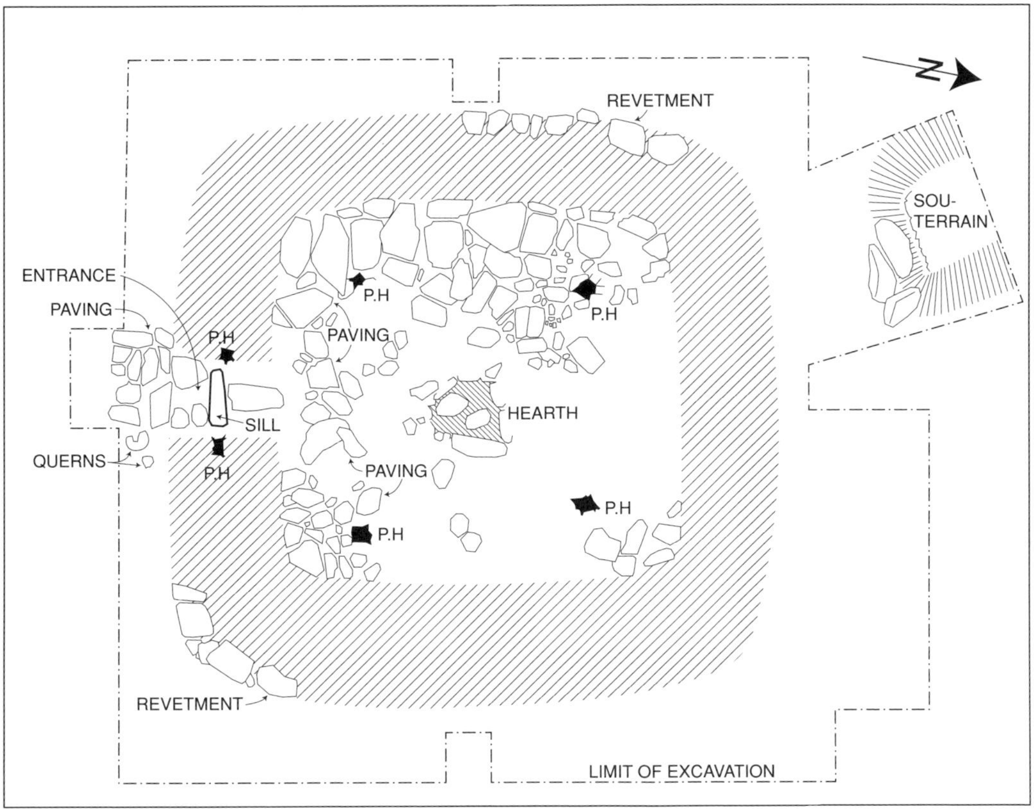

20—Plan of White Fort, Drumaroad, Co. Down, showing sizeable stone uprights remaining in trenches, probably used to support the exterior sod walls of the phase 2 house. *(After Waterman 1956, fig. 4, courtesy of the Ulster Archaeological Society)*

first-millennium AD rectangular structure that in its second phase used stone uprights to brace the external mud or sod walls (Waterman 1956, 73–86) (Fig. 20). Material evidence of the use of sod in domestic and ecclesiastical structures in the early medieval period was sparse until recently.[29]

Parallel trenches holding stone uprights to support sod walls may have been a common regional style on the Iveragh Peninsula. In 1995–2001 Walsh and Hayden found substantial new evidence for sod constuction of huts with stone uprights set in trenches in excavations on the early medieval and medieval settlement on nearby Bray Head, Valentia Island. Among these huts, one well-preserved round house was an excellent example of this technique; the space between the stone uprights still contained sod and small stones. A radiocarbon date from charcoal in the stone-lined hearth indicated that the house was being used sometime between AD 676 and 984 (Fig. 21) (Walsh 1995).[30] Three additional round houses using similar construction were found in this settlement (Hayden 1998).

Period 1 burials associated with the sod oratory

Five closely spaced graves (F211a–e) had been placed behind the eastern wall of the sod oratory (Fig. 22). No bone remained in these simple, unmarked, earth-dug

21—Plan of round house on Bray Head, Valentia Island, Co. Kerry, showing parallel trenches that contained stone uprights to brace sod walls similar to those used on Illaunloughan. Sod still remained in this hut, dated to between the late seventh and late tenth centuries (Walsh 1996). *(C. McHale)*

graves, but their unequivocal association with the structure and its presence in the area later used for the drystone oratory confirmed that it was an earlier oratory. Most of the other graves around the oratories may also relate to this first oratory, as it appears that burial moved to the eastern quadrant of the gable shrine once it was constructed.

Bone did not survive in several of the remaining four/five graves around the oratory (Fig. 23). Two graves, on the north-western and western sides, did contain bone; one (Sk. 103) must have been related to the earlier oratory, as construction of the *leacht*, itself associated with the second drystone oratory, disturbed this skeleton. There were two burials in the second grave; one (Sk. 120) overlay another (Sk. 119); the later burial was radiocarbon-dated to between the late eighth and the late ninth centuries. It was probably associated with the Period 2 drystone oratory because of its position and late date. The underlying third skeleton (Sk. 119) was earlier than Sk. 120 but was otherwise of uncertain date, although it may have been related to the Period 1 oratory because the grave ran under the drystone oratory.

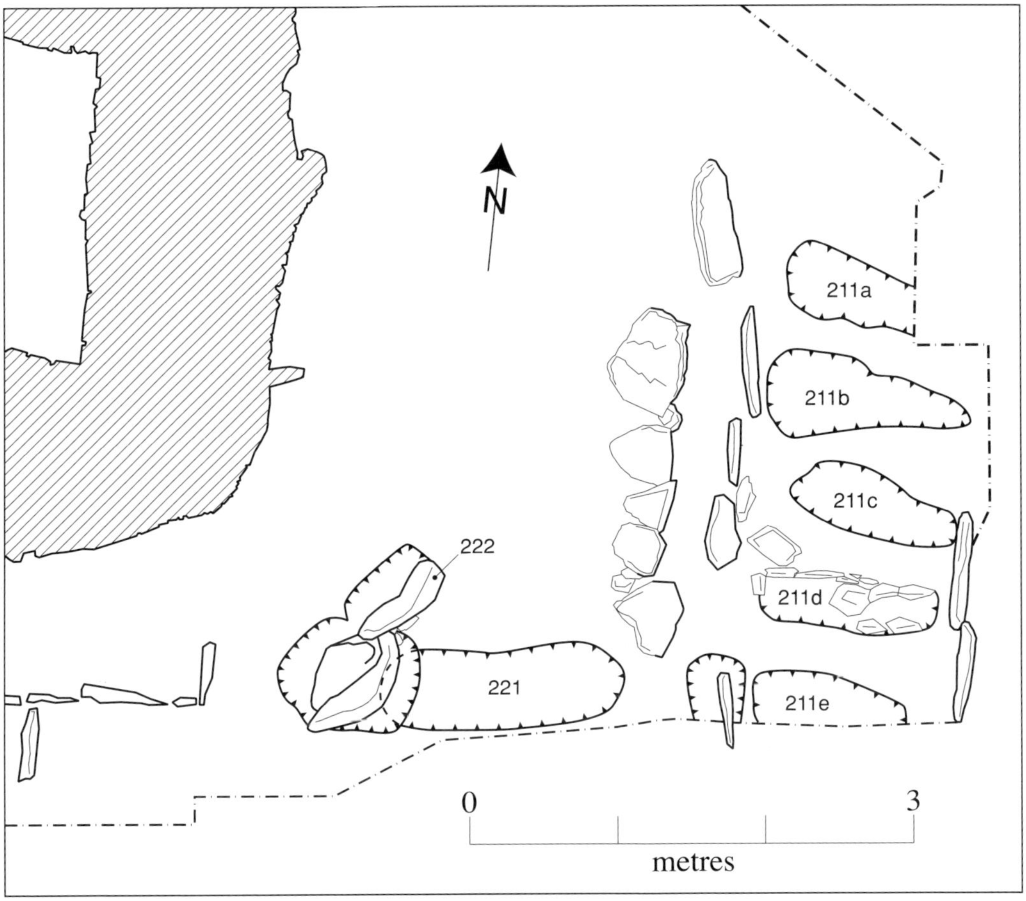

22—Plan of graves behind the Period 1 oratory on Illaunloughan. Kerbstones were possibly placed to mark the eastern end of the Period 1 oratory and the five graves behind it. *(C. McHale)*

Period 1 burials in and under the gable shrine

The translated burials in the reliquary shrine, radiocarbon-dated to between the late seventh and the late eighth centuries, may have been the founder of the settlement and his immediate successor.[31] There are, therefore, including the burials mentioned above, some nine to twelve burials that were most likely related to the period of the primary oratory.

Three graves, earlier than the gable shrine, had been cut into the rock ridge that lay partly under the shrine (Figs 24a and 24b). One (Sk. 216), north-east of the shrine and directly under the corner of it, still held a few fragments of human bone, among them the end of a human femur (Fig. 25). The second grave (Sk. 230) lay west of the shrine and 2.5m west of the first grave. This grave was considerably smaller and contained no bone or quartz in its gravel fill. The third grave (Sk. 223), 2.8m south of the shrine, contained small fragments of bone, one possibly a human ulna; quartz pebbles were found in this grave, as well as with Sk. 216. The three graves were separated from the oratory and clustered together on top of a bedrock ridge; they

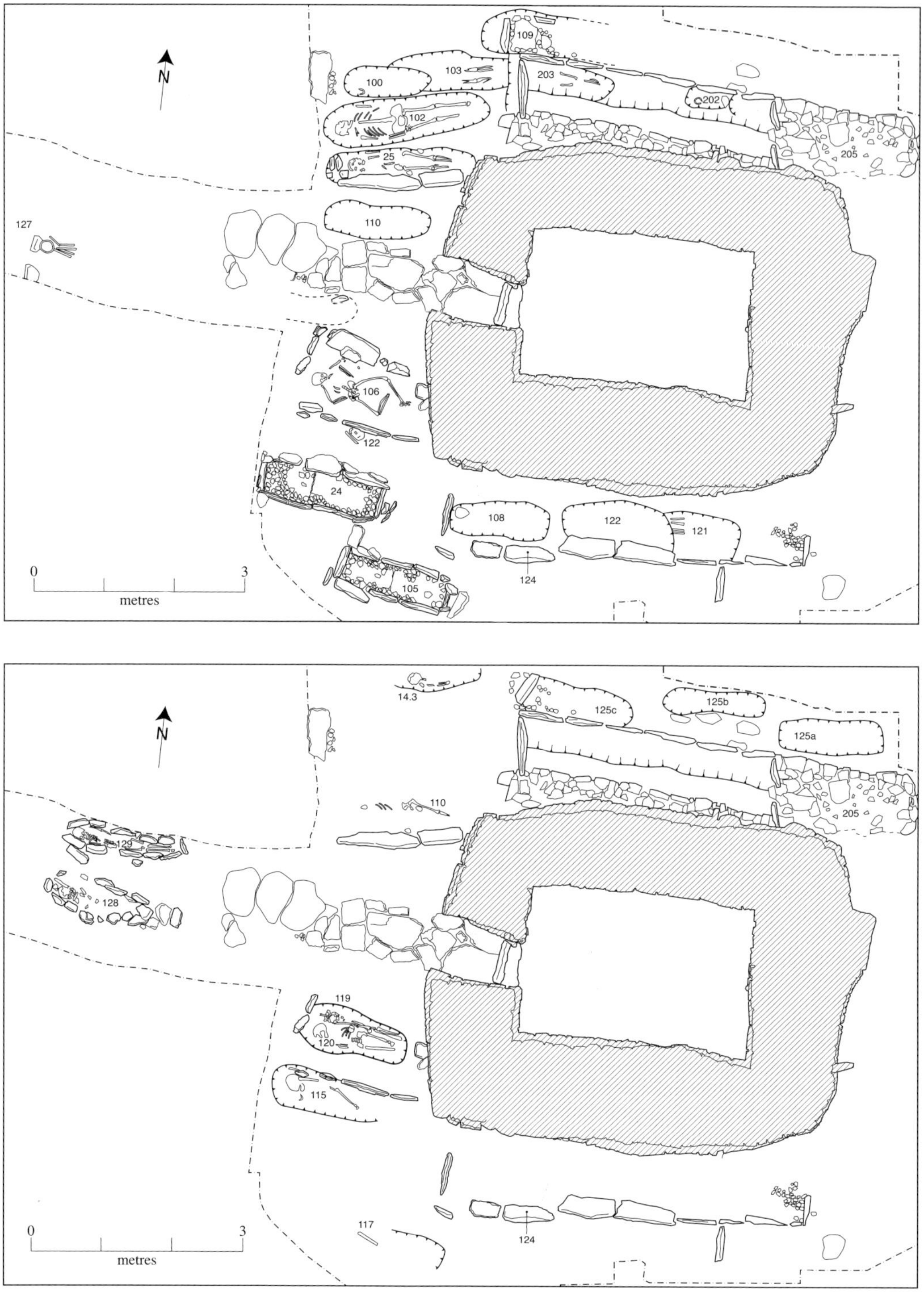

23—Plan of graves around the Period 2 drystone oratory, presented as two plans in order to show the burials in detail. *(C. McHale)*

24a—The gable shrine on Illaunloughan from the north-east in 1994, showing the location of the grave partially under the walling of the gable shrine. This grave, one of three, preceded the construction of the shrine. The other two are west and south of the shrine. *(Con Brogan)*

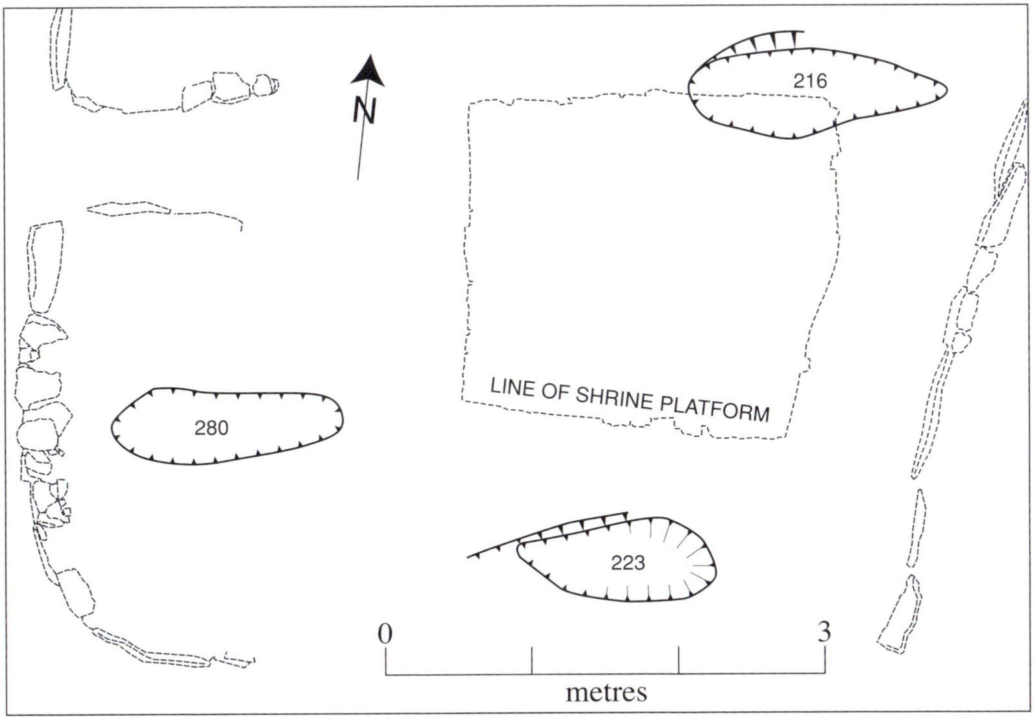

24b—Plan of the three graves under the gable shrine on Illaunloughan. *(C. McHale)*

25—Close-up view of the grave under the north-eastern corner of the walling surrounding the gable shrine on Illaunloughan, showing a small piece of femur remaining in the grave. *(C. Walsh, 1994)*

probably surrounded a no-longer-existing central feature: an earlier shrine, cross or sacred focus that was replaced by the gable shrine. Were these the original burial-places for the three individuals later found in the cists of the gable shrine?

Second oratory or shrine

A second, smaller structure replaced the earlier sod oratory built on the east side of the earlier oratory (Figs 26a and 26b). This diminutive building was only 1.2m wide north–south and of uncertain length, at least 0.80m. No traces of its western wall trenches survived; they were probably covered by the western wall of the later drystone oratory.

Two parallel trenches, each packed with large rectangular sandstones, were reminiscent of the trenches of the earlier sod oratory, although no sod-like material was left between the trenches. A light thatch roof may have rested directly on the walls, as there was no evidence of a roof-support system. Although the distance between the trenches was narrow, no more than 0.25m, this second structure may have had sod walls, provided they were no higher than 1.5m (G.D. Rourke, pers. comm.).

No other feature of this structure survived, and its purpose remains enigmatic, although its location in this area devoted to sacred structures hints that it served an important function. The incorporation of sections of both the first oratory and this second structure in the later drystone oratory appears deliberate and was perhaps

26a—View from the west of the diminutive structure that was built in the oratory space between the Period 1 and Period 2 oratories. *(C. Walsh, 1994)*

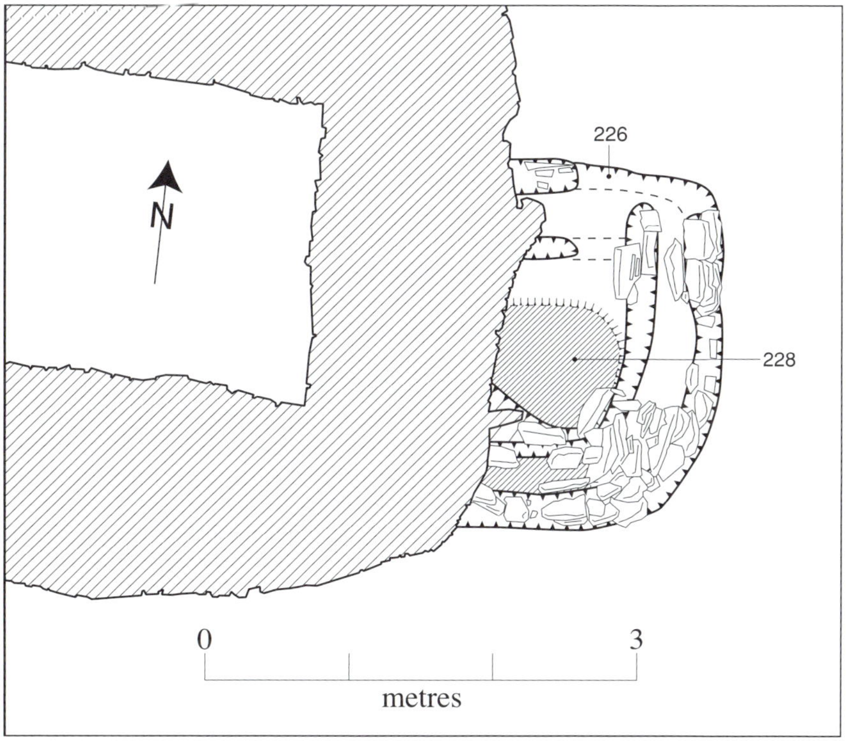

26b—Plan of the diminutive structure built partly upon the eastern end of the Period 1 oratory at Illaunloughan. Little remains of this structure outside of its eastern wall trenches. *(C. McHale)*

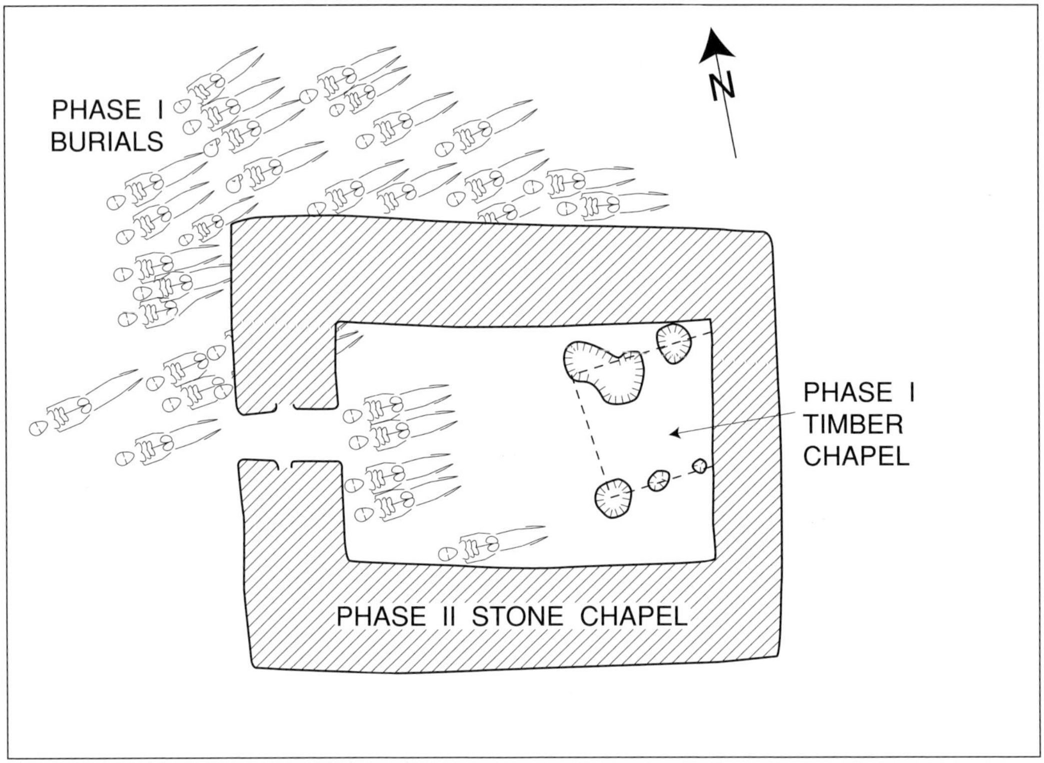

27a—Plan of the post-holes of an earlier structure, possibly an oratory, that remained under the drystone oratory on Church Island, Co. Kerry. *(After O'Kelly 1958)*

intended to create a physical and spiritual link between them. Even the upright stones of the small structure were left untouched and upright where the drystone wall of the later oratory was laid on top of them.

Excavation has revealed the remains, usually imperfectly preserved post-holes, of small timber structures that preceded later stone churches at St Vogue's at Carnsore, Co. Wexford, at Church Island, Valentia Harbour, and at White Island, Co. Fermanagh (Figs 27a and 27b).[32] Similar structures have been found outside Ireland, in Wales, Scotland and Anglo-Saxon England.[33] Interpretation of the function of these structures has varied from that of the first oratory to that of tomb-shrine (Harbison 1982; 1991; Wallace 1982a).

A few small stone oratories also exist, such as the Small Oratory on Skellig Michael, Co. Kerry (2.45m by 1.85m internally), Teampull Dhiarmaid on Inchcleraun, Co. Longford (2.46m by 2.15m internally), and Teach Molaise on Inishmurray, Co. Sligo (2.77m by 2.46m internally) (O'Sullivan and Sheehan 1996, 284; Leask 1955, vol. 1, 51) (Fig. 28). Each of these little stone buildings, however, was one of several oratories on large sites; their names hint that they may have been shrine oratories, built primarily to house the relics of the patron saint, similar to the structure built for St Swithin west of the main church at Winchester.

The small structure on Illaunloughan was the second of three structures built in

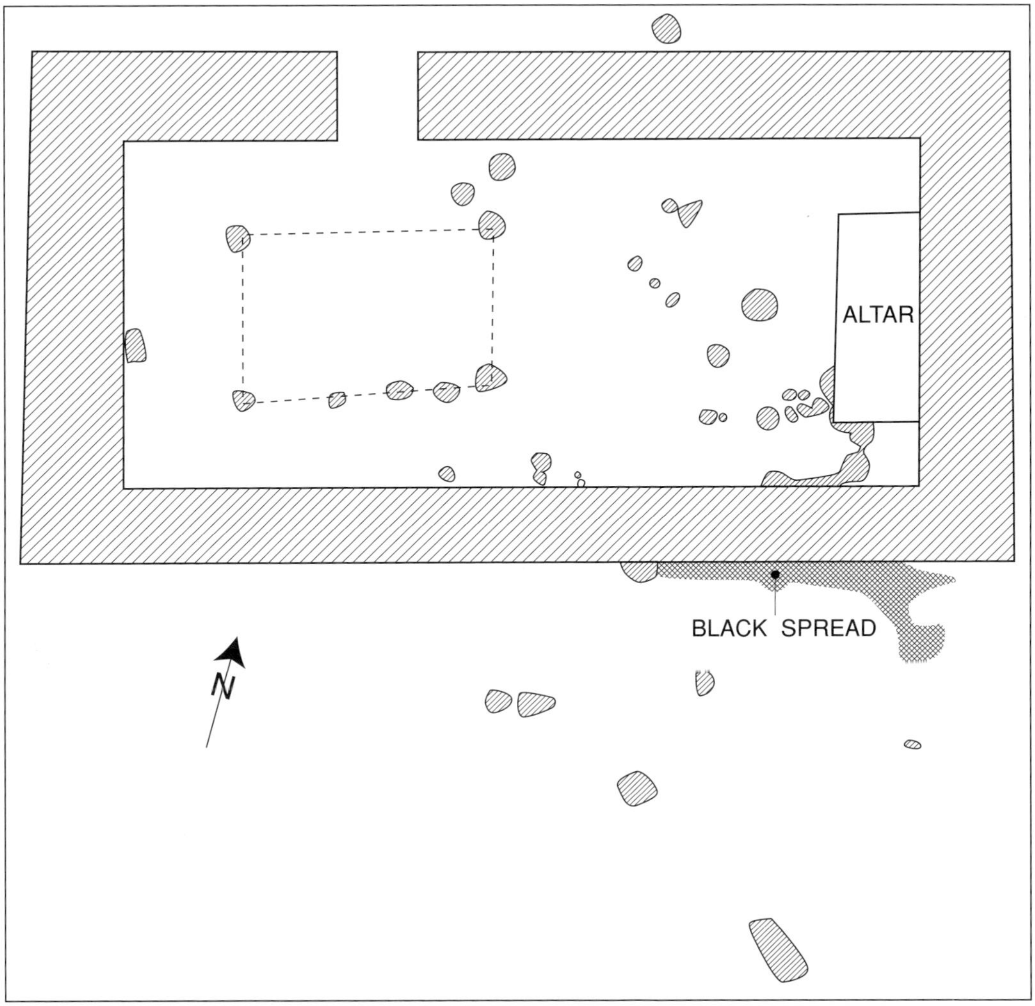

27b—Plan of post-holes under St Vogue's, Carnsore, Co. Wexford, indicating the possible presence of an earlier timber oratory. *(After O'Kelly 1975)*

this location, and, unlike the stone oratories mentioned above, it replaced the primary, sod oratory and preceded the later, drystone oratory. There was no evidence of an oratory elsewhere during its existence. The location of an oratory was carefully considered, and excavation often reveals that successive oratories were built close to or on top of earlier ones. The presence of an earlier and a later oratory here suggests that this structure may also have been one. Its minute size, moreover, would make it the smallest known oratory in Ireland, and it is difficult to imagine that it served the same purpose as the primary or later oratories.

The thin walls and the small size of the structure suggest that it may have been a temporary structure. During construction of the gable shrine and the drystone oratory it may have been used as a short-term oratory serving as a shrine/storage area for the relics that needed to be moved in order to build the gable shrine and to

28—Teach Molaise, Inishmurray, Co. Sligo, one of a number of small stone oratories that still exist on large prestigious ecclesiastical sites along with other, bigger churches. *(Courtesy of the Photographic Section of the Department of the Environment, Heritage and Local Government)*

contain Gospel books and liturgical equipment.

The recent excavation of a mid-twelfth-century structure in Roscommon in the form of a miniature church, 1.5m by 3m, covering a cist burial provides support for the use of oratory-shaped structures for relics and special graves (King 2002; see below, discussion of the *leacht*, Chapter 2, pp 46ff, and discussion of the small reliquary excavated at Roscommon, pp 100–1).

It appears that a construction programme had been planned. The primary oratory was taken down, perhaps because it was subsiding. Then the small oratory/shrine was built, and the relics from the three graves under the gable shrine may have been moved into it. Next, a massive new gable shrine was built, and the relics were deposited in it. Finally, a new drystone oratory was constructed. The entire programme may have been accomplished in a few weeks, with aid from the mainland, or in a few months.

2

Period 2: Eighth to ninth century. Hut D and the drystone oratory

The second period of the community is marked by the transition from sod construction to drystone structures (Fig. 29). During this period a drystone oratory replaced the small sod shrine/oratory. A stone reliquary shrine and its large mound replaced and covered the proposed earlier sacred focus with its surrounding three graves. The community graveyard moved from around the oratory to the eastern quadrant of the shrine mound. A single drystone hut, D, replaced the earlier sod huts, A and B. The building of these drystone structures is a sign that the monastery was thriving and expected to continue to do so; it was willing to invest in longer-lasting structures requiring more work and, in the case of the shrine, of a more monumental nature. They were an investment for the future of the community.

A precise chronological distinction between the end of Period 1 and the beginning of Period 2 based on radiocarbon dating is not possible. A burial, an articulated skeleton (Sk. 192), in the eastern quadrant of the shrine was radiocarbon-dated to the same late seventh- to late eighth-century period as the translated relics in the shrine.[34] The translated bones of three people in the new shrine were strongly related to, indeed likely the inspiration for, the construction of the shrine and its mound and possibly for the entire rebuilding of the monastery. In view of the earlier burials and the activity of Period 1, Period 2 began sometime in the eighth century and may have lasted on a diminished basis into the ninth century (see below and Chapter 3).

Drystone Hut D

Drystone Hut D was built on the south-western edge of the island, overlooking the shallow cove that is one of the closest and easiest landing places for travellers coming from the mainland. The hut is a few metres south of the earlier conjoined sod huts and 22m west of the drystone oratory (Figs 30a and 30b).

The hut was built up against and partly into the rock ridge that traverses the

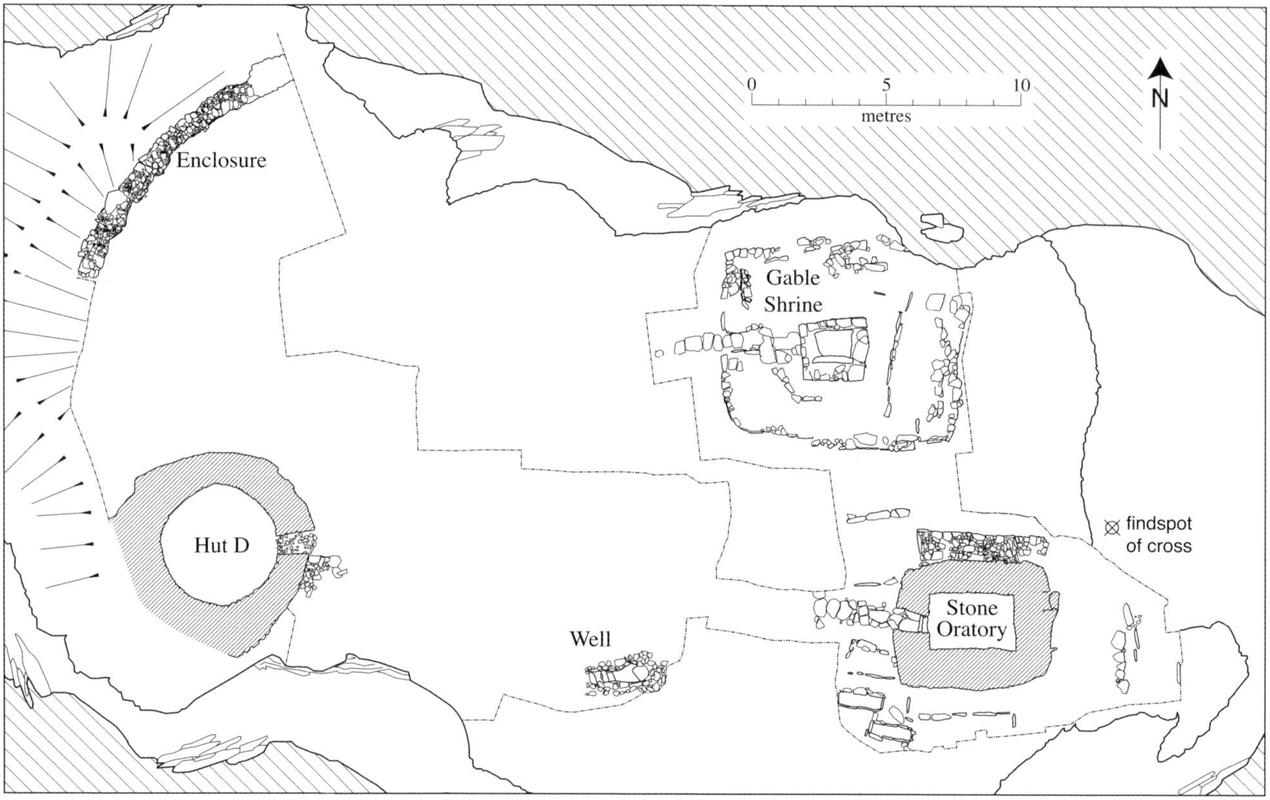

29—Plan of Illaunloughan in Period 2, showing Hut D, the drystone oratory and the large gable shrine. *(C. McHale)*

western end of the island. The ridge, almost 2m high, buffers it from winds and storms coming from the west. No formal flooring was found because the hut interior had been disturbed by later use. It is clear, nonetheless, that its original ground level was below that of the external ground level and that, therefore, soil and probably some of the bedrock needed to be cut out in order to construct the hut. Sunken levels are not characteristic of early medieval Irish huts, but their use here further demonstrates intent to maximise protection from wind and water by using the surrounding ground as natural insulation. The large hut on nearby Beginish Island, itself in a windswept location, was similarly constructed partially below ground level.[35]

The hut was almost perfectly circular, 4.3–4.4m in diameter, with corbelled walls intact to a maximum height of 2.3m on the western side. Hut D has excellent masonry, with walls over 1m thick that are tightly packed and carefully constructed (Fig. 30c). Excavation revealed a considerable amount of stone collapse in the interior of the hut, which confirmed that it was corbel-vaulted. Its masonry style is similar to that of several of the huts on Skellig Michael, but it is closest in masonry, size and shape to the cell found recently on the terrace below the main monastery (G.D. Rourke and E. Burke, pers. comm.). Projecting stones on the exterior masonry

30a—Hut D on Illaunloughan after excavation. A large, well-constructed corbelled stone hut cut partially into the underlying island bedrock, it replaced the earlier sod huts. *(C. Walsh, 1993)*

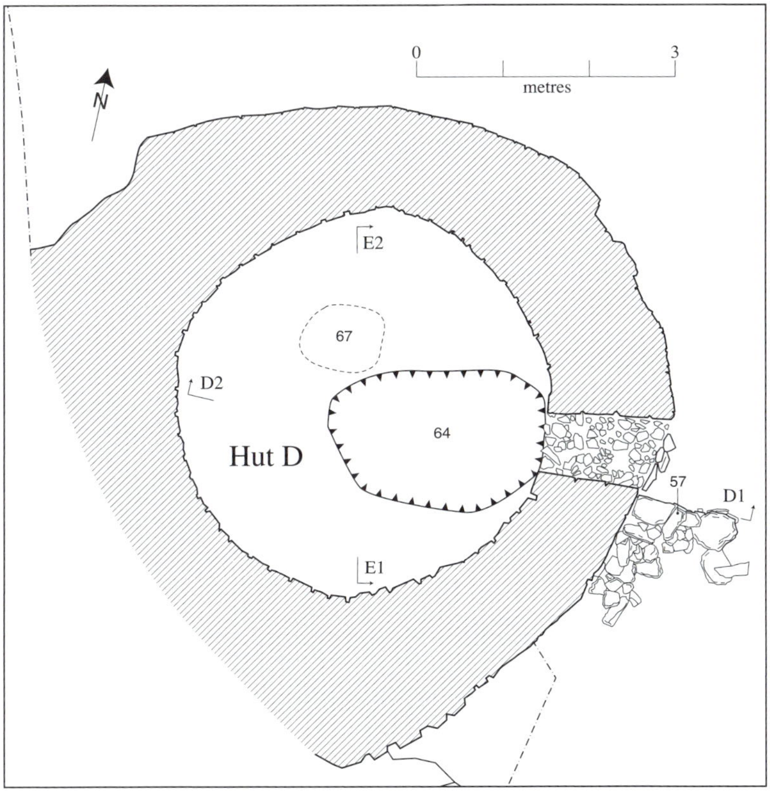

30b—Plan of Hut D, Illaunloughan. The short length of walling that projected from the entrance towards the east probably prevented the drift of midden material into the entranceway of the hut. *(C. McHale)*

30c—Drawing of the interior masonry of Hut D on Illaunloughan, showing the good quality and sturdy nature of the stonework. *(G.D. Rourke)*

31—Cell A on Skellig Michael, Co. Kerry, showing projecting stones similar to those of Hut D on Illaunloughan. These stones probably served as scaffolding during construction and for later repair of the hut. *(G.D. Rourke)*

of Hut D, one on the south-eastern side and one on the north-eastern side, are also seen on two of the larger huts, A and E, on Skellig Michael (Fig. 31). They may have been placed to aid building and repairing of the upper levels of the structures (de Paor 1955, 185).

The external face of the masonry was built on different levels, in a series of steps, and on underlying material of varying degrees of solidity. The north-western masonry, 2.3m high on the interior at the time of excavation, was much lower externally, whereas the south-eastern wall was 1.5m high on both faces. The underlying bedrock on the south-eastern side consisted of thin sheets of slanted, almost vertical sandstone of debased quality, friable and easily fractured. Over a long period of time, sea erosion and subsidence in this area contributed to the south-eastern wall moving outward, whereas the western and northern sections of walling remained quite stable (Figs 32a, 32b and 33). At some later period a revetting wall was constructed here in an effort to halt the outward movement of the wall, which eventually caused the collapse of the dome of the hut. Building techniques were pragmatic and highly eclectic in this period, which is also demonstrated by the shells and cattle bone wedged into a small space under the base walling on the north-eastern side, possibly to level the wall base.

The entrance facing the oratory was on the eastern, most sheltered side of the

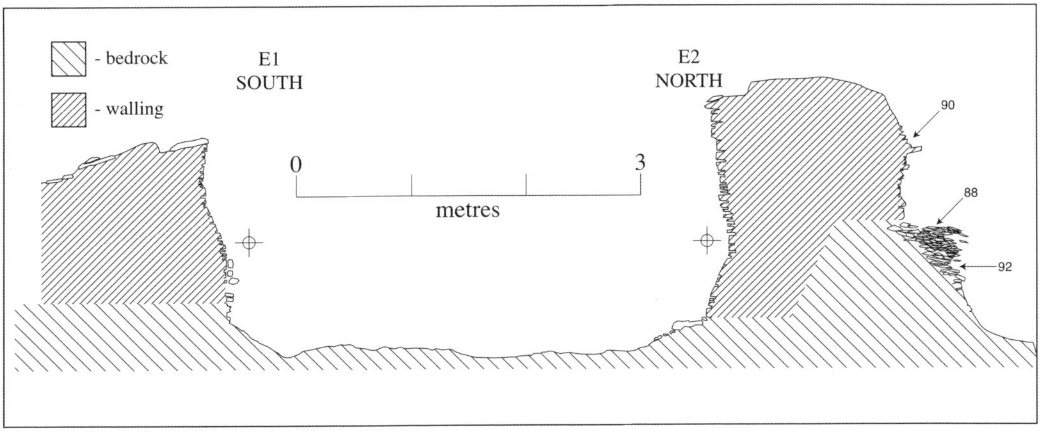

32a—North–south elevation of Hut D, Illaunloughan, showing the hut's construction on different ground levels. *(C. McHale)*

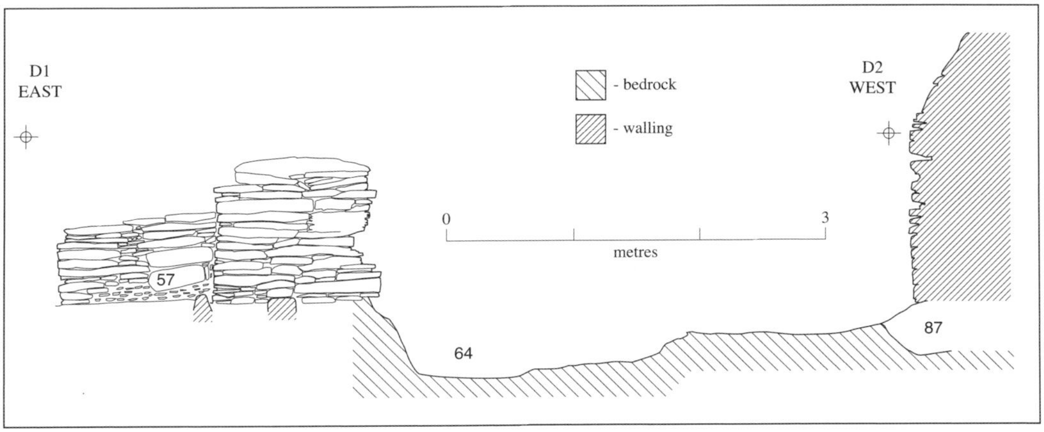

32b—East–west elevation of Hut D, Illaunloughan.

island, like those of the other huts on the island, and was wider externally than internally. The threshold was paved, and underlying the paving was a thin layer of pea-gravel used to level the ground and provide a base for the hut. A short length of stone walling (F57) (Fig. 30b) abutted the southern side of the entrance and extended eastward. The wall was fairly high, standing to a maximum of 0.60m, and was built on gravel and soil deposits associated with Level 1; it pre-dated most of the midden refuse. A similar but more elaborate and longer pair of walls is seen at House 1 on Beginish (O'Kelly 1956). At Illaunloughan the wall provided wind protection and prevented midden refuse from drifting into the entrance.

Before excavation, deposits up to 0.80m thick had accumulated in the interior in the form of stone collapse, soil, burials, and small amounts of animal bone and shell. The interior masonry of the hut was unbroken, with no sign of cupboards, hanging pegs or windows. Excavation revealed little about its original inhabitants from the interior soil layers. Ashy and charcoal deposits dated to the later medieval period indicated post-monastic occupation of the hut for at least a short term and possibly several times.[36] The cell was used again, probably in the nineteenth

33—Hut D from the north-east in 1994, showing its location on the island and also showing the burial under the north-eastern corner of the gable shrine. *(Con Brogan)*

century, for four burials: a neonate, two juveniles and an adult.

Radiocarbon analysis of cattle bones found under the base of the north-western side of the hut dates the construction of the hut to sometime between AD 775 and 961.[37] It is improbable, however, that the hut dates from later than the early ninth century (see below, burials, Chapter 5), and it may have been built in the second half of the eighth century. The extensive refuse deposits associated with Hut D, several times greater than those found for Huts A and B, indicate occupation for a considerable time. Hut D, of less spiritual importance to the settlement than the oratory and the reliquary shrine, may have been the last stone structure built on the island.

Another feature of the monastery on Illaunloughan is the small well. This feature is not fed by a spring but is rather a ground-run water-collection system, similar to that on many islands. Some system of collecting and holding water was necessary for the community. The well on Illaunloughan may have been dug out and enlarged, because it is unlikely that such a deep hole was a natural occurrence. The well is well built of seven drystone steps, each 0.45m wide, leading down to the pool of water, with a large capstone over the pool. Excavation yielded nothing of archaeological significance.

The drystone oratory

Grass and sod-covered debris effectively concealed much of the remaining structure before excavation, particularly on the eastern and western sides (Fig. 34a).

34a—The oratory on Illaunloughan from the west after excavation, showing the oratory walls intact up to a maximum height of 1.29m and some of the burials around it. Remnants of a flagstone path led to the western entry. The wall masonry was strong and tightly made of a large variety of small to medium-sized oblong stones, ranging from 0.1m to 0.8m, with the majority in the mid-ranges. There are no signs of worked or dressed corner stones or door jambs. *(C. Walsh, 1993)*

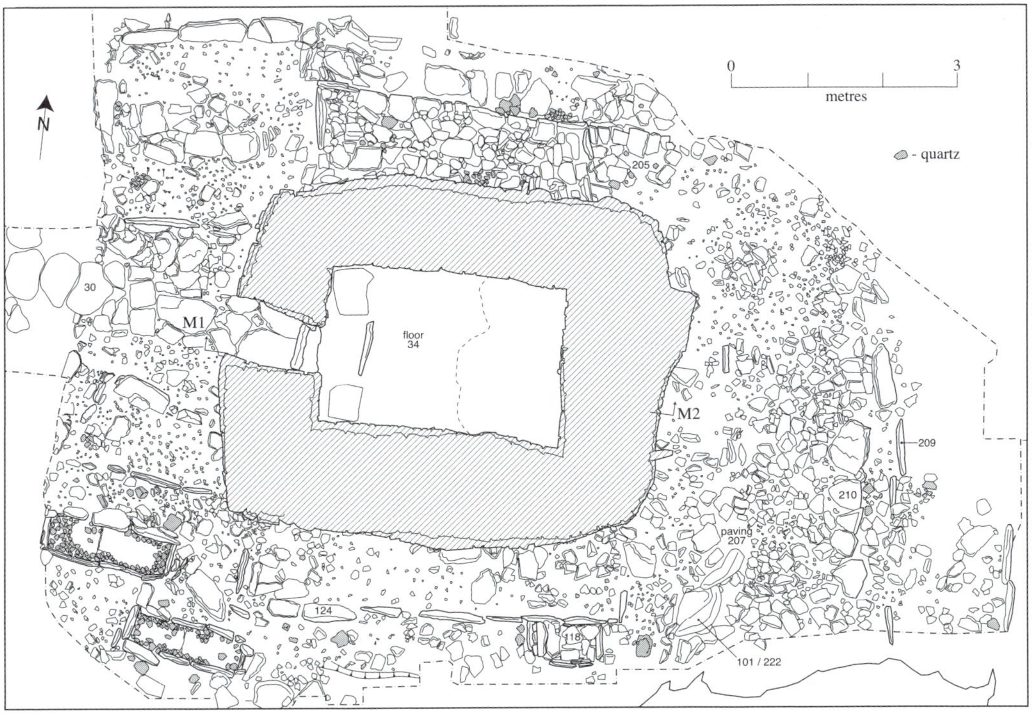

34b—Plan of the drystone Period 2 oratory on Illaunloughan, showing the area east of the Period 1 oratory. Two terraces were formed in this area, before the construction of the Period 2 oratory, by depositing soil and gravel; in addition, kerbstones marked the end of the Period 1 oratory and also the end of the graves. *(C. McHale)*

The collapse of stone from the upper walls of the oratory and the sod and grass that covered the fallen stones were substantial enough to raise the ground level around the structure to as much as 0.66m high. When excavated, the walls were found to stand to a maximum height of 1.29m and were clearly corbelled and battered; the thickness of the wall base varied from 1.3m to 1.6m on the northern and southern walls, and the eastern and western walls were somewhat thinner.

The entrance of the Illaunloughan oratory, in common with all Irish church thresholds, was paved with large flagstones; a well-built path of flagstones led away from the oratory but was broken off a few metres from the oratory threshold (Fig. 34b). The door jambs of the entrance were splayed, varying in width from 0.95m on the outside to 0.62m on the inside, but had no vertical uprights used as facing stones, a feature seen on the Large Oratory at Skellig Michael. There was no evidence of working or dressing on any of the stones. An unusual feature of the entrance was the step down from the threshold paving into the interior, perhaps a consequence of building on top of the earlier sod oratory; the sill stone of the earlier structure, which remained in place, is at this lower level.

No trace of a window was left at Illaunloughan, but a single window in the eastern façade was common in early medieval stone oratories and churches in Ireland; windows tended to be flat-headed with splayed ingoings and inclined jambs with stepped sills. Only one corbelled oratory, Gallarus, on the Dingle Peninsula, has a simple, small, round-headed window.

The exterior masonry of the oratory comprised stones of varying size. The average stone was flat, rarely more than 0.15m high and 0.20–0.30m wide. There was no attempt to create courses, but the stones were well and closely set, with a levelling effect that would have been more noticeable when the oratory was intact, as subsidence and collapse of the upper walls have displaced some stones. Nothing in the masonry fabric indicated more than one period of construction.

Island stone was used for the oratory, and evidence of quarrying on the rock ridge behind the domestic huts was clearly visible. Devonian sandstone is easily prised off with iron tools and makes a strong building stone for corbelled structures.

Surface beneath the oratory

The drystone oratory, the last oratory built on Illaunloughan, was shorter than the sod-constructed oratory, and the eastern wall was set considerably farther to the west (Fig. 17). The width was the same, however, as the northern and southern walls were perfectly aligned with those of the earlier oratory; the western wall was only 0.60–0.80m farther west than that of the first oratory. Over the centuries since its construction, the more western location and its more durable stone material have helped to protect the structure from damage by high tides and storms, but it has suffered some sea damage (see below, Chapter 9). It is also probable that the second oratory was smaller because of the challenges involved in building a rectangular corbelled drystone structure (see Chapter 7).

The earlier sod walls were spread out or levelled, covering the trenches of the first two structures east of the drystone oratory. A substantial bed of pea-gravel and small stones was laid on top of the soil under the drystone walls and on the now-vacant eastern space of the sod oratory. Pea-gravel extended almost 5m east of the present oratory and created a raised area or low platform.

Two sets of vertically set kerbstones were placed here, with one set (F210) marking the eastern wall of the earlier sod-constructed oratory and the second (F209) marking the end of the graves east of this oratory, forming an inner and an outer terrace (Fig. 22). This may reflect a desire to mark out and maintain a tangible link with the earlier structures, as well as to protect the area from erosion. The kerbing has now been largely displaced by erosion. The area containing the remnants of these structures was not used again by the community, not even for burial, which substantiates the idea that the community wished to honour this space.

The pea-gravel under the drystone walls served another purpose. There were no foundations, in the customary definition of sunken underpinnings, usually in stone, for the oratory. Such traditional foundations, common to Mediterranean stone buildings, were not used in early medieval Ireland.[38] The Illaunloughan community was, nevertheless, aware of the necessity of providing a level building surface. The space on which the oratory sits has a slight natural slope running down from west to east; it was, furthermore, prudent to provide a surface on top of the remains of the earlier structures. A level of pea-gravel and shillet, material readily available around the shoreline of the island, was a pragmatic solution, one used for other Illaunloughan stone structures (see discussion on the reliquary shrine in Chapter 3 and the drystone domestic hut, above).

A substantial level was laid down under the walls of the oratory; around the north-eastern corner of the oratory the gravel deposit was 0.20m deep. At the base of the northern and southern walls, those most affected by the sloping terrain, additional measures were taken. Along the southern wall, noticeably large stones and boulders were used along the base, forming an uneven, rather erratic baseline that occasionally projects awkwardly beyond the wall face (Fig. 35). The northern wall was also exceptionally treated, as it was built on a plinth on top of the *leacht* (see below).

Interior of the oratory and post-monastic occupation

Its internal dimensions of 3.2m north–south by 2.2m east–west are average for drystone oratories on the Iveragh Peninsula and similar to the Large Oratory at Skellig Michael and to the oratory at Kildreelig. The interior of the oratory had been filled with collapsed stone, a number of baby burials and covered by grassy sod. Little evidence remained of features of the oratory; no articulation of the walls, windows, cupboards or altars was visible. Indeed, only the remnants of a flagstone

35—The southern wall of the oratory on Illaunloughan, showing the round boulders used along the base of the wall to compensate for the difference in ground level, which dropped slightly from west to east. *(C. Walsh, 1993)*

path leading to a well-set paved threshold with a sill stone still existed.

Several pieces of evidence indicated later medieval use of the oratory, probably on a short-term basis, either for habitation or for industrial purposes, in at least two different time periods. Seeds of *Avena strigosa* from a burnt layer (F31) inside the oratory, near the western and northern walls, indicate occupation between AD 1260 and 1390.[39] Six silver pennies dating from AD 1272 to 1377 were found buried together outside the west doorway of the oratory (see Chapter 10). Later still, between the fifteenth and the seventeenth centuries, the oratory was reused for domestic or industrial purposes. The western doorway was blocked, and a door was cut in the eastern wall. Two stone-lined pits at the eastern end of the oratory contained evidence of ironworking (see Chapter 9) (Fig. 34b).[40]

Northern oratory wall and the *leacht*

Excavation on the northern side of the oratory revealed a sizeable, solidly built *leacht*, clearly a primary feature, the construction of which was integrated with that of the oratory (Fig. 36).

Leachta are simple, quadrangular, drystone structures, easily built and equally easily destroyed. Their origins, purpose and chronology are difficult to determine precisely, and, as a consequence, they have not been thoroughly studied either by survey or by excavation.[41] They are clearly associated with early medieval ecclesiastical, rather than with secular, sites, although not all ecclesiastical sites have

36—The northern wall of the oratory on Illaunloughan, showing the drystone *leacht* that served as a base for the oratory wall. Stones on the eastern and western ends of the *leacht* were keyed into the oratory, indicating that they were integrated together. *(C. Walsh, 1993)*

leachta. A number of settlements such as Skellig Michael, Co. Kerry, have one or more within the ecclesiastical enclosure, whereas others, such as Caher Island, Co. Mayo, Inishmurray, Co. Sligo, and High Island, Co. Galway, have them both inside and outside the enclosure. Surviving examples in Ireland are primarily found in the western coastal areas, but it is possible that their original distribution was more widespread. J. O'Sullivan (pers. comm.) notes that there are *leacht*-like remnants at Glendalough and Clonmacnoise, and Thomas (1971, 169–74) associates *leachta* with settlements outside of Ireland such as St Patrick's Chair, Marown, the Isle of Man, and Ardwall Isle in the west of Argyll, Scotland.[42]

The Illaunloughan *leacht* was 1–1.3m wide (north–south) and ran parallel to the northern wall of the oratory for 3.6m. Lower than the *leachta* on Skellig Michael, at 0.4m high, it appeared to be undisturbed and in its original condition, with its borders strongly defined by sizeable vertical stones interspersed occasionally with short sections of walling. A similar use of vertical uprights combined with walling is found in the kerbing of the reliquary shrine. Each vertical stone of the *leacht* was set deeply in a trench, *c.* 0.50m wide, dug to a depth according to its individual size; on the northern border, small stones at the base further braced the upright stones (Figs 37a and 37b). The interior of the *leacht* was filled with redeposited soil, gravel and small stones and finished with rough layers of larger stones; liberal quantities of white quartz stones covered the top.[43]

The northern wall of the oratory was clearly designed to be constructed on top

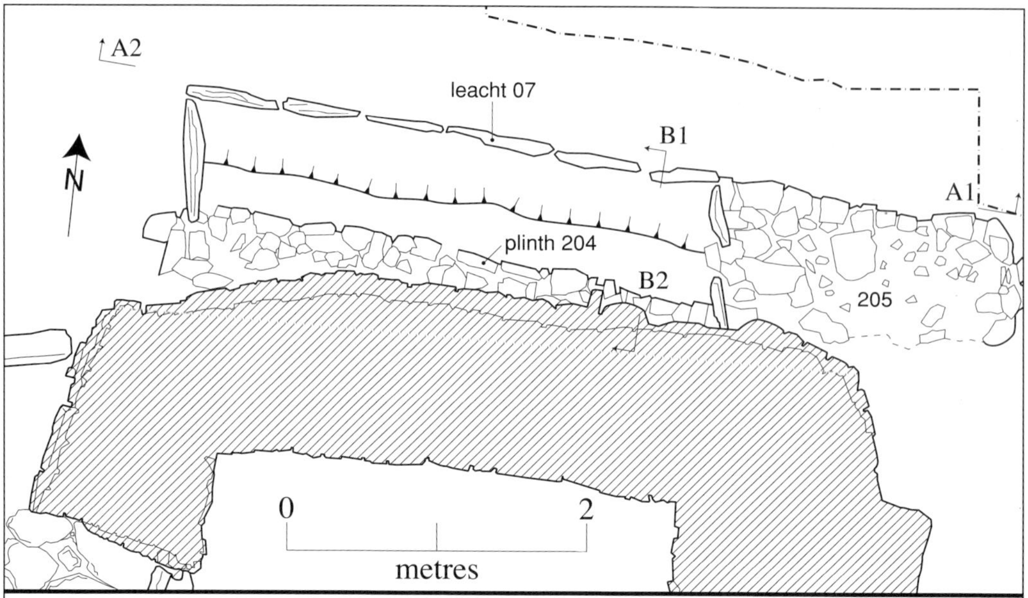

37a—Plan of the *leacht* on Illaunloughan. The oratory's northern wall rose from a plinth, shown by dotted lines, that only extends for the length of the *leacht*. (*C. McHale*)

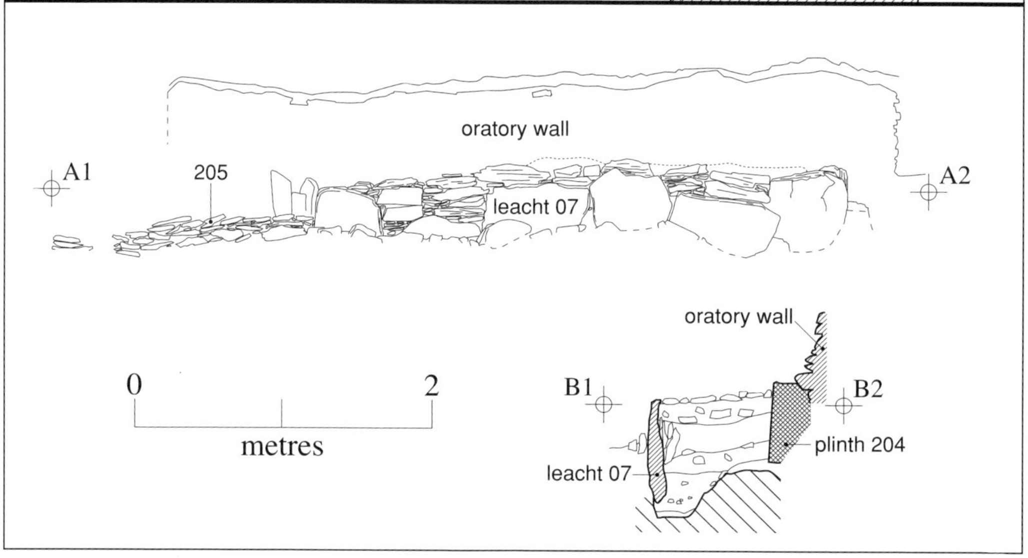

37b—Elevation of the *leacht* on Illaunloughan, showing the kerbing around it which consisted of upright stones sunk into the ground, alternating with short sections of stone walling and the plinth. (*C. McHale*)

of the *leacht*. The kerbstones on the eastern and western sides of the *leacht* were keyed into the oratory wall. A thin plinth (F204) projected from the base of the northern oratory wall and ran along the *leacht* for its entire length, diminishing from 0.40m wide at the western end to 0.20m at the eastern. Effectively, the plinth served as a level base or foundation for this section of the northern wall as it rose above this level. Its full width remains unknown without the demolition of the northern wall, but there was no evidence that it extended beyond the width of the wall; it probably ended under the wall. The deliberate structural integration

38—The Large Oratory and its *leacht* on Skellig Michael, Co. Kerry. The Skellig Michael *leacht* is positioned on the northern side of the oratory and integrated with its construction, like the *leacht* at Illaunloughan. *(G.D. Rourke)*

between the oratory and the *leacht* is unusual and known elsewhere only at the Large Oratory on Skellig Michael, where a similar *leacht* is also found on the northern side of the oratory (Fig. 38).

Function of *leachta*

Interpretation of the function of *leachta* has relied on the meaning of the word and on their traditional use as local pilgrimage, or *turas*, stations. The Irish word *leacht* strongly suggests funereal origins and purposes for these structures: Ó Dónaill's (1977, 757) Irish dictionary defines *leacht* as (i) a 'grave or gravemound', (ii) a 'memorial cairn', (iii) a 'memorial or monument' and, finally, (iv) a 'heap or mound'. C. Thomas (1971, 168–72) noted that the word derives from the Latin and Old Irish words *lectus* and *lecht*, both of which mean 'bed' in the early medieval sense of 'grave'.[44] Thomas further pointed out a reference in the twelfth-century *Life of St Illtud* that describes a burial structure in south Wales that may have been a *leacht* or a cist tomb, both potentially similar-looking structures: 'the body (of Samson) was taken and honourably carried by the clergy and buried in the midst of quadrangular stones [*in medio quadrangularium lapidum*] standing upright in the cemetery, a stone cross being placed above and the insignia of a bishop inscribed below' (Wade-Evans 1944, 217). Burial connotations for the meaning of *leachta* have been common and scholars have suggested that they were used as grave or tomb covers for individual saints, as reliquary shrines containing the bones or belongings of a saint, or as a special type of memorial.

Folk tradition and historical documentation, however, clearly demonstrate that *leachta* have often been used as pilgrimage stations in locations where a burial connection is unlikely. Speculation about their use and purpose has also included, therefore, the idea that they were altars for these stations (C. Thomas 1971; Herity 1995). In 1971 C. Thomas posed questions that have never been satisfactorily answered. Did they begin as special graves that were then treated as open-air altars, or were they simply originally altars? Were they in some fashion imitating the customs of early Christians who, from the early use of graves as altars in the catacombs, next built altars and churches over the burials of the saints?

Excavation of *leachta*

Several recent excavations have provided more information, if no definite answers to Thomas's questions. The first excavation of a well-known pilgrimage station was carried out on Inishmurray, Co. Sligo, which may have the greatest number of surviving *leachta* on any site in Ireland. With over two centuries of documentation, Inishmurray also has the longest record of continuously used and preserved structures of this type in Ireland. In 1794 the artist Gabriel Beranger wrote the first account of the Inishmurray stations following his visit to the island, in which he recorded thirteen 'places of devotion on the island, called Stations, which the Romans Catholicks visit, and where prayers are said'. He then briefly named and described the stations that had altars or *leachta*: 'The first eleven stations consist in or are squares of ten or twelve feet, with a wall of dry stones, breast high, and a cross, altar or pillar in their centre' (Beranger as recorded in Wilde 1870–1, 135). Successive authors, O'Donovan (1836) and Wakeman (1893), used slightly different names and numbers, but their accounts exhibit excellent general agreement with Beranger's stations, and with those listed by Heraughty (1982), who has written the most recent book on the island–the only one written by an islander.[45] He, like Wakeman, described some of the stations as altars and others as memorial altars.

In 1997 O'Sullivan and James excavated Trahaun O Rian, the westernmost of the Inishmurray stations, which had the usual Inishmurray pilgrimage station components of a stone altar, or *leacht*, surrounded by a stone wall, in addition to the remains of a small drystone cell in the western side of the enclosure wall (Fig. 39).[46] They found the altar to be a secondary construction of uncertain date. The primary phase of the station consisted of the cell, with remnants of a small area of paving that the excavators believed may have been the base for a post, perhaps a support for a table altar or a cross. Unfortunately, the primary phase also remained undated (J. O'Sullivan, pers. comm.). In 1999–2000 several other Inishmurray stations were excavated, including the two at the medieval cemetery of Roilig Odhráin.[47] The *leachta* here overlay burials whose calibrated radiocarbon dates ranged broadly between the tenth and twelfth centuries. O'Sullivan (pers. comm., 2004) concluded that the period of construction of these monuments and the

39—Trahaun O Rian, one of a number of stations on Inishmurray, Co. Sligo, that consisted of a *leacht* surrounded by drystone walling. The station also has a corbelled drystone hut—the only station on Inishmurray to have a hut. Trahaun O Rian was excavated in 1997 by O'Sullivan and James. *(After Wakeman 1893)*

period of their use covered a long time.[48]

O'Sullivan and James's excavation substantiates the oral tradition of altars/*leachta* as memorial stations, dedicated to the memory of a saint, or a place that was held in great esteem and functioned as a pilgrimage altar. The excavation also illustrated the problems of establishing a chronology for these structures.

In 1992–3 O'Keefe's excavation of the burial-grounds on the north side of Omey Island, Co. Galway, uncovered a *leacht* that had graves beneath it. However, O'Keefe (1994; 1998, 116) points out that the structure covered no specific grave, and the date of its construction remains uncertain. Nevertheless, he suspects that the *leacht* was linked with burials because of the etymology of the word *leacht* and the custom of depositing white quartz on both *leachta* and burials. He suggests that they may be a form of memorial, structures dedicated to people who were buried elsewhere. O'Keefe's hypothesis is perfectly possible, though difficult to prove. Equally plausible is that a *leacht*/altar may have been erected in graveyards for prayers in remembrance of all the dead, rather than for a specific burial.

The results at Illaunloughan, however, differ from these excavations in that the *leacht* was clearly a primary structure, an original feature of the ecclesiastical site built by members of the community during the early medieval period. The Illaunloughan *leacht* does not fit satisfactorily into a number of proposed functions for these structures. Excavation revealed no evidence that it had been used as a base for a cross stone, nor did it cover any original structures. It certainly was not built as a grave cover for an individual burial, although it rests on top of earlier burials. Its construction partially intersects one or two burials, and consequently its position appears to be fortuitous rather than deliberately marking a specific grave, much like the *leacht* on Omey Island.

The *leacht* post-dates the construction of the first sod-built oratory because the trench for the kerb or border stones of the *leacht* cut through two burials (F203 and F202) on the north-western side of the sod oratory. The drystone oratory, moreover, rests on top of the *leacht*, which means that the *leacht* also pre-dates this oratory, but how much earlier it is remains uncertain. Excavation uncovered a thin deposit of pea-gravel in the lower fill of the trench of the *leacht*; deposits of pea-gravel were laid down before construction of the drystone, Period 2 oratory, which suggests that the *leacht* was built concurrently with the oratory (see Chapter 9). In no case could its construction have long preceded the drystone oratory, as it was planned to be aligned with and part of that structure.

There is no reason to believe that the *leacht* was used as a reliquary, despite the presence of bone. We base this conclusion on comparison with the special structural treatment of enshrined material on Illaunloughan. Unlike the distinctive treatment accorded to the bones in the gable shrine, the bones in the *leacht* were not placed inside small paved cists. There was, moreover, no particular treatment of the area surrounding these bones: the pea-gravel and white quartz found in the gable cists are also absent. The lower part of one burial in the *leacht* was left untouched, but the skull in the southern section had clearly been displaced; the position of the skull appears to indicate respectful treatment of a burial disturbed during construction of the *leacht*.

Conclusions

The significance of the excavation of the Illaunloughan *leacht* is that it demonstrates the building of these structures by ecclesiastics as early as the eighth century. The existing evidence on *leachta* is most consistent with an interpretation of them as altars, substantiating C. Thomas's (1971) and Herity's (1995) hypotheses that they were open-air altars of considerable antiquity. Altars have multiple uses as places for prayer and the saying of Mass; consequently, they can be erected wherever it may be thought appropriate.

Although current evidence shows no link between *leachta* and specific burials, too little is known to assert that there was none. There was, moreover, a strong and well-documented connection between church altars and the saintly dead, dating from the early Christian centuries in the Roman catacombs, and widely practised on the Continent and in Anglo-Saxon England (Herrmann-Mascard 1975; Marshall and Rourke 2000, 92–3, 118–20). The custom of burial near the altar in the church was not common in Ireland during the early medieval period, even for saints, with a few exceptions such as the tomb of St Brigid and Bishop Conláed at Kildare and possibly the burials inside the church at Dunmisk (Doherty 1989, 2:17; Ivens 1989, 17–64). It is entirely possible, however, that one of the purposes of *leachta* in Ireland was to serve as altars for the saintly dead who were buried outside the church. The presence of white quartz on these structures indicates, at least, that pilgrims may have perceived them as such, or, if pilgrimage altars were dedicated to a saint or to a stage in the life of Christ, white quartz may have been placed as a token of reverence and respect.

The intimate connection between the oratory and the *leacht* at Illaunloughan suggests an important, perhaps liturgical, purpose for the structure. It is possible that, in spite of its low height, it served as an altar, perhaps a memorial altar marking the place of the first oratory and honouring the earlier monks buried around the oratory.

There are two further possibilities for the use of this structure as an altar after the construction of the drystone oratory: one relates to pilgrims coming to the island, and the other to the use of multiple altars on ecclesiastical sites in the early medieval period. The size and prominence of the expanded shrine on the island are a strong indication of flourishing pilgrimage visitation, and, if this is the case, pilgrims may have wanted to say additional prayers at the oratory. An outer altar would permit pilgrims to pray by the oratory while preserving the interior for the exclusive use of the community. It is also possible that Irish religious communities adopted the custom, common elsewhere, of having more than one altar. Processional services that went from altar to altar at large ecclesiastical sites had become so common that regulations for them were written down in the ninth century by Angilbert for St Riquier of Centula in Carolingian France and in the tenth century *Regula Concordia* in Anglo-Saxon England.[49] It is not clear to what extent small Irish communities followed this custom.

3

Period 2: The reliquary shrine

The most prominent, immediately visible feature on Illaunloughan is the reliquary shrine on the northern side of the island, *c.* 9.2m north of the church. Before excavation the shrine appeared as two large slate stones on top of a grassy knoll (Fig. 40). It is one of a small group of fixed, open-air structures, each formed by two long stones placed together like a small tent, with smaller, triangular end stones. Scholars have long suspected that these structures were reliquary shrines and labelled them slab shrines, house shrines or gable shrines. At Illaunloughan and similar Iveragh structures the shrine is surrounded by a border of upright stones.

Scholarly discussion of these structures has been limited. Françoise Henry first identified three intact gable shrines in the area of Waterville and Caherciveen, Co. Kerry: Killoluaig, Killabuonia and Illaunloughan (Figs 41 and 42).[50] Henry (1957, 160–1) referred to these structures as shrine-shaped tombs but decided that they were too short to have contained original burials and were, therefore, shrines containing translated bones. In 1971 Charles Thomas agreed with Henry that they were reliquary shrines and further speculated that they were directly inspired by Mediterranean *cella memoriae*, open-air or partly roofed walled yards around the tomb of a saint, in themselves shrines and an early stage in the progressive elaboration of objects or buildings designed to display relics for veneration. The tombs also had openings known as *fenestellae*, which both Henry and Thomas believed were present in the gable or triangular ends of the Kerry shrines, such as that at Killabuonia. Thomas (1971, 139–44) also believed that the Kerry structures were the oldest surviving structures of this type in Britain and Ireland, possibly as early as AD 600.[51] Hamlin (1984, 295–6) pointed out the problems created by the absence of dating evidence for these shrines and further suggested that their closest resemblance was to the twelfth-century shrine of St Manchán, which contains bones assumed to be those of a holy man associated with the site, perhaps the founder.

40—The gable shrine on Illaunloughan before excavation. *(Walter Horn, 1982)*

Only a few gable shrines other than the three in western Kerry remain. There are the remains of a gable shrine at Cill Comhla on Inishmore, Co. Galway (Waddell 1976; 1994, 118), and two larger ones at Temple Cronan, Co. Clare. Waddell (1994, 128–9) has also identified a solitary triangular end stone as part of another at Cill Cheannannach on Inis Meáin, Galway. Other sites that may have had gable shrines, but with less clearly identified elements, include Inishcealtra (N. Edwards, pers. comm.; Harbison 1991) and Aghatubrid (Kilpecan), Co. Kerry. Their current distribution indicates that they were common at ecclesiastical sites on the western coast of Ireland, but their original distribution may have been more widespread, as Westropp (1901, 405) believed that he found part of such a shrine at Slane, Co. Meath.[52]

All of the gable shrines are oriented like churches and burials. Two of the Kerry shrines are also definitely placed on raised areas or mounds surrounded by vertically placed stones, creating a clearly defined sacred space around the shrine. The Illaunloughan shrine was displayed most prominently of all; it sits on an enclosed area that extends for 9m by 7.6m and is 1.5m higher than the surrounding ground level. At Killoluaig the shrine is defined by vertical stones enclosing an area of 2.5m by 4.6m; a shrine mound, clearly formed partly of loose stones, is 0.40m above the present ground level (Fig. 43).

At Killabuonia Henry (1957, 102–3, fig. 18) reported that the shrine was not defined by a surround and not on a raised area of its own but placed on a raised

41—Gable shrine at nearby Killoluaig, Co. Kerry. The shrine is similar in style to that at Illaunloughan, but the mound is considerably smaller. *(J. Marshall, 1995)*

42—Gable shrine at Killabuonia, Co. Kerry, which contained a circular opening that allowed the devout to access the area containing the relics. *(C. Walsh, 1993)*

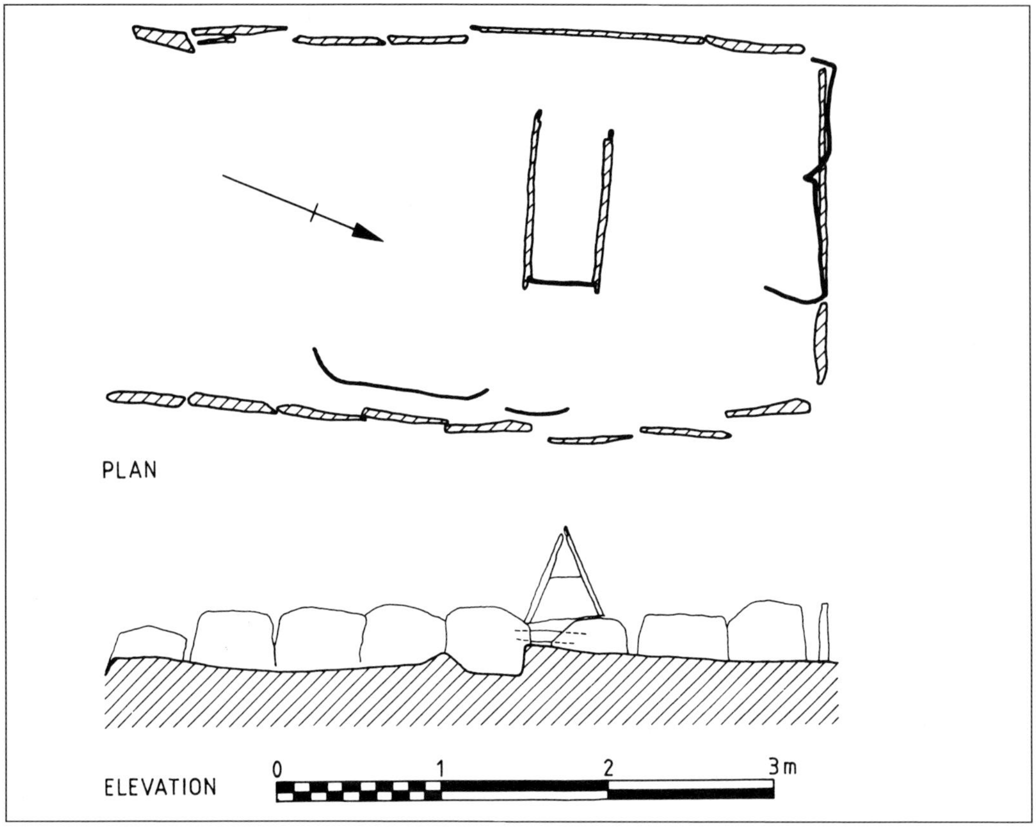

43—Plan and elevation of shrine mound at Killoluaig. *(After O'Sullivan and Sheehan 1996)*

terrace along with the oratory. Closer inspection, however, indicates that the reliquary shrine may have been constructed on a raised mound defined by vertical stones (G.D. Rourke, pers. comm., 1990). A large vertical stone, almost 2m long, forms the western side of the shrine, and others may lie below the present ground level. The ground level around the shrine at Killabuonia has risen over the centuries; a general indication of the amount of soil that has been carried downhill is given by the current height of the ground level at the oratory entrance. A large shrine mound, previously termed the 'garden terrace' by O'Kelly (1958), is undergoing excavation by A. Hayden at Church Island, Valentia Harbour.

Gable shrines outside of the Iveragh Peninsula have no visible evidence of enclosure walls or built-up mounds.

Illaunloughan shrine

Excavation showed that the raised rectangular mound surrounding the Illaunloughan shrine was composed partly of a natural rock outcrop running east-west along the northern, seaward side of the mound; the shrine itself was built upon this rock (Figs 44a and 44b). Where the rock ended abruptly on the southern

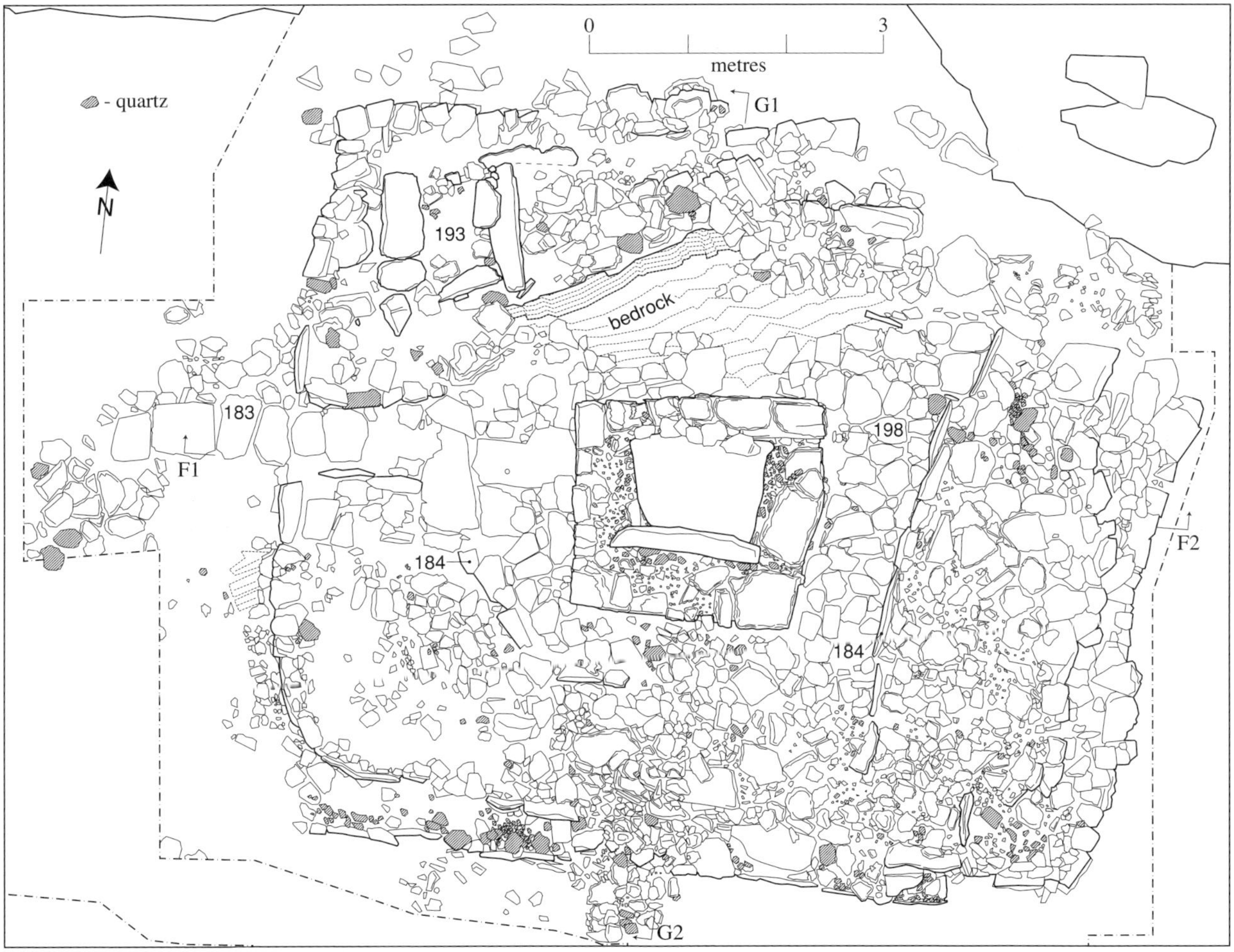

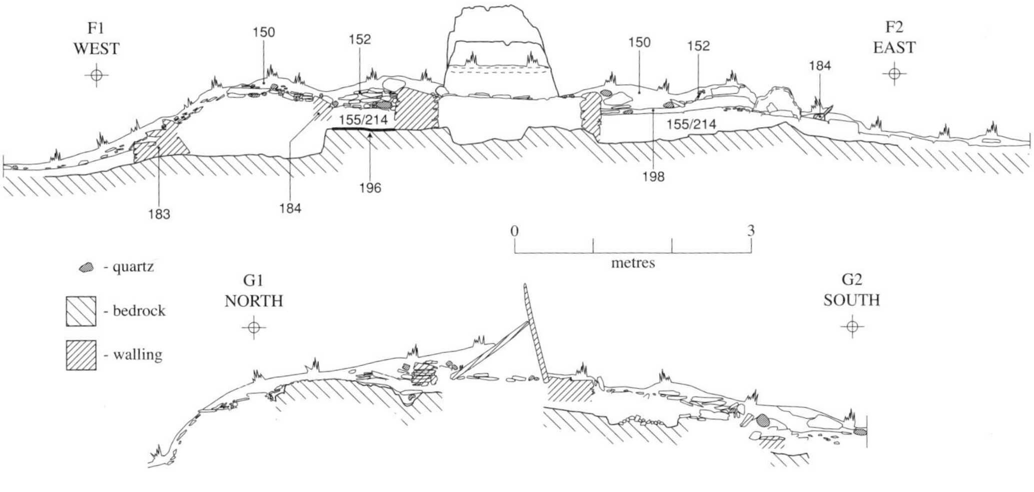

44a (above)—Plan of the gable shrine and its surrounding mound at Illaunloughan, showing the larger size and greater complexity of the shrine compared to that at Killoluaig. *(C. McHale)*

44b—Elevation of the gable shrine and its mound at Illaunloughan. *(C. McHale)*

45—The gable shrine at Illaunloughan from the west with the sod cover removed, showing the gently rising steps on the west leading up to the central section of the mound that contained the reliquary shrine. Quantities of white quartz stones were scattered over the shrine mound. *(J.W. Marshall, 1993)*

and eastern side of the mound, soil, stone and pea-gravel were used to raise the mound to the same level. Numerous white quartz stones of varying size were scattered over the mound (see discussion of white quartz stones below, Chapter 6) and mixed with the gravel forming it. Vertically set stones alternating with short sections of walling defined the southern, western and eastern perimeter. On the northern side the rock outcrop ends abruptly, and substantial erosion here has completely swept away any fill, kerbing or monastic enclosure wall that may have been here originally. The kerbing served the practical function of retaining the mound fill as well as defining the sacred space of the saints. As the mound fill gradually shifted downhill over the centuries, the short sections of walling were less successful than the vertical uprights in retaining it.

The entrance to the shrine was on the western side, where a short, gently rising, flight of sandstone steps led up to a roughly paved area that surrounded the shrine (Fig. 45) A rectangular structure of drystone walling, positioned slightly off-centre on top of the mound, contained the two slate stones forming the gable shrine (Fig. 46). The shrine consisted of only the two long stones, which had been dislodged from their original positions so that the northern stone had slipped below the southern stone; the two smaller end pieces of the shrine were missing. The walling, almost 0.5m high, braced the gable shrine and protected the interior core of material.

46—The slate gable shrine on Illaunloughan, set inside and braced by drystone walling. Flagstone paving ran around the shrine. The two small end pieces of the gable shrine were missing, and the northern slate stone had slipped below the southern one. *(C. Walsh, 1993)*

Interior of the shrine

The upper layer of soil within the shrine had clearly been disturbed by birds and the burial of an infant (F185) in the north-western quadrant. The lack of burial markings and casual placement indicates a later, intrusive burial, likely a *ceallúnach* burial of recent centuries, the only one anywhere in the shrine or its mound. The hasty burial of this infant may be the reason why the end stones of the shrine disappeared and the long stones slipped.

Two stone cists, each shaped like a miniature lintel cist grave, lay sealed below layers of soil, stones, gravel, scallop shells and white quartz stones. Each cist held exhumed bones, mostly the long bones, of two adult males (Sk. 176 and Sk. 188) (Figs 47 and 48). Gravel, quartz pebbles, half-scallop shells and flecks of charcoal were loosely scattered over the bones, and a single scallop shell rested on the lid of one cist. Most of the cists and the gable shrine were made of slate, the only structures on the island not made of island sandstone.

The hypothesis that the structures commonly called gable shrines were in fact reliquary shrines has been settled with the discovery of the translated bones which also demonstrated that the Illaunloughan community venerated more than one saint, as did other communities. St Adomnán followed St Columba into sainthood at Iona, and Bishop Eadbert was buried in the original grave of St Cuthbert after Cuthbert was translated into a new coffin above the grave at Lindisfarne. Bede remarked that 'The miracles of healing that take place from time to time at the tomb bear witness to the holiness of them both' (Sherley-Price 1955, 267).

The presence of the bones of a small child in one cist was puzzling, but there

47—One of the two cists found under the gable shrine on Illaunloughan before excavation, showing the scallop shell and a large piece of quartz placed on top of the cist. Scallop shells and quartz pebbles were also found inside the cist. *(C. Walsh, 1994)*

was no evidence that this layer of the shrine had been disturbed by a later, intrusive burial, and radiocarbon analysis demonstrated that this infant was contemporary with the monastic community. High-precision radiocarbon analysis undertaken at Queen's University, Belfast, returned the following dates for the adult males: one (Sk. 176) was dated to AD 686–794, and the other (Sk. 188) was dated to AD 666–777. The infant skull was sent to the Oxford Radiocarbon Accelerator Unit and was dated to AD 660–780. All three of these dates fall between the late seventh and the late eighth centuries, demonstrating that the infant burial belongs to the same period as the other individuals and was not a later burial. It appears that the bones of the small child in the cist were deliberately deposited, for uncertain reasons. No other case of such an occurrence is known, but a plausible conjecture is that it is connected to a close kin relationship (see further discussion below, Chapter 5).

Good material evidence of the translation of corporeal relics is rare; such evidence has usually long since disappeared or been divided into tiny pieces of uncertain origin and date. Brisk demand for relics made them highly prized objects

48—One of two stone cists, with its stone cover removed, found under the gable shrine on Illaunloughan. The cists, 0.2–0.3m wide, 0.1–0.2m deep and less than 0.7m long, were too small, narrow and shallow to hold articulated burials. They contained exhumed bones of two adults and one infant. *(C. Walsh, 1994)*

of trade and theft. Few relics survived this fervour intact, and many also perished in wars, fires and floods over the centuries. Still fewer survive in their original shrines and close to their original burial-places.[53]

Contact with the relics or bones of a saint was not customary but was, in any case, unnecessary, as the potency of the sanctity of the saints transformed everything associated with them, even several layers of material removed from the relic. Gregory of Tours regularly mixed dust from the tomb of St Martin to settle his troubled stomach (Van Dam 1993). Pilgrims to the Holy Sepulchre chipped away at Christ's stone tomb, packed up soil of the Holy Land, made drawings, drained oil from lamps burning above the tomb and carried home ampullae, medallions and flasks. All became cherished as relics themselves (Biddle 1999b).

White quartz stones lie on many early medieval graves and *leachta*, but the origin of the custom has remained uncertain. Their presence in the reliquary cists closely links their use to the period of the construction of the shrine, perhaps the earliest secure dating for the practice in early medieval Ireland (see Chapter 6, below).

49—A possible shrine north of the entry steps to the gable shrine on Illaunloughan. Pea-gravel and quantities of white quartz stones covered its paved floor. This structure resembled one to the south of the drystone oratory. *(C. Walsh, 1994)*

The great scallop (*Pecten maximus*) is plentiful around the island today, and the midden contents indicate that scallops were present during monastic times but were not a primary element in the diet. A total of 32 scallops were counted, less than 0.1 per cent of the total MNI (minimum number of individuals) of shellfish in the extensive midden sample (see Appendix 4). They are not present anywhere else on the island, except in the gable shrine, where a number of half-shells are on the stone lids of the reliquary cists and inside them, scattered over the translated bones. This close association appears purposeful.[54] The calibrated radiocarbon determination for these shells dates them to AD 665–1048.[55] It is highly probable, therefore, that these shells were part of the original construction of the shrine and not a later insertion (for further discussion about the possible symbolic interpretation of scallop shells see below, Chapter 6).

Secondary reliquary shrine, on the western quadrant of the mound

North of the steps leading up to the shrine is a square feature, measuring 1.3m by 1.3m, defined by four vertically set stones (Figs 45 and 49). Gravel and quartz pebbles covered its roughly paved floor, but no other material survived. The structure, nevertheless, was deliberately built and is identical in design, though larger, to one south of the oratory on Illaunloughan and to two on Skellig Michael: one on the South Peak hermitage (Horn *et al.* 1990, 50, fig. 43) and one on the terrace below the oratories (G.D. Rourke and E. Bourke, pers. comm., 1995).

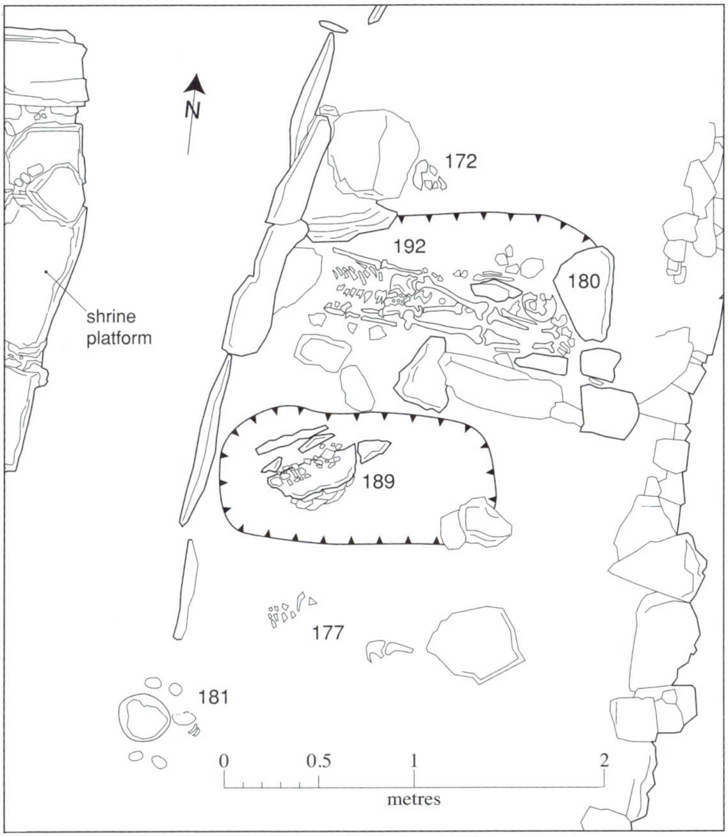

50a—Plan of the burials in the eastern quadrant of the gable shrine at Illaunloughan. *(C. McHale)*

50b—The gable shrine on Illaunloughan in 1994, from the north, showing the excavated eastern quadrant that was used as a monastic cemetery. *(C. Brogan)*

Variations of fixed open-air reliquaries appear to have been fairly common in the region. The remains of a similar, though smaller, structure, measuring 0.90m by 0.85m, at Reask tested positive for phosphate and may have contained bones (Fanning 1981, 84–5). A much larger, more elaborate structure, measuring 2.9m by 1.9m, exists at Caherlehillan, on the Iveragh Peninsula. The Reask and Caherlehillan structures have pillars at the corners, a variation not seen at Illaunloughan or at Skellig Michael, possibly a version of the corner-post shrines seen in northern Britain (O'Sullivan and Sheehan 1996, 265; C. Thomas 1971, 150–9). It is highly probable that all of these structures were reliquary shrines and that some of them contained non-corporeal, as well as corporeal, relics.[56]

Eastern quadrant of the shrine mound

This section of the shrine mound was used as the cemetery. Seven burials, two of which were juveniles under seven years of age, were found here (Figs 50a and 50b). Most of the skeletal material was in poor condition, but one grave with two burials produced a considerable amount of information. The first burial (Sk. 192) was placed in the usual east–west position; however, later, possibly when space had run out, another burial (Sk. 180) was carefully placed on top. The skull and shoulders of the first burial were placed at his feet and, perhaps as a consequence of congestion at the foot of the grave, the head of the second burial in this grave (Sk. 180) was placed farther west than those of the other burials, slightly under the kerbstones and paving of the shrine.

The first burial (Sk. 192) was dated to AD 677–768, and the second (Sk. 180) was dated to AD 683–805;[57] this may have been the last burial in the shrine mound. Superimposed interment is generally a consequence of space constraints and is indicative of later burials. Illaunloughan has only two such examples, which, predictably, have yielded the latest radiocarbon dates for human skeletal material. All of the radiocarbon dates are consistent with the stratigraphical evidence.

In size and visibility the reliquary structure dominates the other Illaunloughan structures; indeed, it is larger than the other known gable shrines, and probably more complex. The prior presence of three burials in this location indicates that it was designated for special burials, perhaps for a shrine, from early in the history of the settlement. Certainly this was the only unused space on the island sufficient for a large shrine with additional burials. A more compelling reason than concern for space, however, may have been the emphasis that the Illaunloughan community placed on the cult of relics, particularly on the corporeal relics of their holy men. The location of the reliquary, in the area most visible to boats heading out to the Atlantic or coming home, suggests that local fishermen venerated the saints of Illaunloughan. The island may also have been part of a larger, regional, maritime pilgrimage that included a visit to Skellig Michael (Harbison 1994).

4

Environmental analysis and the food supply

Emily Murray and Finbar McCormick

Excavations at Illaunloughan allowed the most extensive investigation of an early medieval monastic midden in Ireland. Excavations at contemporaneous monasteries, including Church Island, Co. Kerry (O'Kelly 1958), and Inishkea North, Co. Mayo (Henry 1945; 1952), produced organic midden material, but the reports were superficial by modern standards. Archaeological investigations at other monastic sites, such as Reask, Co. Kerry (Fanning 1981), Moyne, Co. Mayo (McCormick in Manning 1987), and Kiltiernan, Co. Galway (Waddell and Clyne 1995), produced only modest amounts of material.

A wide range of analyses was undertaken on different aspects of the environmental data retrieved at Illaunloughan. The work of individual specialists produced significant results, providing us with data on the diet of the inhabitants of the site and on the farming practices of the surrounding area. The individual environmental reports are provided in their entirety in Appendix 4. The current chapter presents an overview of the results.

Food refuse and midden material were present in several areas on the island. Some was found within the sod and stone huts, but the largest sample came from an extensive area outside of, and contemporary with, the stone hut D. The earliest environmental samples are from the sod huts A, B and C, and some later medieval material was derived from the levels of reuse in the oratory. The following discussion is, for the most part, based on material from the garden soil that extended over much of the western part of the island and was contemporary with stone hut D. This material dates from between the eighth and the ninth centuries AD. The environmental samples recovered from this soil consist almost exclusively of discarded food refuse and can be assumed to represent the diet of the ecclesiastical inhabitants of the site.

Faunal data

Analysis of the well-preserved mammal bone assemblage (Murray, Appendix 4) shows that the principal mammals represented were the usual domesticates found on early medieval Irish sites (Table 1). However, in comparison with contemporaneous secular sites, such as the coastal ringfort at Rathgurreen, Co. Galway (Murray in Comber 2002), fish and bird play a much more significant role in the diet. Sheep was the most common domestic species present, followed closely by cattle, with pig playing a relatively minor role. The predominance of sheep probably reflects the relatively poor farming potential of the area, which comprises mostly heath and boggy pasture. Sheep can generally thrive more successfully than cattle on the coastal areas of south-west Ireland.

The age data for cattle and sheep, as represented by a high occurrence of unfused and porous bones and the limited toothwear data, indicated that a large number of very young animals were culled, much more than have been noted on contemporaneous sites elsewhere in Ireland. This phenomenon has also been noted on Bronze Age Dún Aonghasa, on Inis Mor (McCormick, forthcoming), and on sites in Atlantic Scotland of all periods. Such an age-slaughter pattern is essentially a reflection of marginality in terms of grazing (McCormick 1998). Marginality, in this instance, is one where wetter and windier weather, coupled with poorer and thinner soils, made the area less favourable for agriculture than elsewhere. If domesticates were more fecund than could be supported by available grazing, it would have been necessary to kill and consume animals at a very young age. Many of these excess animals became part of the diet of the monks on Illaunloughan. A low incidence of pig is also a characteristic of Atlantic coastal sites

Table 1—Frequency of mammal bones at Illaunloughan identified to species (after Murray, Appendix 4). NISP = number of specimens; MNI = minimum number of individuals. Bones of rabbit and rat, which are presumed to be intrusive, have been omitted.

Phase	*NISP/ MNI*	*Cattle*	*Horse*	*Sheep/ goat*	*Pig*	*Dog*	*Cat*	*Red deer*	*Seal*	*Whale*	*Total*
1	NISP	374	3	210	80	–	–	–	–	–	667
	% NISP	56.1	0.1	31.6	12.2	–	–	–	–	–	
	MNI	6	1	9	3	–	–	–	–	–	19
	% MNI	29	5	43	14						
2	NISP	493	5	221	111	–	–	–	–	1	831
	% NISP	59.4	0.6	26.5	13.4	–	–	–	–	0.1	
	MNI	7	1	9	2	–	–	–	–	1	20
	% MNI	33	5	43	9					5	
3	NISP	624	12	256	222	1	3	1	4	–	1123
	% NISP	55.6	1.1	22.8	19.7	0.1	0.3	0.1	0.36	–	
	MNI	11	1	6	5	1	1	1	1	–	27
	% MNI	39	3	22	18	3	3	3	3		
4	NISP	477	5	227	169	1	1	1	–	–	881
	% NISP	54	0.6	25.7	19.2	0.1	0.1	0.3	–	–	
	MNI	8	1	7	5	1	1	1	–	–	24
	% MNI	28	3	24	18	3	3	3			
5	NISP	88	2	30	17	–	–	1	6	–	144
	% NISP	61.4	1.4	20.7	11.7	–	–	0.7	4.1	–	
	MNI	3	1	3	1	–	–	1	1	–	10
	% MNI	30	10	30	10	–	–	10	10	–	

Species	Phase 1		Phase 2		Phase 3		Phase 4		Total	
	NISP	% NISP	NISP	% NISP	NISP	% NISP	NISP	% NISP	NISP	% NISP
Cormorant	9	4.4	4	5.9	10	5.7	10	7.9	33	5.7
Crow	–	–	–	–	1	0.6	–	–	1	0.2
Domestic fowl	–	–	–	–	2	1.1	–	–	2	0.3
Eagle?	–	–	1	1.5	–	–	–	–	1	0.2
Gannet	–	–	1	1.5	6	3.4	1	0.8	8	1.4
Godwit	–	–	–	–	1	0.6	–	–	1	0.2
Goose	–	–	–	–	1	0.6	–	–	1	0.2
Guillemot	–	–	1	1.5	–	–	3	2.4	4	0.7
Gull	–	–	1	1.5	–	–	–	–	1	0.2
Kittiwake	1	0.5	9	13.2	22	12.5	6	4.7	38	6.6
Manx shearwater	191	92.7	40	58.8	87	49.4	87	68.5	405	70.2
Puffin	–	–	5	7.4	31	17.6	13	10.2	49	8.5
Shag	5	2.4	6	8.8	12	6.8	6	4.7	29	5.0
Snipe	–	–	–	–	1	0.6	1	0.8	2	0.3
Woodpigeon	–	–	–	–	2	1.1	–	–	2	0.3
Total	206	35.7	68	11.8	176	30.5	127	22.0	577	100.0

Table 2—Frequency of bird bones at Illaunloughan identified to species (after O'Sullivan, Appendix 4).

Species	Phase 1		Phase 2		Phase 3		Phase 4		Total	
	NISP	% NISP	NISP	% NISP	NISP	% NISP	NISP	% NISP	NISP	% NISP
Bass	10	3.3	7	1.7	19	1.4	4	1.0	40	1.6
Cod	–	–	1	0.2	13	0.9	3	0.7	17	0.7
Conger	2	0.7	3	0.7	17	1.2	13	3.2	35	1.4
Flatfish	1	0.3	–	–	3	0.2	–	–	4	0.2
Gadidae	15	4.9	23	5.4	121	8.7	24	6.0	183	7.2
Gurnard	–	–	1	0.2	7	0.5	3	0.7	11	0.4
Haddock	–	–	–	–	–	–	1	0.2	1	0.0
Hake	20	6.6	20	4.7	44	3.1	36	8.9	120	4.7
Mullet	–	–	3	0.7	3	0.2	3	0.7	9	0.4
Pollack	22	7.2	14	3.3	44	3.1	8	2.0	88	3.5
Ray	–	–	–	–	1	0.1	1	0.2	2	0.1
Saithe	1	0.3	–	–	–	–	–	–	1	0.0
Salmon	1	0.3	–	–	1	0.1	–	–	2	0.1
Scad	3	1.0	14	3.3	45	3.2	19	4.7	81	3.2
Sea bream	148	48.5	228	53.9	708	50.7	154	38.2	1238	49.0
Sea scorpion	–	–	–	–	–	–	3	0.7	3	0.1
Shark	2	0.7	–	–	12	0.9	11	2.7	25	1.0
Whiting	–	–	–	–	7	0.5	4	1.0	11	0.4
Wrasse	80	26.2	109	25.8	352	25.2	116	28.8	657	26.0
Total	305	12.1	423	16.7	1397	55.3	403	15.9	2528	

Table 3— Frequency of fish bones at Illaunloughan identified to species (after Hamilton-Dyer, Appendix 4).

		Phase 1	*Phase 2*	*Phase 3*	*Phase 4*	*Phase 5*	*Total*	*% Total*
Sample weight (kg)		10.33	35.52	24.36	13.68	26.36	110.25	
Cereals (Caryopses)								
Cerealia indet.		2	182	374	44	51	653	32.8
Hordeum spp	Barley	3	120	95	7	58	283	14.2
Triticum spp	Wheat	0	51	10	0	0	61	3.1
Avena spp	Oats	1	291	215	19	467	993	49.9
Total		6	644	694	70	576	1990	
Principal weeds								
Anthemis cf. *arvensis* L.	Corn chamomile	–	17	13	–	7	37	7.5
Caryophyllaceae indet.	Pink family	1	6	10	3	7	27	5.4
Cf. *Artemisia*	Mugwort	–	–	10	–	8	18	3.6
Compositae indet.	Daisy family	2	2	9	3	11	27	5.4
Gramineae indet.	Grass family	–	9	8	–	–	17	3.4
Polygonum spp	Knotweeds	2	3	10	1	6	22	4.4
Rumex acetosella L.	Sheep's sorrel	–	5	13	4	9	31	6.3
Rumex spp	Docks	2	52	19	–	11	84	16.9
Sinapis arvensis L.	Charlock	–	3	1	2	2	8	1.6
Stellaria media L.	Common chickweed	–	–	–	–	8	8	1.6
Stellaria spp	Stitchworts	–	16	–	–	–	16	3.2
Vicia spp	Vetches	–	14	–	–	1	15	3.0
Others		4	18	27	8	21	78	15.7
Indeterminate		14	13	47	10	24	108	21.8
Total		25	158	167	31	115	496	

Table 4—Summary of the 'raw count' of cereals and the most common weed taxa identified from Illaunloughan. (See Plunkett, Bentley and Collins, Appendix 4.)

Phase	*NISP*	*Mammal*	*Bird*	*Fish*	*Total*
Phase 1	NISP	674	206	305	1185
	% NISP	56.9	17.4	25.7	
Phase 2	NISP	832	68	423	1323
	% NISP	62.9	5.1	32.0	
Phase 3	NISP	1128	176	1397	2701
	% NISP	41.8	6.5	51.7	
Phase 4	NISP	908	127	403	1438
	% NISP	63.1	8.8	28.0	

Table 5—Relative frequency of the number of identified bone fragments (NISP) of mammal, bird and fish from the early medieval phases at Illaunloughan.

Site	*Phase*	*NISP*	*Mammal*	*Fish*	*Bird*	*Total*
Illaunloughan	Phase 1	NISP	667	305	206	1178
		% NISP	56.6	25.9	17.5	
	Phase 2	NISP	832	423	68	1323
		% NISP	62.9	32.0	5.1	
	Phase 3	NISP	1128	1397	176	2701
		% NISP	41.8	51.7	6.5	
	Phase 4	NISP	908	403	127	1438
		% NISP	63.1	28.0	8.8	
Rathgurreen	Phase 1	NISP	674	2	3	679
		% NISP	99.3	0.3	0.4	
	Phase 2	NISP	1392	8	22	1422
		% NISP	97.9	0.6	1.5	
Doonloughan		NISP	115	314	—	429
		% NISP	26.8	73.2	—	

Table 6—Frequency of identified bone fragments of mammal, fish and bird from the early medieval phases at Illaunloughan, Rathgurreen, Co. Galway (after Murray in Comber 2002; Hamilton-Dyer in Comber 2002), and Doonloughan, Co. Galway (Murray 1999).

of all periods. The general absence of mature forest, which could provide beech and oak mast, their main source of fodder, partially accounts for this. Additionally, bogs, heath or machair areas do not provide good grazing for pigs.

The poor grazing available to the domesticates at Illaunloughan is supported by the occurrence of hypoplasia on two of the sheep teeth (Fig. 51) found on the site (Murphy, Appendix 4). This abnormality, which is due to a disturbance in the development of the enamel, is caused by physiological stress when the affected tooth was developing. In a detailed study of the occurrence of this pathology on pig teeth, it is proposed that birth, weaning and periods of undernourishment probably encountered during the first winter of the animal's life may be the main

51—Sheep's teeth from the midden, Illaunloughan; the tooth to the left shows evidence of hypoplasia.

52—Tooth of a young killer whale (*Orcinus orca*) found in the midden on Illaunloughan (identified by Jerry Herman of the National Museums of Scotland, Edinburgh).

causal agents (Dobney and Ervynck 1998).

A few horse bones were present among the food refuse. The eating of horse was condemned by the church (Bieler 1963, 161); despite this, horse bones generally occur on ecclesiastical sites, in small numbers. Horse bones were found in the midden on nearby Church Island (Roche in O'Kelly 1958, 133), at Moyne, Co. Mayo (McCormick 1987, 60), and at Iona, where horse leather was also identified (McCormick 1997, 62). It is probable that the few dog and cat bones represent pets, and it is unlikely that they were eaten.

Wild mammals were represented by bones of red deer and seal and by a tooth from a young killer whale (Fig. 52). Most of the small red deer assemblage was antler and may represent industrial waste. A single post-cranial bone, however, may represent venison consumption. The whale tooth may represent cetacean hunting, but it is much more likely to have derived from a beached whale. A perforated tip of a sperm whale 'back tooth' was found at Lough Faughan Crannog, Co. Down (Jope in Collins 1955), and this might be interpreted in the context of an early Irish law that indicates that a 'beautiful tooth', which a gloss identifies as being of a whale, was regarded as an object of great value (Kelly 1997, 285). Lough Faughan is a secular site, but whale teeth were also highly regarded by the church. In 752 the Annals of Ulster record that a whale was washed ashore in the territory of Mourne, in modern County Down. Rather fancifully, this whale was supposed to have had three gold teeth, one of which was placed on the altar at Bangor, Co. Down (Hennessy and McCarthy 1887–1901, 217). The bringing of a large tooth into a church seems odd, and one might wonder if there is any parallel with an incident recorded by St Augustine in his *City of God*: a large tooth was found on the shore near Carthage, and St Augustine records that it was brought into the church to be displayed as evidence of the existence of giants in former ages (Cohen 2002, 23–4). Seal bones were also found at Illaunloughan, in two different contexts in the midden. They were not identified to species level. Seal bones have also been found at the nearby monastic Church Island (Roche in O'Kelly 1958, 134) and at the island monasteries of Iona (McCormick 1997, 58) and Inishkea North (Stelfox in Henry 1945, 154–5). Though absent from the coastal ringfort at Rathgurreen, they were noted at secular Dún Eoghanachta, a cashel site on Inis Mor (Murray 1999).

Thirteen bird species were identified at Illaunloughan (O'Sullivan, Appendix 4), with the most common being the Manx shearwater, which comprised 70 per cent of the bird elements identified to species. The other species present are shown in Table 2. A gannet humerus was the only bone to display a cut-mark, and this was consistent with the removal of the wing. Most of the bones came from adults, and O'Sullivan ruled out the possibility that the accumulations were natural; the absence of any definite signs of gull predation and the distribution of body parts (see Appendix 4) clearly indicated that the bones derived from butchery waste. Seabirds and their eggs would have been readily available to the inhabitants of Illaunloughan, principally in the summer months. Domestic fowl were kept but not in large numbers; only two specimens were noted.

Fish played a very important role in the diet at Illaunloughan (Hamilton-Dyer, Appendix 4). A wide range of species, at least twenty, were represented, but sea bream dominated the assemblage, accounting for 50 per cent of the material identified to species level (Table 3). These are most likely to have been red, rather than black, sea bream. Sea bream is a summer migrant to the Irish coast, and its dominance here has not been recorded at any other Irish or British site. It is a fine food fish, frequenting rocky outcrops, and could have been caught quite close to the island. The same can be said of the Ballan wrasse, which was also common in the assemblage and could easily have been caught from the island shore at high tide. The absence of small wrasse suggests that smaller specimens were thrown back, which implies a plentiful supply of fish in the area. Other species present, such as the larger cod, hake and shark, would have necessitated fishing from a boat. There is evidence of the use of both nets and hooks during this period. The Life of St Moling refers to catching salmon with a net (Kelly 1997, 289), and a possible net-sinker was found at nearby Beginish (O'Kelly 1956, 179). Iron fish-hooks have been found on the coastal site of Dooey, Co. Donegal (Ó Ríordáin and Rynne 1961), and in Viking Dublin (Wallace 1998, 209).

Most of the early literary references to fishing deal with salmon fishing, usually on rivers (Kelly 1997, 291). The remains of salmon, along with those of sharks and rays, were present, but uncommon, at Illaunloughan, although this may be in part due to differential preservation. The bones of salmon returning to spawn become decalcified, whereas rays and sharks do not have fully ossified bones, which makes their bones more susceptible to decay (Hamilton-Dyer, Appendix 4). The same is probably also the case with very oily fish. Mackerel, for example, is the easiest fish to catch along the Irish coast but is virtually absent from the archaeological record. In summary, the most frequent fish remains from this site are of species that are expected to be common around the coast of south-west Ireland, and most of the fish identified favour weedy, rocky coasts, as is the case in and around Illaunloughan.

The shellfish assemblage was dominated by gastropods, in particular periwinkles (79 per cent) and limpets (20 per cent), both of which inhabit rocky shorelines, as at Illaunloughan and the surrounding locality (McLoughlin and Murray, Appendix 4). The occurrence of bivalve species, of which oyster was the most common, was minor and unimportant. Such bivalves are found only in sandy beach and bottom areas. There are patches of sand in the vicinity of the island, and the few oysters and scallops found on the site may have been derived from these areas. The shellfish may have been exploited during winter when other wild resources, namely fish and bird, were in short supply. A seasonal preference for exploiting shellfish during winter has been noted on prehistoric island settlements in Scotland (Mellars and Wilkinson 1980).

A number of scallop shells (*c.* fifteen) of the common Atlantic species *Pecten maximus* were found in the shrine associated with the burials. Four of these had small perforations, but many of the others were incomplete. The size and irregular shape of the holes in the valves rule out the possibility of their having been bored by carnivorous whelks, and so it is likely that they were man-made. As scallops are associated with religious pilgrimage, the holes in the Illaunloughan specimens may have been made so that they could be strung to hang on one's person (see Chapter 6).

Non-meat component of the diet

Unfortunately the non-meat part of early diet leaves very little evidence in the archaeological record. It is often only secondary evidence, in the form of plough parts or querns, that provides any indication that plant foods were consumed on a particular site. A quernstone was found at Illaunloughan (see Finds Report below), suggesting that the inhabitants ground some of their own flour. Carbonised cereal grains and weed and fruit seeds were also recovered, although processing by-products, such as chaff, an indicator of a 'producer' site, were not abundant in the Illaunloughan assemblage. This, coupled with the frequency of calcifuge crop weeds, which grow on acidic soils, indicates that crops were grown and processed off the island.

The carbonised cereal assemblage from Illaunloughan was dominated by oats, accounting for half of the identified cereal grains, followed by barley and with wheat found infrequently and in only a small number of samples (Plunkett, Bentley and Collins, Appendix 4). This predominance of oats is unusual when compared with contemporaneous sites, where barley is typically the most common cereal (Monk 1991). There is, however, a high representation, and indeed dominance, of oats at other Munster settlements, including the ringforts at Lisleagh II, Co. Cork, Lisnagun, Co. Cork, and Ballyegan, Co. Kerry (Monk 1998, 68–9). The high incidence of oats may, therefore, be a regional phenomenon.

Two old Irish legal texts class oats as the least-valued cereal (Kelly 1997, 226–7), and, given its dominance at Illaunloughan, it is interesting that a number of records of oats and oat consumption are associated with ecclesiastics. A miracle recounted in the Life of St Ciarán describes how a bag of oats that he had was transformed into a much more valuable bag of wheat (*ibid.*, 244–5), and in the famous Irish wonder tale *Aislinge Meic Con Glinne* the Armagh scholar Aniér MacConglinne is contemptuous of an oaten ration given to him when visiting a monastery in Cork (Meyer 1974, 14–16). Cereals would have played an important role in the diet of the monks. They would have been consumed in the form of bread, porridge or a thin gruel that was a feature of penitential and ascetic diets, such as that associated with St Máel Rúain of Tallaght (Kelly 1997, 332 and 348).

What is perhaps more significant, however, is the apparent importance of naked two-row barley. Previous studies (e.g. Monk 1991) have tended to suggest that hulled six-row barley was more common during this period in Ireland, and in

Britain it has been suggested that the dominance of hulled barley from the mid-first millennium BC may be due to its use principally as animal fodder rather than human food (van der Veen 1992). The fact that animal fodder would not have been an issue at Illaunloughan, and the cereals must have been for the monks' consumption alone, may explain why hulled barley was less common in the assemblage (Plunkett, Bentley and Collins, Appendix 4).

With the exception of a single seed of the cabbage family, there was no evidence of vegetables in the macro-botanical assemblage from Illaunloughan (Plunkett, Bentley and Collins, Appendix 4). Their absence, however, is not surprising, as such (easily degradable) food is usually identified by the presence of seed, and vegetables are generally harvested before the setting of the seed. The early literature indicates that the range of vegetables grown in Ireland was fairly limited. Peas, beans, onion, cabbage, chives and probably celery, carrots and leeks were the main garden plants cultivated at the time (Kelly 1997, 248–59). Other potential food supplements represented by the plant macrofossil assemblage from Illaunloughan include raspberry, burnet rose, rowan, hazelnut, vetch, charlock, docks, common chickweed and common nettle.

Plaggen soils and gardening on Illaunloughan

Most of the archaeo-environmental material was retrieved in a deep deposit of rich organic soil that covered much of the western, 'domestic' half of the site. This was an artificially made plaggen soil, which must have derived primarily from organic material brought to the island that was augmented and enriched by discarded food waste. This must have been deliberately imported in order to create a garden soil. The location of the garden on an exposed island would have made cultivation at Illaunloughan rather difficult, but the adverse affects of the wind were partially mitigated by a protective wall along the western part of the island. This would have afforded some shelter for the plants from the prevailing winds.

Artificial garden soils have been noted in later monastic sites in Scotland (Barber 1981, 359–60; McCormick 1993, 80), although examples that can be definitely attributed to the early medieval period are difficult to identify. It could be assumed that the soils on the terraced gardens on Skellig Michael (Horn *et al.* 1990, 36) are of early medieval date, but this has not been proven. Kelly (1997, 251) notes that the gardener is listed as one of the seven officers of the church, but there is no mention of gardeners being among the servants employed by a king or lord. It is also to be noted that the Irish saint Fiachra founded a monastery with a fine garden at Breuil near Meaux in France and later became the patron saint of gardeners in that country (Reeves-Smyth 1999, 108). One can surmise from these various strands of evidence that gardening must have been an important aspect of early monasticism. Gardens would also have allowed the monks to produce more of their food and to be self-sufficient; documentary sources also suggest a medicinal motivation for gardening (Binchy 1938). At Illaunloughan, a number of the identified herbs present, such as coriander, mugwort, nettle and sorrel, may have had remedial uses.

Monastic diet

The question arises of whether the diet noted at Illaunloughan constitutes a specific 'monastic' diet. It is a question that has also been considered elsewhere, where the evidence from Illaunloughan has been compared in detail with that from Iona in the Inner Hebrides (Murray *et al.* 2004). The documentary evidence indicates that some clerics were vegetarians. It is stated that St Tigernach of Clones, Co. Monaghan, lived exclusively on barley bread, watercress and hot water (Kelly 1997, 344). It is very unlikely that anyone could have survived on such a diet, and, indeed, a passage in the monastic rules, the Monastery of Tallaght, describes a meeting that took place between the saints of Ireland to discuss this very problem (Gwynn and Purton 1912, 157–8). Barley and watercress alone do not supply some vital amino acids and would have needed to be supplemented by the occasional consumption of beans, dairy produce or meat. Possibly the greatest disadvantage of Tigernach's diet is that watercress is available only from about May to October. In general, the diets of monks or nuns were supposed to be frugal but well balanced. The Teagasc Maoil Ruain is another set of regulations dealing with the monastery of Tallaght, Co. Dublin. It states that typical monastic fare consists of 'bread with a condiment of fish, butter, cheese or hard boiled egg' (Kelly 1997, 344); cabbages or leeks could also be eaten (*ibid.*), while the Monastery of Tallaght states that, if meat was to be consumed, it was to be of 'deer or a wild swine' (Gwynn and Purton 1912, 129). In the same section it is noted that other meat, presumably that of domesticates, was reserved for guests. It should be noted that these rules at Tallaght pertain to the Céle Dé reformist movement, and the diets mentioned may have been more austere than elsewhere.

There is no evidence of wild swine at Illaunloughan, and the deer bones are essentially incidental. Evidence elsewhere, however, partially confirms aspects of the diet recorded at Tallaght, with its emphasis on wild meats. The ecclesiastical site at Moyne, Co. Mayo, produced the highest incidence of red deer bones known from an early medieval site in Ireland (McCormick 1987, 67), although the diet there was still predominantly of domesticates.

The exploitation of fish and wild bird makes the diet at Illaunloughan so unusual. Is this a 'monastic' phenomenon or simply a reflection of a coastal diet in general? It is known, for instance, that bird and fish are common on Atlantic Scottish sites of all periods (McCormick and Buckland 1997, table 6.3). Large quantities of bird and fish bone were also found in the Bronze Age levels at Dún Aonghasa on Inis Mor, Co. Galway (Cotter, in prep.). However, a comparison between Illaunloughan and secular early medieval west coast sites suggests that the site is exceptional.

Rathgurreen ringfort (Comber 2002) is *c.* 1 mile from the shore of Galway Bay. The site was excavated in 1948 and 1949, and there is no evidence that the animal bones were collected other than by hand. Nonetheless, bird and fish comprised less than 2 per cent of the identifiable bone (NISP). Excavations in the sand dunes at

Doonloughan in west Connemara included the investigation of an early medieval secular unenclosed hut site (McCormick and Murray, in prep.; Murray 1999). All material from the site was extensively sieved, and only a small sample of bone was retrieved. No bird bones were present, but fish bone greatly outnumbered those of mammal, comprising about 75 per cent of the total. The high incidence of fish may be as a result of sieving, which was not undertaken to the same extent at Illaunloughan. The species represented were far more limited than at Illaunloughan, comprising for the most part scad (horse mackerel) and wrasse. Scad is a schooling fish that could have been caught very easily, and wrasse can be easily caught from the shore. Most of the scad bones were from a single context and may reflect only a single fishing occasion. Essentially, there was no evidence of extensive fishing at Doonloughan, and certainly there was no evidence of deep-water fishing. Fish, however, played an important role in the diet of the Columban monks at Iona (McCormick 1998, 59–60), where there was evidence of deep-water fishing.

On balance, it seems likely that the high incidence of bird and fish at Illaunloughan is a reflection of its monastic status. The inhabitants were integrating a monastic preference for 'wild foods' with an attempt to be as self-sufficient as possible, given the environmental limits. Finally, fish and wild birds may also have been regarded as fasting foods. The eating of fish on fast days in later periods is well known, and birds seem to have been held in the same regard, at least in later times. In an eighteenth-century account from Kerry concerning the Skelligs, it is reported that 'They eat them [gannets] in Lent and on their fast days as well as fish' (Smith 1756, 112), and Roderic O'Flaherty (1846, 67), writing in 1684, observed that 'Here [Connemara] are ayries of hawkes and birds which never fly but over the sea and therefore are used to be eaten on fasting days'.

Regarding the faunal remains from Iona, McCormick (1997, 58) has suggested that seals were considered to be more fish than mammal and were therefore allowed in a monastic diet. It is interesting that the references to seal in the contemporaneous literature are confined to the Lives of two saints, St Brigid (Stokes 1890, 196) and St Columba (Sharpe 1995, 143). In the case of Columba, it is clear that the seals breeding near Iona were regarded as the private property of the monastery. In the Life of Brigid a seal was hunted to provide food for some guests at a monastery, while at Iona sealskin was used for leatherwork (Groenman-van Waateringe in Barber 1981, 318). Additionally, the *Liber Hymnorum*, which records miracles attributed to St Brigid, records the use of a sealskin basket (Stokes and Strachan 1901–3, Vol. 2, 347). Seal has also been recorded at the coastal monasteries at Church Island (Roche in O'Kelly 1958, 134) and Inishkea North (Stelfox in Henry 1945, 154–5). Its presence, however, is not confined to monastic sites, as it is also recorded at the coastal cashel at Leacanabuaile, Co. Kerry (Stelfox in Ó Ríordáin and Foy 1941, 95–6).

Supply of foodstuffs to the island monastery

In terms of subsistence, the question arises of whether the settlement was independent and self-reliant, was supported by secular society or was, perhaps, even affiliated to a monastic 'mother house'. The molluscs, seabirds and fish could have all been caught by the inhabitants of the island. The domesticated animals and cereals, however, must have come from elsewhere, although it is not possible to attribute the source of these foods. The grain was almost certainly grown off the island, given the limited garden area available and the presence of calcifuge weed species. The absence of chaff also suggests that grain was not processed on the island, but it must be remembered that burnt chaff is less likely to survive than burnt grain, and so this evidence is equivocal. It is likely that these foodstuffs were from a 'mother house' off the island or from the laity, either as payments for specific spiritual services or as part of the rent due by monastic clients.

The early medieval settlement at Bray Head—which, because of the inscribed crosses, may have had a monastic connection—presents one possibility for the source of cereals and it may indeed constitute the 'mother house' for Illaunloughan. The settlement comprises an extensive complex of early and late medieval sites, which Mitchell (1989, 102) suggests may have provisioned the small monastic communities on the other islands in the area, including Illaunloughan. Excavations at Bray Head so far, however, have produced only very small quantities of carbonised oats and wheat, along with a few fish bones. There are two extant grain kilns at the site, as well as an extensive, early medieval field system, indicating that the area was intensively farmed at this time (Hayden 1997; 1998).

Alternatively, or even additionally, the laity may have supported the monastic community. The high incidence of young calves and lambs, while reflecting the agricultural marginality of the area, shows a clear resonance with the dues to be rendered to the church by its lay tenants as outlined in the early Irish canons. These comprised one tenth ('tithe') of the flocks and fruits of the ground, in which first fruits and first-borns were frequently emphasised (Etchingham 1999, 240, 245; Bieler 1975, 8). This theme also occurs in a reference made by the seventeenth-century cleric John Lynch (1848–51, vol. 2, 509) to tributes given to monasteries: 'Every house in Uí Maine, a district in Connacht, paid yearly to their patron St Grellan, three pence and the first little pig, the first lamb, and the first foal, whence it is evident that the ecclesiastics received not only first fruits and cattle but also voluntary oblations'.

Conclusion

The monks of Illaunloughan enjoyed a varied diet. This comprised the flesh of numerous species—marine fish, shellfish and seabirds—the use of which is not attested in contemporaneous literature, as well as the more traditional beef/veal, mutton/lamb and pork. They clearly did not adhere to a strict vegetarian regime. Provisions also included oats, barley, raspberries and, presumably, vegetables and dairy produce. Most of these foods would have been available only on a seasonal basis, so the diet would have changed throughout the year. Most of the birds and fish would have been confined to the summer, and, to counterbalance their absence, it is likely that the shellfish were consumed more during the winter. These foods would also have allowed the clerics to be as self-sufficient as possible in their dietary requirements.

5

Burial patterns

Excavation and observation of ecclesiastical sites in Ireland have commonly demonstrated that Christian burials, particularly those of the ecclesiastical community, centred around the church by sometime in the eighth century.[58] Successive or additional churches, accompanied by burials, tended to be situated in the same general area, except at larger sites such as Inishmurray and Glendalough, where churches and their associated burials were at a considerable distance from each other. The monastic burials on Illaunloughan, however, were spaced around two focal points: the oratory and the gable shrine (Fig. 53). The concentration of burials around a feature other than a church was unusual, but the gable shrine at Illaunloughan, to the north-west of the oratory, was clearly used for this purpose and was delineated and separated from other site features.

The closest parallel may be information from excavation around the west and south high crosses at Clonmacnoise (King 1994). Under modern graves, there was a small cluster of graves that appeared to have been grouped around a sacred focus (wooden crosses?) earlier than, but in the same location as, the high crosses.[59] It is likely that excavation will reveal more unexpected burial patterns.

The entire eastern quadrant of the mound of the shrine was used for burials; conversely, burials were absent from the other mound quadrants. Indeed, when space was used up in the eastern area, one grave was reused. Does exclusive use of this quadrant indicate a preference for burial to the east? It is possible that the earliest burials around the oratory were on the east; however, burials were found on all sides. The three rock-cut graves under the gable shrine were also distributed on three sides, one each on the north-eastern, southern and western sides.

Excavation has not revealed a spatial preference for burial deposition at other sites in the region. Burials around the first oratory on nearby Church Island were to the west and north-west of the little structure (O'Kelly 1958, 59), whereas at Reask on the Dingle Peninsula, Co. Kerry, the burials were largely to the north and south

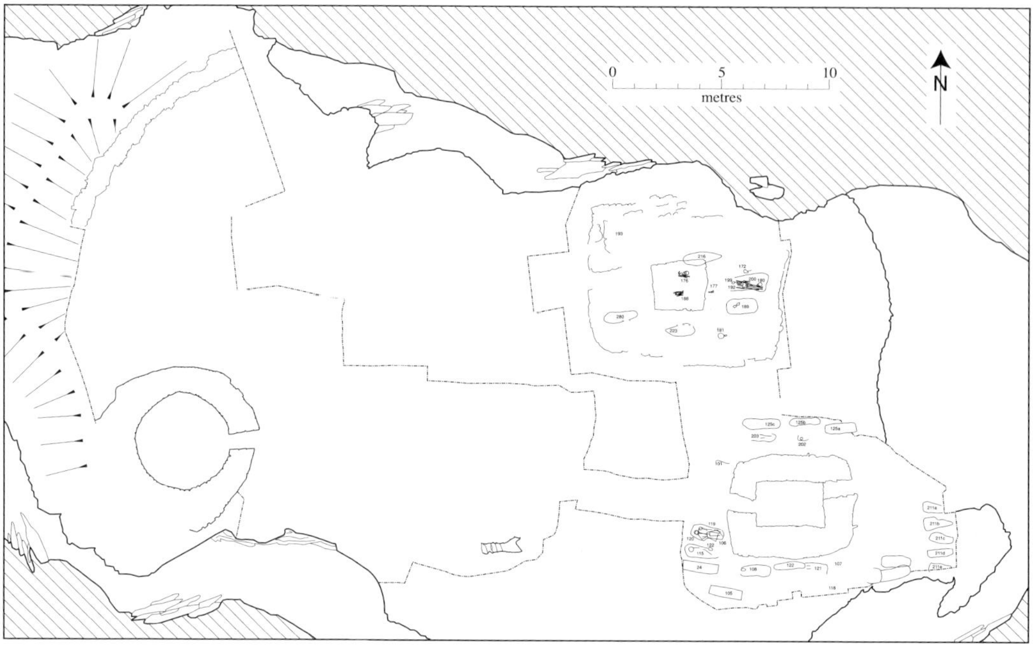

53a—Plan of burials of the monastic period on Illaunloughan, around the oratory and in the eastern section of the gable shrine. *(C. McHale)*

53b—Plan of burials of the medieval period on Illaunloughan. *(C. McHale)*

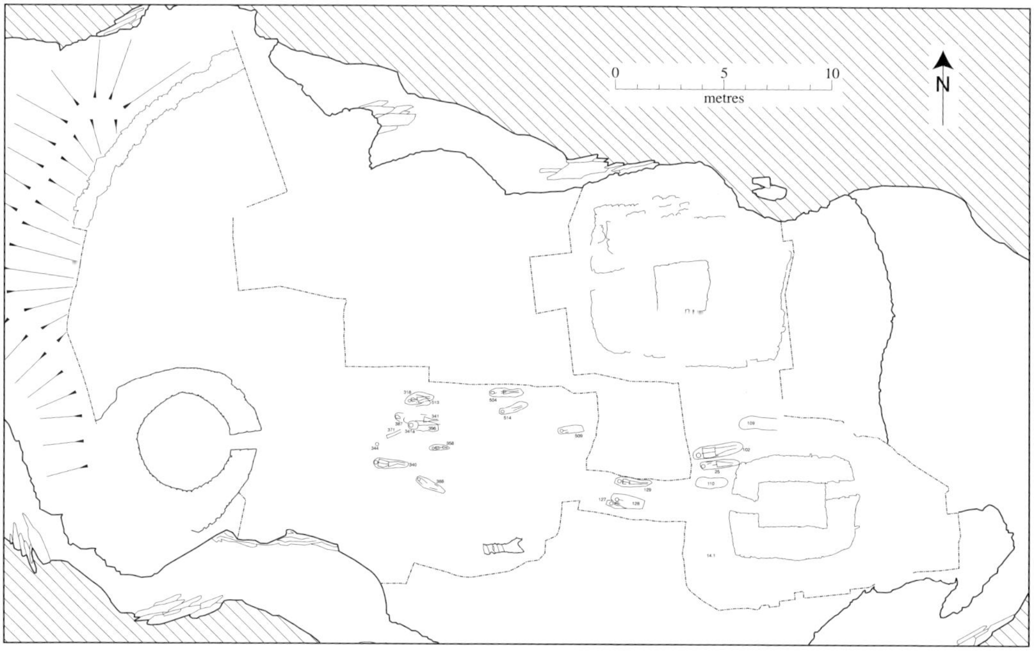

53c—Plan of burials of the post-medieval period on Illaunloughan. There were also a few infant burials at a high level inside the oratory.

of the oratory. It remains possible that there were spatial preferences that shifted with time, reflecting the changing attitudes of the monastic community, but definite evidence is lacking.

Pragmatic concerns may partially explain the burials in the eastern quadrant of the gable shrine. The mound was built up with pea-gravel, soil and rock to raise it to the level of a large ridge of rock running east–west. The rock outcrop, part of the natural bedrock of the island, surfaces largely on the northern part of the mound; consequently, placement of burials on the northern side would have been awkward. The shrine, itself oriented east–west, had its entrance steps on the west. Oriented burials lying side by side were more easily placed in the eastern quadrant than in the southern. Burial was also easier in the eastern quadrant because no rock outcrop existed in this area. The eastern quadrant, separated from the rest of the shrine and mound by a row of upright kerbstones, appears to have been planned as a cemetery.

The original plan may have been to use the other quadrants of the shrine eventually, in anticipation that the monastery would eventually need the burial space. The two monastic burials positioned in existing graves were the only radiocarbon-dated skeletons that possibly date from the ninth century; one (Sk. 180) was dated to AD 683–805 (see n. 55 for full details), and the other (Sk. 120) to AD 787–884.[60] They both may have been placed with the knowledge that full-time occupation of the monastery was soon to end.

Style of graves and demographics of burials

Most of the Illaunloughan graves were simple, earth-dug graves into which bodies, presumably shrouded, had been laid. All of the graves east of the reliquary shrine and most of the graves around the oratory were fashioned in this manner. Some of the graves west of the oratory, however, were more elaborate and had stones lining the sides, a simple form of cist burial, with quartz stones present in or on them. Two of these on the western and south-western corner of the oratory were more structured still. They (F104 and F24) had, in addition to stones defining the sides, large stone-lined grave bases; moreover, each grave was lined with white quartz pebbles (Figs 23 and 34a). These two graves were more elaborate than the other graves around the oratory and may have been the graves of special people, perhaps abbots.

The only other grave style used on Illaunloughan was found in the two stone cists in the centre of the reliquary shrine that contained the translated bones; these were small versions of lintel cist graves, that is, stone-lined graves with stone covers. O'Brien (1992, 132) excavated fifth-century lintel cist graves at Ballyshannon, Co. Donegal, and believes that lintel cist graves evolved from simpler cist graves in the early medieval period, possibly as early as the fourth century in Ireland. Lintel cist graves were found at Reask, Co. Kerry, which the excavator believed pre-dated the stone oratory, but none was found on Church Island, Co. Kerry.[61] Lintel cist graves were common in the sixth-century graveyard at Whithorn, Galloway, Scotland (Hill 1997, 37, 94–105).

Only seventeen skeletons survived among the approximately 24–25 graves associated with the ecclesiastical community; fourteen were adults, and three were juveniles (see Buckley in Appendix 5). The twelve adults whose gender was detectable were males, which strongly suggests that the population was all male, confirming the original working hypothesis that Illaunloughan was a monastery. General age categories could be determined for eight of these men; five or six of them were older men, at least fifty years old, a much higher proportion of older men than a normal random selection would suggest. Buckley cautioned, however, against drawing age conclusions from the small percentage of the population whose age was determined.

The presence of three juveniles (Sk. 172, Sk. 176 and Sk. 181) in an early monastic island cemetery was unexpected, as was their high percentage of the monastic population. Historical documents, nonetheless, record that six- or seven-year-old children were sent to be raised in ecclesiastical communities. In the early eighth century the Anglo-Saxon monk the Venerable Bede attached a small biography of himself to his *Ecclesiastical history*, in which he remarked that 'at the age of seven I was, by the care of my relations, given to the most reverend Abbot Benedict...to be educated. From that time I have spent the whole of my life within that monastery' (Bede 1896, ix, x). Alcuin of York, another Anglo-Saxon monk of the late eighth century, wrote to his brothers at York of his hopes to return to them: 'Perhaps God will pity me, so that he whom you raised in childhood you will bury in old age' (Chase 1975, letter of 795–6). Irish hagiographies also frequently mention saints who were sent to monasteries, such as the notation about St Berach: 'When St Berach had completed seven years, he was taken to Daigh Mac Cairill to study; and he learned the wisdom of the Son of God, so that he became a sage' (Plummer 1922, 2:25; see Plummer for other examples).

Irish children of six or seven were commonly sent to be raised by another family in the early medieval age. This custom, known as fosterage, frequently lasted until children were fourteen to seventeen years old and served the purpose of building strong alliances between families. Fosterage, moreover, often involved a fee paid to the foster family, as well as a set legal contract with guarantees and expectations of benefit for both parties (Kelly 1988, 86–90). The church would naturally be included in this arrangement, a point mentioned and explained in the Life of St Declan: 'On the completion of seven years [of fosterage with his uncle] Declan was taken from his parents and friends and fosterers to be sent to study as Colman had ordained [at his baptism]. It was to Dioma they sent him, a certain devout man perfect in the faith, who had come at that time by God's design into Ireland having spent a long period abroad in acquiring learning...There was given him also, to instruct, together with Declan, another child, scil, Cairbre Mac Colmain, who became afterwards a holy learned bishop. Both these were for a considerable period pursuing their studies together' (Power 1914, 13–15; see also Bitel 1990, 106–7). Illaunloughan has revealed plausible material evidence of the practice of fosterage to the church.

Among the hagiographies in *Vitae Sanctorum Hiberniae* a few refer to the presence of infants in monasteries; in two of these lives the miraculous gift of milk by a doe solved one of the more immediate practical problems associated with the adoption of such young children. St Brendan of Clonfert was one of these examples, and the detailed description of his childhood notes that after a year of being nurtured he was sent to St Ita, one of his foster-mothers, where he spent five years, before being sent on to study with Bishop Erc.[62] Although the hagiographies mention infant adoption, and its difficulties, at large mainland sites, it is difficult to account for an infant presence on a small windswept island. In early medieval times, however, there were no social institutions other than the kin group and the church. The Illaunloughan monks, probably members of local families themselves, may have intervened in the absence of the secular family.

Fosterage, nevertheless, does not adequately explain the presence of a small child in the reliquary cist of the shrine or the small size of one of the three earlier graves under the present shrine. In this exceptional situation it seems probable that this child was a close relative, perhaps even a child, of the adult with whom he is buried.

Post-monastic burials

Illaunloughan continued to be used for interment long after its full-time occupation as a monastery ceased. The demographics of the burials were different in the later medieval (twelfth–seventeenth-century) group and different again in the nineteenth- and twentieth-century groups, although it was not possible to determine the age or gender of a number of incomplete skeletons. These population changes doubtless reflect changing local attitudes toward the site over time.

A small number of post-monastic, later medieval graves, approximately 25, were found (see below, Part 2, Stratigraphic Report). The first identifiable female burials on Illaunloughan were part of this group and, indeed, dominated the adult population. Buckley noted that the demographic pattern was atypical of a normal graveyard, with too few juvenile burials, only 20 per cent of the total, and twice as many adult females as males; she cautioned, however, that the small population size might be influencing the male/female ratios (see Appendix 5). Nevertheless, the pattern is in marked contrast to that of the early medieval one of all males. The chronology of these burials was not extensively investigated, although one individual (F340), a woman, was radiocarbon-dated to the seventeenth century.

The oratory was being used for secular habitation by the late thirteenth to fourteenth century, as indicated by the Edwardian silver pennies buried near its western doorway, radiocarbon dates from the ashy deposit, remnants of a fire, on the southern interior of the oratory, and midden debris (see below, Part 2, Stratigraphic Report). There is no evidence to suggest that the medieval burials are linked to this activity, but this is the first indication that respect for the site as a religious one had waned and that secular people felt comfortable occupying it, even for a temporary period.

In the post-medieval (post-seventeenth-century) period the site was used primarily as a *ceallúnach*, a children's burial-ground, according to local tradition. This tradition also encompassed a few adults, unbaptised people who could not be buried in consecrated burial grounds or who lacked the burial fees; some of these may have been Famine burials, and one was reputed to have been a typhoid victim. O'Sullivan and Sheehan (1996, 323) note that there are 116 *ceallúnaigh* on the Iveragh Peninsula, thirty of which are at recognisable early medieval sites like Illaunloughan.

This last grave population was 91 per cent juveniles and 9 per cent adults. The chronology of this population was not investigated in detail, although Buckley's (Appendix 5) analysis revealed increased dental caries, the presence of clay pipes, which are post-medieval artefacts, and an apparent increase in anaemia and other deficiencies. The general change in demographics and pathology bolsters local traditional belief and the original archaeological classification of these skeletons. Portmagee tradition is that the last known burial on the island was in 1940. It is clear that continuing reverence for the old religious site made it an attractive place for unofficial burials.

6

White quartz, scallops and shrines

White quartz and scallop shells appear on Illaunloughan structures in distributional patterns that cannot be random but serve no apparent function. Commonly found on the nearby shore, they are not inherently meaningful and are found occasionally on the island in ordinary, casual locations, such as scallops in the midden or quartz as a component of Hut C. White quartz was scattered abundantly in and on a number of Illaunloughan structures: on the *leacht*, in several graves, in the two small quadrangular shrines, on the gable shrine and in the cists in the shrine. Scallops were not as numerous and were limited to an invisible presence in the fill over and in the cists of the gable shrine.

Church literature makes no specific mention of white quartz or scallop shells, but historical and archaeological contexts may suggest logical inferences. Christian religious metaphors strongly influenced the lives spent on this small island. Reliquary shrines and graves themselves were fundamental, evocative features of Christianity, shaped and displayed for their spiritual and symbolic meaning. It is plausible that objects closely associated with them also carried similar or related messages.

White quartz

These stones are common on graves or *leachta* of early medieval ecclesiastical sites in Ireland, Wales and northern Britain (Crowe 1982), but the custom of depositing them must have lasted for centuries, because they are also found occasionally on nineteenth- or twentieth-century graves, such as the O'Connell family graves at the old abbey in Derrynane, Co. Kerry, on graves around the church on Inishglora, Co. Mayo, and on graves on Inishark, Co. Mayo.[63]

Their presence has generally been associated with pilgrims, but, because of the duration of the custom, the origins and chronological details of the tradition have remained uncertain. Recent excavation evidence, however, shows that ecclesiastics also used them in the early medieval period, in more readily dated contexts, such as graves. The earliest were in western Britain, at Whithorn, where enormous quantities of white quartz were used as pebble covers on the graves. Late Period I, the second half of the seventh and the early eighth centuries, had the highest concentration, although they continued in use in later periods: the proportion of graves with white pebbles peaked at almost 50 per cent late in Period I (Hill 1997, 472–3).[64]

Evidence of white quartz in early medieval graves is scarce in Ireland, apart from Illaunloughan and two special burials at High Island (Marshall and Rourke 2000, 111). On Illaunloughan the stone is present in graves west of the oratory, especially the two cist graves, F24 and F105. On Church Island O'Kelly (1958) recorded a vast quantity of white quartz stone, some 6800 stones, but they were not found in the earliest burials. There were, however, 298 in the fine gravel of the tomb/shrine, possibly an original layer, that was below the modern layer of soil. White quartz stones were not found in either the lintel cist graves or the shrine at Reask (Fanning 1981, 79–84). White quartz has, however, been found in and around some of the graves at Caherlehillan (J. Sheehan, pers. comm., 2004).

The deposition of the white quartz stones on Illaunloughan, however, can be dated to the time of the monastery because they were found in the two cists of the reliquary shrine, as well as in the quadrangular structures also believed to be shrines; all of these structures fit into a broad chronological range of late seventh to late eighth century. It is also clear that the ecclesiastics, rather than pilgrims, placed the white quartz in these structures. It is probable, therefore, that much of the quartz seen on the other Illaunloughan structures also dates from the period of the active use of the monastery.

White quartz is one of a number of stones imbued with symbolic meaning in this period. Stones, generally naturally shaped and occasionally decorated, were used for various purposes, such as altar stones, cursing stones and cure stones (Ritchie 1971–2; Higgins 1987, vol. 1, 18–21). This is probably based on ancient traditions that were easily Christianised, as in the famous story of St Columba picking up a white stone from a river, blessing it and ordering the water into which it had been dipped to be used to cure sick people (Anderson and Anderson 1961, 399–405).

There are no official church statements about the liturgical use of white stones. It is, therefore, unlikely that they were deposited as part of an established protocol for a religious rite. Hill (1997, 472), however, cites two references that contain a strong clue about their significance. The first is from Apocalypse 2:17: 'To him who conquers I will give...him a white stone, with a new name written on the stone'; the other is from Bede: 'although you may write the name of the devil on a white stone, nevertheless, he signifies the uttermost darkness'.

The importance of white quartz appears to relate largely to its colour, and it seems to have become meaningful only when placed in sacred areas. Ferguson (1954) noted that white has traditionally been the Christian colour of purity, innocence and a holy life. This is the interpretation specifically stated in the *Leabhar Breac* of the meaning of a priest's white vestments; other examples are that Christ wore white garments after his resurrection, and that St Columba ordered the Iona monks to wear white habits for a special Mass in honour of St Colman.[65] In the seventh century an Irish monk wrote in *Augustinus Hibernicus* relating white to divine power: 'Why then did his [Christ's] garment have the whiteness of snow, seeing that they were neither human nor divine?', and concludes that it was because 'the flesh illuminated by that divinity shone through the garments' (Carey 1998, 70). In the *Pseudo Historical Prologue to the Senchas Már* white is associated with sacred script: 'white language of the Beati would come, i.e. the law of Scripture' (Carey 1998, 143). The composer of the *Félire Oengusso* implores the saints, 'a shining host', and mentions them as standing around God 'in white garments' (Carey 1998, 70, 143). When the Sil Muiredaig sought the aid of St Mochua of Balla against the yellow plague, they promised 'to do the will of the white pure cleric' (Stokes 1890, 143, 287).

A number of other casual references in Irish and biblical sources confirm the importance of the colour and suggest that this meaning was never debated or discussed but was taken for granted (see also Marshall and Rourke 2000, 110–11). The deposition of white stones appears to be a spontaneous gesture rather than a formal ritual act, one based on popular belief, a cultural attitude that needed no discussion or official recognition. White stones may have been placed as a token of respect and reverence for the holiness of the person or feature, a sign of devotion that created a memorial of its own.

Scallop shells

Scallop shells, some perforated, were found in the shrine, mixed with gravel and quartz in a soil layer above the reliquary cists, and also in the cists containing the translated bones (Fig. 54a). A scallop was also on the lid of one of the cists. The calibrated radiocarbon determination for these shells dates them to AD 665–1048.

Scallops are abundant near the island and are easily harvested from the mudflats at low tide today. They were, however, rare in the midden remains and were not present elsewhere on the island.[66] The artificial perforations on the shells and their scarcity in other locations raise the possibility that their presence in and around the cists in the reliquary shrine is deliberate and meaningful. They may have been suspended from a leather strap and worn around the neck or attached to a personal article in a similar fashion to the scallop shells found in Tuam, Co. Galway, and one found at Winchester, England, dated to the twelfth–thirteenth century (Fig. 54b).[67] The scallops at Illaunloughan, however, considerably pre-date these examples.

In the Mediterranean, scallops were used as ceremonial, symbolic imagery for centuries before the beginning of Christianity. Greco-Romans believed them to be an attribute of Aphrodite/Venus, who was associated with birth/creativity and the sea. Shells were common on mosaics, wall paintings and funerary monuments,

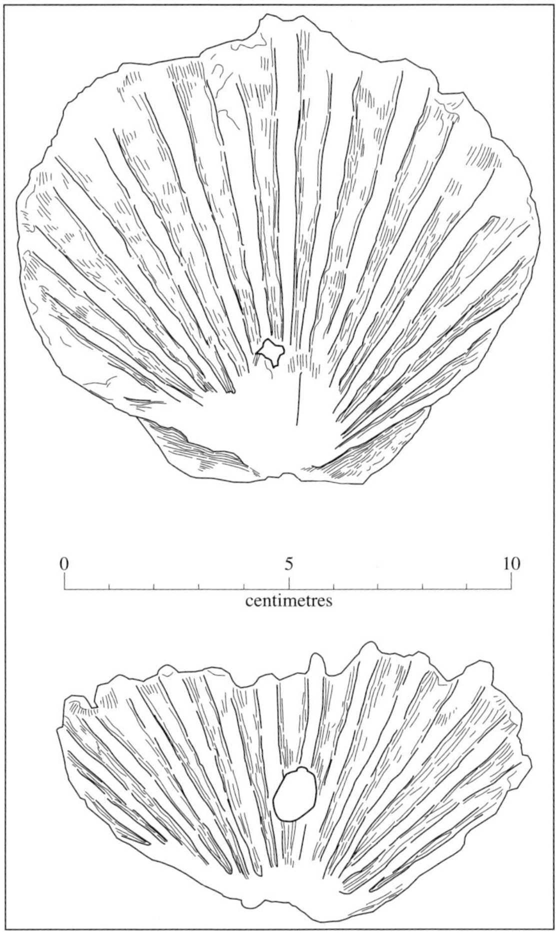

54a—Perforated scallop shells found within the gable shrine on Illaunloughan. A leather cord may have been threaded through the single, man-made perforation on each shell. The perforation on these shells was in a different place than those on the shell shown in Fig. 54b. *(C. McHale)*

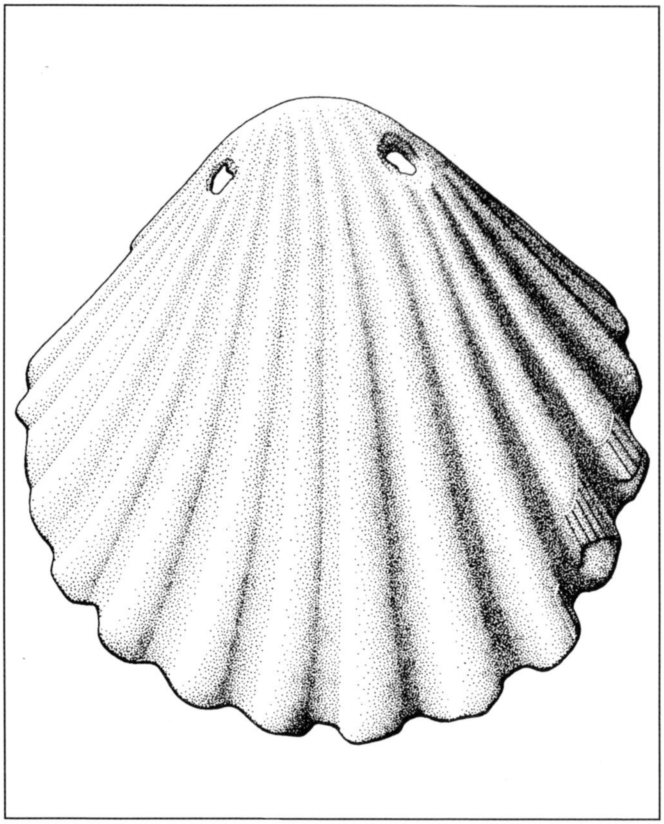

54b—A later medieval shell, with double perforations, related to the pilgrimage to Santiago de Compostela, found during the Winchester excavations (after Biddle 1990, vol. 2, 801–3); it is similar to one found in a grave at St Mary's Cathedral, Tuam, Co. Galway (Clyne 1987–8, fig. 5, no. 42; 1990). These scallop shells were probably attached to the pilgrim's satchel or script.

particularly in niches above cinerary urns in mausoleums and as a framing device or halo behind the head of the deceased on a sarcophagus. Eventually the Romans used the scallop for purely decorative purposes on household items such as hand mirrors, lamps and flasks or as an honorarium behind the head of Caesar.[68]

The importance of the scallop shell as a symbol transcended religions as well as cultures in the Mediterranean. In the second or third century, Jews of the region used it on Torah shrines, on sarcophagi and over doorways or windows on synagogues. The Torah shrine, encompassed by a small structure (*aedicule*), was the point of orientation for prayer in the synagogue at Dura Europos (AD 245); a shell made in plaster is placed above the Torah, and another is above the entrance of the Lost Temple painted on the *aedicule* above (Fig. 55).[69] Later still, the shell is found in one of the early sacred places of Islam, the cave beneath the Dome of the Rock in Jerusalem (Goodenough 1958–65, vol. 8, 104), and on the early eighth-century mosaic depiction of a mosque in the Umayyad mosque at Damascus, Syria.[70]

Christianity, a Mediterranean religion, naturally adopted scallop imagery, as part of a structural vocabulary shared and understood in the region. One of the earliest, and certainly the most influential, Christian uses of the scallop was on the Tomb of Christ in Jerusalem. In AD 325–6 Constantine ordered extensive work to preserve and embellish the newly rediscovered Tomb of Christ in Jerusalem. A small structure known as the *aedicule* ('little house'), a two-chambered building, was built around the tomb; then the Rotunda of the Anastasis enclosed both the tomb and its surrounding structure. Immediately above the entrance to the tomb was a large scallop shell, and shells, according to an early seventh-century poem by Sophronius

55—The Torah shrine inside an architectural structure known as an *aedicule* (small structure); it was the focal feature of the synagogue at Dura Europos (AD 244–5) and is now in the National Museum in Damascus. There is a scallop shell in plaster above the shrine as well as above the entry to the Temple of Jerusalem above it. The commonality of architectural motifs in the Mediterranean is seen in the similarity of the Temple to the later *aedicule* around the Tomb of Christ. *(Courtesy of Yale University Art Gallery)*

56—Reconstruction drawing of the original *aedicule* around the Tomb of Christ as it looked in the fourth century AD. *(After Wilkinson 2002, 367, fig. 7)*

of Jerusalem, were also found around the exterior of the *aedicule* (Fig. 56):

> And as I venerate that worthy Tomb,
> Surrounded by its conches
> And columns surmounted by golden lilies,
> I shall be overcome with joy.[71]

Schematic representations of the façade of the *aedicule* found on small cast-pewter flasks of the late sixth to early seventh century, such as at Bobbio and Monza in Lombardy, aided in the reconstruction of its original appearance. A similar pewter medallion is now in a museum in Stuttgart (Fig. 57).[72] The façade of the *aedicule*, flanked by the three Marys, represented the Tomb of Christ and likely, therefore, the Resurrection. The scallop as a feature of the *aedicule* may have survived or been restored after the extensive damage done to the Holy Sepulchre

57—Late sixth- to early seventh-century medallion showing the Holy Women at the façade of the *aedicule* for the Tomb of Christ. *(Courtesy of Stuttgart. Württembergisches landesmuseum inv. Nr. 1981-165)*

58—Scallop shell above the head of St Simeon Stylites sitting on his pillar as he confronts the Devil in the form of a great serpent. This representation is on a gilded plaque, a sixth-century Syrian reliquary. *(Courtesy of the Louvre Museum, Paris)*

59—The Riha Paten. This Syrian embossed silver and silver-gilt paten, stamped with the seal of Justin II (565–78), shows a scallop shell placed above the Divine Liturgy, Christ administering the Eucharist to his disciples. *(Courtesy of the Dumbarton Oaks Collection)*

in 1009 by Caliph al-Hakim but was clearly changed sometime later.[73]

Between the fourth and the sixth centuries there is substantial evidence of the use of symbolic scallops in the eastern Roman empire. For example, scallops occur on Christian sarcophagi, such as the fifth-century sarcophagus of Constantius III, husband of Galla Placida, and another, sixth-century, sarcophagus in the church of St Apollinare in Classe in Ravenna.[74] On a gilded silver plaque, a sixth-century ex-voto offering, the scallop shell hovers above the head of St Simeon Stylites, who sits calmly on his pillar as the Devil in the form of a great snake twines around the pillar (Fig. 58). On the sixth-century Riha Paten in Syria a scallop shell was placed centrally above the scene depicting Christ serving communion to his disciples (Fig. 59). The late fourth-century Hetoimasia relief depicts Christ as a dove flying from the scallop down to an empty throne. And there is a scallop on an ivory relief of St Menas standing in front of his church. On these items the scallop appears to have explicit meaning as a marker of divine presence and a sign of life after death.

Scallop motifs were not found in western Europe during the first thousand years AD, outside of areas strongly influenced by the Roman empire.[75] The popularity of this motif diminished everywhere after the sixth century, until its revival centuries later at Santiago de Compostela and for a short time at Mont St Michel.

Scallop shells are famous as a symbol of the apostle St James the Great and the celebrated pilgrimage to Santiago de Compostela in Spain. In the later Middle Ages

60—The Areobindus plaque, a fifth-century Byzantine ivory plaque showing a procession of relics. A patriarch in a carriage holds the reliquary box. *(Courtesy of the Cathedral Treasury in Trier)*

61—A sixth-century Byzantine marble reliquary shaped like a small sarcophagus with acroteria at its corners in imitation of larger sarcophagi reliquaries; it is typical of those found throughout the Byzantine empire. An opening on the crest of the lid may have been made for libations. Such small reliquaries have been found under altars. The drawings and engravings on the side date from the eighteenth century. *(Courtesy of the Metropolitan Museum, New York)*

St James was viewed as the great intercessor for the dead, and he and his scallop became symbols of pilgrimage and of salvation of the soul (Alexandre-Bidon and Treffort 1993, 167–79). The first written references to St James's grave in Galicia are in the ninth century, but they make no mention of scallops, nor was St James the Great associated with scallops in the eastern Mediterranean.[76] The earliest statement connecting the scallop to St James is in the early twelfth-century *Liber Sancti Jacobi*; scallops on pilgrims also begin to appear in the mid-twelfth century, on Romanesque architectural sculpture on French and Spanish cathedrals built along the pilgrimage routes to Santiago.[77] The first use of pilgrimage badges at a western European site may have been at Santiago early in the twelfth century.[78] It is, therefore, evident that the use of the scallop at Santiago de Compostela considerably post-dates its use at Illaunloughan.

There is no evidence of the use of scallops, particularly those worn on a cord, as a souvenir of any pilgrimage that might connect the tomb of Christ with a simple ecclesiastical site in western Ireland in the eighth century. The presence of a scallop shell over the door of the most celebrated Christian shrine, nevertheless, was likely the inspiration for the presence of the scallops in the shrine at Illaunloughan and for its later, more famous, adoption at Santiago de Compostela.

The structural model for the reliquary shrine

Small portable reliquaries existed as early as the fifth or sixth century, in Constantinople. Examples are seen on the sixth-century ivory diptych of Areobindus, which shows a patriarch holding a reliquary during a procession, and in the small sixth-century Byzantine marble reliquary, modelled on stone sarcophagi, which is typical of those found under church altars (Figs 60 and 61).[79] By the seventh/eighth century small reliquaries were appearing on the Continent and in Ireland and Scotland, but the stylistic details of the reliquary differ from Byzantine models. A number of these small reliquaries had been modified to include ridge poles and finials, motifs reminiscent of wooden houses or churches (Figs 62 and 63).[80] In function, form and chronology the small reliquaries appear closely related to the gable shrine at Illaunloughan, although the larger, permanent structure at Illaunloughan has no decoration, no ridge pole or finials.

The shape, finials and ridge poles on the portable reliquaries also resemble the illustration of the church found somewhat later on the Temptation of Christ page in the Book of Kells, as well as the later small stone structures found on the top of high crosses such as Muiredach's Cross at Monasterboice and the Cross of the Scriptures at Clonmacnoise (Fig. 64). Similar forms are also seen on Irish structures assigned to the twelfth century, such as St Manchan's reliquary in County Offaly, the mortuary houses in counties Down and Derry and a stone sarcophagus at Clones, Co. Monaghan; the latter two have ridge poles and finials.[81]

Scholarly speculation about the original model for these reliquaries has varied. An early opinion was that gable shrines derived from both churches and tombs, which in turn derived from the outline of early Christian and non-Christian temples (Thomas 1971, 164). More recently, scholars have viewed them either as miniature versions of late antique sarcophagi (Blindheim 1984; Ó Floinn 1994, 14, 15; Harbison 1999b, 133–4) or as house shrines (Rollason 1989, 29; Ryan 1989, 129–34). Ryan remarked that Irish versions of portable reliquaries were shaped like 'small models of hip-roofed buildings with prominent gable finials and applied decorations of metal'; he also, in addition to the comparisons mentioned above, cited their resemblance to extant small stone churches. He suggested that their ultimate origin may be in the long-vanished Temple of Jerusalem.[82]

62—Late seventh/early eighth-century portable French reliquary (purse or house?) of silver- and copper-gilt plates over wood. It has finials and ridge poles. *(Courtesy of the Musée de Cluny, Paris)*

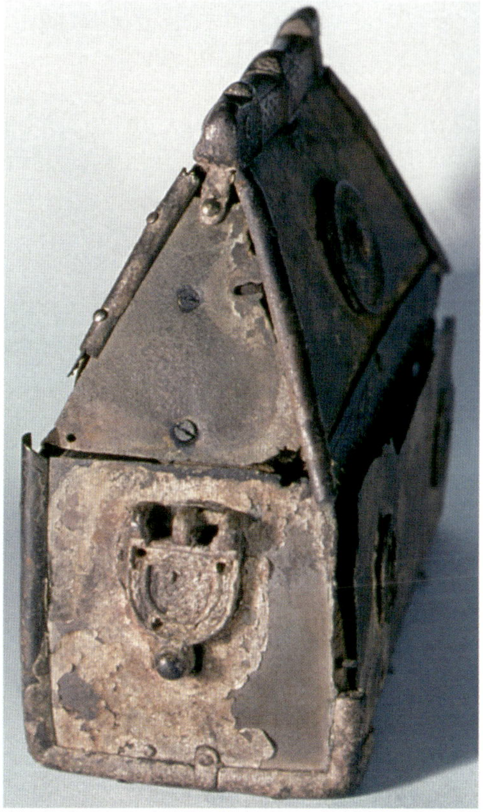

63—The Lough Erne shrine, the larger, outer part of a two-piece portable reliquary dating from the late eighth to early ninth century. The outer section is shaped like a hipped-roof structure with a ridge-pole; the shrine has a wooden base with sheets of copper alloy fastened to it. At the centre of the ridge-pole is another hipped-roof structure. *(Courtesy of the National Museum of Ireland)*

Very little contemporary written evidence of the nature of these reliquary shrines exists, but all of it is connected to the use of the word 'house'. In the early eighth century Bede wrote of a reliquary constructed over the burial-place of St Chad at Lichfield in Mercia: 'Chad's burial place is covered by a wooden tomb made in the form of a little house [*domuncula*] with an aperture in the wall through which those who visit it out of devotion may insert their hand and take out some of the dust'. The word *domuncula* was used by the hagiographer of the Irish saint Fursey, whose remains were translated to a 'little house' east of the altar at Péronne, Gaul.[83] Clearly, the word 'house' was being used to describe a saint's reliquary or tomb. This was a variation of the use of the word, which had traditionally been used by Christians to describe a church or temple. The use of the word was universal, so that the expression 'The house of Christ', or the house of a specific saint, was common in late antique Christianity. It was still used in tenth-century Scotland; for

64—Small church-shaped structure on top of the high cross at Monasterboice, Co. Louth, which bears a close resemblance to the small portable reliquaries made of wood and metal. *(Courtesy of the Photographic Section of the Department of the Environment, Heritage and Local Government)*

example, when the son of King Aed became an abbot and retired to 'a church on the sea's edge...the house of the apostle'.[84] Ireland, following this tradition, still calls a number of small stone churches that date from approximately between the eighth and the tenth centuries 'the house of [the saint]', among them Teach Molaise on Inishmurray, Co. Sligo, and St Columb's House in Kells, Co. Meath.[85]

Pagan gods and goddesses, Christian saints and the Jewish Ark of the Covenant were all depicted in temples or shrines on coins, ampullae and stone reliefs (Figs 65 and 66).[86] The architecture of the protective structure stood for the holy power sheltered within; in all of these the structural form was meaningful to the contemporaneous population.

The design of Irish reliquaries appears to have elements of both tomb and church, a combined structure that perfectly reflects Christian doctrine. Emphasis on

65—Stone relief of Mercury and a goddess standing in a temple, from Gloucester, England. *(Courtesy of Gloucester Museum)*

the tomb and resurrection of Christ and the tombs of Christian martyrs and saints led Christians to merge the tomb and the temple into one building in a pointed change from the customs of earlier religions, which venerated both but kept them distinctly separate.[87] When Christianity became the official religion of the Roman Empire, the cult of the saints increased, churches were constructed over the tombs of the saints near the main altar, and, later, saintly relics were placed in or on the altar of the church.

The placing of a saint's tomb at or near the altar, the most sacred part of the sanctuary, architecturally expressed the potent relationship between God, Christ and the local saint. This place was the entrance to heaven, where God and the saint might best hear prayers and the saint might, as a human friend and intercessor, plead for humans with God. Traditional veneration of local saints further increased confidence in accessibility to God (Doherty 1984, 95; Lucas 1986, 7; Ryan 1989, 129). Churches themselves became viewed as the saint's shrine, and his tomb-shrine was seen as his dwelling because his spiritual power continued to be active there (Brown 1981). This attitude is represented in the famous inscription on the tomb of St Martin: 'Here lies buried Martin the bishop of holy memory, whose soul is in the hand of God, but he is entirely here, present and manifest in all the grace of his virtues' (LeBlant 1856–65, vol. 1, no. 180). The distinctions between tomb and shrine, church and saint's dwelling, were fading.

There is no question that the reliquary shrine at Illaunloughan was the tomb of the three individuals found in the cists. It is unlikely, however, that any of the Irish

66—A clay pilgrim's ampulla, approximately sixth-century, from Smyrna, showing St Peter holding a cross and a key. He is shown inside a gable-shaped structure with twisted columns that may represent the church. *(Courtesy of the Louvre Museum, Paris)*

gable shrines were intended to be a literal rendition of a Merovingian or late antique sarcophagus, as sarcophagi were neither manufactured nor used by the Irish (Edwards 1998, 227); indeed, coffins were exceptionally rare in Ireland in the seventh and eighth centuries, almost certainly made of wood and used for special burials.[88] Sarcophagi were not part of a readily understood architectural vocabulary, but tombs certainly were. The image of a church may have been used as a visual metaphor for a tomb or saint's house, just as the façade of the tomb *aedicule* represented the tomb of Christ, the intent being to represent the tomb by using a familiar structure, a contemporary Irish church.[89]

Although archaeologists such as Harbison (1984; 1991, chap. 11), Herity (1995, 277, 280) and Marshall (1989) have speculated about a functional similarity between gable shrines, small churches and the mortuary houses found in the north of Ireland, chronological and excavation evidence has been lacking until the excavation of Illaunloughan and of a small structure in Lough Key, Co. Roscommon. King's (2002) excavation of the small structure, measuring 1.5m by 3m, north of the church on Church Island, Lough Key, supports Harbison's earlier arguments. The small, stone-roofed, mortared structure was clearly shaped like a miniature medieval church, with a round-headed window and a possible entrance in the southern wall, part of another window in the eastern wall, and two *piscinae* in the interior near the entrance. The structure, set upon a plinth or platform, probably dated from the late twelfth century, and was built around a cist grave, which contained an articulated skeleton; another, unarticulated skeleton was found on the southern plinth. Illaunloughan and Church Island, Lough Key, clearly demonstrate the longevity of the gable-shaped design for fixed, outdoor reliquaries.

The construction of the saint's reliquary/tomb/shrine in the form of his own church on the exterior of the main church is another indication that many Irish communities maintained the strictures of the early church against burial inside the church into the twelfth century. In the early medieval period Irish saints were not buried inside the church but entered the church translated into small reliquaries (E. O'Brien, pers. comm., 1997; Marshall and Rourke 2000, 91–3).

There are still other symbolic possibilities. Ryan (1989, 134) has compared the form and decoration of the church in the Temptation of Christ in the Book of Kells to the Temple at Jerusalem as seen in the seventh-century Ashburnham Pentateuch's depiction of the Tabernacle (Weitzmann 1977, pl. 47). Ryan concludes that the use of this image on the small, portable reliquaries was also likely modelled on 'a traditional representation of the long-demolished Temple, a building which was of particular significance in both the Old and New Testaments' O'Reilly (1994) agrees and carries this allusion to the Temple of Jerusalem further by stating that it represents the importance of patristic exegesis of the temple as a symbol of the body and church of Christ, present and future, on earth and in heaven. Insular familiarity with the importance of the patristic exegesis, she argues, is clearly demonstrated in Bede's treatise 'De tabernaculo, de templo':

> The house of God which king Solomon built in Jerusalem was made as a figure of the holy universal Church which...is daily being built through the grace...of its redeemer. It is still partly in pilgrimage from him on earth and partly...already reigns with him in heaven...But (it was a figure) of him as the uniquely chosen and precious cornerstone laid in the foundation and of us as the living stones built upon the foundation of the apostles and prophets, i.e. on the Lord himself...the figure (of the temple) will apply to our Lord himself in some respects, in others to all the elect.[90]

Irish ecclesiastics were certainly familiar with all of the themes mentioned here—the significance of the saint's tomb, the concept of a tomb-shrine, the shapes of late antique and Merovingian sarcophagi, the church as the house of God—and with the important Christian shrines at Old St Peter's in Rome and the Holy Sepulchre in Jerusalem. The various interpretations of gable-shaped shrines and structures as tomb or temple or house do not conflict but are complementary. The shrine is a tomb, as it contains the bones of the saint; it is also the house of the saint in that his/her spiritual presence remains there, and it is further a declaration that the saint is part of the eternal church and an exhortation to the faithful to become 'living stones'. The imagery and possible meanings are so interwoven that, in the absence of specific contemporaneous statements, it is impossible to distinguish between them or to attach one specific meaning. It is perhaps more likely that multiple meanings were always intended. All of the possible interpretations relate to the hope of resurrection and the triumph of the church; all declare the status of the saints as members of the elect.

7

The drystone oratories of western Kerry

G.D. Rourke and J. White Marshall

The corbelled, drystone oratory on Illaunloughan belongs to a type of small stone church found in western Ireland, often called the Gallarus style, after the well-known Gallarus Oratory on the Dingle Peninsula, Co. Kerry. The construction technique is the same as that used for the domestic cell on Illaunloughan, except that the cell is round on plan and the church is rectangular.

History of drystone corbelled structures

The history of corbelled vaults is thousands of years old, and they are widespread in Europe. In prehistoric times this tradition appears to originate in monumental tombs such as Maes Howe in the Orkneys, in the royal tholos tombs such as the Treasury of Atreus in Mycenae, Greece, and in the Boyne Valley tombs in Ireland such as Newgrange. These tombs are among the oldest surviving structures still standing, dating to 2500–1500 BC, which led Colvin (1991, 1), a well-known architectural historian, to remark that 'Architecture in western Europe begins with tombs'. The stone fabric of these tombs, both in Ireland and elsewhere, was not visible but covered by mounds of soil and stone (Fig. 67). The purpose of the stonework, therefore, may relate to the durable and permanent qualities of stone construction rather than to any exterior aesthetic appeal.

There is no evidence that domestic structures in Ireland were commonly of drystone construction at the time that these high-status tomb/ceremonial sites were built.[91] Although stone continued to be used for prominent tomb structures for some centuries in various forms, such as wedge tombs and small passage graves, house remains with stone as a component are rare, comprising only 12.8 per cent of excavated Bronze Age structures (Doody 2000, 141); Doody speculates that this stone was most likely used only for foundation courses.

It is not until many centuries later that drystone, corbelled structures, built on a smaller scale, become a prominent feature of vernacular architecture in Ireland, where they are most common in the western coastal regions, with a particularly dense concentration in western County Kerry.

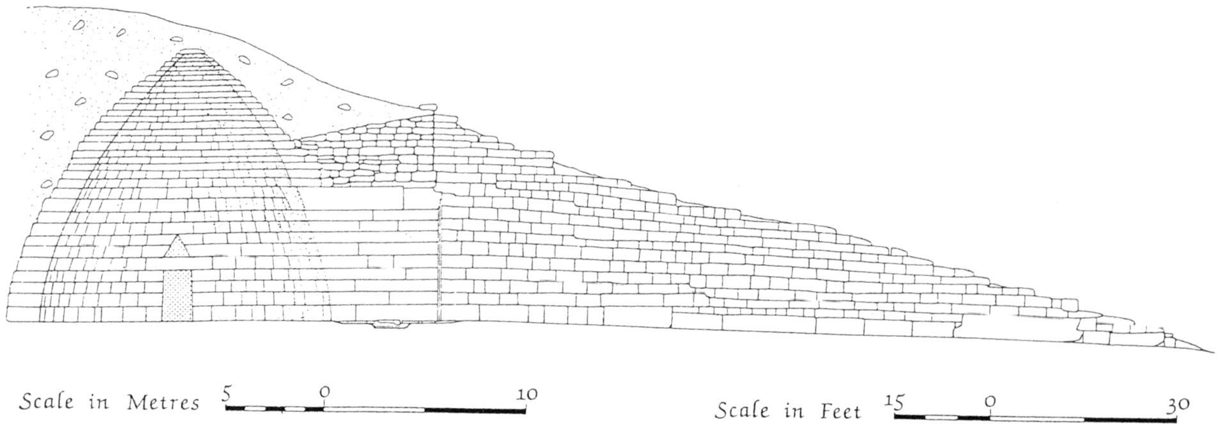

67a—Drawing of an ancient drystone corbelled tomb, Ile Longue, in Brittany, France. *(After Colvin 1991, 10, fig. 10)*

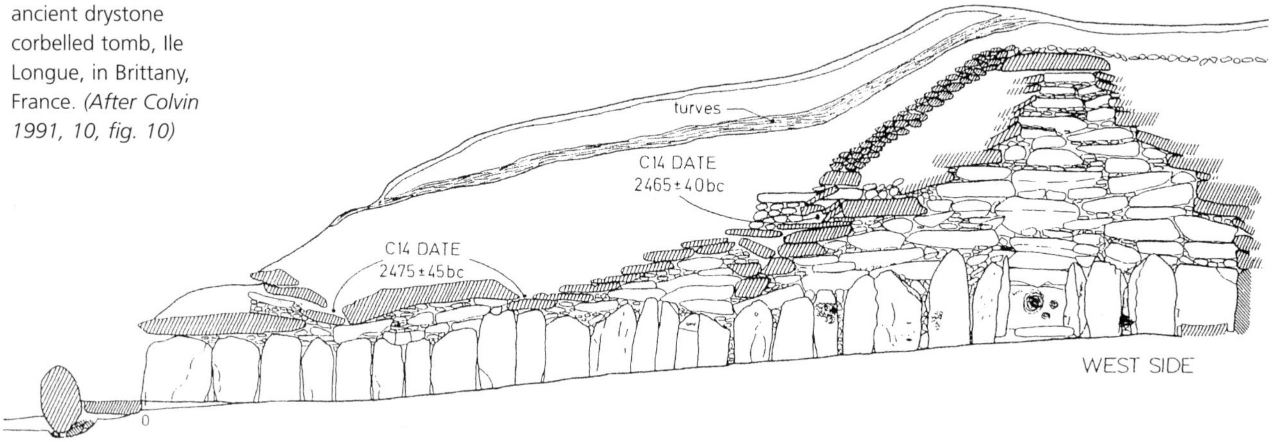

67b—Elevation of the west side of the passage before excavation at Newgrange, Co. Meath. *(After O'Kelly 1982, 94, fig. 17).*

The earliest drystone building known on the Iveragh Peninsula is a Late Bronze Age structure at Coarhabeg on Valentia Island, dating from the seventh century BC; the excavator was uncertain whether this building, perhaps used as a sweat house, was corbelled, but it was not corbel-vaulted (Hayden 1994b) (Fig. 68). Individual stone buildings remain difficult to date unless excavation reveals datable associated material, such as charcoal or bone from hearths. The widespread presence of stone buildings in secular and ecclesiastical settlements of the early medieval period strongly indicates the commonality of the type at this time. Their presence in the secular ringforts is particularly striking. O'Sullivan and Sheehan (1996, 135) remarked that, among the ringforts alone: 'Definite or probable remains of houses or other buildings are apparent in 36 per cent of the raths and in 47 per cent of the cahers. Most of these remains are of circular stone buildings.' Cuppage (1986, 99) noted an even higher frequency of—mostly round—stone buildings in Dingle Peninsula ringforts, where they are found in 40 per cent of the raths and 69 per cent

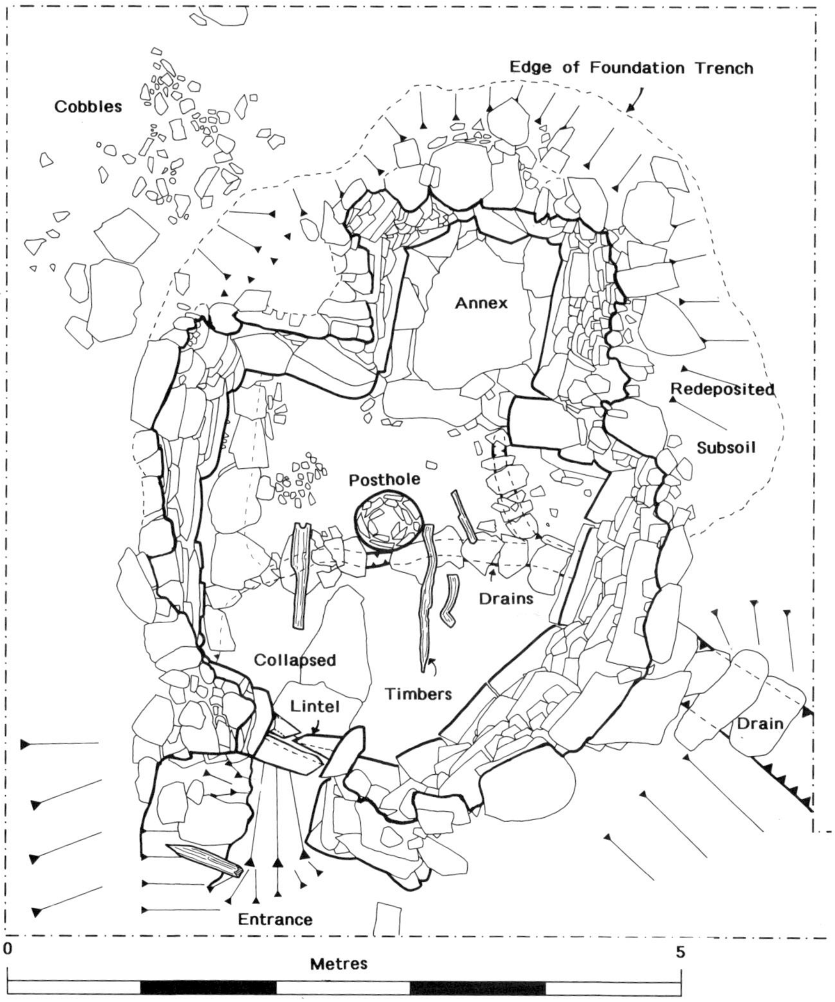

68—Plan of the late Bronze Age drystone structure at Coarha More on Valentia Island, Co. Kerry, which dates from the seventh century BC. This is one of the few domestic structures in stone known from this period. *(A. Hayden, 1994)*

of the cashels, or cahers.[92] Excavation on a number of these sites, such as the secular sites of Beginish, Cool West, Loher, Leacanabuaile and the ecclesiastical sites of Reask, Church Island, and Illaunloughan, has further confirmed this chronological placement.

The question, nevertheless, remains: why did these stone, corbelled structures become so prevalent in western Ireland in the early medieval period? Wood and sod are warmer, better-insulating materials than stone for the western climate. The prevalence of stone buildings during this period may relate to a combination of factors, such as easy access to good building stone, a long local tradition of building drystone walls, climatic constraints, increasing population, decreasing availability of timber, a desire for more permanent and solid structures, and a perception of stone as a desirable, status-enhancing material.

If causation is difficult to determine, there has been a clear, if uneven and often slow, shift from construction in organic materials to construction in stone in Europe over the last 1500 years. Extensive excavation in England has revealed a change in vernacular architecture from sod, clay or timber to stone, starting in the late twelfth century in the south and south-west of the country and gradually spreading. The Hound Tor excavations in Devon (Beresford and Hurst 1971, fig. 14) revealed that stone walls replaced sod walls without disturbing the uprights used on the sod-wall construction.[93] In Kerry the trend appears to have started earlier than in Devon.

Corbelled drystone construction technique

Drystone construction in Ireland consists of carefully laid inner and outer faces with often, but not always, an inner core of smaller rubble stones. Corbelled construction generally, and in all of the Kerry oratories, involves the construction of a masonry vaulted roof constructed from the walls of the structure; each horizontal layer of the stones is laid so that it slightly overhangs on the interior. Construction continues toward the apex, which is then closed by one or more capstones. In this method each stone, or corbel, must be laid so that its long end is set well into the wall as a counterweight, keeping the centre of gravity within the wall. In circular structures, the most common shape, the corbel stones are tapered so that their edges radiate from the centre of the structure to facilitate tight construction (Figs 69 and 70).

Another principle of circular corbelled construction is that the stones of each course are given a slight outward slope or inclination (roughly 15 per cent), which serves two important functions. Inclined stones help to deflect wind and impede water penetration. Any rain falling is deflected outward, keeping the interior of the structure dry and providing a better internal environment.[94] The second function is structural: the outward inclination of the stones helps to compensate for inward thrust and to achieve a better structural balance.

As the corbelled vault is constructed, each successive course of stones laid in this way holds the lower stones firmly in place. Flat stones are preferred, as they allow for a good bond between the stones, and this helps to reduce any movement. As the corbelled vault settles under gravity, the masonry tightens and the structure stabilises. This form of drystone construction can accommodate slow, differential movement or settlement at any stage in the life of the structure. It is an extraordinarily flexible method of construction.

The shape of the vaults, therefore, is a primary influence on the nature and amount of thrust and hence on the strength and stability of the structure (Norton in Oliver 1997, vol. 2, 360). Round corbelled structures are the most stable form, as the inward movement serves to wedge and tighten the inner ends of the stone. The

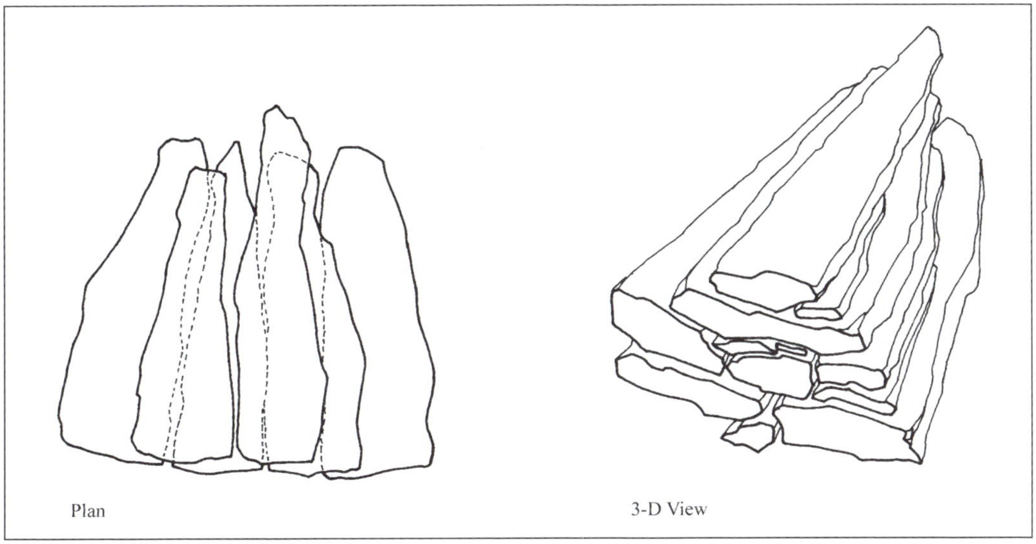

69—Drawing showing the radiating technique used in the placement of stones in circular corbelled structures. *(G.D. Rourke)*

70—The interior of the Small Oratory on Skellig Michael, Co. Kerry, showing the tendency of the lateral walls to sag inwards. *(G.D. Rourke)*

balanced and harmonious distribution of weight and pressure in a circle is disrupted in a rectangular structure by the angular divergence of the corners. The differentiated stresses of inward thrust then cause the longer walls to move inward, particularly at the centre, which often leads to the collapse of these walls. The Small Oratory on Skellig Michael demonstrates this kind of deformation (Fig. 70).

Drystone oratories in County Kerry

The remains of drystone oratories, like those of other drystone structures, are found primarily on the western coast of Ireland, most on the western sections of the Dingle and Iveragh peninsulas, Co. Kerry.

The corbelled drystone oratory is the most common form of stone church architecture from the early medieval period remaining on the Iveragh Peninsula. The survey of the Iveragh Peninsula (O'Sullivan and Sheehan 1996, 247) noted that there was evidence of 28 stone oratories at 26 ecclesiastical sites. Three were medieval, and five had left no surface traces. Six of the remaining twenty stone oratories, 30 per cent of the total, are complete enough to allow us to be certain that their roofs were corbelled: Ballycarbery (927: Church Island), Ballynabloun (929: Templecashel), the Large and the Small oratories on Skellig Michael (948), Kildreelig (951), and Killabuonia (954).[95] Fieldwork done in 1990 by Rourke and Marshall on drystone oratories indicated that another six oratories with visibly corbelled walls should be added to the total of such oratories on the Iveragh Peninsula: Beginish (932), Cappanagoun (935), Clohanelinaghan (937: Killobarnaun), Illaunloughan, Kilkeaveragh (953) and the South Peak Oratory of Skellig Michael (948).

The scant remains of another six or seven stone oratories survive, consisting only of stone base courses or sod-covered walls, such as Baslickane (930), Feaghman West (945), Loher (963: Kildreenagh), Long Island (966) and Scariff Island (967).[96] Whether these were drystone corbelled oratories remains uncertain until they are excavated, but they resemble the known corbelled oratories in wall thickness, plan and size and are found on the same type of small sites.

The few remaining, essentially intact, drystone oratories in Kerry, such as the Large and Small oratories on Skellig Michael, Templecashel on the Iveragh Peninsula, and St Brendan's and Gallarus on the Dingle Peninsula, are corbel-vaulted. Excavation evidence, currently limited to three County Kerry oratories, Illaunloughan, Church Island (O'Kelly 1958, 61–3) and Reask (Fanning 1981, 76), further reinforces the hypothesis that all of the drystone oratories were corbel-vaulted. The presence of collapsed stones in and around the structures and the absence of post-holes to support wooden or thatched roofs were particularly significant at Reask, where little was left of the structure, with walls ranging from base courses to a maximum height of 0.45–0.50m.[97] On the nearby Dingle Peninsula the most common style of early medieval oratory surviving is the same as that of the Iveragh Peninsula. This prevalence of drystone vaulted oratories in

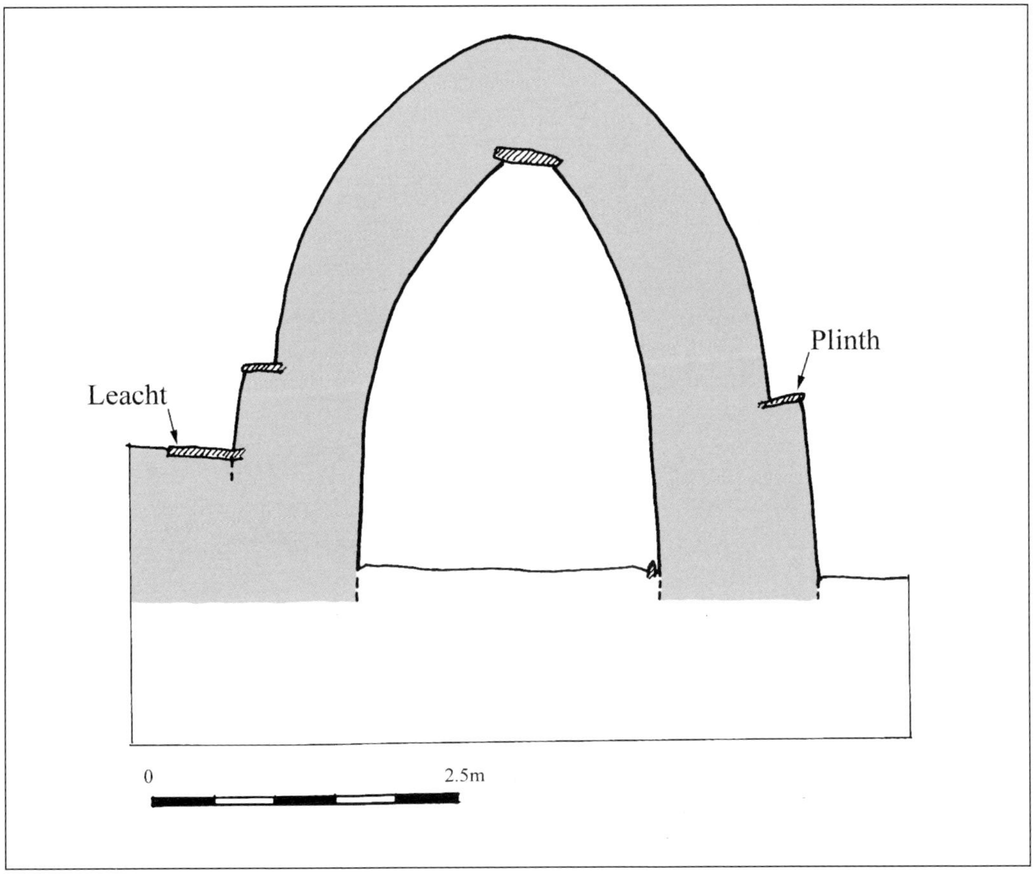

71—Cross-section of the Large Oratory on Skellig Michael, Co. Kerry, showing the straight lower section and the upper rounded dome resting on an offset or plinth. *(G.D. Rourke)*

western Kerry is in sharp contrast to that of other areas, such as west Galway, where none of the 22 stone churches listed for this period is a drystone corbelled building (Cuppage 1986, 257–347; Gosling 1993, 89–90). Similarly, County Donegal has no evidence of drystone oratories (Lacy 1983, 326); in County Cork most surviving churches are late medieval (fifteenth–sixteenth century), with only a small number of earlier, Romanesque churches (Power *et al.* 2000, part 2, 552).[98]

Outside of Kerry, only two island sites, in County Mayo, Duvillaun More and Inishglora, have such structures. Drystone oratories probably existed in a number of the western coastal counties, as it is unlikely that the original distribution was limited to Kerry and Mayo, because of the remaining evidence of the use of other forms of drystone architecture in these areas.[99] Continuous occupation of a number of sites and replacement of original structures by more modern churches or by secular structures have probably obliterated some evidence of their original distribution pattern. Western Ireland, nevertheless, is still mainly rural countryside, and it is, therefore, unlikely that the prevalence of drystone oratories in western Kerry is accidental. Drystone oratories must always have been a favoured regional

72—The offsets on Tory Bhrennell, a large round hut inside the monastic enclosure on Inishmurray, Co. Sligo. *(Courtesy of the Photographic Section of the Department of the Environment, Heritage and Local Government)*

style here, one that perhaps originated in this area and may not have been as widely adopted elsewhere.

The architecture of the drystone oratory

Drystone oratories resemble mortared masonry churches of the early medieval period in many basic respects, differing primarily in their corbelled vaults and in structural elements and masonry styles related to those vaults. The normal style for both is that of a simple, one-room structure, with the walls interrupted only by a door in the western façade and a window in the eastern façade.[100] Corbelled oratories tend to be both smaller and simpler than the Irish mortared masonry churches. Decorative architectural elements such as finials and antae, characteristics derived from wooden churches, were translated into stone and used on mortared masonry churches. Antae do not occur on corbelled oratories, but finials are present on three of them: Church Island, on the Iveragh Peninsula, and Gallarus (839) and Templemanaghan (824: Ballymorereagh) on the Dingle Peninsula. Finials may have been rare on the drystone oratories, but the collapse of most vaults makes it difficult to establish how many were present originally.[101]

There are differing styles of oratory, quickly visible in the outer masonry of buildings such as the Large and Small oratories on Skellig Michael and Gallarus Oratory. On the Large Oratory of Skellig Michael there is no single architectural form on the exterior (Fig. 71). This sturdy and practical structure is divided into two separate parts, really two elements, one on top of the other, differentiated by an

73—Gallarus Oratory on the Dingle Peninsula, Co. Kerry: a drystone oratory using sharply angled corners and walls uninterrupted by offsets. *(Courtesy of the Photographic Section of the Department of the Environment, Heritage and Local Government)*

offset, or plinth, running around the structure at an upper level.

Offsets, a term used interchangeably with plinths, can vary in height, even on a single structure. On the Small Oratory on Skellig Michael the offset is at its highest on the entrance side in order to clear the lintel. The offsets on the other three sides are lower and run below the east window, whereas in the Church Island and Illauntannig (Fig. 77b) oratories the offset runs above the east window. Large domestic cells occasionally used offsets in this manner, such as Cells A, E and F on Skellig Michael and Tory Bhrennell on Inishmurray, Co. Sligo (Figs 31 and 72). The offsets were clearly designed as a base for the vaulted structure above and also provided a working platform for the builders as they constructed the vault.

The offset marks the interface of the two elements of structure. Below, the solid, thick walls act as a stabilising base for the vaulted roof; the lower plan is rectilinear, with relatively vertical walls, often with a gentle batter and showing little or no sign of corbelling. Above the offsets the corbelling begins; the wall thickness is immediately reduced by the width of the offset; and, in the case of the Large Oratory on Skellig Michael, the corbelled roof resembles that of the cells in many respects. Externally, the corners are rounded, and an elongated dome shape is achieved; internally, the rectilinear shape is retained to a higher level, with the corners articulated.[102]

The other intact Skellig Michael oratory, the Small Oratory, while demonstrating the same technique, displays a somewhat different form externally and internally. Externally, above the plinth levels, the shape of the vault is not an elongated dome but retains its rectangularity right to the top, with defined corners rising all the way to a long ridge (Fig. 76a). This is almost mirrored in the interior construction, except that a series of narrow capstones forms the apex of the roof.

At Illaunloughan much of the architectural detail of the structure has been lost, as the walls survive only to 1.29m in height. Its lower masonry, nevertheless, can be clearly identified as similar to that of the Large Oratory on Skellig Michael: the masonry walls of the western façade are battered but show no visible corbelling on the external walls, and the initial internal corbelling starts at a similar level to that of the Large Oratory above the ground. The construction and thickness of the extant lower walling would easily have supported a stone corbelled roof. The amount of collapsed stone uncovered in excavation around the oratory further indicated that this oratory was corbel-vaulted. Illaunloughan, the same size as the Large Oratory on Skellig Michael and Kildreelig oratory, would also have used offsets to carry the upper, roof, structure.

Another very distinct style is represented by Gallarus Oratory on the Dingle Peninsula (Fig. 73). This style of oratory is also present on the Iveragh Peninsula, at Templecashel (926: Ballynabloun), and on the Dingle Peninsula at Templemanaghan (a.k.a. Teampall Geal) (824: Ballymoreragh) and St Brendan's (818: Kilmalkedar). In the Gallarus style the entire structure is an uninterrupted, graceful arc, a unified whole from base to top externally and internally. The corbelling begins almost at the base externally and continues evenly and smoothly to the apex, with the corner angles sharply defined inside and out. There is a very low plinth just above the base of the structure, which provides support to counter the outward thrust of the sloping walls. By constructing the vaulted roof gently almost from ground level, the builders managed to reduce the height of a wide, supporting base wall almost to foundation level.

The corbelling on these structures appears effortless but is a feat of sophisticated craftsmanship, the result of experience and skill in working with stone. They are an eloquent display of achievement in drystone building, one based solely on the simple, severe beauty of the structural form and the placement of its stones. None of these structures has as yet been dated, but it is difficult to believe that their confident mastery of drystone technique places them among the early drystone oratories (see Harbison 1970; 1984).

The evolution of the drystone oratory

From the available evidence, there is clearly a range of types or styles of oratory, and it is possible to put them into a typology with related chronological implications, which demonstrates a very definite building-style evolution. The chronology is not, as yet, definitively established.

The traditional beehive construction was a circular cell. Later a rectilinear or square plan evolved, but the desire to revert to a rounded form was so strong that in the earliest of these structures the interior plan developed rounded corners as

74a—The Large Oratory, Skellig Michael, Co. Kerry, showing a fully rectilinear lower section, whereas the upper section is an elongated dome. *(G.D. Rourke)*

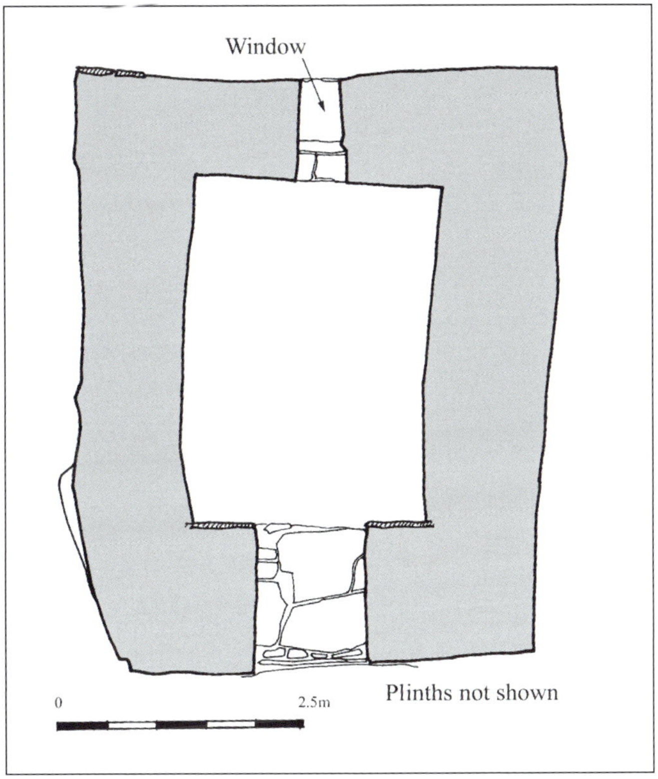

74b—Plan of the Large Oratory, Skellig Michael, Co. Kerry, showing the sharp lower angles in contrast to those of Beginish and Illaunloughan. *(G.D. Rourke)*

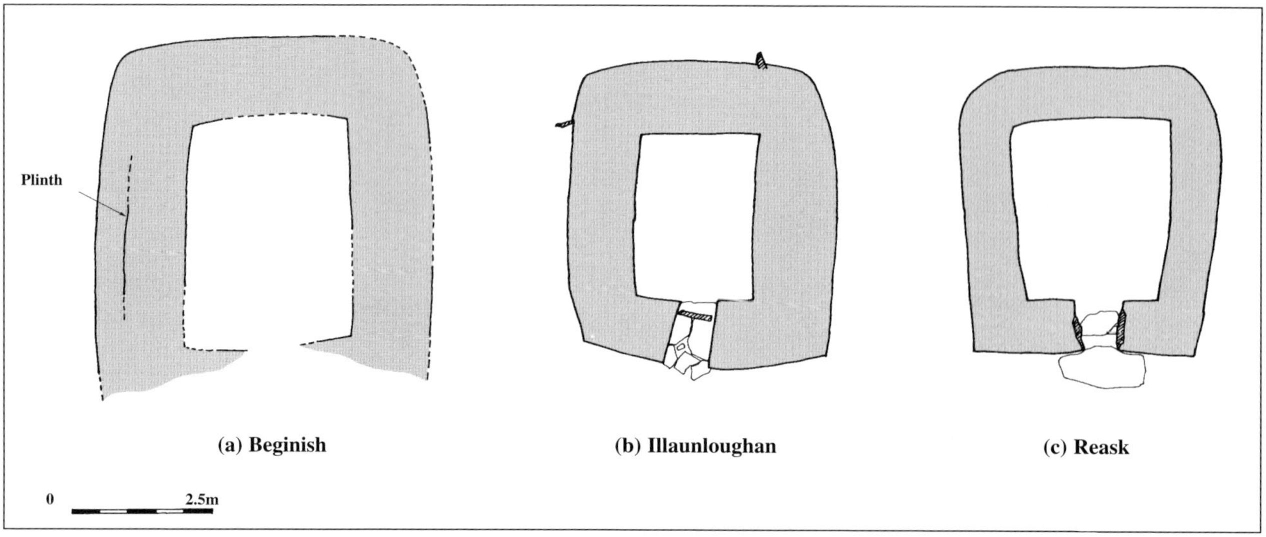

75—Plan of the oratory on Beginish, Valentia Harbour, Co. Kerry, showing externally rounded eastern corners at base level. The surviving remains at Illaunloughan and Reask also show externally rounded eastern walls. The walls of the three oratories were too low to determine the original existence of other architectural features, such as windows. *(G.D. Rourke)*

the walls were raised, the overall shape becoming ovoid as it rose to the apex. This is clearly visible in Cells A and F on Skellig Michael (Fig. 31). Externally the cells remained rounded. In the later cells, Cells B and C on Skellig Michael, the square plan is retained on the interior all the way to the apex, culminating in a capstone; however, the external shape continues to be rounded.

The plan of the Illaunloughan oratory shows clearly that both corners on the east side are rounded right down to ground level. In addition, the front wall is somewhat bowed or rounded. As described previously, this oratory had a vaulted roof, most likely with an offset, on which the vault was constructed, running around the structure. In many ways this oratory is like the Large Oratory on Skellig Michael (948): it would have had its offset or plinth at a similar level, probably at lintel level. If reconstructed, this oratory would look remarkably like the Skellig Michael structure, except that two of the lower exterior corners are rounded, whereas the base of the Large Oratory on Skellig Michael has definite square corners (Figs 74a and 74b).

That the rounded shape was superior and more stable was clearly well understood, and there was an obvious reluctance to abandon it, particularly on the exterior shell, which bound the cell together. The small, early churches required a rectangular form, and this was easily achieved when they were constructed of timber. In their desire to make more permanent structures of stone the builders on the west coast looked to their tradition of drystone construction and adapted it to accommodate the rectangular shape of a church. The small size of the churches was ideally suited to the use of this form of construction. The builders of the Large Oratory on Skellig Michael constructed the lower level in the necessary rectangular form and above this built an elongated dome, quite rounded, a somewhat stretched

76a—The Small Oratory on Skellig Michael, Co. Kerry, showing more sharply angled, articulated corners than the Large Oratory but still retaining the plinth. *(Courtesy of the Photographic Section, Department of the Environment, Heritage and Local Government)*

version of the dome of the rounded cell, the familiar form.

The Illaunloughan oratory seems almost one step back, with its rounded corners on the lower walling. However, this is not unique and is found on the oratories at nearby Beginish (932) and Reask (874), on the Dingle Peninsula (Figs 75a, 75b and 75c). Both of these oratories also appear to have a slightly bowed external west wall. In their desire to create rectangular drystone buildings, the builders were reluctant to abandon fully the construction technology with which they were comfortable and familiar. And so, in creating a rectangular structure, the builders first created oratories that retained some of the

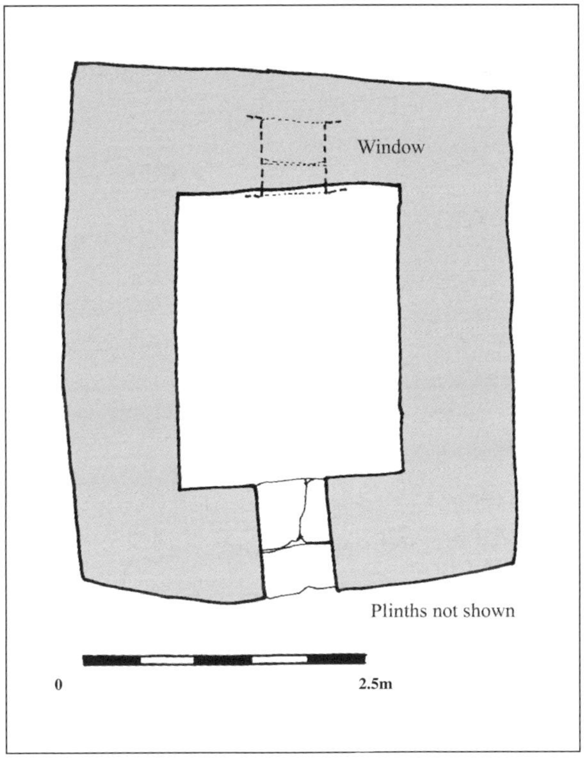

76b—Plan of the Small Oratory on Skellig Michael, Co. Kerry. *(G.D. Rourke)*

77a—Church Island, Valentia Harbour, Co. Kerry: internal south-east corner before conservation works (2003–4). The corbelling on this oratory is similar to that of the Small Oratory on Skellig Michael, Co. Kerry, with corners articulated internally and externally from the base to the apex. *(G.D. Rourke)*

77b—Illauntannig, Co. Kerry. The corbelling on this oratory also resembles that of the Small Oratory on Skellig Michael in form, although the masonry is quite different. *(Courtesy of the Photographic Section, Department of the Environment, Heritage and Local Government)*

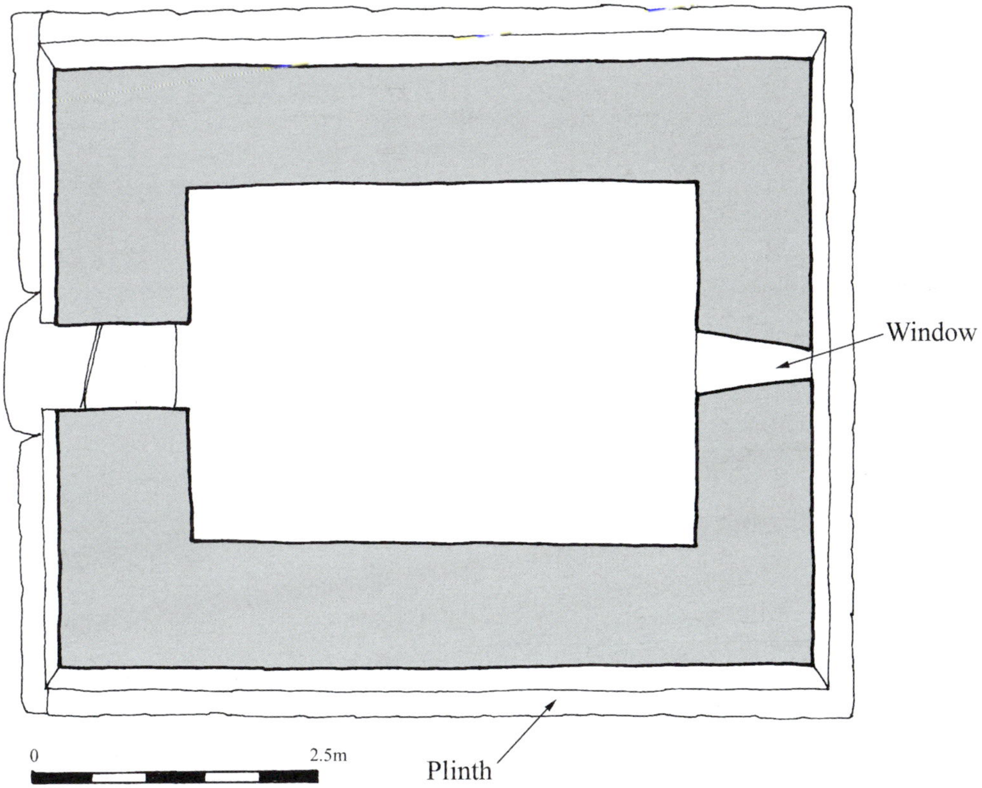

78—Plan of Gallarus Oratory, Dingle Peninsula, Co. Kerry. *(G.D. Rourke)*

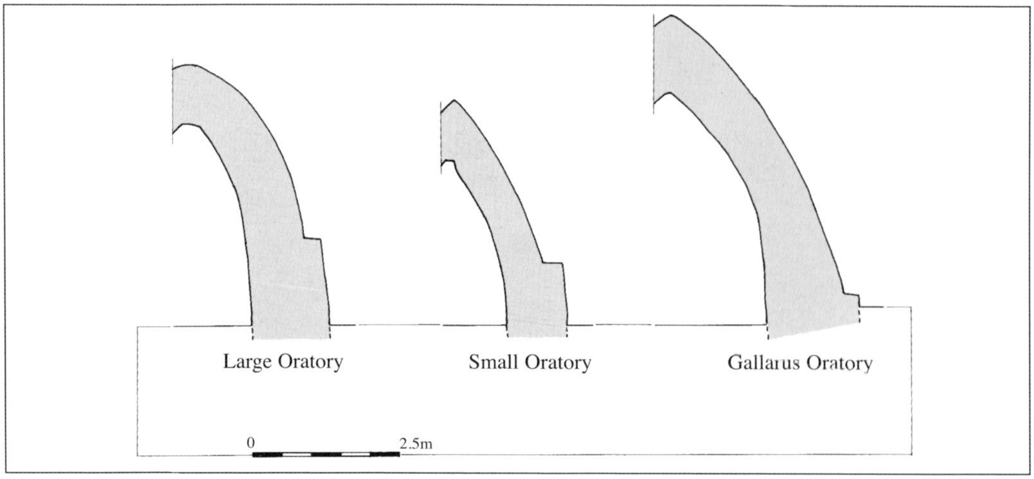

79—Cross-sections showing the progressive lowering of the plinth to form a kind of foundation. *(G.D. Rourke)*
(a) The Large Oratory, Skellig Michael, Co. Kerry.
(b) The Small Oratory, Skellig Michael, Co. Kerry.
(c) Gallarus Oratory, Co. Kerry.

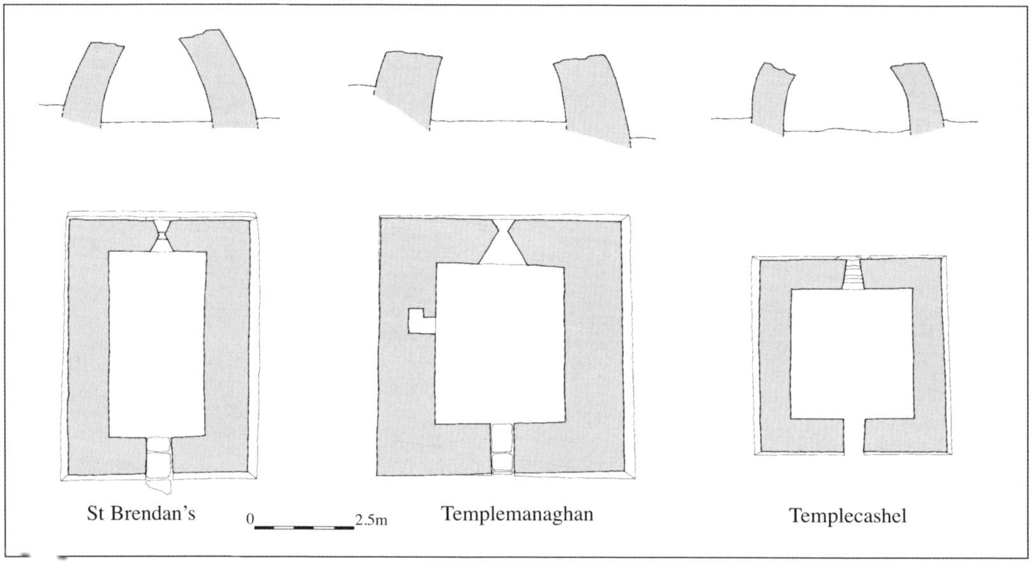

80—Cross-sections and plans of (a) St Brendan's and (b) Templemanaghan on the Dingle Peninsula, and (c) Templecashel on the Iveragh Peninsula.

characteristics of the rounded cell. By the time that the Large Oratory on Skellig Michael was constructed, they felt comfortable enough to construct a fully rectangular lower structure but still felt the need to use a domed roof, albeit elongated (Fig. 74a). On the interior they were more ambitious, retaining the rectilinear shape to a height of *c.* 2.0m above floor level, where the corners become less defined and rounded; this change occurs a little over 1.0m below the capstones. Kildreelig (951) demonstrates similar construction, and the oratories at Killabuonia (955) and Ballywiheen (827) probably fall into this category.

The next development was fuelled by the desire to express the rectangularity of the oratory right up to the apex, and this is evidenced in the Small Oratory on Skellig Michael (Figs 76a and 76b). By this stage the knowledge of drystone

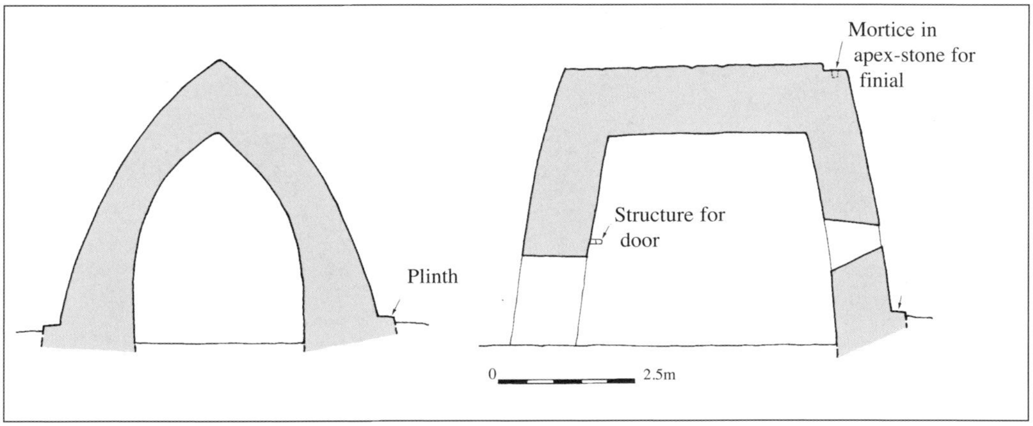

81—Cross-section and long section of Gallarus Oratory, Dingle Peninsula, Co. Kerry, showing the lateral and gable walls. There is a distinct difference in the corbelling profile between the two. *(G.D. Rourke)*

construction and the use of stone had developed sufficiently for the builders to be more daring. If stones were more carefully chosen, a better bond could be achieved, and consequently a thinner wall, or vault, would be able to do the work of the earlier, thicker ones. Understanding of corbelled construction led the builders to realise that it might be possible to begin the construction of the vault at a lower level. In the Small Oratory the offset on the lateral and east walls has been reduced, with the western, entrance side treated differently because of the demands of the doorway. The corbelling begins lower down; the thickness of the vault is somewhat reduced and the corners are articulated all the way to the top, both inside and out. The oratories on Church Island, Valentia Harbour (927: Ballycarbery West), and on Illauntannig (843) also fall into this general category but are not as finely crafted (Figs 77a and 77b); the oratory at Kilkeaveragh (953) may also belong to this category.

In this logical progression, and based on the masons' increased understanding of stone and structure, Gallarus Oratory (839) represents the final phase of the development of the drystone oratory (Figs 73 and 78). Here the stones are carefully chosen and crafted to get maximum value from them, creating the best bond possible using just the one material–stone. The vault starts almost at ground level on the exterior and is constructed in a very gentle arc. By doing this it was possible to reduce the lower walls down almost to ground level, so that they become a kind of foundation (Figs 79a, 79b and 79c). From just above the ground right to the apex, there are no longer any offsets: the wall rises gracefully in an arc that runs to the sharply defined ridge. Other examples exist at Templecashel (929: Ballynabloun) on the Iveragh Peninsula, which is very finely constructed, with long horizontal stones on the interior, and St Brendan's (856: Kilmalkedar) and Templemanaghan or Teampall Geal (824: Ballymorereagh) on the Dingle Peninsula (Figs 80a, 80b and 80c). These three oratories have their interior corbelling beginning almost at ground level in a similar fashion to the exterior.[103]

However, this is not the case with Gallarus, and in some ways Gallarus Oratory

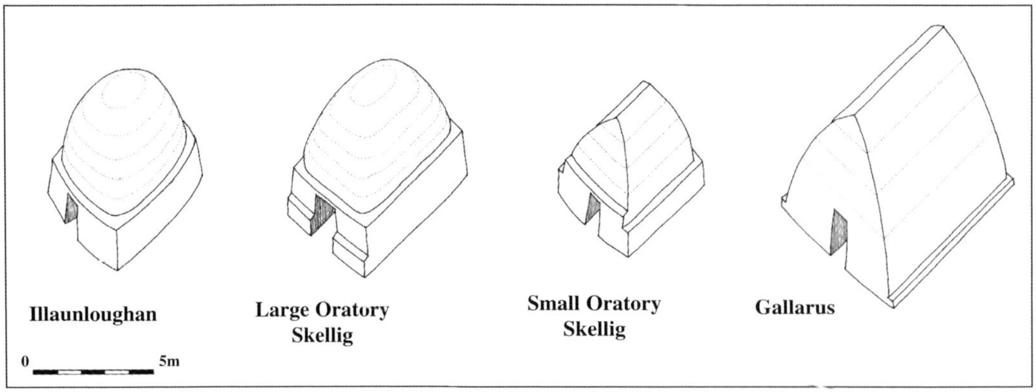

82—The evolutionary progression of drystone corbelled oratories on the western coast of Ireland as they developed from circular drystone structures. *(G.D. Rourke)*

may be the very last structure from this final phase of development. The masons at Gallarus must have been particularly aware of the problem of the lateral walls of these structures, and they made two adjustments that created a more stable structure; in fact, this is probably why it is the only oratory of its type still fully intact. Curiously, the profile of the inner walls varies (Fig. 81). The gable walls start corbelling from the base, but both lateral walls rise almost vertically for a little over 1m before gently corbelling inward. This is no accident. Realising that the lateral walls were vulnerable, the masons treated them differently from the gable walls and in doing so gave these walls a greater ability to resist inward thrust. Secondly, they must have recognised that the tighter the bond between the horizontal layers of stone, the better the resistance to movement. The individual horizontal stones in Gallarus have been carefully selected and worked to maximise the surface area contact between them and so create a stronger bond to combat deformation. These masons were extraordinarily skilful in executing this project, and they created a truly remarkable building.

The oratory on Illaunloughan is limited to a broad eighth-century date. This is not based on direct dating evidence from the oratory itself but on logical inference based on radiocarbon dates, largely from site burials, and the stratigraphical sequence of structures and burials on the site. An eighth-century date for the Illaunloughan oratory is consistent with the assumption that its form is among the earliest of drystone oratories. The Large and Small oratories on Skellig Michael represent the next known phases of stylistic development. The Large Oratory is not far removed from the Illaunloughan type, whereas the later, Small Oratory is a similar construction to the oratory on the South Peak of the island, which has been broadly dated to the ninth century.[104]

The final group of oratories is the most sophisticated structurally, demonstrating a considerable knowledge of both the building material and the structure. There is much more working of the stone, and in the case of Gallarus a very finely crafted doorway and round-headed window. This would be consistent with placing this structure at the end of the period stylistically (Fig. 82).

Of course, there are structural problems with a fully rectangular drystone structure. It does not have the structural equilibrium of the rounded cell. The lateral walls are weaker at the centre and tend to move inward; this has clearly led to eventual collapse in most cases. However, these structures may well have lasted intact for the duration of their use. The builders may have been aware of this shortcoming and used stones that were more worked and flatter in later structures to achieve a better bond and so help to counteract this inward movement. Gallarus Oratory, perhaps the last of these oratories to be constructed and certainly the most sophisticated, is a wonderful testament to the great endeavour to achieve a fully rectangular oratory constructed entirely of drystone.

Drystone oratories were in existence on the Iveragh Peninsula by at least the eighth century, although attempts to construct such oratories may well date from the preceding century. By the ninth century the shape of these structures had evolved quite considerably. Given that there is not a huge leap developmentally to Gallarus Oratory, it is unlikely that this final phase dates from later than the tenth century or early eleventh century. This gives a broad range for drystone oratory construction from the seventh to the eleventh century.

Drystone oratories and mortared masonry churches

A number of scholars have long suspected that drystone oratories are earlier than mortared stone churches because of a relationship to the drystone building tradition (see O'Keefe 1998, 114, for the most recent expression of this view). The chronological relationship of drystone oratories to mortared masonry churches, however, cannot be determined with conviction at present because of the paucity of dates for all stone churches.

At Illaunloughan the stone oratory belongs to the eighth century and was built as part of a remodelling of the monastic structures from organic materials into drystone. At present it is the most closely dated of all of the drystone oratories and is the beginning of the establishment of a chronological framework for them.

Churches with straight, mortared masonry walls and wood, thatch or shingled roofs were beginning to be built in Ireland at around this time. Hamlin (1984) pointed out a reference in the late seventh-century *Collectanea* by Tírechán: 'beside Dom Liacc, that is, the house of stones, of Cíannán' (Bieler 1979, 146, 147). Another reference to this church occurs in the *Annals of Ulster* in 724, referring to the death of Aldchu of Damliag.[105] There is no evidence that mortared masonry churches were being built on the Iveragh Peninsula at this time. The only surviving examples of mortared masonry on the Iveragh Peninsula are much later and are found on island sites: the two phases of St Michael's Church on Skellig Michael and Church Island, Lough Currane.[106] Areas of substantial population that have been continuously inhabited, such as Caherciveen, almost certainly had earlier churches, but the evidence is no longer visible.

The question of the origins of mortared masonry churches on Iveragh cannot be answered currently. The evidence from survey and excavation, however, suggests that drystone oratories were largely used instead of mortared churches in the early centuries of the early medieval period in this region. Drystone oratories may have begun to be built in the late seventh/eighth century on small ecclesiastical sites in the western regions of the Iveragh and Dingle peninsulas of County Kerry, as a parallel, regional expression of the construction of mortared masonry churches on high-status sites elsewhere in Ireland at this time. Drystone construction works well for small structures. Ease of construction suggests that their presence was due to the expansion of a familiar, regional building tradition rather than to ignorance of new mortar technology. Harbison (1970) suggested that mortared masonry architecture came from Anglo-Saxon England or the Continent, and further that drystone architecture is not a predecessor of, or related to, the architectural development of this alternative form of stone architecture in Ireland. Indeed, mortared stone masonry churches may have served only as a stimulus for building in stone.

Ecclesiastical and secular distribution patterns

The Iveragh Peninsula has the most substantial land mass of the four peninsulas that run into the Atlantic from south-west Ireland. Its irregular coastline and high terrain, the most mountainous in Ireland, and the distribution of good soils largely limited to the river valleys and along the coast, have influenced its settlement patterns (O'Sullivan and Sheehan 1996, 1–8). Both ecclesiastical and secular settlements of the western end of the peninsula, therefore, are highly concentrated along the river valleys and coastal areas, with another settlement area found in the level land north of Macgillycuddy's Reeks, on better, mostly brown podzolic soils.

This pattern is similar to that found by Swan (1983, 273) in his aerial survey of ecclesiastical enclosures, where he noted concentrations of enclosures in Limerick, in north Kerry, on the Cork and Kerry peninsulas and on coastal and lake islands: 'The sites seldom occur above the 120m contour, and almost never above 180m; they also tend to follow a riverine distribution'. Stout (1997) agreed with Swan and added that there is a highland/lowland dichotomy between secular ringforts and ecclesiastical sites in the midlands, where the ringforts tend to be found at higher altitudes than ecclesiastical sites. Unlike the ecclesiastical sites, which are situated on or near communication arteries, the secular ringfort is distanced from them, perhaps for defensive purposes. Stout (1997, 100–9; 1998, 36) also noted the good grazing for the cattle-based economy at the ringfort sites.[107]

Iveragh does not entirely conform to the upland/lowland distribution pattern for the midlands, largely because of its unusual topography. Indeed, in Iveragh, although the majority of both ecclesiastical and vernacular sites are found in the low-lying areas, a greater proportion (65 per cent) of secular than ecclesiastical sites (58 per cent) is found below 100m. A greater proportion of ecclesiastical sites (11.5 per cent), moreover, than secular sites (7 per cent) is found at altitudes of over 150m.

In the twenty sites on the Iveragh Peninsula containing drystone oratories, the distribution is even more markedly different. Contrary to the general distribution of ecclesiastical sites, more than half of the sites with drystone oratories (55 per cent) are found above 100m where the land is more inhospitable. Three of these are found on only one site, Skellig Michael.

Small church sites or small monasteries

There is a distinct coastal distribution of the extant drystone oratories on the west coast, one particularly obvious on the Iveragh Peninsula, where eight (40 per cent) of the sites containing drystone corbelled oratories are on islands and most of the others are in sight of the sea. Among the islands, only the large island of Valentia, with its good soil, and, to a lesser degree, Beginish offer possibilities for secular settlement of any size.[108] It is clear that sites containing drystone oratories have a different settlement distribution pattern, one that may relate to the nature and function of the sites.

Opinions on the nature of the small ecclesiastical enclosures in this region have varied. Henry (1957, 154–7) treated all of these as small monastic sites, writing of 'a countryside dotted with tiny hermitages'. Hurley (1982), however, pointed out that few ecclesiastical sites in south-west Ireland are found in remote or isolated areas, but rather in valleys or along the coast in areas of good land, where settlement was quite dense. His conclusion, that most of them were probably not eremitic sites but should be regarded simply as small church sites serving the local community, is generally accepted today. On Iveragh a number of the mainland sites are found on better agricultural land in areas coinciding with the secular ringforts and hence may be either small church sites or small monasteries (O'Sullivan and Sheehan 1996, 246).

The large proportion of drystone oratories in Iveragh on islands and at high altitude, both isolated areas of no economic advantage, strongly suggests that a number of these sites were in fact monastic and that the monastic movement was robust in the area. T. Ó Carragáin (2003, 130, fn. 4) provides another reason to doubt that many of these sites were pastoral: in some areas of western Iveragh, church sites are as numerous as secular sites. He also points out that their small size makes them unlikely to have been adequate for congregations. The large number of small sites with reliquary shrines, he proposes, may indicate a number of flourishing small independent churches in the northern part of the Iveragh Peninsula (2003, 142–6) in the mid-eighth to ninth century. (For another possible explanation of their small size see Hunwicke 2002.)

O'Sullivan and Sheehan (1996, 248) pointed out that excavation evidence from Church Island in Valentia Harbour (O'Kelly 1958), Caherlehillan (Sheehan 1996, 248), Reask on the Dingle Peninsula (Fanning 1981) and Illaunloughan indicates that these sites were in existence by the eighth century. Other scholars have also believed that these were early sites (see Fanning 1981; Hamlin 1982, 291–3). The excavated sites provide little evidence of a long duration of ecclesiastical activity, such as extensive burial, reuse of burial space or accumulation of additional churches, such as on Inishglora, Co. Mayo, and on Skellig Michael, Co. Kerry. If these sites were in existence in the eighth or ninth century, it is unlikely that most of them lasted more than a century or two, and only a few may have been active by the eleventh or twelfth century.

The drystone oratories are small; the smallest examples are the auxiliary oratories on Skellig Michael of the South Peak Oratory (2.1m by 2.55m) and the Small Oratory (2.45m by 1.85). Illaunloughan (3.4m by 2.1m) belongs to a mid-range size, similar to the Large Oratory on Skellig Michael (3.65m by 2.45m), Kildreelig (3.25m by 2.25m), Ballywiheen (3.8m by 2.6m) and Reask (3.5m by 2.7m).

All of the drystone oratories on the Iveragh Peninsula are suitable in scale to the small, simple ecclesiastical settlements on which they are found, and all, except those of Skellig Michael, are the sole oratory on the site. Indeed, O'Sullivan and Sheehan (*op. cit.*) note that none of the extant ecclesiastical sites on Iveragh developed into a major centre, with the average ecclesiastical enclosure being 33m in diameter. The modesty of these sites possibly reflects a low population density and may also reflect a large number of small hermitages or monasteries in the area.

8

The monastic community of Illaunloughan

The monastery on Illaunloughan did not begin as a hermitage site occupied by one or two men who sought solitude on a small island, as the evidence suggests happened on Church Island, Valentia Harbour. Excavation revealed, instead, that a small monastery, consisting perhaps of five to six men, was established here, possibly in the second half of the seventh century. The founding community occupied two or three huts and built an oratory with sod walls.

Earlier interpretations of Illaunloughan as a monastic site were confirmed by the excavation of a cemetery with no female burials, eliminating the ambiguity found at Church Island. The spatial arrangement of the cemetery as part of the gable shrine also expressed the intent of the community to stay together near their saints after death as they had in life and, by stressing their unity, underlined their separation from the secular community. The absence of contemporary secular burials of mixed gender is not, therefore, surprising. It is difficult to compare the Illaunloughan burial evidence to other regional ecclesiastical excavations. The pathology of the Church Island burials was never done, and the site was excavated before radiocarbon dating was common. At Reask no skeletal material remained in the acidic soils. The clear, dated record of a male burial population in the late seventh to late eighth century on Illaunloughan will provide a useful comparative base for future excavations.

A number of ecclesiastical settlements in Ireland, particularly the larger ones, were clearly multifunctional and contained bishops and priests as well as monks, a practical arrangement in a rural society.[109] Settlement on Illaunloughan, a small island of no discernible economic or political advantage, points to a narrower purpose for a small population. These were men who sought to remove themselves from everyday life and go into 'exile for the love of God', to spend their lives primarily in prayer and contemplation rather than pastoral care of the laity. Such a community remained the classic, treasured goal of monastic, indeed of Christian, life and as such merited support by ecclesiastics and laity alike. The size and complexity of the reliquary shrine indicate that the community, and probably the

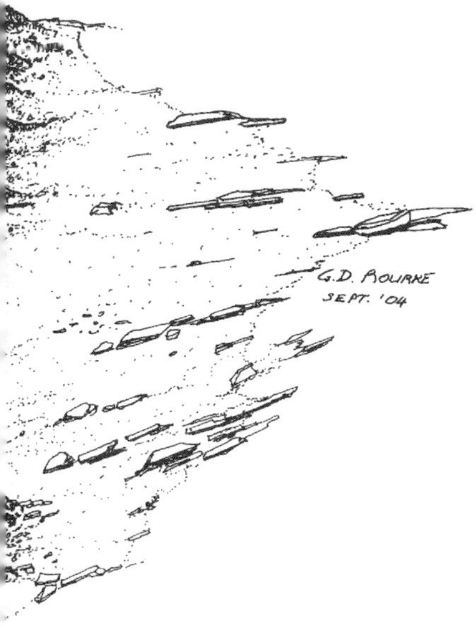

83—Conjectural reconstruction of the monastery of Illaunloughan, showing the corbelled Hut D on the west of the island, the large gable shrine on the north-west and the drystone oratory on the west. *(G.D. Rourke)*

local population, respected and venerated the lives led on the island and that the island enjoyed local and probably even regional fame for a time.

The unusually tight and consistent range of high-precision radiocarbon dates from Illaunloughan, primarily from human skeletal material, has provided most of the firm chronological framework for the lives of the monks, the general time range of the structures associated with them and the duration of the monastery. The late seventh to the late eighth century was a peak time for the monastery.[110]

During this time the community replaced its first sod structures with new stone structures, a corbelled drystone oratory, a single drystone corbelled domestic hut, a sizeable reliquary and a new monastic graveyard. When the single drystone hut replaced the two conjoined sod huts, the monastery was probably reduced in size. Reduction in size of the community is also consistent with the fact that more burials connected with the primary oratory were found than in Period 2, where burials were placed largely in the eastern mound of the reliquary shrine. By the time that the superimposed burial (Sk. 120) was placed in front of the oratory, it is possible that only one or two men remained on the island. Radiocarbon determinations indicate that only two burials, both of which overlay earlier burials, possibly date from as late as the ninth century. These two graves are the last substantial evidence of occupation of the monastery as a separate settlement. The monastery, therefore, may have lasted only for 150–200 years, from the mid-/late seventh century to the mid-ninth century. Its appearance today probably belongs to the eighth century (Fig. 83).

Sacred space and domestic space

Division of activities into separate functional spaces was apparent and remained the same for the duration of the monastery. Cooking, eating, deposition of waste material, sleeping and industrial activities all took place on the western end of the island, near the domestic huts. All of the oratories were on the eastern end of the island, placed so closely together that their boundaries overlapped. Only burials, a *leacht* and a shrine accompanied them. Orientation of churches was normal during the early medieval period, and the location of a church or oratory in the eastern section of an ecclesiastical site is standard; the oratory on Church Island, Valentia Harbour, in the western section of the island, is an exception. Although there was no formal separation of the oratory space—such as an enclosure wall around the oratory as at Reask or Killabuonia, Co. Kerry, High Island, Co. Galway, and Caher Island, Co. Mayo—the absence of later activity in the space east of the drystone oratory and the efforts to preserve and delimit this space with uprights clearly demonstrate a distinct separation of secular and sacred space.

The most defined space on the island is that occupied by the reliquary shrine and its mound on the northern side of the island; both the mound and its shrine are oriented like the oratory (Fig. 43). The shrine is the principal structure on the island and, unlike Hut D and the oratory, its space is unmistakably divided into external and internal areas by stone uprights and walling. Access to the shrine is well marked by a paved path, in the western quadrant of the shrine mound, that leads up to the central paved area, which contains the gable shrine, itself enclosed by stone walling. The entrance steps pass another, smaller shrine set in the mound to the north of the path.

Paving around the main gable shrine indicates that passage around the shrine was expected, but no access to other sections of the shrine mound was provided. The formality of the structure emphasises its importance as the sacred focus of the island. Its visibility from the sea channel and the clear marking of traffic circulation to and around the shrine suggests, in addition, that this was a public space. The importance of the shrine is further indicated by the use of the eastern quadrant as the monastic graveyard.

Corporeal relics and burial near the saint

A number of Irish scholars, drawing on Irish hagiographies and ecclesiastical documents, believe that the custom known as *translatio*, removal of the bones of a saint from the original grave to a shrine, as well as their dispersal to a number of different shrines and locations, even to distant continents, began in Ireland in the late seventh or the early eighth century.[111] The greater complexity of the gable shrine than the smaller shrine south of the oratory demonstrates the increasing attention to relics on Illaunloughan, as well as interest in the translation of corporeal relics at this time.

The graves in the eastern quadrant of the shrine mound also provide explicit evidence of Irish adoption of Christian customs relating to the cult of relics. The dominant motivation underlying the evolving focus on relics was the passionate belief in the physical and spiritual presence and power of the saint. The clergy and the secular population both assumed that close contact with the saint, in whatever form, might aid in physical and spiritual redemption; even after death, the holy man could intercede in the salvation of a person's soul. Emphasis on burial near the tomb of the saint began as an extension of this conviction, although the origins of the custom are unknown. The practice had certainly begun by the fifth century, when Paulinus wrote to St Augustine, asking about its effectiveness. St Augustine, the great authority on ritual for the dead, denied its relevance to salvation, but the practice continued.[112]

The burial of a saint in a churchyard would attract shrines and other burials close by, although this was a custom more typical of the earlier stages of a saint's cult. If the cult expanded, the original burial shrine might be replaced by a later small chapel or by building a church in the saint's honour, with the bones moved into a new shrine inside the church (C. Thomas 1971; Herrmann-Mascard 1975; Van Dam 1993). Excavation at ecclesiastical sites in Britain has revealed two such sites. One is at Whithorn, Galloway, where a succession of shrines apparently developed around focal points, perhaps a cross, pillar or small shrine, and formed a centre for surrounding burials (Hill 1997, 34, chap. 3, figs 3.16 and 3.17). The other site is at the Old Minster of Winchester, where only the grave of St Swithin (d. 862), at the western door of the church, was specially treated with its own structure and became the focus of the most important graves of the period; other graves at Old Minster were grouped all around the church. Archaeological evidence for this practice remains rare, however, on Anglo-Saxon sites (Biddle 1986).

Archaeological and historical evidence from the Continent and England shows that burial near the saints continued when saints were moved into the church, in spite of sporadic strong objections from church councils and synods to burial of anyone other than saints within the church, as first prestigious clergy and then secular élites followed the saints into the churches.[113] In Ireland, evidence of burial near the saints is not clear until the later medieval period, when burial began inside churches. At Reask, Co. Kerry, phosphate levels indicated that the shrine had contained bones, and the excavator believed that a few burials may have centred on the shrine. Unfortunately neither shrine nor burials could be dated (Fanning 1981, 84–5).

Irish texts of the second half of the seventh century mention corporeal relics: Tirechán relates the request of the lonely St Bruscus to move his grave from his deserted church, and Cogitosus describes the bodies of St Brigid and Bishop Conláed to the right and left of the altar in the church at Kildare.[114] Illaunloughan may present the first unequivocal material evidence that the cult of corporeal relics and burial near the saints had become widespread in Ireland by the eighth century. This is the earliest and most substantial evidence known, but it is unlikely that the small monastery of Illaunloughan was a solitary case.

The Christian cult of the saints and the desire to be close to them changed burial patterns throughout Europe, initiating the gradual movement of the cemetery from outside the town to churches in the centre of the town, and then from outside the church to within it. And so, too, in Ireland burial patterns were changing to focus on Christian saints.

Environmental evidence

The location of Illaunloughan on a small sea-channel island of little potential use for later generations and its good soil conditions have resulted in excellent preservation of material, particularly of environmental remains. This has facilitated analysis and dating that have yielded considerable information about the economic and social strategies of the residents.

The Illaunloughan diet was based on a mixed arable/dairying economy that also made excellent use of its marine location.[115] The evidence shows that the community used domesticated resources, such as cereals, cattle, sheep and pig, and wild resources, such as shellfish, seal, fish and birds, in order to maximise readily available food supplies in their seasonal variations (see Murray and McCormick, Chapter 4). Similar use of a wide range of dietary resources is evident from Church Island (O'Kelly 1958), Beginish (O'Kelly 1956), Co. Kerry, Inishkea North, Co. Mayo, and Iona (McCormick in Barber 1981; 1993; 1997) and Whithorn, Scotland (McCormick 1997, 605–13).

Murray and McCormick have clearly demonstrated that the diet of the inhabitants of Illaunloughan was not the ascetic one mentioned by the monastic documents of the time (see Chapter 4); excavation evidence to date has shown that a more ordinary diet may have been common at ecclesiastical sites.[116] An austere diet would have been particularly hard to maintain on a small Atlantic island, where a physically active life would require more calories, particularly more fat and protein, than an ascetic diet would provide. The midden showed clearly that processed cereal grains, largely oats with some barley, and meat were brought in for/by the monks. Trace evidence of berries and other plant foods also exists, and food that left no material traces, such as milk, cheese and butter, as well as other vegetables and fruits, was also likely brought in for the community.

It is quite clear from the environmental evidence that the island was not self-sufficient, although Murray and McCormick point out that the Illaunloughan community was probably largely responsible for the wild component of their diet—fish, seabird and some seal—a substantial part. There may have also been a kitchen garden for growing vegetables, but such a garden was most probably associated only with Period 1, during the time of occupation of Huts A and B. The depth and extent of the midden associated with Hut D and the layers of stepping stones thrown over it to facilitate passage make a garden in this area impractical in Period 2.

Murray and McCormick make good arguments for the possibility that

Illaunloughan was in an environmentally marginal area, citing the unusual number of young cattle (7–18 months old), the small size of the sheep, the scarcity of pig bones and the dominance of oats in the cereal grains. They add that these may be evidence of a wet, cold environment with poor, acidic soils that strained resources, such as is found in western Scotland and on the Aran Islands, Co. Galway.[117] Illaunloughan was, moreover, geographically remote from the main political and social centres of seventh–eighth-century Ireland, another characteristic of marginal environments.

Murray and McCormick, however, provide an alternative, or additional, explanation for the young animals found at Illaunloughan, in the custom of offering first fruits to the church, donations in consideration of services. This suggestion was first made by McCormick to explain the similar quantity of young animals found at Iona (McCormick 1993, 99), based on information found in Lynch 1848–51, vol. 2, 509. This may be a particularly important element of the Illaunloughan economy because an island of 0.1ha could not produce the basic supplies, such as wool, leather, wood and iron utensils, Gospel books, liturgical equipment and fuel, needed to run an early medieval religious community. The environmental evidence demonstrates substantial ties to mainland communities but does not explain the nature of the mainland support. Most logically, Illaunloughan would have been a subsidiary unit of a mainland ecclesiastical establishment that provided a steady supply of sustenance and materials. The mainland community may have received regular donations from the secular population, some of which were used to support the island monks. Secular people may also have contributed directly to the maintenance of Illaunloughan on a more spontaneous and irregular basis. Analysis of the environmental remains of Illaunloughan needs to take account of its special situation as a recipient community.

There is insufficient evidence to allow a conclusive position on these propositions; however, both merit serious consideration in comparing future environmental evidence from early medieval excavations with that of Illaunloughan. The determination of a marginal environment for the seventh–ninth-century landscape is complicated and subject to many variables, many of which involve human activity and adaptability (Mills and Coles 1998). A few of the questions that relate to this issue are raised below.

The windy marine climate of Kerry is somewhat balanced by the mildness of the climate, where grass grows most of the year, good conditions for a mixed dairying economy. Kelly (1998, 42–3) raises the additional possibility in maritime regions of using seaweed as a substitute for grass in case of fodder shortage. The great Munster butter roads of the late eighteenth century led into Iveragh as far as Caherciveen, a possible indication of surplus at that time.[118] The dairy production of Iveragh relative to the needs of its population in the early medieval period is unknown.

In the early medieval period the soil and climatic conditions suitable for raising cereal crops would have played an important part in the economy of the region. The *Atlas of Ireland* (1979, 25) shows that brown podzols are the basic soil on Valentia Island and on a small portion of the mainland around Portmagee today. The *Atlas* (*ibid.*, 28) classified this land as wide-use land with no serious limitations, and Gardiner and Radford (1980) more narrowly categorise these soils as having reasonable to good qualities for both pastoral and arable use.[119] Brown podzols may have been more extensive 1200–1300 years ago and since been degraded by rising population and over-use of soils.[120]

A hint that the local environment has been modified by human activity is found in the evidence of the fuel used on Illaunloughan (see O'Carroll, Appendix 4). O'Carroll identified the charcoal as hazel, alder, oak, yew and blackthorn and speculated that the evidence suggested the exploitation of a mixed light forest of oak and ash, with hazel, alder and blackthorn growing as an understorey or in glades. This is in striking contrast to the situation today, where peat would be used as fuel.

The main supplies for Illaunloughan probably came from an area close to the island, either on the mainland, near Portmagee, or Valentia Island, in the areas where brown podzols exist today.[121]

The large proportion of oats, over 50 per cent of the identifiable cereal grains found in all periods, found on the island is unusual but not completely out of line with evidence from other Munster sites, especially considering that no cereals were used as animal feed on Illaunloughan. Consumption of oats was substantial at Loher, a cashel close to Illaunloughan on the Iveragh Peninsula, and at the County Cork sites of Lisnagun, Lisleagh I and Lisleagh II (Monk 1991, 315–24; Monk *et al.* 1998). Oats and barley may have been the dominant cereals in this region, crops well suited to the climate and soil conditions. Oats prefer cool, moist climates, require more water than other small grains and do well in soils with a high water-holding capacity. They are also one of the few species that can withstand high coastal winds and can be grown on poorer soils than wheat or barley.[122] Oats are not very sensitive to acidic soils, but oat production is affected by lack of the nutrient nitrogen, a problem that fertilising with seaweed could mitigate.[123]

Oatmeal is easily made into gruel, porridge or soup, using milk, butter, vegetables, honey, scraps of meat and bone (see Sexton 1998); and oats are superior to wheat, barley and rye in their total nutritional values, as they are generally almost as high, or higher, in protein as the other grains and always higher in oil (Findlay 1956, 196–7). The practical and nutritious advantages of oats are clear, but equally clear was a cultural preference for wheat or barley.

Did the high proportions of oats and young or small animals indicate a marginal environment at this time, or was the Illaunloughan diet simply a more modest but healthier version of the ordinary secular diet suitable to a monastery? It is possible that both an increasingly marginal local environment and the position of

Illaunloughan as a beneficiary site are reflected in the environmental evidence. The extensive evidence of the Illaunloughan economy will have to be compared with future quantitative studies of both secular and ecclesiastical local sites in order to understand it fully.

The island after the monks

The religious community appears, because of the burial evidence, to have left the island sometime in the ninth century, for reasons that are not apparent in the material remains. It is probable, however, that the shrine continued to be maintained by people from the mainland, perhaps by the community who had sponsored Illaunloughan. It is also possible that the monastery was still occupied on an occasional basis, perhaps seasonally or as a solitary retreat. An eleventh-century coin found under the paving around the shrine and an eleventh-century charcoal date obtained from the midden suggest that the site was being used or maintained before clear secular occupation of the island in the fourteenth/fifteenth century.

Centuries after the monastery ceased to be actively occupied, Illaunloughan continued in use as a special secular graveyard, particularly in the nineteenth and twentieth centuries. Local people came to the island and used it as a graveyard; the old monastic structures, such as the oratory and dwelling cell and the open spaces between and around them, were used for more than 110 graves. These medieval and later burials all avoided using the space (7.5m by 9m) occupied by the reliquary shrine and its mound. Only one intrusive burial, an infant, was found in the upper levels of the north-west quadrant of the central shrine. The absence of burials in the reliquary mound shows continuing respect and reverence for the shrine by the local population.

Illaunloughan was a small monastery off the Atlantic coast of Ireland (Fig. 84). Its limited size and monastic nature will always differentiate it from the average secular site, but the information derived from its material is, nevertheless, a good reflection of its time and place. The new evidence presented here establishes an eighth-century benchmark for the construction of drystone oratories and *leachta*, as well as that of a large gable shrine. The reliquary shrine and its mound, more complex than expected, encompassed not only corporeal relics but also a monastic graveyard that revealed the importance for the community of burial near the saints. The use of white quartz and scallop shells for symbolic spiritual purposes can also be dated to the construction of the gable shrine. In a slightly more extensive framework, from the mid-seventh to the ninth century, belongs the evidence of sod construction of oratories, of the casting and designing of fine metalwork on small sites, and of the fosterage of young children on monastic islands. Widespread dissemination and penetration of Christian ideology and customs from other parts of the world and their adaptation to a regional monastic format are also evident here. The quantitative analyses of diet and economy, integrated with cultural customs and the chronological evidence, provide substantial comparative material for the Irish early medieval period.

The excavation of Illaunloughan shows the importance of complete excavation of sites with good preservation of material and dating evidence, particularly for the small island sites. Too insignificant to be fought over or disturbed by later generations, its spiritual nature respected by the local population, Illaunloughan retained clear material records of its era.

PART 2:
ARCHAEOLOGICAL EXCAVATION

Claire Walsh

9

Stratigraphic report

Introduction

This report details the four seasons of excavation carried out on Illaunloughan, Portmagee, Co. Kerry, from 1992 to 1995.

The first season lasted for eight weeks in the summer of 1992. The second, in the summer of 1993, was of ten weeks' duration. A third season, lasting eight weeks, was undertaken in the summer of 1994. The final programme of work, which completed the excavation, lasted for five weeks, from July to August 1995.

Location

The island is located in a relatively sheltered position in the Portmagee channel, just 125m from the shore at high tide (Fig. 1). At low tide the water channel is reduced to less than 25m in width and is less than 0.8m deep. The island measures approximately 0.1ha at high tide (0.305 acres) and is subject to erosion, particularly along its southern and eastern flanks. The underlying rock is Old Red Sandstone, which on nearby Valentia varies in refinement from conglomerate to fine-quality slate (Mitchell 1989, 1). The heavily weathered sandstone foreshore of Illaunloughan is of medium coarseness, with the weathering cracks all running north-west/south-east (Fig. 6).

Summary of excavation seasons

1992

Three areas were selected for excavation in 1992. Area A, on the northern side of the drystone hut, was designed to establish the presence and structure of an enclosure at the western end of the island, and to reveal the relationship of the hut to the enclosure. A trench encompassing one half of the interior of the drystone hut (hut

D) also encompassed the midden, which was located immediately to its east, and established the relationship of the hut with a later drystone wall at the south side. Part of an earlier structure (hut C) was uncovered beneath the midden. Area B, initially designed to test the surviving drystone structure at the east end of the island, was soon doubled in size as excavation revealed that the remains of this building, an oratory, were substantial.

1993

The west side of hut D was excavated, as was the remaining part of the earlier hut C. Trenches through the midden were extended to uncover the outer part of hut D at the north and east sides. The trench that encompassed the enclosure at the west side of hut D was completed.

Work continued on the oratory trench, concentrating mainly on exposing and removing the many skeletons interred to the west of the oratory. Most of the effort in the 1993 season was focused on a trench measuring *c.* 9.5m by 11.5m, which was centred on the gable shrine and which extended from the north side of the oratory trench. The central part of the shrine was completely excavated.

1994

The midden and underlying layers to the east of hut D were excavated in full, and upwards of 120 skeletons were removed. An exploratory trench was opened over the enclosure wall at the north-west of the island and was fully excavated.

The shrine mound was excavated in full and reinstated. The *leacht* on the north side of the oratory was excavated and reinstated. The area to the east of the oratory was fully excavated.

1995

Area A was extended to the east, to encompass the well and graveyard and to connect with the western extent of area B. The area to the north of the drystone hut was expanded, uncovering the remains of two hut structures and the enclosing element of the settlement. The interior of the oratory was re-excavated, to re-examine the presence of the earlier sod-walled structure that underlay the stone structure.

The total area excavated is indicated on Fig. 6.

Layout of the report

Each excavation area is described in full, and the features found therein are phased. The features are described in summary. Interpretation and discussion of the archaeological remains have been incorporated into the main body of the report. The original feature numbers have been maintained throughout all sections of the report.

All the artefacts recovered have been conserved and carry the excavation

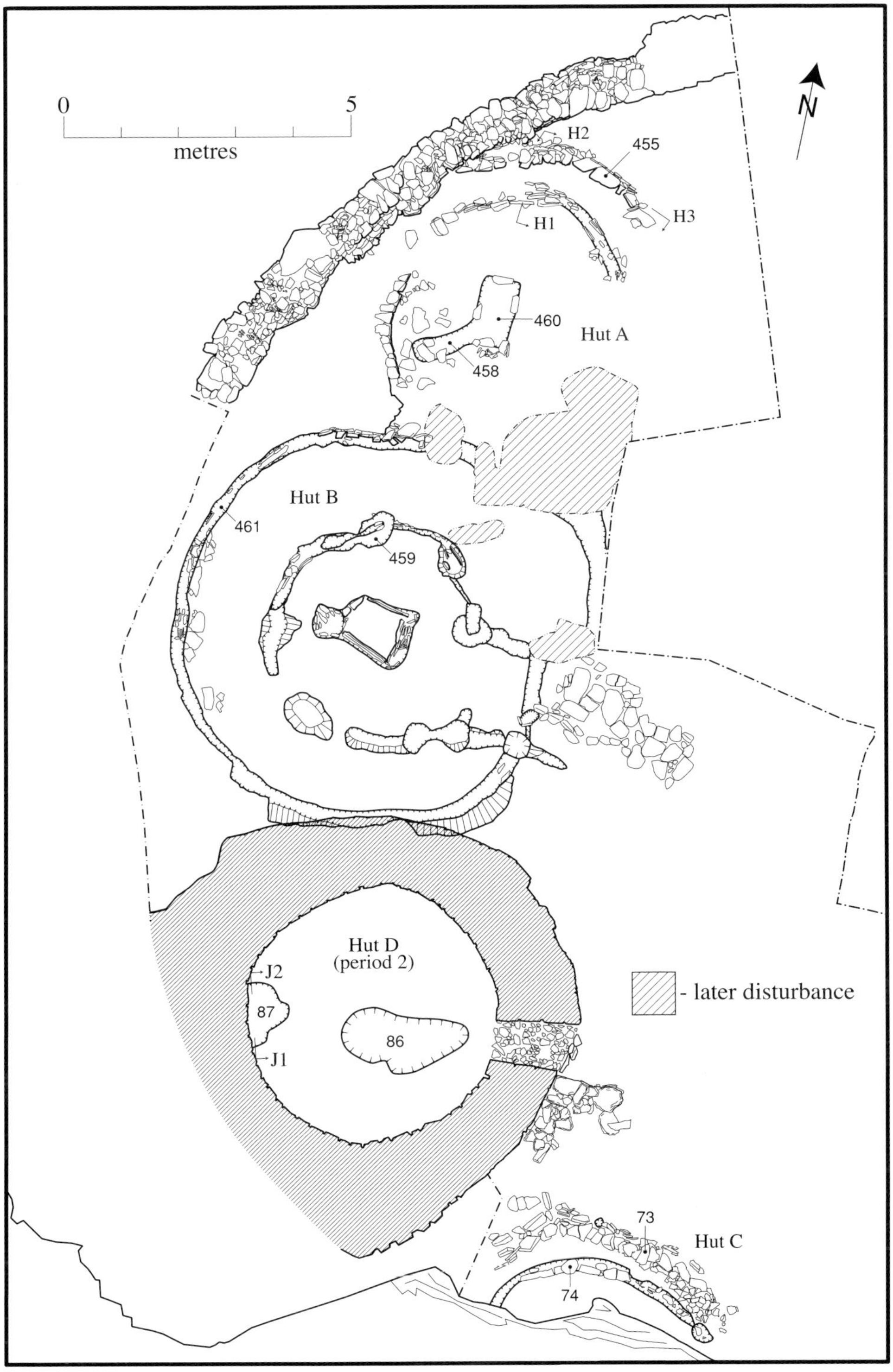

84—Period 1 huts and pits. (*C. McHale*)

number 92E87, the number of the layer where found, and an individual find number. They are stored in the National Museum of Ireland.

Area A: the habitation area, midden and enclosure (Fig. 84)

By the close of excavation in 1993, an area measuring over 11.2m north/south by 10.2m east/west had been excavated around hut D. This was extended eastwards for a further 2.2m at the eroded south face of the island. This trench was extended in 1994 by almost 7m eastwards, and spanned between 10m and 13m north-south to encompass the entire area of the midden. It was further extended eastwards in 1995, incorporating the drystone well and connecting with the westward limit of area B.

The earliest levels in this area represent the remains of three timber and earthen structures, two (huts A and B) to the north of hut D, the other (hut C) on the south shore of the island.

Huts A/F432 and B/F440

These two circular huts were uncovered and excavated in 1995. They appear to have been constructed simultaneously and to have been conjoined. Both huts pre-date the construction of hut D on their south side. A sample from the hearth of hut B yielded a date range of 640–751 at 2 sigma (UB-4357), while bone from the foundation material of the north wall of hut D returned a date between 775 and 961 at 2 sigma (UB-3860).

Hut A (F432)

Hut A was built up against the enclosure wall. It had an internal diameter of 3.8m. No evidence for internal roof supports was recovered. The construction of hut A is interesting: the well-preserved wall structure of the north-west side is similar to that of the sod-walled structure found beneath the drystone oratory (see below). Thin slabs remaining *in situ* in the narrow trenches acted as kerbs for a core of grey silt, a construction which can readily be interpreted as an earth-walled hut.

The hut utilised the enclosure wall as the outer component of walling. On the inside, the earth core was revetted with horizontally laid drystone walling (F455, Fig. 85), which stood to a height of 0.26m above subsoil and continued for a distance of 1.78m, curving gently. It used small stones, which averaged 0.2m in length and 0.08–0.09m in height, with a depth of up to 0.4m. The masonry was not close-fitting and incorporated occasional rounded stones. It is possible that the outer wall kerb was also of drystone masonry, laid in horizontal courses, as there was no evidence for a slot for orthostats in this area.

The orthostats occupied a very definite construction trench through subsoil, which was lined with thin stones and filled with dark silt. The overall width of the wall was 0.6m between the stones, and this was infilled with a distinctive compacted grey soil, which probably represents decayed sods. The sockets for the

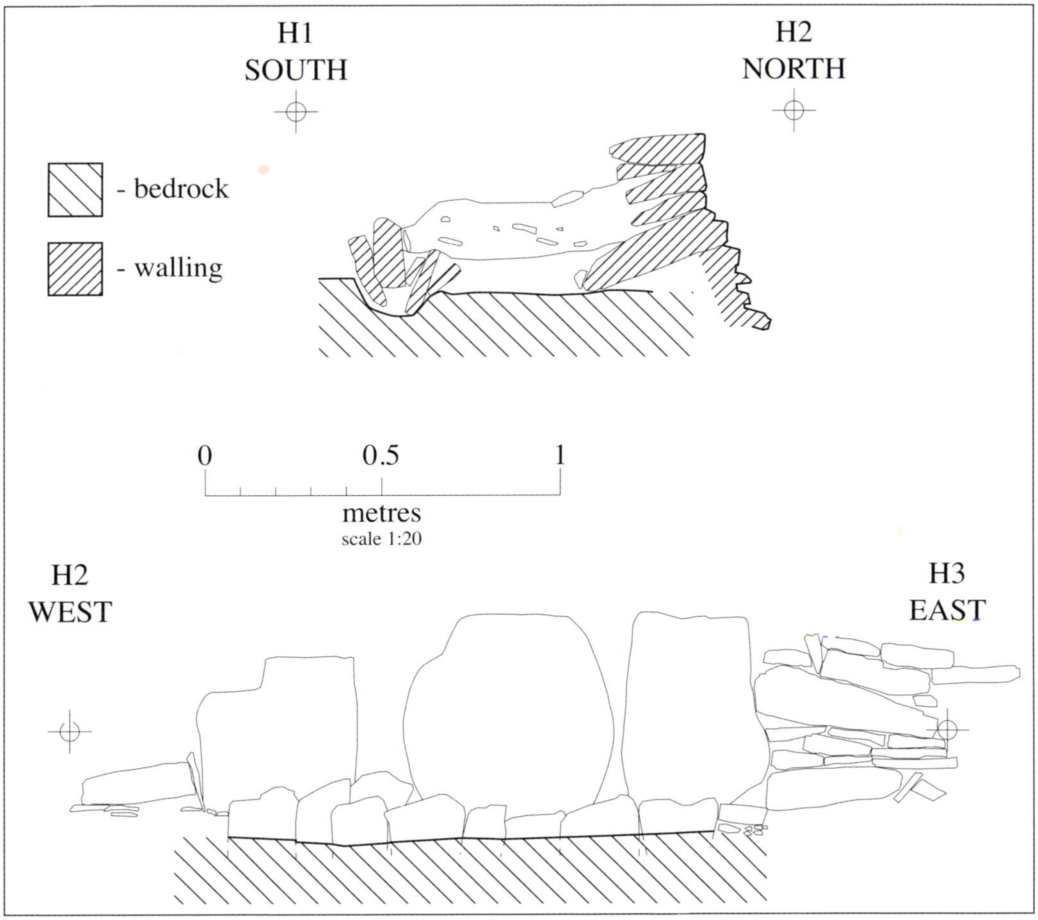

85—Detail of wall structure, hut A. *(C. McHale)*

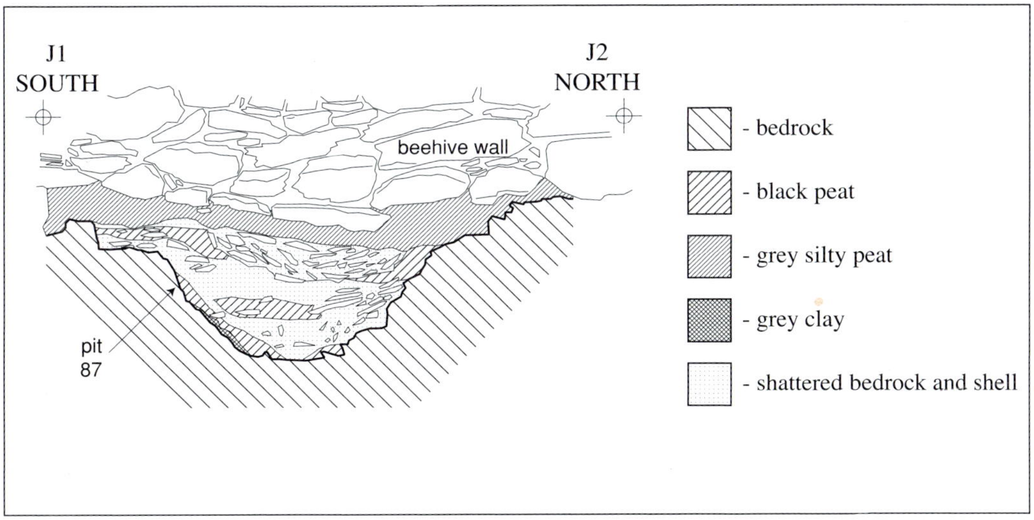

86—Section of pit F87 beneath walling of hut D. *(C. McHale)*

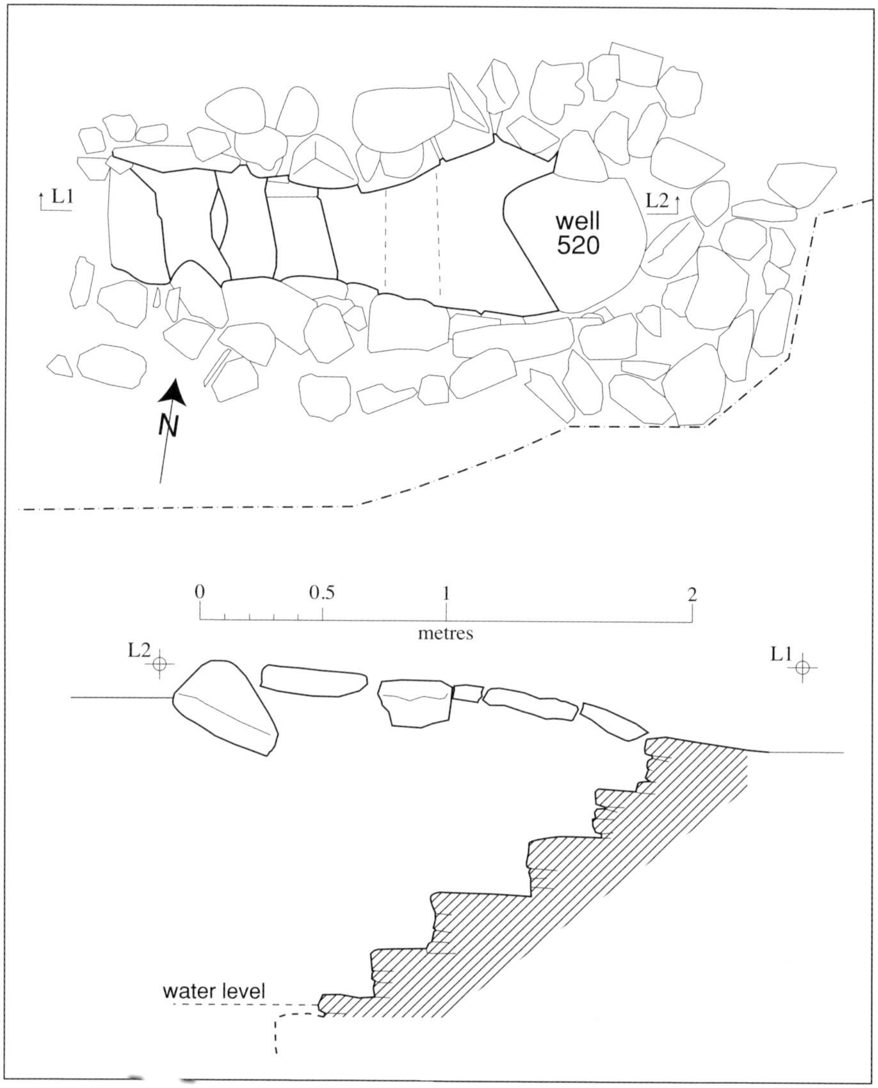

87—Plan and elevation of well F520.

stones were not fully excavated, as the stones were retained *in situ*. Three thin slabs, 0.05–0.09m in width, were extant (section H2–H3, Fig. 85). These were of weathered sandstone and stood to a height of 0.59m above the level of the subsoil.

There was no evidence for any formal flooring within hut A. The primary hearth was a spread of red ash, F460, which was set into a rectangular hollow and centrally placed. It measured 0.75m by 1m north–south, and three of the original kerb stones, set on edge, remained *in situ*. The ash was 0.2m deep. No finds were recovered from the hearth deposits.

The ash was cut by a pit or small secondary hearth, F458, which was associated with a curving gully. The fill of both was a crumbly dark grey charcoal-flecked loam, and thin stones remained set on edge along one side.

Deposits of rubble and silt (F433), shillet (F434), and loose soil with slag (F441) overlay the structure. These deposits were cut into by several later graves and constitute a probable contaminated horizon.

Hut B

Hut B (F440), which measured 6.7m in overall diameter, was set into a semicircular arc that cut vertically through the bedrock outcrop on the west side of the site to a depth of 0.7m. To the west of the vertical cut, the bedrock ridge rose to a further height of *c.* 0.75m. This sharply cut arc defined the outer wall of the hut (1.5m thick on average) on the west side. The interior of the hut averaged 3.5m in diameter.

The walls of the hut were defined by two shallow parallel trenches, F459 and F461, which cut through the underlying bedrock. Both trenches were poorly defined and filled with quite compacted shattered bedrock and inorganic silt. Narrow stones, vertically set against the sides of the trenches, occasionally occurred. The inner trench, F459, averaged 0.4m in diameter and 0.3m in depth. It was not continuous, particularly towards the eastern side. Several post-holes, between 1.5m and 2m apart, and 0.15–0.25m in depth, were cut into the bedrock on the line of the slot. The post-holes could have held upright timbers up to 0.4m in diameter, although smaller uprights are more likely. Several of the post-holes retained small packing-stones. There was a fairly well-defined break in the trench at the east side, where two post-holes set 1.3m apart indicated the position of the doorway (see below). The trench was filled with light brown silt and shattered bedrock fragments, with occasional charcoal flecks throughout. A large, rounded stone with three grooves (92E87:459:1) was recovered from the trench at the western end, as was a very corroded iron object, possibly a knife blade (92E87:459:2).

The outer trench, F461, was shallow, measuring on average 0.08m in depth and 0.22m in width. It was filled with shattered stone in a silt matrix that was slightly darker than subsoil. At the western side, several vertically set thin slabs, up to 0.4m in height, were set into the trench. The line of trench 461 was not continuous across the north side: this is most likely due to disturbance from later grave-cuts and a rise in the height of the bedrock in this area, rather than an indication of an entrance leading from hut 440 to hut 432 (see below). The trench, however, did continue across the entrance threshold at the east side of the hut. Here, post-holes indicated the former presence of an outer set of jambs to either side of the doorway.

The sole internal feature of the structure was a large, centrally placed stone-lined hearth, F439. This measured 1.08m east/west by 0.75m north/south, with a larger cut through subsoil into which the stone kerbing was vertically set. An irregularly shaped pit extended from the west side of the hearth: small stones occurred around the edges of the pit, which was filled with charcoal and ash similar to that in the hearth.

Four distinct deposits with an overall maximum thickness of 0.3m were evident in the hearth. The lowest fill was a brown loam containing moderate amounts of charcoal. Above this was a layer of fairly compacted red/brown ash. The layer above this was similar, and contained mottles of red oxidised earth. The uppermost fill was brown silt with a high charcoal content. No finds were recovered from the hearth deposits, but small fragments of calcined animal bone occurred throughout.

An extensive but patchy spread of heavily charcoal-flecked silt, F453, the sole remaining occupation deposit, overlay the subsoil floor of the hut. This material survived particularly well in the south-east quadrant of the hut interior. Part of this layer had been uncovered in the 1993 season of excavation (then labelled F93 and interpreted as possibly part of a hut floor). Small fragments of calcined animal bone were recovered from the charcoal layer, as were several unmodified, fist-sized beach stones, which may have been used in shellfish exploitation.

A regularly laid, flat sandstone-flagged pathway, F403, uncovered in the 1994 season of excavation, led to the door of the hut. It was oriented north-west/south-east and survived for a length of *c.* 2.5m, being cut away at the east end by later burials. The stones of the pathway were bedded at the west end on pea-gravel, F457, from which a clear six-faceted quartz crystal (92E87:457:1) was recovered. The crystal is unworked but would have been collected elsewhere and then subsequently discarded where found. The pathway, 1m in width, was well laid and regular, composed of flat slabs, some shattered. It may originally have had vertically set kerbing to both sides: this survived in one area where the kerb stones stood 0.2m higher than the surface of the paving. In character the pathway resembles the paving laid outside the west door of the oratory rather than the rough levels of stones present outside the door of the later hut D. It was overlain by dark brown, very friable loam, F402, which had been cut away on either side by later graves. No finds were recovered from this area.

A thick layer of soil and broken rock, rubble and shillet, F434, overlay the walls and interior of the hut. This was up to 0.5m in depth and tailed off to the east with the natural gradient in this area (Fig. 32, section E1–E2). Much of this material is likely to have originated from the construction of hut D (see below). The upper level of the soil/shillet was cut through by closely packed infant graves; while several artefacts were recovered from the shillet, the possibility that they are intrusive should not be discounted.

Level 1, trench A: hut C/F77

Prior to excavation, the original ground surface (OGS, F40) was evident in a *c.* 2m-long section along the eroded south face of the island (Fig. 88). The pale grey, dark-flecked sandy loam (F40) overlay subsoil to a depth of 0.015m. A sample was retained for radiocarbon dating, but proved to contain peat fragments. F40 survived only in localised areas, such as beneath the walls of the drystone hut and within the floor area of timber round house F77. Elsewhere, continuous grave-digging had

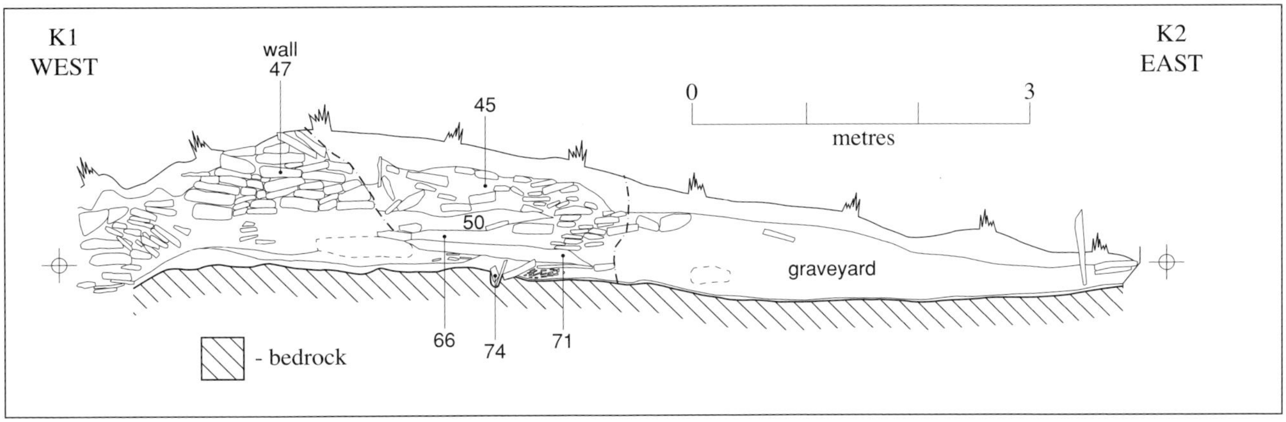

88—Section along eroded face of the island, showing the build-up of midden soils over hut C, period 1, and wall 47 (period 3) outside hut D. *(C. McHale)*

removed all trace, and in the area of huts A and B it is possible that the sod had been deliberately stripped for construction purposes.

The wall-trench F74 described part of an arc that would originally have measured *c*. 4.8m in diameter. It was composed of a slot 0.23m wide, which varied from 0.1m to 0.19m in depth. Very thin (average 0.005m) shattered slate slabs, set on edge, had been placed along the inner (southern) side of the wall-trench. These stood to a height of 0.08m above the flooring level of the structure (see below). Rough quartz pebbles, averaging 0.23m in diameter, were also present along the length of the wall-trench. The soil fill of the trench was a mid-brown, fairly stone-free sticky silty loam with occasional charcoal flecking. No remains of timber survived in the well-drained loamy soils. The regular outline of the trench, the vertical placement of slates and the occasional presence of quartz packing-stones are all suggestive of a standing structure, possibly of small posts and wattle, which decayed *in situ*.

A single post-hole, F74a, 0.38m east/west by 0.24m north/south, with a depth of 0.17m, was present at the eastern end of the wall-trench. This probably held one door jamb of the structure.

A rough but nonetheless regular alignment of sandstone blocks (F73) was sited 0.3–0.4m outside (north) of the wall-slot. The stones, both rectangular blocks and rounded boulders, varied in size from 0.14m to 0.45m. Up to three stones were set on top of one another, giving a maximum height of 0.16m. Many of the stones were set on edge, particularly at the western end, and may have held orthostats, as in the wall construction of hut A. The stones did not extend as far as the eroded cliff face at the western end, where slate feature F75 occurred within the wall-trench (see below). It may have been disturbed here by the later construction of hut D. The stone alignment terminated at the eastern end of wall-trench 74, supporting the suggestion that the entrance to the structure lay in the north-east quadrant, away from the direction of the prevailing wind.

Bounded by wall-trench F74 to the south was a possible flooring level, F76, which overlay the OGS, F40. The flooring was 0.05m thick and comprised a fairly stony, compacted grey clay silt, which contained no evident carbonised debris. Marine shells on the east side of the flooring were sealed by a slate that had partially collapsed from the wall-trench.

A small, slate-covered feature (F75) occurred at the westernmost part of the enclosed floor area. This measured 0.8m east/west by 0.5m north/south. The horizontally laid slates may be the remnants of partial reflooring in this area. This suggestion is reinforced by the presence of a 0.1m-thick spread of coarse orange gravel beneath the slates, which was continuous with floor F76. Large, structured fragments of charcoal were present in the voided pockets immediately below the slates.

No finds were recovered from these levels.

A localised spread of fine pea-gravel, F70, similar to that found on the foreshore of the island, was laid down over the subsoil and sod in an area to the north of hut 77. This layer measured up to 0.02m in depth and was noted in an area measuring *c.* 3.5m north/south by *c.* 3m east/west. The gravel was present around the entrance to the (later) hut D, and extended beneath the walls of that structure. Its spread was contained to the north by a raised, level outcrop of sandstone.

The pea-gravel is no doubt contemporary with the timber round house F77. Pea-gravel was also present beneath the paving associated with hut B (see above).

A deposit of mid-brown, relatively stone-free silty loam, F71/89/411, accumulated between and over the stones of F73. It extended northwards, where it overlay the pea-gravel F70, and eastwards for *c.* 2m beyond the wall of hut F77. This soil was 0.18–0.2m deep. A discrete area of red ash, which measured only 0.46m north/south by 0.74m east/west, occurred between wall-trench F74 and the alignment of sandstones F73. Many fragments of fired clay mould and a bone motif-piece were recovered from this deposit. A similar soil (F72) overlay soil F71.

Period 1: features beneath Hut D

Excavation of the interior of the drystone hut was completed in 1993. Several features and layers pre-dating its construction were uncovered. It cannot be stated with any certainty that these are connected with or contemporary with the occupation of huts A, B or C; nonetheless they are included in period 1.

A thin, compacted, purplish/grey clay silt and peat OGS (F78) survived beneath the wall of hut D at the south-west and south-east sides. This is probably the same deposit as F40 (described above) and did not survive over what was to become the floor area of hut D.

Two pits were cut into the weathered bedrock within the floor area of hut D. F87, which extended beneath the west side of the wall of the hut and therefore pre-dated it, was irregularly shaped, measuring 0.95m north/south with a depth of 0.37m (Fig. 86). It was filled with a grey/black, dry, rooted peaty soil, interleaved with deposits of light brown shattered bedrock and shillet. The pit was capped with dark peat-like soil (possible percolation material) on which the wall of the later hut rested.

Pit F86 was oval, with a maximum depth of 0.36m, and measured 2.2m east/west by 1m north/south. The inorganic fill consisted of redeposited finely shattered bedrock, slightly darker in hue than the parent material. It contained intermittent flecks of charcoal and lenses of ash, and produced several tiny fragments of calcined bone.

It is assumed that F86 pre-dates the drystone hut, as it is difficult to envisage the function of such a large feature in the centre of a dwelling. (See F64 below for further discussion.) No finds were recovered from either feature.

Period 2: trench A, level 2. Hut D/F49

Construction of hut D

Hut D, F49, at the western end of the island, was built against a rising outcrop of sandstone. Before excavation the exterior face of the hut wall was not visible on either the western or northern side. A narrow ridge, an enclosing feature, extended northwards from the north-west side of the hut (see below).

Excavation of the interior of hut D was completed in 1993, while the deposits to the east of the hut were excavated in their entirety in 1994. Earlier deposits to the north of hut D were excavated in 1995.

The drystone wall of the hut was not constructed on bedrock at its northern and eastern sides (Fig. 32, section E1–E2). Instead, it was constructed in a hollow that appears to have been quarried from an outcrop of sandstone. In the north-west quadrant, where the external wall of the hut intersected with enclosure F91 (see below), a total depth of 0.9m of dumped deposits underlay the wall of the hut. These deposits were composed of 0.45m of shattered sandstone shillet and loam, F88, which contained flecks of charcoal. A layer of dark grey/black charcoal-enriched silt, F92, which contained abundant marine shell and animal bone (quite fresh in appearance), underlay the shattered rock. This midden matter was 0.2m deep and overlay a further deposit of shattered rock, F94, which overlay bedrock. Samples of bone from F92, submitted for radiocarbon analysis, gave a date of between 775 and 961 at 2 sigma (UB-3860).

Outside the entrance to the hut, in the north-east quadrant, the wall was built on a 0.4m-thick deposit of shattered sandstone shillet (also F88/94). This overlay the grey/brown loam F71/89/411 of period 1 and the occupation silt of hut B. It appears to have been deposited to provide a firm level surface on which the drystone coursing was laid. The shattered sandstone did not extend fully beneath the walls of the hut, nor did it occur within the floor area of the hut.

In the north-west quadrant the faced external walling of the hut stood to a height of 0.55m, whereas internally the masonry stood to a height of 2.2m. In the north-east quadrant the external walling was 0.9m in height: at this point internally it stood to a height of 1.7m. The height differential indicates that the hut was built as a sunken structure, and also illustrates how it was tucked into the rising ground.

At the point where a break or step upwards in the rising ground outside the hut was apparent, a plinth or projecting course, F90, at the base of the wall followed the circuit of the hut in its north-east quadrant for a distance of approximately 2m. The plinth projected up to 0.3m from the curving wall of the hut, and stood up to three courses in height (Fig. 32, section E1–E2).

Description of hut D (Figs 30b, 32a, 32b)

The drystone hut measured 4.3m north–south by 4.4m east–west, and the walls (internally) stood to a maximum height of 2.3m. The doorway was located at the east side. Prior to excavation, rubble and soil infill had accumulated inside the structure to a depth of 0.8m. The section of the wall in the south-east quadrant stood to a height of 1.5m both internally and externally. Here it had partly collapsed outwards. It measured 1.2m in width. The external face of the wall was of closely fitted rectangular blocks averaging 0.1m in height and 0.7m in length.

In the south-east quadrant, at a height of 0.9m above the footing level of the wall, a stone that was firmly set into the masonry projected outwards for *c.* 0.3m. A second, similar stone occurred in the north-east quadrant, just 0.5m above the base of the wall. This projected outwards for only 0.12m.

The doorway was splayed and measured 1.1m in width, narrowing to 0.7m on the inside. Two sill stones were set into the underlying pea-gravel. On the southern side of the doorway, a short length of faced masonry, F57, extended eastwards from the external face of the wall of the hut and functioned as a passageway into the hut. This walling merely abutted the outside of the hut and was not keyed in. The masonry F57 was well faced on the north side by the doorway, where it stood to a height of 0.6m. The southern side, where it was scarped into the gently sloping terrace of stone debris outside the hut, was of embanked rubble. F57 pre-dated the accumulation of most of the midden refuse (see below) but was built on the gravel and soil deposits associated with period 1. The wall was of dual function: it provided shelter for the doorway and also acted for some time to prevent the midden from spilling over and blocking the access into the hut.

One half of the interior of the drystone hut was excavated in 1992, and excavation was completed in 1993. No formal flooring was recovered, and the original floor level of the interior was found to be below the exterior, contemporary ground level. There is a drop of almost 0.4m from the lowest course of the walling inside the hut to undisturbed bedrock subsoil. Vertically pitched, degraded, thin sandstone slabs, generally oriented east/west, formed an uneven natural flooring to the hut.

Internal features comprised a localised red ash spread, F67, a possible hearth, which measured 0.48m by 0.3m. Around the basal coursing of the northern side of the wall of the hut a band of soft brown silt and shillet was evident. This measured *c.* 0.05m in width and had the texture of decayed wood, but survived only as a superficial stain on the surface of the underlying bedrock and shillet. Its origin and function are uncertain.

A layer of compacted grey/black fine sandy silt, F62, overlay the bedrock floor of the hut but did not extend to the south wall. The silt had charcoal flecks throughout, with rare flecks of shell and some animal bone. Small stones, some of which were set on edge, occurred throughout. Centrally placed in the hut, and occurring in a fairly concentrated area within this layer, was a disturbed area of oxidised clay and compacted ash lenses. This was cut through on all sides by later burials, but may represent a hearth site. No artefacts were recovered.

Cutting through the occupation silt F62 by the doorway of the hut was a stone-capped, silt-filled feature, F64. This measured 1.4m by 0.66m (max.), oriented north-west/south-east, with a maximum depth of 0.3m. It partially overlay the earlier cut F86, although the two are unrelated. The fill was a dark brown, charcoal-flecked gritty silt containing marine shell, mainly oyster and periwinkle. The feature was roughly capped with flattish sandstone slabs, up to 0.7m in diameter. It may have functioned as a sump, gathering water from the entrance and from the sides of the structure, although the fill contained primarily debris and food refuse.

Further silt and small stone layers, F54, accumulated in the hut. Patches of yellow-brown ash with structured pieces of charcoal, probable hearth rake-out, represent the penultimate level of occupation material within the stone hut prior to the collapse of the roof and the walls. A sample of carbonised material from F54 yielded a radiocarbon date of 315 ± 45 BP, AD 1486–1642 when calibrated (UCLA-2873E), indicating that the structure had been occupied into the later medieval period.

Period 3: later disturbance and dereliction of hut D

Four individuals were interred in the hut at an uncertain date. Bones of an adult (F51), two juveniles (F84 and F85) and a neonate (F83) were recovered. Grave-cuts for the burials were not apparent through the overlying rubble, but the skeletons are likely to be of eighteenth/nineteenth-century date. Skeleton F51, of a female aged 20–25, was inserted north-west/south-east just inside the entrance of the hut. Several nails found adjacent to the feet suggest that the individual was interred in a coffin. No trace of timber nor even of a definite grave-cut survived.

Inside the hut, rubble collapse in a dry brown soil matrix, F48, overlay the occupation deposits. Much of the stone derived from the roof of the structure, with slabs up to 1.5m in diameter occurring. Several whetstones and a tanged knife blade were recovered from the rubble. The upper levels of overlying loose soil, shattered sandstone and turf within the hut were numbered F3. A whetstone, some animal bone and shell came from this upper deposit. This material may be related to the period 3 usage of the oratory, from which several whetstones were recovered.

Period 2: the midden

Outside the hut, contemporary with its usage and overlying the level 1 deposits, a sizeable deposit (up to 0.9m) of soil and stones accumulated. This consisted of a mixture of sandstone rubble, quantities of marine shell and butchered animal bone in a charcoal-enriched loam matrix. Little differentiation in the texture or hue was apparent throughout the excavation of the midden, so the soil was removed in a series of 'spits'—artificial layers that attempted to follow the natural contours. The concentration of bone and shell lessened considerably to the east and north of the excavation area, although attempts to excavate the upper levels of the midden in a meaningful manner were frustrated by the sheer number of later infant burials encountered. The midden may once have been fairly contained within an area around the entrance to hut D, but was dispersed and spread out over a wider area owing to considerable disturbance by the burials.

The excavated midden deposits were sieved in their entirety in the 1992 and 1993 seasons through 7mm garden sieves, resulting in the retrieval of all animal, fish and bird bone, as well as a large quantity of marine shell. Marine shell was retained only in the 1992 excavation season, as the sample was considered sufficiently large.

The excavation of a large, open area of the midden in 1994 included a localised area of stratified deposits. A small area within the excavation trench, measuring only *c.* 2.5m north/south by 2.5m east/west, had not been excessively disturbed by infant burials. Furthermore, a succession of rough paved pathways or small yards (four levels in all), outside the entrance to the drystone hut, had sealed the intervening midden layers. Animal bone from each of these 'sandwiched layers' was kept separately, and each layer was sampled for environmental material.

The lowest layer of paving, F410, extended for 1.8m north/south by 2.2m east/west. It was composed of quite roughly placed sandstone slabs up to 0.44m across, bedded in a deposit of pea-gravel. Charcoal-enriched loam, F409, containing animal bone and marine shell was dumped on top of the paving.

A more extensive area of roughly placed sandstone blocks, F408, was thrown down on midden F409. This was more like stepping-stones across the midden than paving, and had a very uneven surface. It covered an area of almost 3m north/south by *c.* 4m east/west.

Further soil and food debris, F407, accumulated on F408. This in turn was sealed by paving F404, which measured 3m east/west by 2.5m north/south. It was composed of fairly large (up to 0.6m in diameter), regularly laid sandstone slabs. Midden F405, which contained packed winkle, limpet and oyster shell, was thrown down over this paving.

A localised area of rough paving, F406, which measured only 0.4m north/south by 0.6m east/west, sealed midden F405.

The uppermost levels of unstratified, disturbed midden soil in the 1994 trench were removed in spits F401, F354 and F301. These equate as follows with the midden spits removed in the previous years from the adjoining areas:

Upper	45= 97= 80	=	301

Middle	50= 98	=	354
Interface			82
Lower	66= 99	=	401

The lowermost spit lay beneath rubble that had evidently collapsed off retaining wall F57 (see above). This midden layer noticeably did not extend into the interior of the drystone hut. It sealed the wall-trench and stones of hut F71. A tanged knife blade, a possible barrel padlock key, a perforated whetstone and some iron slag fragments were recovered from this level, and part of a copper or bronze ring-brooch was found in the 1993 season. Overlying this, a thick spit of similar material, F50, contained noticeable lenses of red ash throughout. The northern limit of the midden was formed by the slightly projecting plinth, F90, on the north side of the hut. Several iron objects—an awl or punch and the head of a decorated bronze ring-brooch—were recovered from this, as was part of a shale or lignite bracelet. Twenty-four small polished bone disc beads were recovered from the midden F50, outside the entrance to the hut. A sherd from the strap-handle of a late thirteenth-century Bristol jug (possibly Redcliffe ware) was recovered from this 'middle spit'. Small pieces of composite antler comb plates were recovered from a localised area within the upper levels of the midden.

Period 3: later activity

When up to 0.8m of midden had accumulated, a retaining wall, F47, was built against the seaward (south) side of the drystone hut. A spread of crushed sandstone shillet, F58, was deposited as a bedding layer over midden F50. In the excavated portion under wall F47 this extended for a maximum distance of 0.95m, sealing the midden beneath. Its maximum depth was 0.28m and it filled a hollow in the midden.

Wall F47 stood to 0.8m in height and was evidently of a different build to that of the drystone hut (Fig. 88). It was 1m in width, with an external face only. This was reasonably well built, of very weathered random coursed rubble, with large gaps between the stones. These averaged 0.23m in width, and the short end of the stones formed the face. This wall was partly removed during excavation to expose the outer face of the drystone hut. The wall is late in the sequence of events on the site, and may reflect the use of the hut as a temporary shelter (see also period 3 of the oratory). Certainly the drystone hut was in an advanced state of collapse when this wall was built. Its function was to prevent the southern part of the hut wall from collapsing outwards.

Further midden material and stones (F45) accumulated, which overlay the basal stones of wall F47. Large stone slabs, with voided pockets, collapsed off the hut walls and sealed the midden in the passage between walls F53 and F57. This rubble, where it continued into the interior of the hut, was numbered F3.

Trench B: the oratory

A trench measuring 9m north/south by 13m east/west, centred on the oratory, was opened in 1992. This was extended in a 5m by 2m cutting westwards in 1993, and for 5.5m northwards, connecting with trench C, opened in 1993 over the shrine. A further 1m at the east end of trench B was opened in 1994.

Prior to excavation, the oratory was evident as a low (*c.* 0.35m high) rectangular structure, with a doorway centrally placed on the west side. Ground level around the structure was markedly higher than that elsewhere in the vicinity, resulting from the collapse of stone from its walls. The whole was covered in a mantle of sod, on which grew short grass, campion and clover.

The oratory was excavated in 1992, while work in this area in 1993 concentrated on the excavation of *c.* 30 graves, which occurred mainly outside the west end of the oratory.

The *leacht* was excavated in 1994, as were two structures pre-dating the stone oratory at the eastern end.

Period 1, trench B, level 1

The earliest activity in this area is evidenced by the remains of an earthen or sod structure, F220. This survived beneath the east end of the stone oratory and projected for some distance beyond it. The structure measured 2m north/south internally and 4.2m north/south externally. The north and south walls extended beneath the drystone walls of the oratory, and the length of the earlier structure is estimated at over 6m. The entrance in the west wall of the structure is represented by a sill stone and socket flanked by two substantial post-holes, interpreted as door jambs (see Figs 17 and 18). The interior of the period 2 oratory was excavated in 1992, and re-excavated in 1994 in an attempt to trace the wall channels of the early structure beneath the later drystone masonry. No further information, however, was recovered by the re-excavation.

The interior of the oratory was excavated to subsoil in 1992. Boulder clay, as revealed within the oratory, was a compact grey/pink, fairly stone-free marl, with nodules of red/brown mineralised accretion throughout. There was no trace of a sod covering on the boulder clay within the oratory.

Several features uncovered at the lowest level within the structure pre-date the oratory. Some of these features were also sealed by pea-gravel, which, however, could not be shown to be continuous with that present beneath the walls of the oratory. Other features that were thought initially to pre-date the oratory have returned radiocarbon dates indicating their usage into the late medieval period. None of these later features appear to relate to the sod-walled building of level 1.

At the north-west side of the excavated interior of the oratory a probable double post-hole, F39c, measured 0.8m in total width. It was circular and extended for 0.06m beneath the north wall of the oratory. In section it had a double-U profile, with a maximum depth of 0.3m. The fill on the east side was of soft, brown, sticky silt, reminiscent of decayed wood, while the fill in general was of quite heavy, inorganic gritty clay silt. This feature was sealed by a large, flat slab. In the south-west corner, a shallow (*c.* 0.12m deep) possible post-hole, F39h, was also sealed by a large flat slab.

A stone sill, F36, was set into a cut or socket, F39b, which was irregular, measuring 0.41m in total depth by 0.3m by 0.7m. The stone measured 0.7m in length, 0.08m in width and 0.4m in height. Only the upper *c.* 0.05m projected above the level of the boulder clay. The sill stone was parallel to and 0.6m away from the inside of the entrance to the oratory. The socket was packed with small rubble, pebbles and loose, sterile gravel. The upper level of the fill contained large pieces of charcoal and some marine shell.

An irregularly shaped cut, F39a, occurred to the west of stone sill F36: this had stones in the fill and is probably a continuation of the socket for the sill stone. It was sealed by a spread of compacted gravel, probably equivalent to F37.

Extending from the east side of F39b, the socket for the sill stone, was an irregular linear feature, F39f. This curved slightly eastwards for 1m and was cut through by a later feature (see level 6, below). The linear feature was a fairly shallow (0.1–0.12m deep on average) U-shaped cut, 0.14–0.17m wide. It was covered with thin sandstone slabs that lay flush with the level of boulder clay. The feature was mainly voided beneath the stones, but had some fill of loose coarse gravel, small stones and large pieces of charcoal. It is likely to have functioned as a drain. Charcoal, hand-picked for radiocarbon analysis, from the fill of the drain returned a date of 805 ± 90 BP, AD 1166–1275 when calibrated. It appears likely that the fill of the drain was contaminated by water backing up from the later feature (F38d, see level 6 below).

A possible post-hole, F39g, was cut through the fill of F39b at its junction with F39f. This measured 0.2m in diameter, with a maximum depth of 0.32m.

The features listed above pre-date the construction of the stone oratory. The scant stratigraphic evidence suggests that F39b was sealed by the general spread of gravel and shillet on which the drystone oratory is built, while F39f was sealed by the laid clay till floor of the oratory (see below).

F39c, h and g are probably post-holes relating to the doorway of the period 1 oratory. F39f is likely to have functioned primarily as a drainage gully—the ground certainly slopes from west to east in this area. The stone sill F36, aligned perfectly as it is with the later threshold some distance higher, is likely too to have functioned as the threshold. This presumably relates to the level 1 oratory.

The main surviving element of structure 220 was the wall construction. This was composed of two narrow, earth-cut trenches, F220 and F225, which were parallel to each other and varied in distance from 0.34m apart at the east end to 0.74m at the south end. The wall-trenches formed three sides of a right-angled structure. The total width of the wall varied from 0.8m at the east end to 1.1m on the northern side. The trenches that defined the walls of the structure were clearly cut through the subsoil in this area. Trench 220, the outer element of the wall construction, measured on average from 0.18m to 0.2m in width and had a depth of up to 0.15m. The profile of the trench varied from a fairly straight-sided V-shape (on the north side) to an eroded, shallow U-shape (on the south side). Much of the sides of the trench was lined with thin sandstone slabs—many of these had been displaced, but enough survived to indicate that the trench had been lined on both sides. The trench had been eroded by the encroaching tide at the north-east corner. Three post-holes, 220a, b and c, were cut through the underlying subsoil along the east side of trench 220. Post-holes 220a and b lay on the eastern extremity of trench 220 and had many small packing-stones in their fill. They were 0.16m and 0.15m deep respectively, with diameters of 0.2m and 0.28m. Post-hole 220c lay along a very eroded stretch of the wall-trench and measured 0.06m in depth with a diameter of 0.2m. No packing-stones survived either in the trench at this point or in post-hole 220c. Post-holes 220a and b were spaced 0.9m apart, with a distance of 1.7m from b to c. A fourth post-hole may well have existed at the north-east corner of the structure, pairing with 220c. The function of these post-holes in the reconstruction of the building is discussed in the main text.

Extending parallel to trench F220 on its inside was trench F225. This was in all respects similar to 220, with a depth between 0.14m and 0.2m and an average width of 0.2m. This trench, too, was lined with thin sandstone slabs. These did not project much above the surviving level of the trench cut. The profile of 225 was as 220 (above).

Some evidence for a repair or refurbishment of the building is given by trench F231. This occurred on the south side of the structure, between trenches F220 and F225. It was narrower than either 220 or 225 and was 0.08m in depth. Few packing-stones survived along its length. Trench 231 is probably best interpreted as the original line of trench 225 along the inner, eastern side of the structure. It lies only 0.2m from trench 225.

A short trench extended for 1m southwards from the southern line of trench F220. This was 0.24m wide and 0.16m deep. It appeared to be continuous with trench 220 at this point and had a similar fill. It was cut away by later activity at its southern end and its function is unknown.

A well-defined soil deposit, F224, was noted between trenches F220 and F225, sealing trench F231 and overlying the boulder clay in this area. F224 was a pinkish/grey, quite compacted sandy silt, with occasional concentrated patches of charcoal on its upper surface. It survived up to a maximum depth of 0.1m in the area between trenches 220 and 225. Similar soil, indistinguishable from F224, filled the upper levels of all three trenches. Soil F224 has been interpreted as the decayed sod walling of structure F225.

No evident flooring levels of the building survived, either within the period 2 oratory or to the east of the later structure. The charcoal patches on the upper surface of 224 may represent occupation/activity traces associated with the use of the structure. Both charcoal and sod 224 were extensively sampled, for botanical and dating purposes. Few botanical indicators were recovered and the possibility of tidal contamination was high. No artefacts were recovered from this level.

Probably related to the usage of structure F220, at a distance of 0.4m east of the outer wall-trench, several graves were cut through the underlying subsoil and rock. Five graves, F211a–e , all oriented east/west and closely spaced, were uncovered. No bone survived in this area of the site. Only one grave had evidence of stone lining, and all were unprotected. The graves were initially unmarked: the terrace kerbings F209 and F210 (see level 4), which roughly marked the ends of the graves, are later than structure 220 and overlie the graves.

Three burials excavated in 1993 outside the west end of the drystone oratory appear to pre-date its construction and relate to the level 1 oratory. F119 and F120 were interred in the one grave: F119 (a young adult male) was the primary burial, which was moved to one side when F120 (an older adult male) was buried. The position of the feet of F120 (now decayed) lay very close to the west wall of the oratory; however, it appears to post-date it. A third, highly truncated skeleton, F103, appears to have had its feet cut away by the construction of the *leacht*, F7.

Several other skeletons had been cut through by later, albeit early medieval, skeletons but it is not possible to determine whether they relate to the level 1 occupation.

Period 1, trench B: level 2

This saw the construction of a small sod or orthostat structure on top of the level 1 sod building. This, too, survived only in part below the eastern wall of the drystone oratory. The remains comprised two parallel well-defined trenches, F226, which extended for 1.5m east of the later drystone oratory and cut through the level 1 structure in this area. They described a small structure measuring only 1.2m north/south by over 0.8m east/west (this dimension unknown).

Trenches 226 measured from 0.62m to 0.8m in width and survived to a depth of 0.25m. They were packed with large, rectangular weathered sandstones, up to 0.5m in diameter. These had slipped and fallen in from their original positions, and no stones survived at the northern end of trenches 226 where they extended beneath the walls of the later drystone structure. The gap between the two trenches measured on average 0.25m: this seems somewhat narrow for a sod- or earth-walled structure, and it is possible that the stone-packed trenches could have held orthostats in place. The soil that remained between the stones lining the trenches was a fairly inorganic brown gritty silt, with numerous small stones throughout. The nature of this soil fill also indicates that sod may not have been the principal component of the walls of structure 226.

A single large stone was laid over the trenches, centrally placed in the east side of 226. This initially resembled a sill stone: when it was lifted, however, a socket into which it had originally been vertically placed was apparent.

Mixed soil deposits, F228, with a depth of 0.15m, occurred within the area enclosed by trenches 226. These constituted lenses of sod, redeposited subsoil and brown inorganic soil similar to that in trenches 226. These appear to have been deposited randomly, and may largely have been derived from the dereliction levels of the underlying building. An upper lens of charcoal-flecked stony loam relates to the construction and utilisation of structure 226.

Period 2, trench B: *leacht* F7 (Fig. 37)

The *leacht* F7, built under the north wall of the drystone oratory, was excavated and reinstated in 1994. There was no surface indication of the presence of this structure prior to excavation. A deposit of fine pea-gravel, F37, with a surviving depth of up to 0.1m, overlay the structures of levels 1 and 2. The presence of gravel in the lower fill of the *leacht* (see below) indicates that the construction of F7 post-dates the abandonment of the level 2 structure.

Description of the leacht

The *leacht* measures 3.6m east/west by *c.* 1m north/south at the east end, widening to 1.3m at the west end. It stands to a height of 0.4m, with sandstone slabs, set vertically on edge or alternately coursed, forming a kerb around it. The top of the *leacht* is rather uneven, consisting of sandstone slabs up to 0.5m in size overlying looser small stones and gravel. Significant quantities of quartz pebbles were scattered over the surface of the *leacht*: these were sealed by up to 0.5m of dereliction rubble and soil.

The construction of the *leacht* pre-dates that of the oratory, but possibly not by a significant period. The end stones of the *leacht* are keyed into a plinth, F204, which projects for *c.* 0.4m at the west end and *c.* 0.2m from the oratory wall at the east end. It does not extend the full length of the north wall of the oratory but rather is the same length as the *leacht*. Moreover, the north kerb of the *leacht* runs parallel with the plinth rather than with the north wall of the oratory. It is unlikely that the *leacht* was constructed to be a free-standing structure: the evidence of the plinth suggests the possibility that the construction of *leacht* and oratory was carried out in tandem.

Leacht F7 was constructed as follows: a foundation trench *c.* 0.5m in width was dug a short distance out from plinth 204, into which the vertically set kerbstones of the *leacht* were set. The foundation trench cut through a thin deposit of pea-gravel, F37, which overlay subsoil. The depth of the foundation trench varied according to the size of the kerbstone to be inserted. The eastern and western slabs were the largest and were keyed into plinth 204. The slabs along the north kerb had been levelled into position with small stones wedged beneath their bases.

The foundation trench of *leacht* F7 cut through one or possibly two earlier inhumations in this area. Grave 203 extended for 1.3m into the area covered by the *leacht* and was dug to a depth of 0.35m below subsoil. The grave fill was quite well defined. The left and right femurs and the left tibia and fibia of the individual survived, albeit in very poor condition. At the east end of the *leacht*, part of a badly preserved skull and mandible, F202, was deposited behind one of the kerbstones, at a depth of 0.2m. Skull 202 may belong to individual 203 or to another inhumation cut away by the eastern end of the *leacht*. The *leacht* was infilled with a mixture of redeposited subsoil and grey-brown sandy loam. Layers of stones were then laid within the structure to brace the corner kerbs. Further layers of soil with small stones were capped with flat stones and dressed with quartz. The upper level of the *leacht* extended over plinth 204.

Period 2, the drystone oratory

The gravel terrace

The oratory was built on a deposit of pea-gravel and shillet, F37, which sealed the structures of period 1 (Fig. 89). The gravel extended beneath the walls of the drystone structure. Outside the east end of the oratory the gravel was revetted by two parallel series of vertically set slabs, F209 and F210, which formed an inner and outer terrace extending 4.8m east of the outer wall of the oratory.

The kerbing F209 of the outer terrace was largely eroded by the tide and extended for only 1.5m east/west. The kerbstones F210, set 1.6m west of the outer kerbs, demarcated the line of the east wall of structure 220 (see level 1, above). The sockets for the kerbstones had cut through and truncated the earlier wall-trench F220 at its northern end. The apparent significance of the positioning of kerbstones 210b in relation to the earlier structure must be weighted by the practical considerations of the builders. Levelling of the soil walls of the level 1 structure, on dereliction, would have resulted in a platform, apparent to the builders of the drystone oratory, roughly along the line of the east wall. Revetting the edge of the soil platform with kerbstones would stabilise the soil mound and protect against tidal erosion. The terrace kerbs post-date the group of burials 211, but also serve to mark the location of these graves. It is probably significant that no further burials took place within this terraced area until the later activity around the orthostats F222 (see below).

A deposit of pea-gravel, F208, 0.25m in depth, was spread between kerbstones 209 and 210. This sealed graves 211 of period 1 and contained numerous small white quartz pebbles, particularly along the lines of the kerbstones. A small sherd from a crucible (92E87:211:1) was recovered from the pea-gravel, possibly linking this spread of material with the metalworking activity of period 1.

Attached to the east side of the *leacht*, and sealed by quantities of pea-gravel, F37, was a 1.5m length of drystone masonry, F205. This had a height of up to 0.18m and stood up to four courses. This masonry appears to be a revetting face for the gravel terrace or platform on which the oratory was built. The masonry was removed in

1994, and features uncovered beneath were excavated.

A localised area of dark grey, rooted silt, F206, up to 0.04m in depth, underlay masonry 205 and pea-gravel 37, indicating that the features below belong properly in period 1. Silt 206 sealed a cut in the subsoil, F218, which measured up to 1.8m east/west by 0.9m north/south. It had a depth of 0.4m. Cut 218 appears to have been disturbed at its west end by the construction cut for the kerbing stones for the *leacht* (level 3). The fill of the cut was an inorganic, grey/brown gritty silt, F219, which contained very rare flecks of charcoal and frequent stones set on edge. The upper level of the cut was capped with small stones up to 0.15m in diameter, set on edge.

The function of cut 218 is uncertain. It may have been a grave, although it is considerably larger than most of the other graves excavated on the island. The site was marked by the construction of the drystone terracing 205, which, although later than cut 218, certainly appears to respect and delimit the earlier feature.

Excavation of the graves at the south side of the oratory exposed a pit, F130, which clearly underlies the south wall of the oratory. The fill of the pit, which measured *c.* 1m in width and *c.* 0.5m in depth, was of rounded sandstone boulders. It appears to be a deliberate infilling of an early feature with material more suitable for building on. The pit could not be further investigated owing to the risk of instability of the drystone structure.

Description of the oratory

The structure measures 3.2m east/west by 2.2m north/south internally, and the walls stand to a maximum height of 1.28m. The long walls measure 1.3m in thickness and are battered (on the south wall) to almost 1.6m towards the base. The north wall had a substantial external batter but had weakened and collapsed forward somewhat on the interior. The east wall measures 1.5m in width: here, too, later disturbance has resulted in a rupture of the face of the drystone masonry. The east wall measures 1.2m in thickness, with a batter widening this to 1.4m towards the base.

At the west wall, where excavation had revealed the basal stones of the oratory, it was evident that the structure had been built on a deliberately laid deposit of pea-gravel and shillet, F37 (see above for details). The ground here, as elsewhere, was not perfectly level before building began: beneath the basal course of the wall, occasional stones were pitched in to provide a better and more level bedding. Stones used in the wall are generally long and flat, of weathered grey sandstone; there are, however, variants. The building stones measure up to 0.8m in length. Rough coursing is apparent throughout the structure, with the use of small, tightly packed stones up to 0.12m long in places. Some stone is shattered *in situ.* The doorway in the west wall splays from 0.95m on the outside to 0.62m internally (Fig. 91). The facing of the door ope on the south side is excellent, while that on the north has collapsed somewhat.

There is a step down (height 0.32m) into the oratory, over a sill stone 0.07m

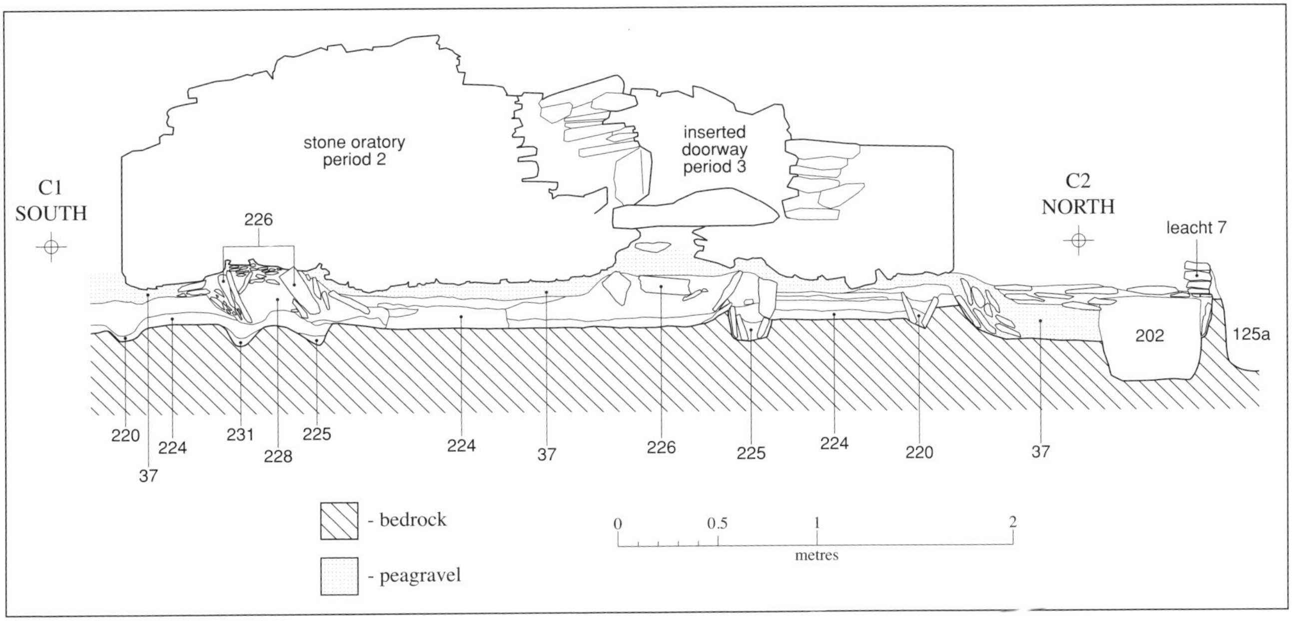

89—Elevation of east wall of drystone oratory, showing features of period 1 and period 3. *(C. McHale)*

wide. This feature, to date, appears to be unique to the Illaunloughan oratory (information from Grellan Rourke), although other examples may come to light through excavation (Fig. 90). While Reynolds (1978, 42) has suggested that the Temple of Jerusalem, as portrayed in the Book of Kells, may have had a sunken floor level because the lower part of Christ's body is shown below the doorway, this was to emphasise the possible Anglo-Saxon connections in the portrayal of that building. That form of construction, however, was more widely undertaken in wood. The Illaunloughan oratory is built on a shallow terrace on a very gentle slope from west to east. The basal courses of the drystone walling were constructed more or less on one level, with the downslope end levelled up with redeposited gravel. This dispensed with the sort of ungainly steps that occurred in the construction of the drystone hut (see trench A above), which also caused instability and rupturing of the outer fabric of the masonry in that structure. It must be taken into account that considerable scarping of the underlying levels may have taken place in the construction of the oratory, and features that pre-date the oratory survive better at the east end of the structure.

The upper surface of the sill is worn quite smooth. Underlying the vertically set sill stone is a horizontally laid sandstone slab, forming the step. The paved pathway F30, which continues westwards for a distance of 4m outside the oratory entrance, is also worn smooth. The paving stones are level and well-fitting, and the west wall of the oratory appears to be built on them.

The outer face of the oratory on the west side is considerably bowed, with angular corners, while those on the east side are rounded.

The south wall is built on a slope from west to east. The basal course is ragged, with crude projecting blocks at its west end and stones akin to beach boulders forming the lowest part of the masonry at the east end.

The east wall stood on large blocks of sandstone, gravel and shillet. The later doorway (see below) had caused a breach measuring 0.78m externally and 0.7m internally, off-centre in the east wall. A 'step' in the internal masonry of the east wall, which probably dates from the same time as the inserted doorway, was refaced with small (average length 0.2m), tightly fitted stones. This had reduced the thickness of the east wall from 1.5m to 1.04m. Around the later doorway, the facings through the east wall were very poorly executed, with evidence of collapse.

The rounded north-east corner of the building sat on a *c.* 0.2m-thick deposit of pea-gravel, F37.

The north wall

The north wall of the oratory is built on top of *leacht* F7 (see above). The coursing of the north-east corner of the oratory is very poor, with the lower stones of the wall pitched at an angle up against the upright slabs of the *leacht*.

The north wall proper stands to a height of 0.7m above the *leacht* and is quite heavily battered at its west end. The basal course of masonry, where it overlies the *leacht*, is of rounded stones and small pebbles.

Interior of the oratory

A formal grey-white pebbled clay/till flooring, F34, was laid down over the central part of the oratory. This stopped short of the east wall of the structure by 0.8m in a somewhat irregular band, where it was cut through by later features (see below). Its western boundary was more regular, where it was kerbed by the earlier sill stone F36. Patches of further flooring (also F34) of yellow, pebbled clay and purplish silt overlay the boulder clay at the west end.

The flat stones sealing F39c and h, at the west end of the oratory, were exposed at this level. These overlay the post-holes of the period 1 structure.

No finds relating to this period of usage were recovered, and no significant level of deposits relating to the primary occupation of the drystone oratory survived. The later pits cutting through the east end of the oratory have removed any traces of an altar that may originally have been there.

Period 2: outside the oratory

Further removal of gravel F37 at the south side of the oratory, and excavation of several intrusive graves in 1993, defined a rectangular setting of stones, F124, which extended for 1m from the south wall of the oratory. It measured 5m in length. A regular alignment of sandstone slabs, set vertically to form a low kerb, it may represent the very truncated remains of a *leacht*. Stone and quartz occurred at the east end of the feature, where a further stone-kerbed, paved, quartz-littered feature,

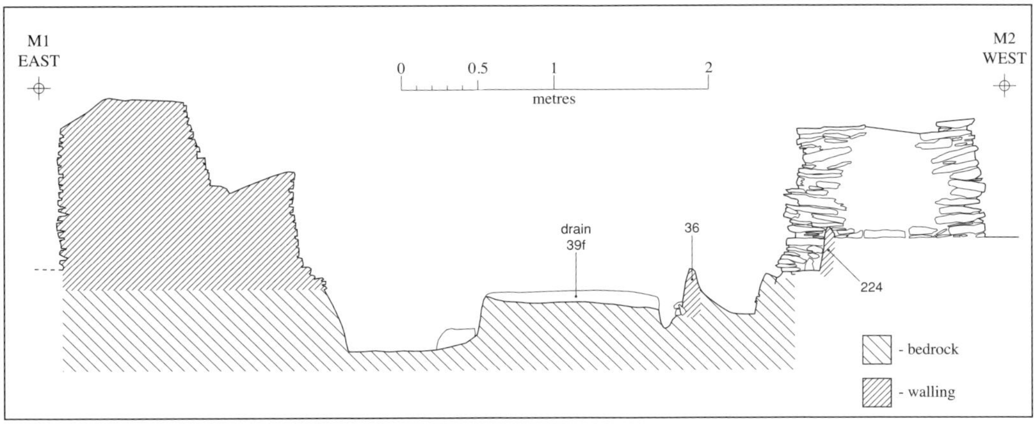

90—East–west elevation across oratory. *(C. McHale)*

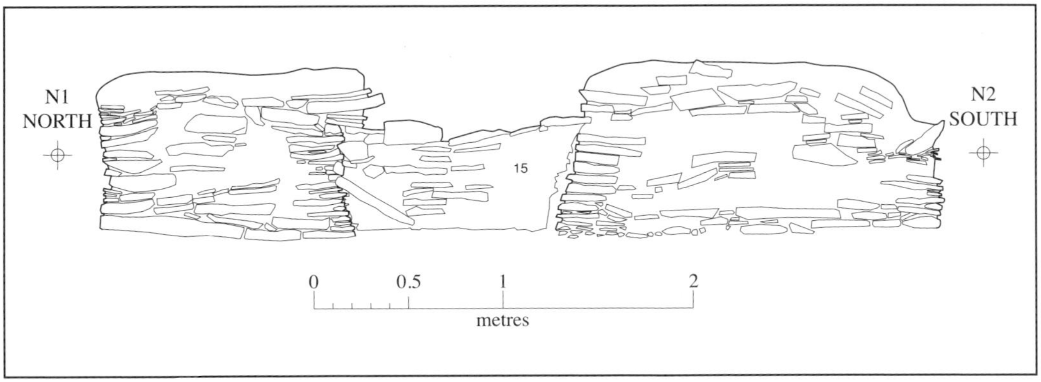

91—Elevation of west wall of oratory, showing original doorway and period 3 blockage F15. *(C. McHale)*

F118, was sited. F118 measured 0.76m east/west by over 0.6m north/south. Kerbstones, set vertically into the underlying pea-gravel at the east and west sides, stood to a height of 0.09m above the paved base of the feature. These were lifted in 1994, and the underlying deposits excavated. Pea-gravel, grey silt and white quartz pebbles filled the space between the kerbstones to a depth of 0.2m. No bone or other artefact survived. In size and plan, F118 resembles most the truncated remains of the putative slab shrine excavated at Reask (Fanning 1981, 84, 85).

Three large, vertically set sandstone orthostats, F10, were set in a low mound of stones, F222, at a distance of 1.5m from the south-east corner of the oratory. The stones stood to a height of *c.* 0.75m above the low mound of stones in which they were set. The stone mound clearly overlay paving 207, which sealed the pea-gravel outside the east end of the oratory. The stones were unmarked, and all leaned sharply towards the south-east. They do not relate to the kerbing 210 around the terrace, which they post-date; rather, they appear to mark the west end of a grave. The grave 221 was unlined, and no bone survived in it. The top of the grave was protected by regularly laid sandstones. This is the only grave at this end of the oratory, and the marking stones are not of the usual variety.

Period 3: trench B

This level saw the probable partial dereliction of the oratory. A deposit of red ash, F31, was spread over the south side of the structure, directly overlying floor F34, and banked up against the south and west walls of the oratory. The ash measured up to 0.16m in thickness, extending to 0.87m from the south wall of the oratory and tailing off. Several discrete patches of the ash remained at the west and north sides of the building. Samples of this deposit were taken for radiocarbon dating and for environmental analysis. The charcoal yielded a date of 1315 ± 105 BP, i.e. AD 640–790 when calibrated (UCLA-2873C). This may represent the 'old wood' effect as the sample contained oak. Redating of seeds from the sample (*Avena strigosa*) in Oxford returned a date of AD 1260–1310 (OxA-10133). The ash appears to represent *in situ* burning of some organic material within the oratory. While the ash adhered closely to the drystone walls on the south and west sides, minimal scorching of the stones appears to have occurred, and the clay/till flooring beneath showed no evidence of oxidisation. The ash deposit, which appeared to be undisturbed, was greater than one would expect to have been generated by a hearth.

The ash F31 was overlain by a thick deposit of crushed sandstone shillet and silt, F28. Animal and fish bone was present throughout this. Several large rubble blocks, F20, including one over 1m in length, were laid adjacent to the entranceway. This appears to represent the initial collapse of the oratory, but formed a roughly level surface that may have been utilised as a flooring of the oratory in the following level.

Period 3: later medieval usage of the oratory (Fig. 92)

Overlying F20, the large rubble blocks, was a *c.* 0.3m-thick deposit of black silty loam, shillet and small stones, F19, which was similar in consistency to the underlying F29. Some of this material spilled into the entranceway on the west side. Two whetstones and a flint flake, as well as animal and fish bones, were recovered from this layer.

A deposit of black gritty loam and food refuse, F29, occurred in the doorway of the oratory but not within the structure itself. This midden deposit was sealed by a deliberate blockage of the west doorway (Figs 91 and 92). The blockage, F15, was a length of drystone masonry, well faced on both sides, generally utilising small stones. It stood to a maximum height of 0.6m and had a fairly level surface on the top. It measured 0.58m in width and was not perpendicular to the doorway. Charcoal from beneath the blockage was submitted for radiocarbon analysis and yielded a date of 520 ± 45 BP, cal. AD 1400–1431 (UCLA-2874A).

Possibly at the same time as the blocking of the west door, a second entrance, F16, to the structure was made in the east wall (Figs 89, 92). This was very crudely achieved, leaving two courses of stonework beneath the new threshold. The threshold was uneven. The breach for the insertion of the doorway was over 1m wider than the doorway, and this part of the wall was reconstructed. The narrowing and refacing of the east wall (see above) probably occurred at this time also. This narrowing or 'step' on the interior of the east wall occurred at a height of 0.7m above the base of the wall, and reduced its width by 0.55m. Some soil and shillet, F27, deposited in the doorway contained animal bone and shell, and is probably a continuation of the soil F19 within the oratory.

At the east end of the interior, two large features were cut into the boulder clay. F38e was ovoid in plan and measured 1.1m east/west by 0.7m north/south. The sides sloped steeply to a depth of 0.5m. It projected by 0.08m beneath the north wall of the oratory. The fill of the cut was a fairly sterile orange/brown mixed gravel and till. Large, thin fractured sandstone slabs, pitched into the upper fill of the feature, had probably originally functioned as a lid on the pit.

F38d, sited very close by, measured 1.12m east/west by 1.09m north/south and was square in plan. It had vertically cut edges, with a depth of 0.65m. Thin sandstone slabs were set on edge around the east and south sides of F38d. The fill was a very heavy, dark grey/black gritty clay silt, which was continually wet during excavation as water bubbled up from the base of the pit. A sample of charcoal, retrieved from the fill by flotation in sea-water, yielded a date of 365 ± 55 BP, cal. AD 1448–1636 (UCLA-2873H).

Both F38d and F38e were dug to precisely the same depth below ground level. The notable elements of these two pits are the thin slab linings of the square pit and the deliberate attempt to provide them with stone lids. A deposit of dark, charcoal-enriched silts, F35, accumulated over the pits at the eastern end. This contained stones pitching downwards into F38d, and disturbing somewhat the stone capping of the pit. A thin sandstone slab, F33, was set into the underlying silts F35 at the east side of the oratory.

Outside the oratory, a fairly thick accumulation of dark soil, F17, with a high food refuse content, was banked up against the blockage of the west doorway. Several sacks of marine shell and quantities of animal bone, including cattle horn, were retrieved from the soil. It filled a hollow directly in front of the doorway, where the paving F30 had not been cut away by graves, and had evidently been kept clear of rubble and debris. At least two episodes in the deposition of the midden were apparent, separated by a layer of large rubble blocks. Several of these slabs had evidently toppled off the oratory structure. The presence of the midden-type soil in this location suggests that it was deposited by the occupants of the oratory, and that blockage F15 never did reach the full height of the original door lintel, its function being more that of a half-door or window.

No similar material would have survived outside the east doorway of the structure, as the sea would have encroached here in winter storms and presumably washed much of the soil away.

Deposits of soil/shillet and small rubble blocks were excavated from the immediate vicinity of the oratory. Spits of this material at the east end were numbered F12; contemporary with midden F17 at the west end was rubble and

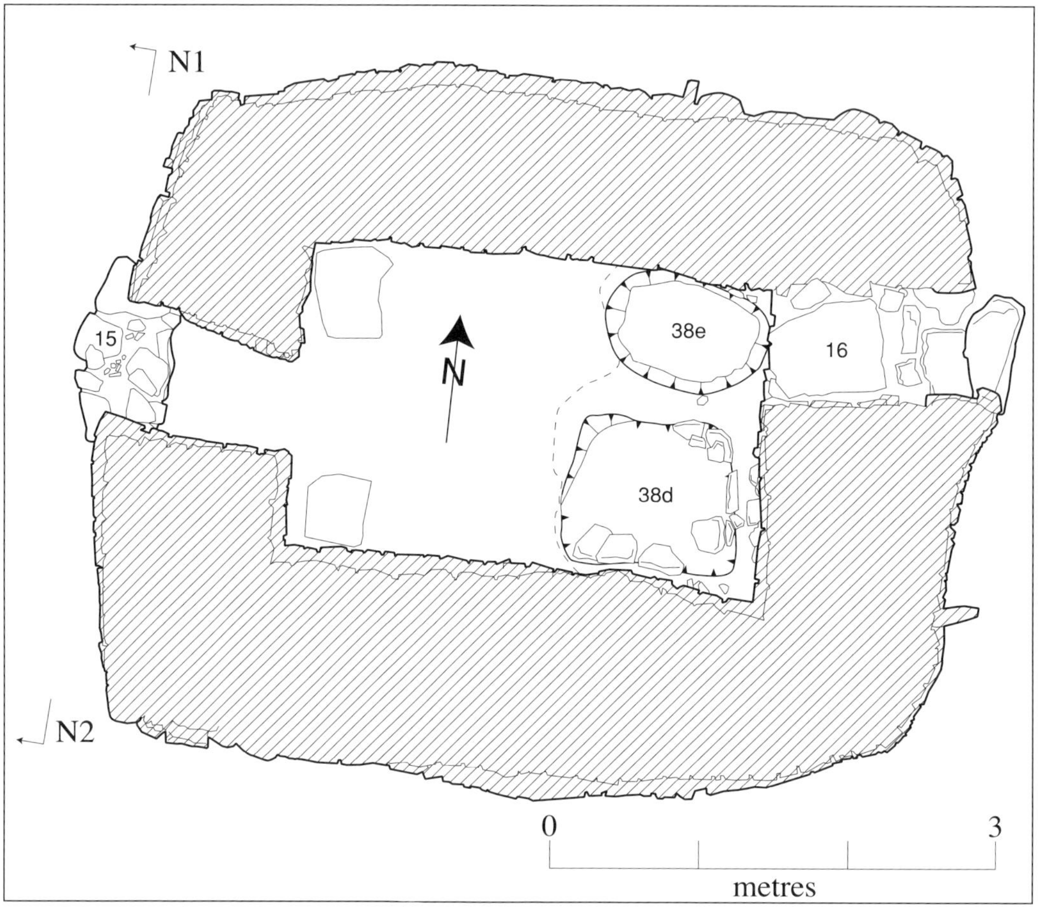

92—Period 3 features inside the oratory. *(C. McHale)*

shillet F18, which, in contrast, had a low food refuse content.

The dereliction of the oratory continued. The interior was infilled with rubble, F9. This comprised some enormous slabs, notably at the west end of the building. One of these, which measured over 1.75m in length, is likely to have been the lintel head over the west doorway.

Outside the oratory, rubble spill F2 (0.7–0.8m in maximum depth) accumulated over the graves to the east of the church and *leacht* F7. The accumulation appears to have taken place from the late thirteenth century through to the eighteenth century. Outside the west doorway of the oratory a small hoard of silver pennies of Edward I were deposited, at a depth of *c.* 0.3m below the sod level (see finds catalogue). The pennies were minted some time after 1279.

Two pieces of post-medieval musket shot were recovered from the rubble spill that overlay the *leacht* F7, and a three-pound cannon ball was recovered from the rubble on the north side of the shrine. These may date from the usage of the island as a mooring-point for the ships of pirates and smugglers in the eighteenth century.

An account of 1728 relates one particular episode involving the brigantine of the Widow Magee, moored off Loughan Island (Pochin-Mould 1978, 54).

A second usage of the oratory, dating probably from the later eighteenth and nineteenth centuries, was as a *ceallunach*. Small areas within what was by then a rubble mound appear to have been used as infants' graves (F4 and F6). No bones survived, but darker, more humic soil occurred within small, regularly set stone placings in the upper levels of the rubble. A small stone-lined grave, F14.4, occurred outside the oratory. Otherwise, babies' graves were concentrated in the midden around the drystone hut (see trench A). Further loose soil, F5, occurred beneath the turf layer F1 within the oratory.

At quite a late stage, probably when the rubble had filled the oratory, the doorway F16 at the east end was deliberately blocked up with crudely faced masonry, F11. A mound of large rubble slabs, F8, appears to have been subsequently deliberately deposited outside the east end of the oratory. The mound stood to a height of 0.7m and tailed off to the east in a roughly trapezoidal shape. It was unrevetted.

The medieval graveyard

Towards the eastern side of trench A, excavated in 1994, ranks of extended adult burials were uncovered. Several of these were badly truncated and disturbed by later infant interrals, but in no case could it be seen that an adult interral post-dated an infant burial. In one case an adult burial, Sk. 387/396, had been partially cut away by another adult burial, Sk. 341. Several of the graves were lintelled, i.e. covered with large flat slabs, while most of the others had the remains of stone lining along the sides, with smaller stones on top of the body, and could be termed 'long cists'.

None of the adult burials at Illaunloughan produced grave-finds; the presence of a hollow bone cylinder from grave 340 (see below) is more than likely coincidental. Few graves of adults contained evidence for coffins, and it is probable that these are late. Included in these are a group of burials outside the west doorway of the oratory and another at the very northern margin of the site, just inside the enclosure wall in trench D (burial F418). One section of the coffin planks from this latter grave were held together with a long, copper-coated nail, and may have been reused from a boat.

Ranks of graves, all oriented west/east and concentrated outside the west doorway of the oratory, were excavated in 1993. Two, at least (F24 and F104), are of a lintel grave variant, and had small, regularly sized quartz pebbles placed neatly around the edges of the slab bases of the graves. All the other graves had quartz present, and all had slabs along their sides. All were filled or sealed by redeposited gravel and shillet. The preservation of bone varied from excellent to complete absence.

Several skeletons appear to have been interred as part of family groups, and several graves were reused. A summary of grave types and burials is presented in Appendix 5.

Burial F340, a female placed in a classic lintel grave, some distance from the west door of the oratory, was initially taken to be medieval in date. However, radiocarbon analysis returned a date of AD 1638–1955 (UB-4109).

The *ceallunach*

The area outside the drystone hut was utilised as a *ceallunach* or burial-ground for infants. There is scant literature on the practice of utilising 'holy places' as burial-grounds for unbaptised infants, but it may have continued in some parts of the country into the 1950s. The insertion of the infant graves resulted in considerable disturbance to the underlying midden, as the graves were dug quite deep.

Over 100 discrete infant burials were excavated. Most of the graves were marked by crude headstones. Many of the infants had been buried in small wooden coffins, where, apart from the nails, timber in fragmentary condition survived. This was identifiable in many cases as Scots pine, imported from the eighteenth century onwards (Deevy and O'Sullivan, Appendix 4).

Many of the infants were additionally protected by placement in stone-lined and slab-covered graves. A small number of infant burials yielded shroud pins; otherwise there were no grave-goods, apart from quartz pebbles. Children up to the age of perhaps three or four also formed part of this group of late burials, although most of the remains were of neonates. It seems likely that children of such an age would have been baptised, and it is curious that they would have been interred in irregular burial-grounds. It was notable that the preservation of bone of the neonates was better than that of the older children, a factor apparent at other excavation sites (Mays 1993, 886). A full report on the burials, including the *ceallunach* phase, has been undertaken by Laureen Buckley (Appendix 5).

Trench C: the reliquary shrine

The main focus of excavation work in 1993 was concentrated on the reliquary shrine, and the large mound on which it was sited. A trench measuring *c.* 8.5m north/south by 11m east/west, encompassing the shrine and the mound, was opened. Semi-erect kerbstones were apparent in the mound structure, particularly on the south side, prior to excavation, and an 'entrance feature' on the west side, noted in Henry's survey, was visible. Full excavation of the reliquary was accomplished in 1993, and excavation and reconstruction of the substantial rubble mound was completed in 1994.

Period 1: the shrine

Several features that pre-date the construction of the shrine mound were excavated in 1994. A fairly extensive old ground surface, F196, was sealed beneath the mound material of the shrine. This was a soft grey/black peaty silt that occurred between the bedrock ridges. It was clearly cut by three graves.

Grave 216 cut through bedrock and measured 1.8m east/west by 0.6m north/south by 0.41m in depth. The fill, F217, was a dark brown inorganic shillet and silt. Few fragments of disarticulated bone were retrieved from the fill, but among these was a piece recognisable as the end of a human femur (see Appendix 5). Several quartz pebbles were also recovered from the fill. The central reliquary shrine (see below) had been constructed on top of this grave.

F230 was some 2.5m further east of grave 216, and also quite clearly cut through the old ground surface silt. It measured 1.6m east/west by 0.45m north/south, with a depth of 0.51m. No bone remained in the gravelly, inorganic fill.

The third grave, F223, lay 2.8m south of 216. It measured at least 1.3m in length (east/west), 0.6m in width and 0.52m in depth. There was a clear edge cutting the old ground surface on the north side of the grave, but the south side was unclear where the later kerbing of the mound had been inserted. Fragments of bone from a human ulna (Laureen Buckley, Appendix 5) were recovered from the fill. This grave had been covered with small rocks and white quartz pebbles.

All three cuts are evidently graves. All are oriented east-west. The presence of disarticulated human bone in grave 216, particularly the femur fragment towards the western (head) end of the grave, suggests the possibility that these may originally have been the graves of the individuals later translated into the reliquary shrine. Testing of this theory through DNA comparison with the bone from the reliquary shrine has not been conclusive, however (see Appendix 3). These three graves are evidently special, set as they are in a place away from the oratory and clustered together on top of a bedrock ridge. It is possible that at least one of these graves was marked in some way prior to the construction of the shrine mound and the reliquary, which would have removed most of the traces of an earlier structure. This special focus is paralleled at Whithorn (Hill 1997).

Period 2: construction of the shrine mound (Fig. 44)

The old ground level F154 (equivalent to 196, where it occurs beneath the shrine mound) was a thin (*c.* 0.1m max.) layer of dark grey peaty silt, which directly overlay the iron-stained boulder clay around the western side and part of the southern side of the shrine mound. It occurred only in the immediate (*c.* 0.2m) environs of the stone kerb of the mound, where it was adequately protected, through gravel slippage, from weathering and other disturbances. The silt contained small fragments of carbonised matter, probably peat.

Removal of the sod cover F150, which averaged 0.15–0.2m in thickness, exposed rubble and shillet slippage that covered the mound proper. This was removed to display the kerbing of the mound and various features around the shrine.

The shrine mound was constructed on uneven ground, with an east/west ridge of bedrock at its northern (seaward) side, which falls sharply away to both north and south. The builders overcame this problem through the deposition of large quantities of fine pea-gravel, which could be gathered from the shore of the island. This is similar material to that comprising the terrace on which the oratory is built. The gravel, F155, was retained in a sequence of kerbs (F184). Over time much of the gravel had spilled downslope over the stones of the kerbing, where it sealed an old ground surface.

Overlying the gravel slip, the ground level around the mound was overlain by brown/grey loam and rubble, F152. This consisted mainly of rubble spill from the mound. No stratification was evident in the *c.* 0.4m-deep deposit.

The mound measures 9m east/west by 7.6m north/south. It has sustained considerable erosion of the kerbing and the rubble/gravel core material on the west side, but the overall planning of the kerbing is evident. The shape is rectangular and the structure is generally angular, but with predominant rounded corners, in contrast, at the south-west side. It consists of three quite closely spaced kerbs, which occur towards the outside of the mound. These are composed of both vertically set slabs and drystone coursed masonry—these two methods occur side by side. The vertically set slabs were evidently preferred, however, and have proved to be the wiser choice.

The mound rises from ground level on the south side to a height in excess of 1.5m in the central part and drops away sharply at the north edge of the island (see Fig. 44). Rubble and gravel core material up to 1m in depth had been deposited over the original ground surface, to create a level platform on which to build the reliquary shrine. Excavation did not result in the total removal of this gravel, as it was thought unwise to destabilise the kerbing of the mound. A depth of over 0.4m of gravel was excavated at the east end of the mound (see below), and all the redeposited material was removed from beneath the central, paved area.

Quartz pebbles occurred in profusion throughout the gravel, as did minute pieces of marine shell and charcoal. While the quartz could have been collected with the gravel from the shore, its sheer quantity indicates its special significance to the builders. The mound, too, was littered with small quartz boulders and pebbles.

A flight of rough, shallow steps, F183, on the west side of the mound led to a level paved area, F198, around the tomb and reliquary shrine. The steps were composed of thick sandstone slabs and had a gentle rise. Vertically set slabs, set parallel to the steps at a distance of 0.8m on their northern side, extended from the outer kerb of the mound. No evidence for such slabs on the south side of the steps was apparent. The paved area, F198, which abutted the drystone kerbing of tomb 186, measured 4.5m north/south by 5.2m east/west and was delimited by a low kerb on the south and north sides. This was not set into the core of the mound, as was the case on the east side. The paving was quite loosely bedded into the underlying gravel F214 and was not closely fitted, except on the west side, where it was composed of a number of large slabs. One of these, of slate, had a quarrying hole. The paving was numbered (for reinstatement) and removed in 1994, and the pea-gravel F214, in which it was bedded, was removed. This measured up to 0.15m in depth. A silver penny, 214:1, of Irish Viking type with a circulation date of AD 1020–35 was recovered from the gravel. The gravel underlay the drystone masonry of the reliquary shrine.

The tomb on which the slabs of the shrine were set was placed off-centre to the mound, towards the south-west side. The tomb was almost square in shape, measuring 2.3m north/south by 2.56m east/west at its widest point. The drystone masonry of its outer face was well coursed and remained in good condition. Care had evidently been taken in choosing the stones. It stood to a maximum height of 0.45m (4–5 courses) above the paving that surrounded it.

The two large slabs that were set on top of the tomb were removed prior to excavation of the underlying structure. These slabs, of Valentia slate, had evidently slipped from their former position, and the precarious position in which they had rested for some time was apparent on removal. The northern slab was entirely dependent on the southern, and the structure was held upright only by the sod. When this was removed, both slabs were loose in their shallow sockets. The socket, F166, for the southern slab was narrow (the width of the stone), measuring from 0.16m to 0.3m in depth.

The southern slab is 1.35m high, 1.3m wide and 0.12m thick. It stood 19° from the vertical, inclining to the north. The top of the slab is irregular, with two distinct semicircular notches. A circular hole approximately halfway down the stone most likely resulted from quarrying.

The northern slab inclined at an angle of 52° from the vertical, resting on the southern slab. It measures 1.28m in length, 1.38m in width, and is 0.12m thick. It, too, has a semicircular notch in the top. Both stones are weathered, and coated with lichens on their outer faces.

The end slabs of the shrine are missing. No likely candidates were recovered during the 1993 season of excavation.

The upper level, F169, inside the shrine consisted of rooted topsoil and pea-gravel, with abundant quartz pebbles occurring throughout. A fragment of bottle glass and numerous bird bones (shags used the shrine for shelter) indicated that the upper levels were disturbed. Fragments of decayed, disarticulated animal and bird bone were also recovered.

The semi-articulated bones of an infant, F185, were recovered from the north-west quadrant of the tomb. Only the pelvis and legs survived. No grave-cut in the gravel was evident, and the grave was not marked in any way. This burial is likely to date from the use of the island as a *ceallunach* in the eighteenth/nineteenth centuries. The burial contaminated the underlying deposit, F182 (see below). It is likely also that the insertion of the infant aided in the displacement of the northern slab of the shrine.

The undisturbed soil beneath F169 consisted of pea-gravel and brown silt, F171, with occasional beach pebbles and abundant quartz. A fragment of human cranium, possibly from Sk. 185 (above), was recovered from the north-west quadrant. Scallop shells, some with perforations, were recovered in quantity.

Further flat slabs and gravel with quartz and scallop shell (F173), which produced fragments of human bone, were removed to expose the slabs of cist 174 (Fig. 93), in the north-east quadrant of the tomb. It measured 0.6m east/west by 0.3m north/south. Inclined sandstone slabs were placed at the east and west ends, and a large sandstone slab formed most of the floor. The cist was 0.1m deep and contained the translated bones (Sk. 176) of an adult individual (report by Laureen Buckley, Appendix 5). The bones present were six long bones, a clavicle, several ribs, a mandible and much of the cranium. The mandible held one tooth only, and it was noted that the occipital was extremely thin. The brow area had been crushed. Gravel and quartz (F175/179) were scattered loosely over the bones and the cist was covered with a large slab.

A second cist, F187, lay to the south of 174. This was formed from pieces of slate set on edge into the gravel, with a (tilted) slab of sandstone set on top. A single scallop shell was placed on the lid. The cist measured 0.6m east/west by 0.2m north/south internally, with a depth of 0.2m. A large sandstone slab formed the base. Human long bones were packed into the cist. Gravel, containing quartz pebbles, scallop shell and occasional flecks of charcoal, was scattered loosely over the bones.

In the north-west quadrant of the shrine the bedrock had a small crevice, and traces of a black, peaty soil cover, F196, survived. The uneven ground was levelled with deposits of gravel, F191, F195 and F182. This contained abundant quartz pebbles and scallop shells.

Some of the scallop shells from the shrine have been perforated, and they may have been suspended from cords. The sea in the immediate area of Illaunloughan is still a rich harvesting-ground for scallops.

The shrine is reputed locally to cure sore eyes.

The shrine mound (Figs 44a and b, 50a)

Excavation of the east side of the mound in 1993 resulted in the removal of *c.* 0.45m of the gravel core. Several extended burials, in varying degrees of preservation, were uncovered.

All were oriented east/west, with the head to the west. Sk. 181 and Sk. 172 survived as skulls only. Sk. 181 appears to have been disturbed when the inner eastern kerb of the mound was constructed. Sk. 189 survived as patches of bone only, and Sk. 177, on the extreme northern side of the mound, was likewise in very poor condition.

The best preserved, Sk. 180, overlay the earlier Sk. 192 in the same grave. What are probably the skull and shoulders of 192 (labelled 197) were placed towards the feet of the later skeleton. The skull of Sk. 180 extended beneath the inner, eastern kerb of the mound. These burials are all contained within the eastern kerbing of the shrine mound. Their insertion had caused several of the kerbstones to slip from their original position. All post-date the construction of the mound.

On the north-west side of the mound, a square cist-like area, F193, delimited by parallel, vertically set slabs, was apparent in the mound matter. It measured 1.3m in diameter, with a depth of nearly 0.4m. A ridge of bedrock formed the south side, while the north side was formed by the (collapsed) secondary kerb of the mound. The floor was roughly paved. The area was filled with gravel, throughout which numerous quartz pebbles occurred. The structure was covered with rubble. No bone survived, although the feature is likely to have been a grave. It is too small to have held an extended inhumation, and may perhaps have been constructed to hold translated bones.

The enclosure: trenches A and D (Fig. 84)

An area immediately to the north of the drystone hut F49 was excavated in 1993, to examine and establish the nature of the enclosing ridge, F91, at the west side of the island. Where the site for the hut had been quarried, an outcrop of bedrock, *c.* 1.1m wide, had been left *in situ* by the builders. Two to three courses of large stones, up to 0.6m in diameter, were closely set along the top of the rock ridge. These were not removed during the 1993 season of excavation. The remaining height of the enclosure above bedrock is *c.* 0.8m.

Rough paving, F96, overlay the dumped deposits of sandstone shillet to the north of the hut, extending eastwards from the enclosure F91 to the plinth F90.

A thin sod covering, 0.12m deep, overlay the enclosure and the rubble collapse both from the enclosure and from the drystone hut.

Trench D was opened in 1994 and measured 10m north/south by 2m east/west, with a projection of 2.8m eastwards at the southern end. It is clear from the pre-excavation site survey that the height of the enclosing ridge tailed off eastwards, where the north face of the island had been eroded by the sea. Removal of the turf and earth overlying the enclosure revealed, however, that a substantial stone-faced construction, F91, stood in this area to a height of almost 0.5m. The wall here measured 1.6m in width and was faced internally and externally with rectangular sandstone blocks. The core of the enclosing wall was of rubble and tightly packed shillet. Surprisingly little rubble debris occurred within the wall, where a localised area of what appears to be the original sod covering (OGS) survived in the lee of the enclosure. This layer, F418, was a dark, greasy grey/black peaty silt. Late burials, including those of many infants, were found in this area up to 0.5m from the enclosure wall.

Outside the enclosure, the ground sloped steeply down to the sea. Considerable

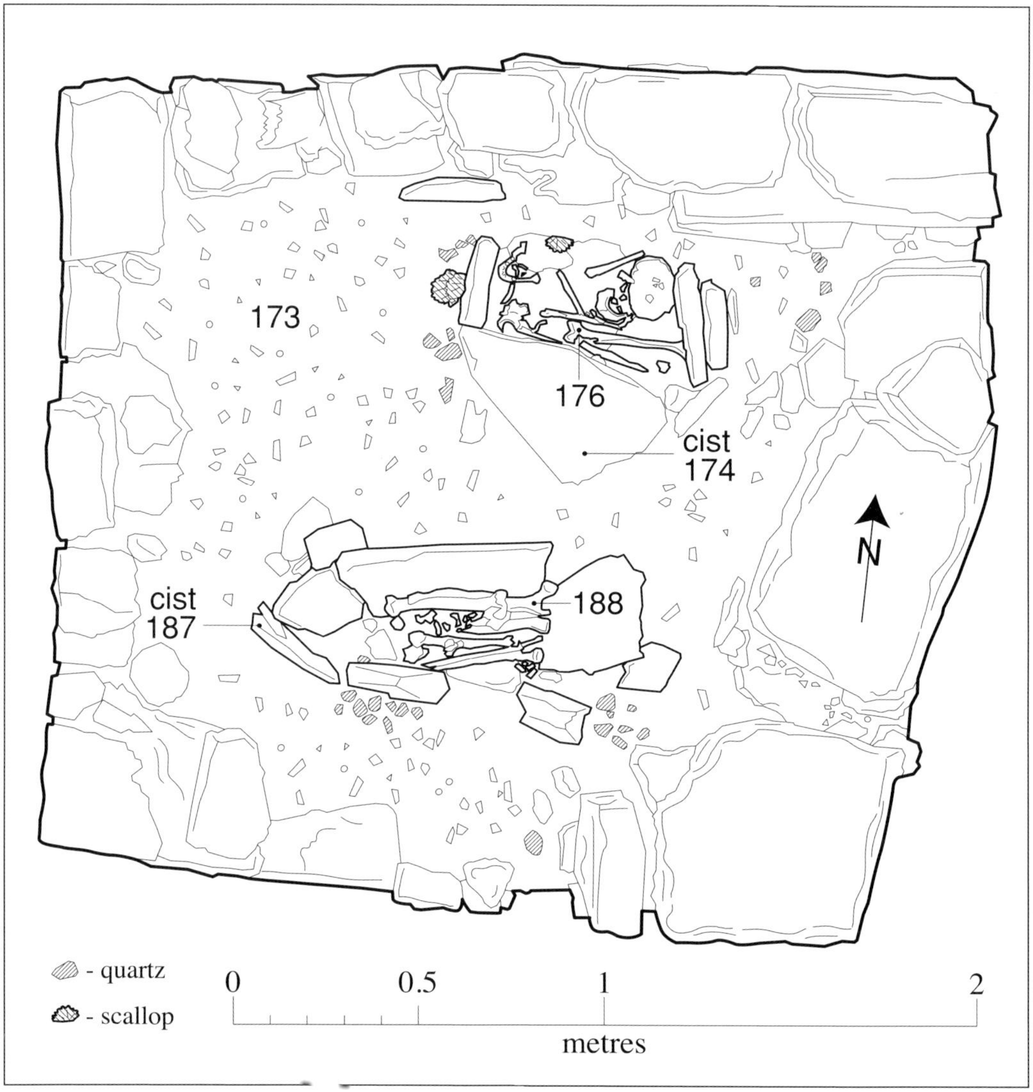

93—Detail of translated bones in the cists, reliquary shrine. *(C. McHale)*

erosion of the north face of the island had occurred, but the outer face of the wall was still evident. A plinth, with a roughly paved surface, extended for 1m from the north face of the enclosure wall. Probing of the area indicated that the plinth widens out a short distance to the west of trench D, and it is possible that the remains of a rough stone shelter exist here.

The overlying topsoil cover, F419, within the enclosure was thin (up to 0.2m) and rooted, containing shillet and small stones throughout. Huts A and B were built up against the enclosure, indicating that this dated from the initial monastic occupation of the island.

PART 3:
THE FINDS

Claire Walsh

10

The finds

The finds are catalogued by material type. All are labelled with the site prefix 92E87 and the number of the feature from which they came. The date and context of each find are given, where applicable.

The assemblage can be paralleled at other sites of a similar period; however, the quantity of small personal decorative objects of copper alloy from this site is notable. Several personal objects of bone or antler were also recovered, along with a fragment of a glass bead. Carved bone pins, fragments of antler comb plates and drilled bone beads are present. Fragments of two stone or lignite bracelets were also recovered.

Many of the objects are mundane domestic tools, such as whetstones and knives, awls or punches. No pottery was associated with the primary use of the site, and in contrast to Church Island, Valentia Harbour, only a single sherd of medieval pottery was recovered. There was a notable absence of imported wares from the primary levels; however, E-ware was not present at Church Island, Valentia Harbour, nor from the sites of comparable date at Bray Head (Hayden and Walsh, forthcoming).

Several of the finds have strong Scandinavian or Hiberno-Scandinavian cultural associations. These include the coin 214:1 (below) of *c.* 1020–35, the perforated whetstone (401:7) and the hollow bone cylinder (340:1). The suspension mechanism for a balance (60:1) is also indicative of Scandinavian contact. None of these finds were recovered from primary levels on the site. They indicate a strong contact with local settlement of probable Norse origin within the area. The settlement on Beginish, excavated in the 1950s by O'Kelly, has recently been subjected to a more thorough interpretation of the evidence (Sheehan *et al.* 2001). These authors conclude that there is strong evidence for a tenth/eleventh-century Scandinavian settlement on Beginish.

There is a wide-ranging assemblage of finds associated with the casting of fine copper-alloy objects from the primary phase of occupation. This is discussed as a separate grouping.

There are few finds that can be related directly to the religious use of the site, apart from the highly significant placement of quartz pebbles and perforated scallops in the reliquary shrine. Several crudely fashioned crosses were recovered as surface or unstratified finds from the site. None have any surface decoration or other distinguishing marks. These are similar to crosses found at Skellig Michael. None were utilised as burial-markers.

Coins (kindly identified by Michael Kenny, National Museum of Ireland)
92E87:214:1. Silver coin (Fig. 94). This was recovered from gravel F214 beneath the paving on the shrine. The coin is silver, of Irish Viking type, probably minted in Dublin, with a circulation period of 1020–35. It is a reduced-weight imitation of a Long Cross penny of Aethelred II, and belongs to the generally earlier grouping, Phase II. The head faces left, the eye is set back, and there are no ears. Clothing is represented by four strokes, fastened at the left by a button. There is a pellet in front of the nose, and a cross with rounded terminals behind the neck. A series of meaningless strokes represent pseudo-lettering: the coins were minted by illiterate moneyers. There are several corrosion holes in the coin, and the reverse is pitted and very worn.

92E87:2:1–6. Six silver pennies were recovered in a group from the rubble spill F2, outside the west doorway of the oratory trench. The coins were deposited in a group, possibly in a grave.

The coins are, with the exception of no. 4, standard issues of Edwardian silver pennies. No. 4, from the mint of Berwick-on-Tweed, differs in style from the normal classes. The town changed hands on a number of occasions between the English and the Scots and some of the material produced is of very crude workmanship.

1. Edward I (1272–1307).
O.: + EDW R ANGL DNS HYB. Late S, barred A.
Crescent-shaped contraction marks.
R.: CIVITAS LONDON.
Fox Class III (1280–1).

2. Edward I (1272–1307).
O.: +EDWAR R ANGL DNS HYB. Bifoliate crown.
R.: CIVITAS LONDON.
Fox Class 10b (1302–10).

3. Edward I (1272–1307).
O.: + EDWA R ANGL DNS HYB. Bifoliate crown.
R.: CIVITAS CANTOR (Canterbury).
Fox Class 10. North Class 101 (1302–10).

4. Edward I (1272–1307).
O.: + EDW R ANGL DNS HYB.
R.: VILLA BERRE (WYC) 1 (Berwick-on-Tweed).
North Class II (1297–8).

5. Edward III (1327–77).
O.: + EDW R ANGL DNS HYB. Annulet stops.
R.: CIVITAS LONDON.
Florin type (1344–51).

6. Edward I (1272–1307).
O.: + EDW R ANGL DNS HYB.
R.: CIVITAS VATERFOR (Waterford).
North Class 11 (1280–3).

Copper/bronze alloy

92E87:82:2 (Fig. 94). Spiral-ringed, baluster-headed ringed pin (Fanning 1994, 13–14). Faceted baluster head, lozenge decorated with three incised dots; abraded collar. 'Plain' ring, with narrowed ends, and shallow pin-rest towards one of the terminals. Ornamentation of three irregular groupings of incised lines on ring. Shank broken, curve evident. L 34mm, D 24mm.

Raghnall Ó Floinn (pers. comm.) has commented that pins of this type have been recovered from E-ware contexts at Garryduff and Lagore, and from Phase Y at Moynagh Lough, dated to *c.* 740–80. Thus a seventh–eighth-century date is indicated, rather than the longer chronology proposed by Fanning.

Ring and pin found separately, but in close proximity, in trench A, lower/middle level of the midden.

92E87:50:9 (Fig. 94). Annular brooch-pin head. Plain ring, undecorated flat back, with expanded, D-shaped, fused terminals. D-shaped panel of parallel incised grooves above an extended piece in the form of an animal with large round eyes and round snout. The pin, now missing, was hinged, held in a constriction in the centre of the hoop, with raised buffers to either side. The pin shaft extended from the animal's mouth, and may have been held fast between two small projections at the back of the brooch: this may, alternatively, have held thread attached to the clothing. D 17mm.

Ó Floinn (1989, 194) observes that the plain ring with D-shaped cross-section is a feature of Irish brooches normally dated to the ninth century, while the small size of the ring and movable pin is more comparable with brooches of the ninth century and later. Ó Floinn (pers. comm.) now believes that this type is more likely to date from the seventh/eighth century. There is a group of late zoomorphic

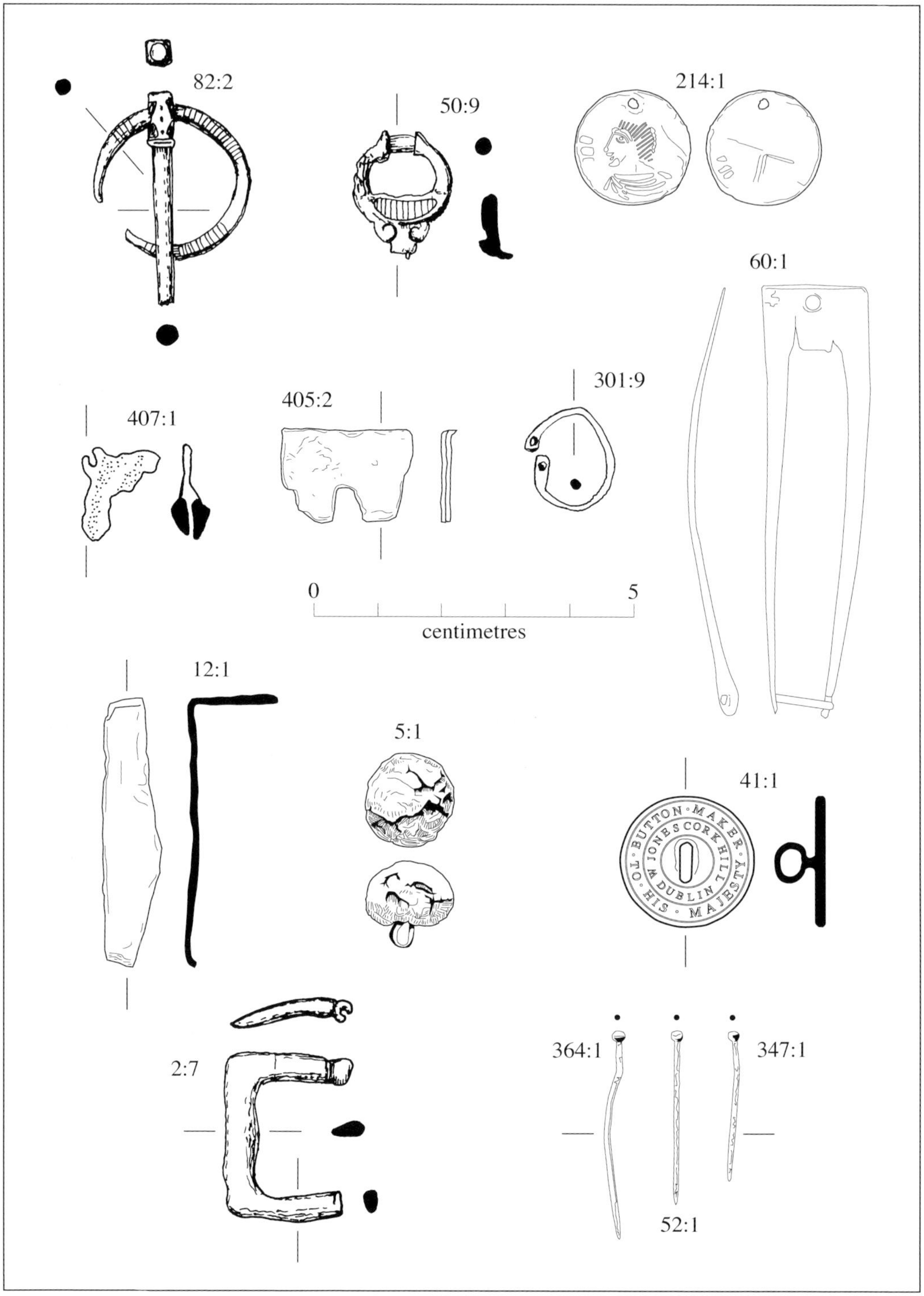

94—Small finds: silver and copper alloy.

penannulars with hoops of D-shaped cross-section (Kilbride-Jones, type D), one of which, from Gransha, Co. Down, comes from levels containing E-ware. The decoration on the terminals would be consistent with such a date.

From trench A, midden, middle level.

92E87:407:1 (Fig. 94). Very corroded copper-alloy object. A small, broken, semicircular projection from one end suggests that it may have been part of a small ring-brooch or other such item. Flat, where not corroded. D 15mm. From sealed midden deposit, trench A, level 2.

92E87:405:2 (Fig. 94). Copper-alloy flat object, of folded sheet metal, possibly a belt end or part of a buckle plate, now broken at both ends. Part of a possible angular rivet-hole remains. W 21mm. From sealed midden deposit, trench A, level 2.

92E87:301:9 (Fig. 94). Fastener or loop. Plain round-sectioned loop, with ovoid eye at one terminal and small hammered rivet present in similar eye at other terminal. Probably used as a cloth-fastener. D 16mm. From upper, disturbed level of midden, trench A.

92E87:60:1 (Fig. 94). Suspension mechanism for a balance. Undecorated rectangular end with round perforation for chain or loop. Hinged pin holds the two springing arms; pointer missing. L 68mm, W 17mm. Recovered from a disturbed context, an eighteenth/nineteenth-century infant's burial, trench A.

In the eighth and ninth centuries, a currency system with a basic unit of an ounce of silver replaced the earlier system of exchange based on the *set* (a heifer or half a milch cow) (Ó Corráin 1972, 73). Balances such as this one were widespread throughout the Viking world, and were used for weighing precious metals in exact quantities (Crawford 1987, 126). They are found in Hiberno-Norse urban centres such as Dublin (Wallace *et al.* 1988), Waterford (Hurley *et al.* 1997, 466) and York (Richards 1991, 96), and are a particularly significant element of the grave-furniture of the Vikings of the Western Isles (Crawford, *op. cit.*).

92E87:12:1 (Fig. 94). Undecorated strip of copper-alloy sheeting, cut straight along one side. Bent at both ends (one broken at bend) to a right angle, and tapering to a blunt, narrow end. From trench B, level 6.

92E87:5:1 (Fig. 94). Copper-alloy button. The head is domed and has exploded, and is very pitted and corroded, with no apparent ornamentation. A simple loop is set into the back. Buttons were probably in use in Ireland from the thirteenth century onwards. Similar buttons, dated to the thirteenth century, are recorded from excavations in London (Egan and Pritchard 1991, 275). D 12mm. From level 7, trench B.

92E87:41:1 (Fig. 94). Modern button, probably originally cloth-covered and possibly part of a uniform. Inscription on back reads 'W. JONES CORK HILL DUBLIN BUTTON. MAKER. TO. HIS. MAJESTY'.

92E87:2:7 (Fig. 94). Plain, square to rectangular single-loop buckle frame, incomplete. Separate bar, missing. Pin missing. Sides concave and D-sectioned. Similar buckles are known from medieval London (Egan and Pritchard 1991, 61, 62), as well as from many medieval Irish sites. They have a wide date range. D 26mm. From trench B, level 6.

Shroud pins
Ten shroud pins were recovered from the post-medieval burials of the *ceallunach* phase of the site. Three are illustrated (Fig. 94). All are wire-drawn dress-maker's pins. Two types are represented: spherical-headed (92E87:364:1) and globular-headed (92E87:52:1).

92E87:363:1. Copper-alloy shroud pin fragment, lower half missing. L 8.7mm.

92E87:351:1–4. Copper-alloy shroud pins. Two globular-headed: pin 1, L 21.5mm; pin 2 (in two pieces), L 22.6mm. Two spherical-headed: pin 1, L 23.7mm, with horizontal groove around head; pin 2, L 23.2mm.

92E87:347:1. Copper-alloy shroud pin. Spherical with groove running round head. L 27.7mm.

92E87:308:1. Copper-alloy shroud pin, globular-headed with groove on head. L 25.3mm.

92E87:518:1. Copper-alloy shroud pin, spherical-headed, complete. L 32.5mm.

92E87:505:1. Copper-alloy shroud pin, complete. Lightly corroded. Globular-headed. L 23mm.

92E87:505:2. Copper-alloy shroud pin. Complete but in three pieces. Head quite corroded. L 24.8mm.

Iron
All the iron objects recovered were in a poor state of preservation, and the function of several remains speculative, despite conservation. A range of household tools is present, including knives, possible shears and two possible barrel padlock keys.

Knives

92E87:48:1 (Fig. 95). Knife, broken at tip. Cutting edge severely corroded. Straight back, triangular blade section. Whittle tang off-centre on blade, sloping shoulder. Similar to one from the monastic period at Church Island (O'Kelly 1958, fig. 12, 1). L 84.5mm, W 18.5mm. From the rubble infill of the drystone hut, trench A.

92E87:66:2 (Fig. 95). Knife, complete but extremely corroded along blade and tang. Curved back, centrally placed whittle tang, triangular-sectioned blade, now exploded. Pronounced shoulder above tang. L 115mm, W 12.5mm. From lower level of midden, trench A.

92E87:401:4 (Fig. 95). Iron object, incomplete. Rectangular-sectioned shaft tapers at one end, which is highly corroded and chipped. The wider end is unevenly fractured. Possibly part of a blade. L 46mm, W 15mm. From middle level of the midden, trench A.

92E87:459:2 (not illustrated). Extremely corroded iron object, possibly a knife blade. L 80mm, W 18.8mm, T 14mm. From the foundation trench of hut B, period 1.

Possible shears

92E87:411:2 (Fig. 95). Object with looped head. Quite corroded, flat-sectioned, possibly rectangular shank, with massive accretion. Probably a double-shanked, hollow-centred object. There is some suggestion of a widening of the shanks in the centre parts (the recess); the object would therefore most closely resemble a small set of shears, with the ends of the blades fused. The tip is broken. L 114mm, W 26.5mm. From level 1, trench A.

Possible barrel padlock keys

Both of these looped objects correspond to the smaller scale of keys for simple barrel padlocks. These are known from Hiberno-Norse Dublin (Wallace 1998, 212) and from sites in Britain of an early pre-Conquest date (Goodall 1990, 1001). The padlocks would have been used to secure storage chests or boxes.

92E87:66:3 (Fig. 95). Object with looped head, broken at narrow end where beginning of an outward curve is apparent. Square-sectioned shank. Possible barrel padlock key with bit missing (see London Museum Catalogue 1940, fig. 45, and Donaghy 1997, fig. 15.25). L 96mm. From lowest level of midden, trench A.

92E87:411:3 (Fig. 95). Object, very corroded, with looped head and rectangular-sectioned shank. Incomplete and in two pieces. Possibly part of a barrel padlock key. L 54.5mm. From level 1, trench A.

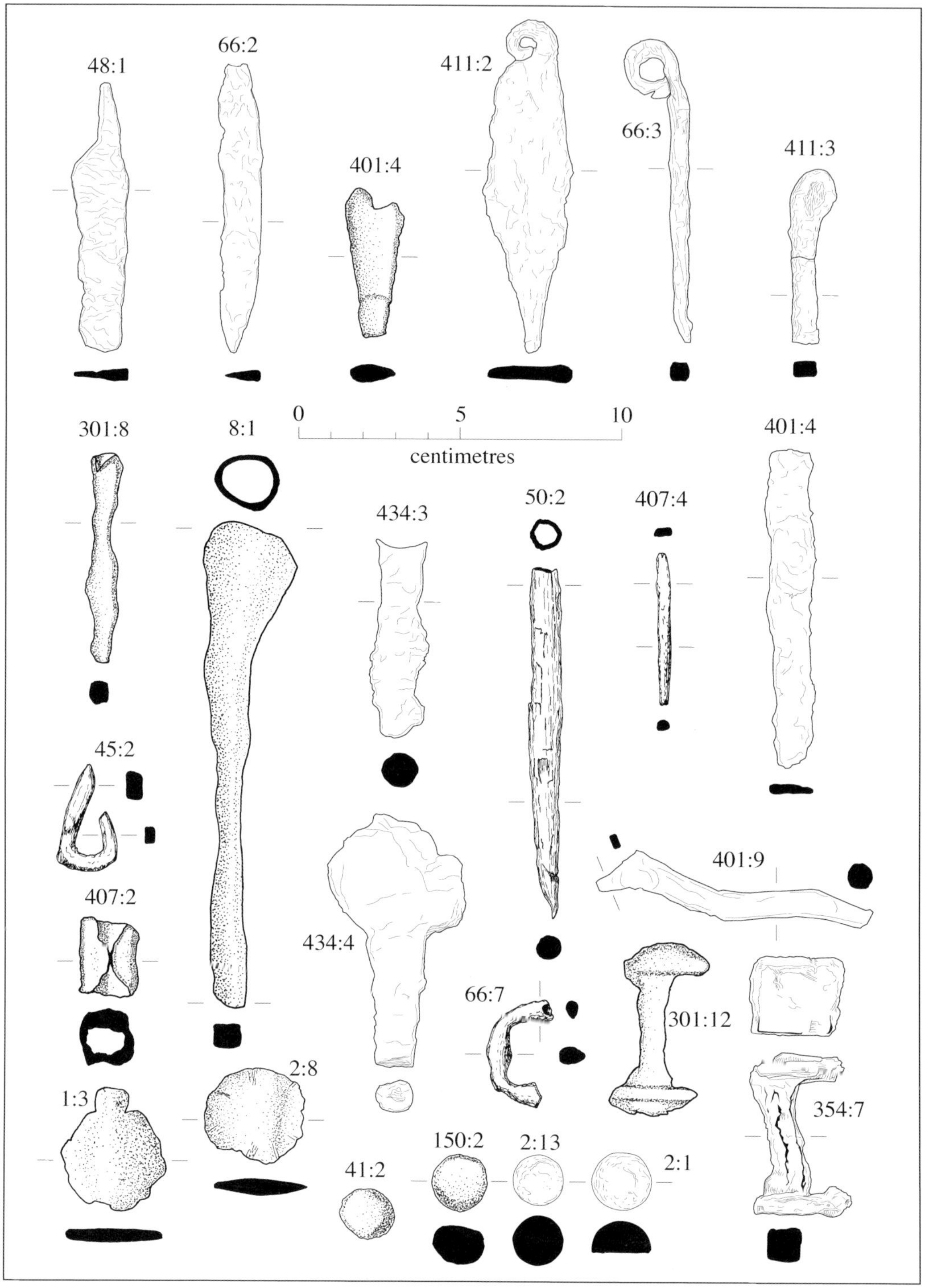

95—Small finds: iron and lead.

Awls and punches

92E87:301:8 (Fig. 95). Socketed punch or awl. Corrosive adherents; tip missing. Round-sectioned socket, square-sectioned shaft. This could have been a centre punch, used in metalworking. L 65.5mm, D 10.5mm (socket). From upper level of midden, trench A.

92E87:8:1 (Fig. 95). Socketed punch. Corroded, in two parts. Round-sectioned socket, square-sectioned shank, tip broken. Punches could have been used by ironworkers, stonemasons or blacksmiths (Goodall 1981, 51, 53). L 151mm, D 19mm (socket). From trench B, level 7.

92E87:434:3 (Fig. 95). Socketed punch or awl. Very corroded. Round shank, rounded blunt tip. L 62.8mm, D 14.4mm (socket). From clearance over hut A.

92E87:50:2 (Fig. 95). Socketed centre punch or awl. Part of tip present. Round-sectioned socket, shaft probably originally square. Function as for 92E87:301:8 above. L 110mm, D 11.5mm (socket). From middle level of midden, trench A.

Miscellaneous tools

92E87:407:4 (Fig. 95). Tool. Small rectangular-sectioned bar, with one narrow end and one slightly splayed end. Could have been used as a small punch. L 48mm, W 4mm. From a sealed level of the midden, trench A.

92E87:401:4 (Fig. 95). Corroded flat strip of iron, starting to curve at broken wider end. Rectangular, flat section. Function unknown; incomplete. L 103.5mm, W 13.5mm. From middle level of midden, trench A.

92E87:45:2 (Fig. 95). Iron hook. Rectangular-sectioned shank. D 18.5mm (head). From upper level of midden, trench A.

92E87:407:2 (Fig. 95) and 92E87:407:3. Two similar objects, perhaps once part of the same piece, although the ends of 407:3 appear to be complete. Corroded folded hoops of iron with hollow centres. Function unknown. D 21mm. From sealed level of the midden, trench A.

92E87:401:9 (Fig. 95). Curved, round-sectioned object, incomplete, with tapering, rectangular-sectioned end, probably incomplete. Possibly a handle. L 90mm. From middle level of midden, trench A.

92E87:514:1 (not illustrated). Curved object, very corroded and incomplete. Function unknown. L 31.2mm. From the fill of a late juvenile's grave.

92E87:434:4 (Fig. 95). Iron object, one end (head?) heavily corroded. Three-sided ovoid section, hollowed shank. Function unknown. L 78.1mm, T 11.5mm. From debris over hut B, period 1.

Buckle
92E87:66:7 (Fig. 95). Buckle, incomplete. Part of the corroded frame only survives, insufficient to determine the true form, whether rectangular, square or D-shaped. W 33mm. From the lowest level of the midden, trench A.

Button
92E87:177:1. Button, of modern type. Corroded iron circular object, with dished upper surface and a central projecting loop on the underside. D 24mm, T 5mm. Recovered during clearance of rubble over grave 177, trench C.

Cannon ball
92E87:150:1. Cannon ball, three-pounder. D 72mm. Recovered from the rubble spill over the north side of the reliquary shrine, trench C.

Unidentified iron objects
92E87:9:1. Very corroded head of iron object. No shank, square in section. From the oratory, period 3.

92E87:12:2. Highly corroded iron object, circular-sectioned shank. L 37.5mm. From the oratory, period 3.

92E87:20:1. Iron rivet or nail in two pieces, heavily corroded on bottom half of shank. Head flattened and partly circular. Shank rectangular in section. L 70mm, D (of head) 19.1mm. From the oratory, period 2.

92E87:54:1. Extremely corroded flat iron strip. L 36.5mm, W 16mm. From ash/charcoal in hut D, period 2.

92E87:66:11. Iron object, heavily corroded with hollowed core, oblong in section. L 24.3mm, W 29.8mm, D of hollow 9.8mm. From the lowest level of the midden, period 1.

92E87:405:3. Heavily corroded, partly circular flattened head of an iron object, probably a nail. D 40mm. From midden over paving outside hut D, period 2.

92E87:433:1. Iron object, heavily corroded. Rectangular-sectioned end. Function unknown. L 42.5mm. From rubble built up against the wall of hut A, period 2–3.

Clench bolts
Two roved nails or clench bolts, both from disturbed levels in the midden, were recovered. These are characteristically used to hold planking together in ships.

92E87:301:12 (Fig. 95). Round-sectioned shank, circular domed nail head and a subrectangular rove. From upper level of midden, trench A.

92E87:354:7 (Fig. 95). Rectangular-sectioned shank, trapezoidal-shaped nail head and a subrectangular rove. From middle level of midden, trench A.

Several nails, apart from the ubiquitous coffin nails, were recovered from the site. The presence of coffin nails is noted in Table 2, Appendix 5.

Lead

Six objects of lead were recovered from the site. All come from the upper levels and date from the late medieval period or later.

92E87:1:3 and 92E87:2:8 (Fig. 95). Exploded musket shot. Recovered from the clearance rubble in the vicinity of the oratory.

92E87:150:2 (Fig. 95). Exploded musket ball. D 16mm. Recovered from the rubble spill over the north side of the shrine. Probably eighteenth-century.

92E87:41:2 (Fig. 95). Musket ball. D 16mm. Recovered from clearance levels at the north side of trench A, close to button 41:1.

92E87:2:13 (Fig. 96). Two musket balls, one with minimal flattening on one side, D 15.7mm, and the other flattened on one side, D 18.2mm.

Bone and antler

Twenty-six circular bone beads were recovered from a localised area within the midden. Various feature numbers have been ascribed to the area over three seasons: F45, F357 and F301 (92E87:301:1 illustrated, Fig. 96). The beads are small, D 9mm, L 3.5, with central to off-centre circular perforations and flattish profiles. Several are quite abraded, with pitted exteriors. Some retain partially polished faces.

The beads appear to have been lathe-drilled (there are frequent notches on the faces) and finished. A few have chatter-marks, apparently saw-cuts, on their faces, where they have been imperfectly finished.

Bone beads are infrequently found in contexts dated to before the medieval period (McGregor 1985, 99). The Illaunloughan beads more closely resemble the well-finished beads of similar manufacture from Northampton (Williams 1979, 318) than the crude examples from the Anglo-Saxon cremation at Spong Hill, Norfolk (Hills 1977, 33 and fig. 135). The beads were recovered from the upper, disturbed levels of the midden, and as incidental finds from eighteenth/nineteenth-century children's burials in trench A. They are likely to derive from a necklace.

Comb fragments
There are four fragments from composite bone or antler combs, two from double-sided combs and two from single-sided combs. Only two combs appear to be represented.

92E87:301:2 (Fig. 96). Tooth-plate of double-sided comb, teeth broken. The plate is pitted superficially and is flat in cross-section. Circular rivet-hole present. There is no evidence of the former presence of the rivet. The teeth are coarse (three per cm) and there is no difference in their gradation on either side. L 12.5mm, D 26.5mm (incomplete), T 2.75mm. Too little survives for classification (Dunlevy 1988, 350).

92E87:301:4 (Fig. 96). Part of tooth-plate of a double-sided comb, teeth broken. Flat in cross-section. Circular rivet-hole present; no evidence for the type of rivet. The teeth are coarse, four per cm. Possibly part of the same comb as 301:2 above. L 8mm (incomplete), W 29mm (incomplete), T 3.5mm. Unclassifiable.

92E87:301:3 (Fig. 96). Tooth-plate of single-sided comb. Flat in cross-section. The teeth are of medium fineness, eight per cm. Part of a single rivet-hole has iron corrosion. L 17mm, W 24mm, T 2mm. Unclassifiable.

All three pieces were recovered from the upper disturbed level of the midden, trench A.

92E87:367:1 (Fig. 96). Tooth-plate of a single-sided comb. Flat in cross-section. Teeth as no. 301:3 above. Part of a rivet-hole has iron corrosion. L 12.5mm, W 29mm, T 2.5mm. Unclassifiable. Probably part of no. 301.3 above. Incidental find in the fill of a medieval grave, trench A.

Pins
92E87:401:1 (Fig. 96). Pin roughout, incomplete. Circular perforation, drilled from both sides. Flat-sectioned and roughly smoothed on one side only. L 47mm (incomplete). From trench A, middle level of the midden.

92E87:401:13 (Fig. 96). Lower part to point of bone pin. Traces of original well-polished surface extant. Undecorated. L 43.3mm. From Trench A, middle level of the midden.

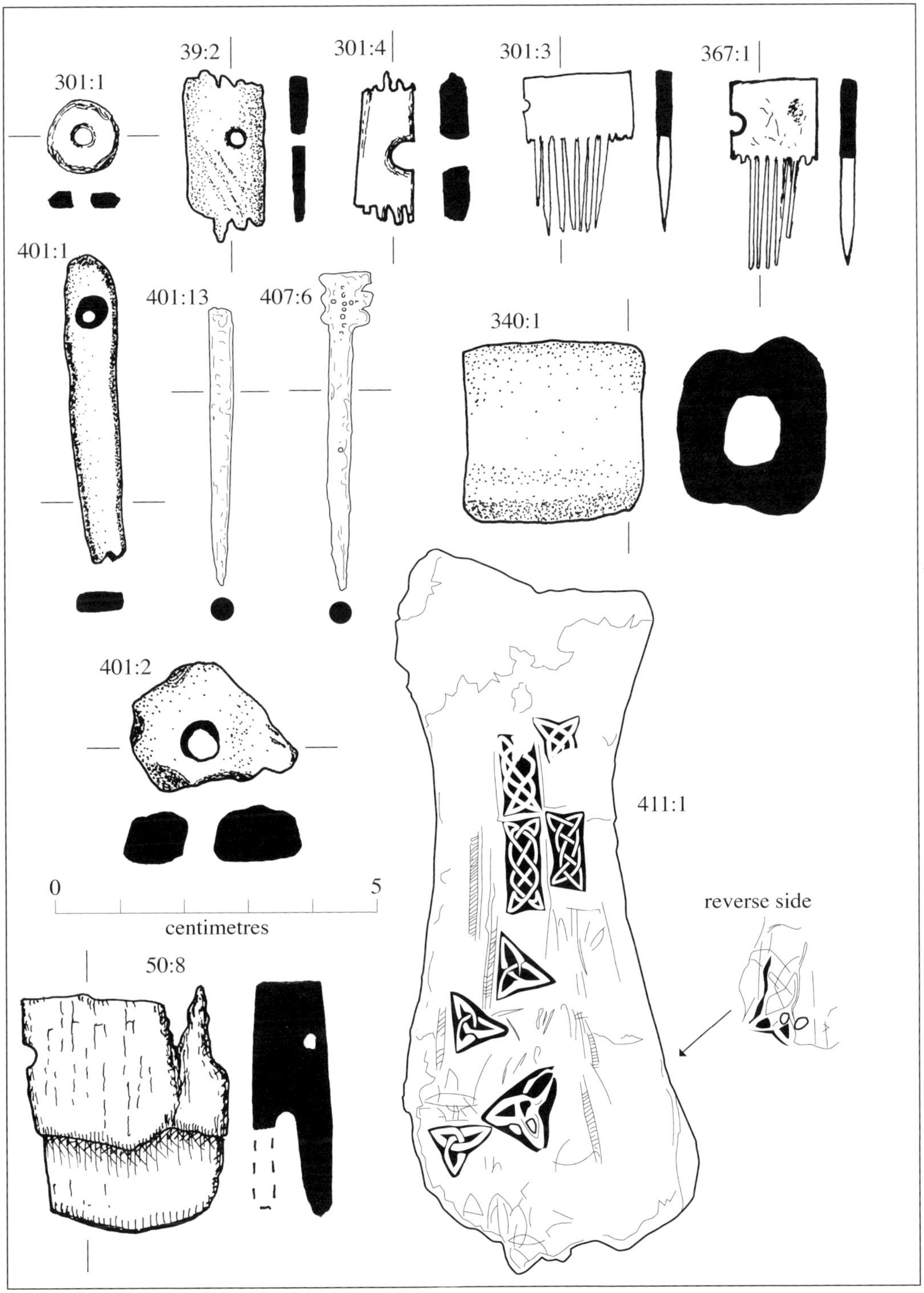

96—Small finds: bone and antler.

92E87:407:6 (Fig. 96). Bone pin with three incisions into the head on either edge, crudely worked. The bone is extremely abraded and demineralised. The top of the head is flat and the head is slightly off-centre to the shaft. The front has a series of deliberate small indentations. The short shaft is slightly curved. L 49.5mm. From a sealed deposit of midden overlying paving 406, hut B, period 1.

Hollow bone cylinder
92E87:340:1 (Fig. 96). Hollow bone cylinder, partially pitted after deposition, otherwise polished. Very common finds from Hiberno-Norse to late twelfth-century levels in Irish towns, these are encountered in both a polished (internal and external) and unpolished state. Seven roughly cut and unpolished cylinders, strung together with a leather thong, were uncovered at Christchurch Place (Gowen 1993, fig. 22). The function of these objects is unknown. An incidental find from the fill of a medieval grave, trench A.

Miscellaneous objects
92E87:401:2 (Fig. 96). Perforated bone. This is a piece of demineralised animal epiphysis, with a round perforation. Function unknown. From the middle level of the midden, trench A.

92E87:50:8 (Fig. 96). Bone object, incomplete. The bone is extremely demineralised and brittle. The object is rectangular, flat-sectioned, with one sawn end. The other end has been divided with a lateral, semicircular groove and is broken on one side. There is a lateral perforation through the object, which is punctuated by a crude rectangular stopped incision. Its function is unknown: it approximates to no recognisable object. L 37mm, W 32mm, T 12mm. From the middle level of the midden, trench A.

Motif-piece
92E87:411:1 (Fig. 96). Motif-piece made from a scapula, possibly of a sheep. The bone has become demineralised and brittle and is fragmented at both ends. One panel of ornamentation is incomplete owing to post-deposition abrasion. Most of the ornamentation occurs on one face. There are some light sketches as well as carved, finished ornamentation in relief. There are two principal recurring motifs. Four of these are rectangular panels of interlaced knots, with another four of triquetra knots in differing sizes. There are four unfinished bands of diagonally hatched motifs; these are similar to the borders on some of the panels on a motif-piece from Lagore crannog, dated to the eighth–early ninth century (Ó Floinn 1989, 176). There are also three areas of very lightly incised motifs: an outline for a rectangular panel, a triquetra knot motif and an enclosed band of diagonally hatched lines. The other side has a single rectangular panel of interlaced knotwork. This has been sketched and carving was started: the motif backs on to a large

triquetra knot on the other face, at the thinnest part of the bone, and the design was abandoned as the bone was pierced through.

Motif-pieces are an Insular Celtic, perhaps Irish, phenomenon; they provide evidence for design as well as manufacture (O'Meadhra 1987, 159). Several have been found at workshop sites such as the workshop at Moynagh Lough, Co. Meath, in use in the first half of the eighth century (Bradley 1993, 76). The designs on the Illaunloughan piece are frequently encountered throughout the early medieval period.

The Illaunloughan motif-piece was recovered in association with the ceramic mould fragments (see below), level 1, trench A.

Glass

Fragments of three glass beads were recovered from the excavation. Two are of the common blue variety (Edwards 1990, 94) and one is two-coloured, grey and blue. A small chip of blue glass was also recovered. None of the pieces, apart from 208:1, came from securely sealed contexts. Glass beads are frequent finds on sites of the early medieval period.

92E87:354:3. Fragment of dark blue barrel-shaped glass bead. L 6mm. From middle level of midden, trench A.

92E87:1:2 (Fig. 97). Fragment of a two-coloured glass bead. The body is grey and opaque, with tiny air bubbles throughout: threads of dark blue glass have been smoothed into the surface in a random pattern. D 8.5mm, L 7mm. Stray find, from trench B.

92E87:311:1 (Fig. 97). Incomplete barrel-shaped dark blue glass bead. Circular perforation. Similar to a bead found at Reask (Fanning 1981, fig. 19, 152). D 7.5mm, L 5.5mm. Incidental find from the feet area of an eighteenth/nineteenth-century child's burial, trench A.

92E208:1. Tiny chip of mid-blue glass. L 7mm. From gravel infilling the terrace, trench B, level 3.

Stone

Quernstone/cross shaft?

92E87:341:1 (Fig. 97). Red sandstone with quartz veins. This was originally identified as part of a lower stone of a quern, but a straight groove lying 120mm from the outside edge and running parallel to it for 75.5mm has given rise to possible suggestions that this may have been (reused?) part of a cross-slab. One side is flat and smooth, the other rough and uneven. The rounded edge is not even or smoothed. The outside edge runs for 203mm. T 48mm, W 153.5mm.

92E87:1:5. A flat and smooth piece of sandstone with regular and tapering edges, suggesting that it may be part of a cross or decorative slab. Rectangular in section. L 289.6mm, W 149.4mm, W at base 90.4mm, T 20.9mm. Unstratified find from rubble clearance, trench A.

Unidentified stone with grooves
92E87:459:1 (Fig. 97). Stone with three grooves at the edges, otherwise appears unworked. Grey fine-grained sandstone, with striations of quartz. The grooves extend from the edge on the flatter side of a rounded beach stone. The grooves are deep and smooth; one is set at a right angle to the others, which themselves are set at 180° to each other. The grooves superficially resemble those on ingot moulds, although considerably smaller and incomplete. There is no evidence for wear on the stone, such as might have arisen with cords or ropes. Its function is unclear. L 228mm, W 205mm, T 93mm. Recovered from the fill of the trench of hut B, level 1.

Unidentified stone
92E87:1:9 (Fig. 98). Stone with flat base; two notches in upper face, one quite crudely done. The upper surface is very smooth. Surface find.

Quartz crystal
92E87:457:1 (Fig. 97). Unworked clear quartz crystal, six-faceted. While a naturally occurring stone, this was found in gravel outside the entrance to hut B, beneath the paving (level 1). It had been deliberately collected. L 30.6mm, W 15.6mm.

Architectural stone
These stones were recovered during clearance of the spoil-heaps and rubble, following excavation, by National Monuments staff. The stones are surface finds, but they are likely to date from the monastic occupation of the island. They are paralleled in finds from Bray Head, Valentia Island, a settlement that encompasses occupation from the eighth century to the late eleventh century (Hayden and Walsh, forthcoming).

Spud stone
92E87:1:7 (Fig. 98). Round stone with central depression that slopes from one side; U- shaped base, with worn smaller hollow. Weathered upper face, flat base.

Pivot stone
92E87:1:8 (Fig. 98). This stone is incomplete, but the partial perforation suggests that it would have projected from the upper courses of a building and would have

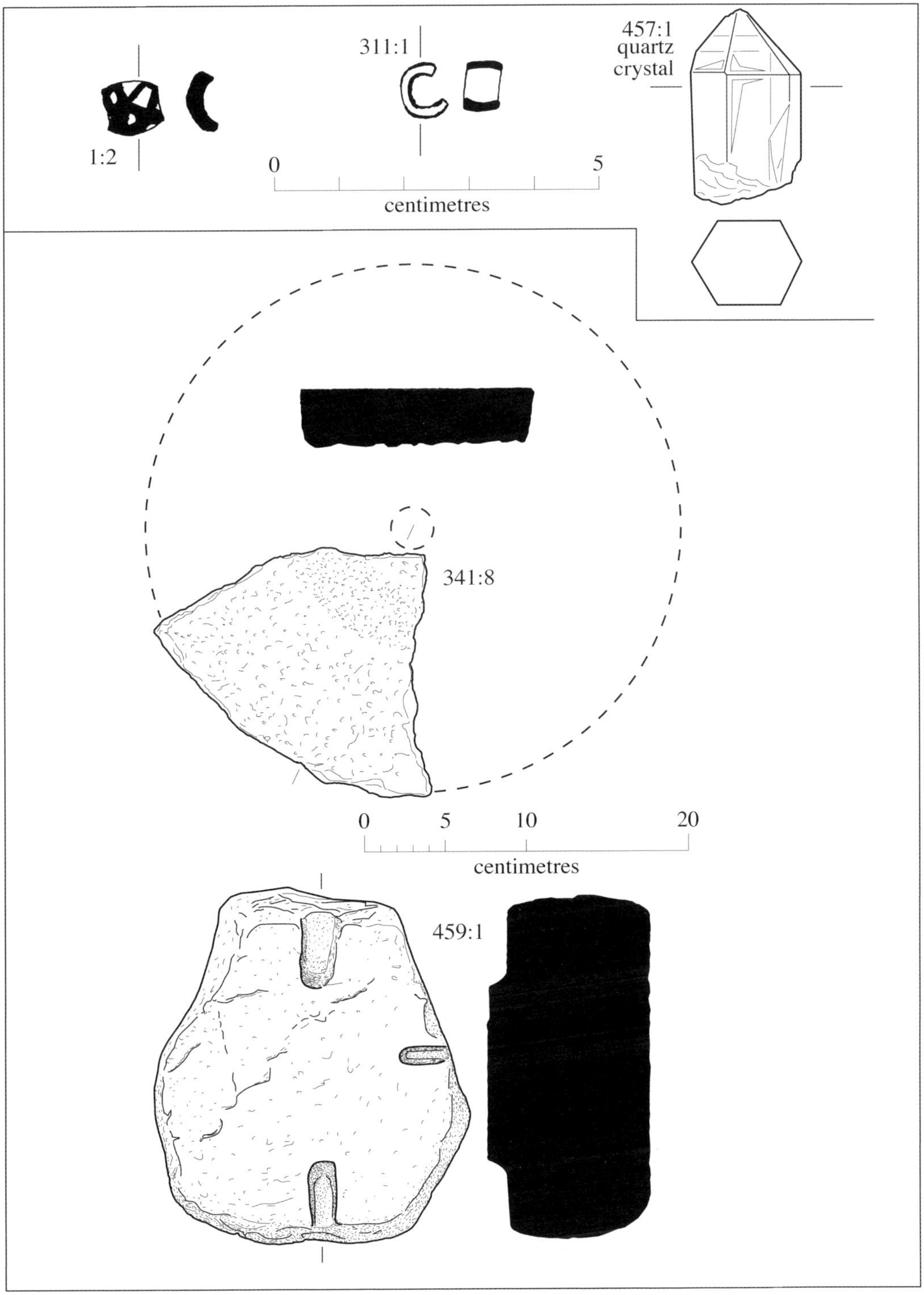

97—Small finds: glass and stone.

held the top section of a door post. Similar stones have been uncovered in the excavations of structures at Bray Head, Valentia Island (Hayden and Walsh, forthcoming).

Perforated stones

Stones of many different forms with perforations are common finds on sites of this period. They appear to have been used for a variety of purposes, including weights possibly for line or even net fishing. None of these stones were large enough to have been used for holding down roofing material, and none were used as roof slates. Spindle-whorls are a separate category of rounded perforated stone (see below).

92E87:26:2 (Fig. 99). Rough flattish sandstone with circular perforation, incomplete. The perforation is slightly hourglass-shaped and worn smooth. The stone is quite shattered. D 41mm, T 12mm. Incidental find from a grave, trench B, level 4.

92E87:354:1 (Fig. 99). Perforated irregular piece of flat, soft yellow claystone. The perforation is circular and incomplete. L 60mm, T 14mm. From middle level of midden, trench A.

92E87:354:2 (Fig. 99). Part of a roughly circular, flattish, perforated soft sandstone. The perforation (incomplete) is circular, slightly hourglass-shaped and worn smooth. D 57mm, T 9mm. From middle level of midden, trench A.

92E87:401:6 (Fig. 99). Part of an irregularly shaped perforated soft sandstone. The stone is flat and smooth on one side. The perforation (incomplete) is circular and hourglass-shaped. L 42mm, T 12mm. From middle level of midden, trench A.

92E87:500:1 (Fig. 99). Part of a flattish yellow-green sandstone with a circular perforation. The perforation is worn smooth. Stone slightly shattered. L 90.5mm, T 14.5mm. Diameter of perforation 9.8mm, widening to 11.3mm. From clearance in the vicinity of the well.

92E87:501:1 (Fig. 99). Part of a roughly oblong-shaped, flattish, perforated, soft yellow sandstone. Edges slightly rounded. The perforation is complete, worn smooth, circular and hourglass-shaped. L 79.8mm, W 42mm. From clearance over the midden.

92E87:452:3. Part of a regularly shaped, flat, perforated soft sandstone. The perforation (incomplete) is roughly oblong and worn smooth. L 105mm, W 51.5mm, T 11.2mm, D 15.5mm. From the fill of a pit, of unknown date, that cuts the wall of hut 2, periods 2–3.

92E87:452:4. Part of an irregularly shaped, flattish perforated sandstone. One side is flat and smooth. The perforation (incomplete) is roughly oblong and worn smooth. L 105mm, T 22.8mm, D 12.5mm. From the fill of a pit, of unknown date, that cuts the wall of hut 2, periods 2–3.

92E87:3:1 (Fig. 99). Part of a flat sandstone perforated stone. The perforation is circular and incomplete. L 48.5mm, T 9.6mm, D 8.8mm. From a clearance level.

Spindle-whorls

92E87:152:1 (Fig. 100). Roughly made, flat, circular spindle-whorl, of fine-grained sandstone, with slightly off-centre circular perforation. D 37mm, T 8mm. Found beneath the rubble collapse, south-west side of reliquary shrine, trench C.

92E87:301:7 (Fig. 100). Circular spindle-whorl of fine yellow claystone, complete although fragmented. Hourglass perforation, oval section. D 33mm, T 11mm. From the upper level of the midden, trench A.

92E87:72:1 (Fig. 100). Fragment of a circular spindle-whorl of fine yellow claystone. Flat in section with cylindrical perforation. Two crudely incised circular lines occur on one face, while a single similarly poorly executed circular line is present on the other face. Similarly decorated spindle-whorls were found at Reask (Fanning 1981, 125), at Church Island (O'Kelly 1958, 101, fig. 14, 7), and in the backfill of the *fulacht fiadh* trough at Coarhamore, Valentia (Sheehan 1990, 31). D (projected) *c.* 500mm, T 11mm. From trench A, level 1.

Bracelets

Polished stone bracelets are quite common finds on early medieval sites; a fragment of a siltstone bracelet, as well as one of jet, was found at Reask (Fanning 1981, 123, 127).

92E87:50:10 (Fig. 100). Fragment of a polished shale or lignite bracelet, with a projected external diameter of 7cm. D-shaped cross-section. From the middle level of the midden, trench A.

92E87:301:15 (Fig. 100). Fragment of a polished light grey-brown sandstone bracelet with a projected external diameter of 7cm. D-shaped cross-section. T 8.9mm, L 40.5mm, W 9.9mm. From the upper level of the midden, trench A.

Whetstones and polishing stones

A large number of whetstones and other stones with evidence for wear and polishing were recovered from the site. Many of these finds are associated with the late use of the drystone oratory for ironworking (trench B, level 6). One whetstone is perforated, and retains part of the iron suspension ring (401:7, Fig. 101). It is considered to be a Norse type. All of the stones are of local origin.

92E87:2:12 (Fig. 101). Part of a rectangular, flat, pink/red, micaceous sandstone whetstone. Edges flat, smooth and squared. Short edge rounded and smooth. Pin grooves. L 53.5mm, W 28.7mm, T 13.8mm. From clearance over rubble in oratory.

92E87:18:1 (Fig. 101). Whetstone of very fine-grained micaceous red sandstone. Incomplete. Two grooves are present on one face: one is sharp and clear, the other is shallower. O'Connor (1991, 57) suggests that these grooves result from bringing objects like pins and awls to a point, and also probably from working the ends of knives. The whetstone edges are partially abraded and fragmented. Both surfaces are flat, worn smooth and polished. Rectangular section with rounded edges. Tapers to end. W 68mm, T 23mm. From trench B, level 6.

92E87:18:5 (Fig. 101). Flat, pink/grey, hard sandstone. Possible whetstone. Incomplete. One surface flat and smooth and slightly convex. Long edges flat, smooth and squared. Short edge rounded and smooth. Bottom surface rough and uneven. Rectangular in plan and section. L 91mm, W 40.4mm, T 20mm. From trench B, level 6.

92E87:19:1 (Fig. 101). Whetstone of very fine-grained micaceous red sandstone. Incomplete. One well-defined groove is present in the centre of one face. The whetstone is well made, rectangular in cross-section, with rounded edges, and is well polished and smoothed. It tapers to the surviving end. W 43mm, T 28mm. From trench B, level 6.

92E87:19:2 (Fig. 101). Well-made complete whetstone of very fine-grained micaceous grey sandstone. Rectangular in section and oblong in plan, it is not greatly worn. There is an area of iron corrosion across one face of the stone. L 127mm, W 33mm, T 14mm. From trench B, level 6.

92E87:66:5 (Fig. 101). Part of a very worn and polished whetstone of very fine-grained grey sandstone. Rectangular in cross-section, and used on both faces. There are a series of lightly incised grooves on one face. W 35mm, T (max.) 15mm. From lowest level of midden, trench A.

92E87:71:2 (Fig. 101). Cylindrical, round-sectioned column of unidentified stone. This has an outer layer of pyrites approximately 1mm thick, which has shattered at one end. The outer part of the stone is extremely smooth and polished, suggesting its use as a polishing or grinding implement. L 63mm, D 17mm. From trench A, level 1, debris over timber round house.

92E87:321:1 (Fig. 101). Whetstone, complete, of soft fine-grained micaceous sandstone. Tapers slightly towards both ends. Rectangular cross-section with slightly rounded edges, much abraded, flat and well finished on the faces. L 110mm, W 45mm, T 17mm. Incidental find from a grave, trench A.

92E87:178:1 (Fig. 101). Part of a small whetstone, similar to 92E87:401:7, but perforated end is absent. Fashioned of fine micaceous red/grey sandstone, it is rectangular in cross-section and smooth on all faces. Tapers slightly to a rectangular-sectioned end. L 41mm, W 13mm, T 9mm. From a possible grave in the shrine mound, trench C.

92E87:301:10 (Fig. 101). Modified beach pebble, broken, of fine-grained micaceous grey sandstone, probably used as a whetstone. It is ovoid in cross-section, and tapers to the extant end. It has been polished along one side. W 21mm, T 11mm. From the upper level of the midden, trench A.

92E87:401:7 (Fig. 101). Perforated, well-made small whetstone of very fine, micaceous, hard, red/grey polished sandstone. Broken at one end. Rectangular in cross-section, it tapers at the head. Part of the iron suspension ring (broken and corroded) is present in the cylindrical perforation, and a corrosion stain is present across one edge by the perforation. Perforated whetstones of this type are accepted as a Viking form (O'Connor 1991, 56; Fanning 1981, 132) and are common finds from urban Hiberno-Norse levels in this country. A perforated whetstone was recovered from rubble outside the round house at nearby Church Island, Valentia Harbour (O'Kelly 1958, 100). L 12mm, T 9mm. From the middle level of the midden, trench A.

92E87:401:8 (Fig. 101). Modified beach pebble, of fine-grained micaceous grey sandstone. Flattened on one side, ovoid in cross-section, it has been polished. A series of light blade-marks occur on one side and across the face. L 90mm, W 23mm, T 8mm. From trench A, middle level of the midden.

92E87:402:1. Flat oblong possible whetstone in two pieces. Piece 1: L 200mm, W 89.5mm, T 28.5mm, worn in middle. Piece 2: L 73mm, W 33mm, T 16.7mm. From hut B, period 1.

92E87:434:1 (Fig. 101). Part of a medium-sized micaceous hard purple sandstone, probably used as a whetstone. Shattered along the interior horizontally, the outer part also shattered (about one third). Three of its four edges are smooth, slightly rounded and polished. Quadrangular, with slight taper from edge not smoothed. Triangular-sectioned. L 120mm, W 48.9mm, T 12.8mm. From debris over hut B, periods 1–2.

Modified beach stones

A variety of beach stones were found throughout the occupation levels of the site. Several of these showed evidence of wear and/or had been modified in some manner, while others, with no evident pattern of wear, could have been used as 'limpet scoops' or as rough hammers. The latter have not been illustrated.

92E87:1:1. Circular flat beach stone. D 49.4mm, T 13.5mm. From clearance over oratory, late.

92E87:18:4. Large, grey trapezoid-shaped stone, polished on one surface, with two smooth and rounded edges where it tapers to rounded butt. L 227.5mm, W 97.2mm, T 46.4mm. From trench B, level 6.

92E87:48:3. Oblong beach stone of hard red/grey sandstone with rounded edges, one surface polished, tapering to a rounded point. One edge slightly shattered. L 150mm, W 52mm, T 37.8mm. From rubble within hut D, period 3.

92E87:48:4. Flat purple micaceous sandstone. One side very flat. Triangular in plan with rounded base edge and snub-nosed point edge. L 152mm, W 66.7mm, T 23mm. From rubble within hut D, period 3.

92E87:48:5. Hard red sandstone beach stone. One surface flat and slightly polished. Rounded edges and quite oblong in plan. L 200mm, W 100mm, T 50mm. From rubble within hut D, period 3.

92E87:48:6. Hard grey sandstone beach stone. One surface partly polished, flat and slightly concave. Other surface rougher and with pronounced ridge. All edges rounded and smooth. Possibly a whetstone? L 142mm, W 51.5mm, T 39.2mm. From rubble within hut D, period 3.

92E87:50:4 (Fig. 101). Pink/brown sandstone, almost brick-like in shape and appearance. Heat-shattered. Surfaces smooth and flat. Edges smooth and rounded. Medium gradient from one larger edge. L 69mm, W 71mm, T 40mm. From midden, period 2.

92E87:50:12. Light grey to pink sandstone beach stone. Oblong in plan with smooth rounded edges. One surface smooth and slightly convex in section. Other surface rough and uneven. L 172mm, W 66.8mm, T 29.7mm. From midden, period 2.

92E87:50:13. Dark grey oblong beach stone. One surface smooth and flat. Rounded edges. Tapers slightly in plan. L 155mm, W 50.2mm, T 25.5mm. From midden, period 2.

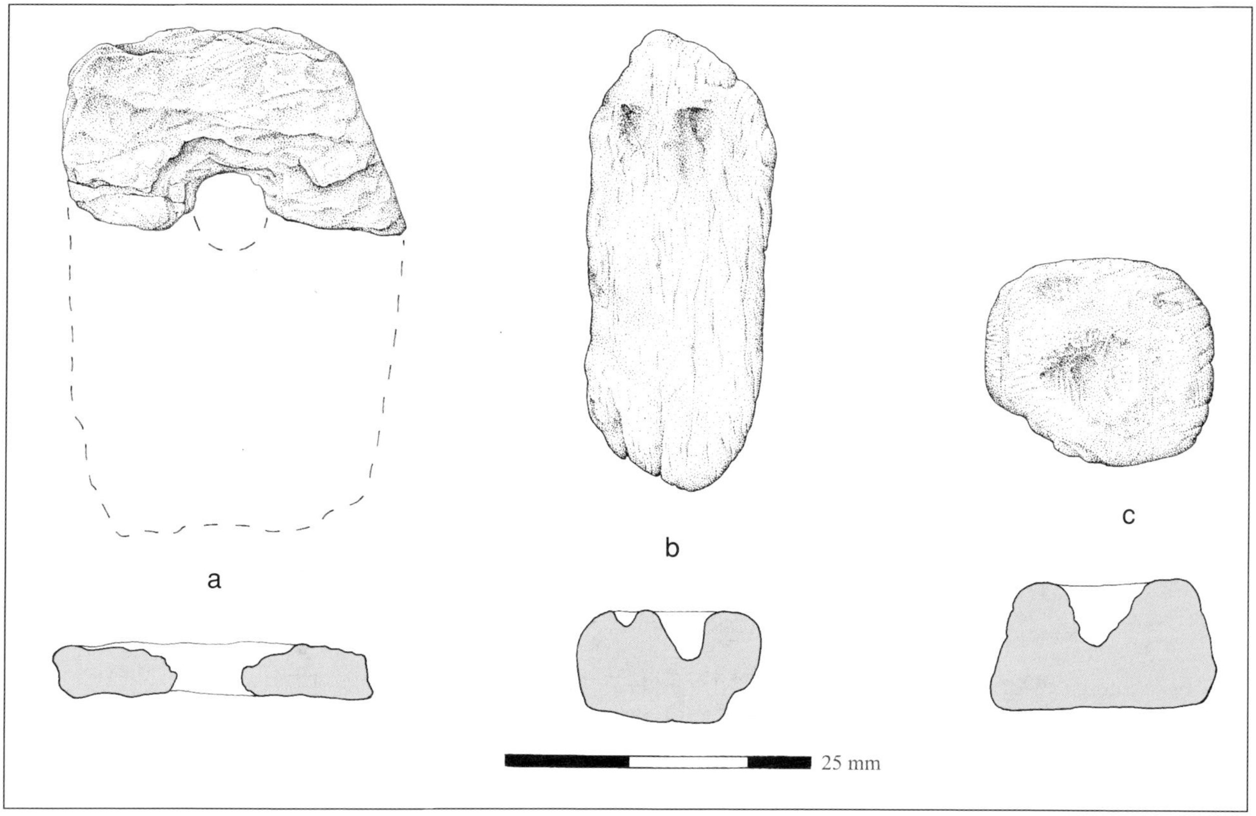

98—Stone artefacts and architectural stone. *(P. Johnson)*

a—Worked stone (0.25m by 0.17m) broken off at one end. Possibly used to hold the top of a door post. (1:8)

b—Unidentified stone. (1:9)

c—Spud stone. (1:7)

92E87:66:10. Pendant-shaped beach stone of hard grey sandstone. One surface flat and smooth (partly polished?), the other partly shattered. Rounded and smooth edges. L 109mm, W 43mm, T 20mm. From midden, period 1.

92E87:301:5 (Fig. 101). Grey stone, quite polished on three sides, wedge-shaped. L 72.4mm, W 32mm tapering to 11mm, T 24.5mm. From upper level of midden, trench A.

92E87:407:5. Flat circular beach stone. D 90mm, T 27.2mm. From midden, periods 1–2.

92E87:446:1–3. Three beach stones, possible limpet scoops.
1: Flat and circular, one side partially shattered. D 94.5mm, T 26.5mm.
2: Flat and oblong. L 59.5mm, W 50mm, T 12.5mm.
3: Trapezoidal beach stone. One side flat and smooth. Pink-hued sandstone. L 109.5mm, W 62.5mm, T 24.8mm.
All from clearance over hut B, period 1–2.

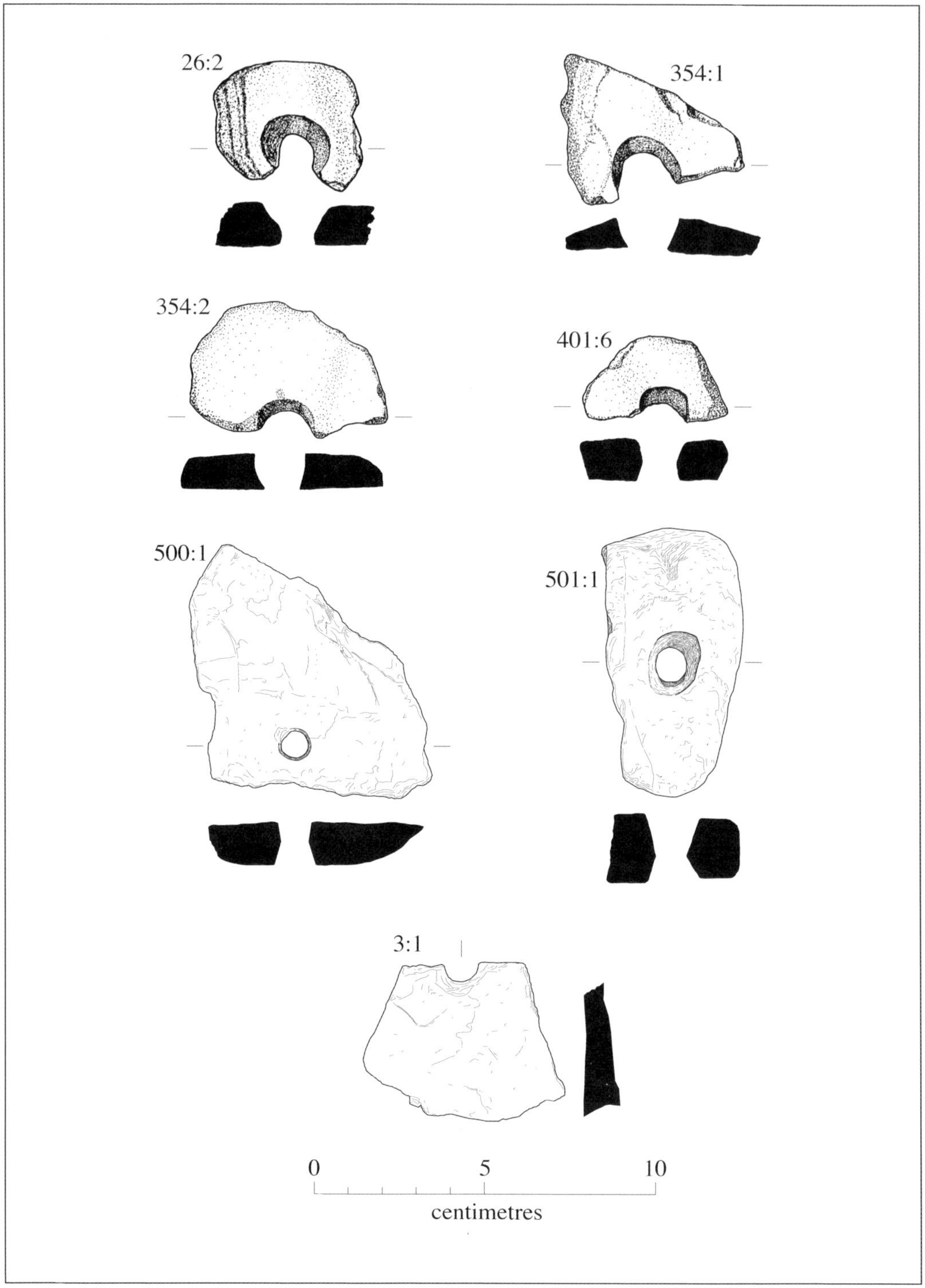

99—Small finds: stone.

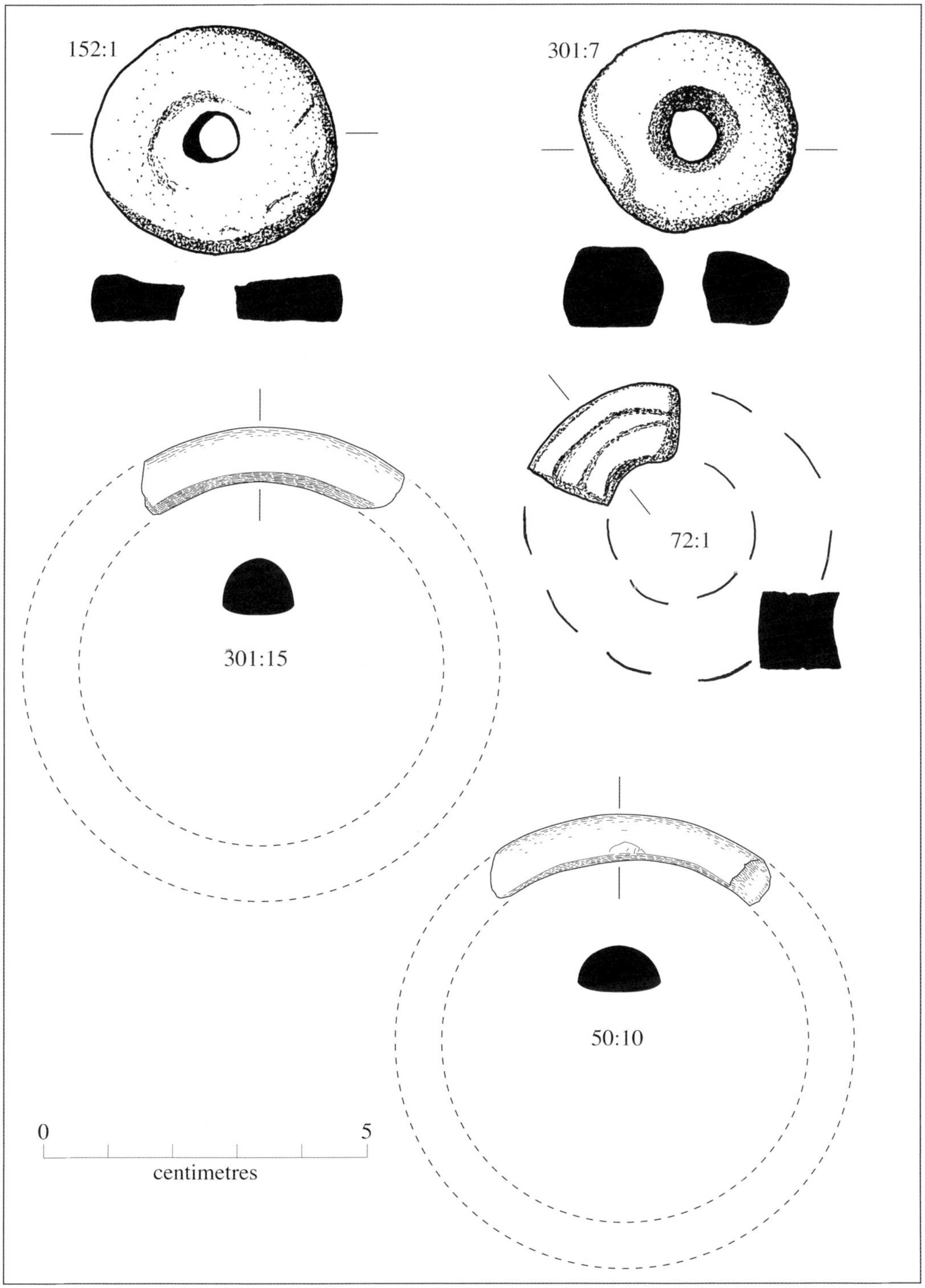

100—Small finds: stone.

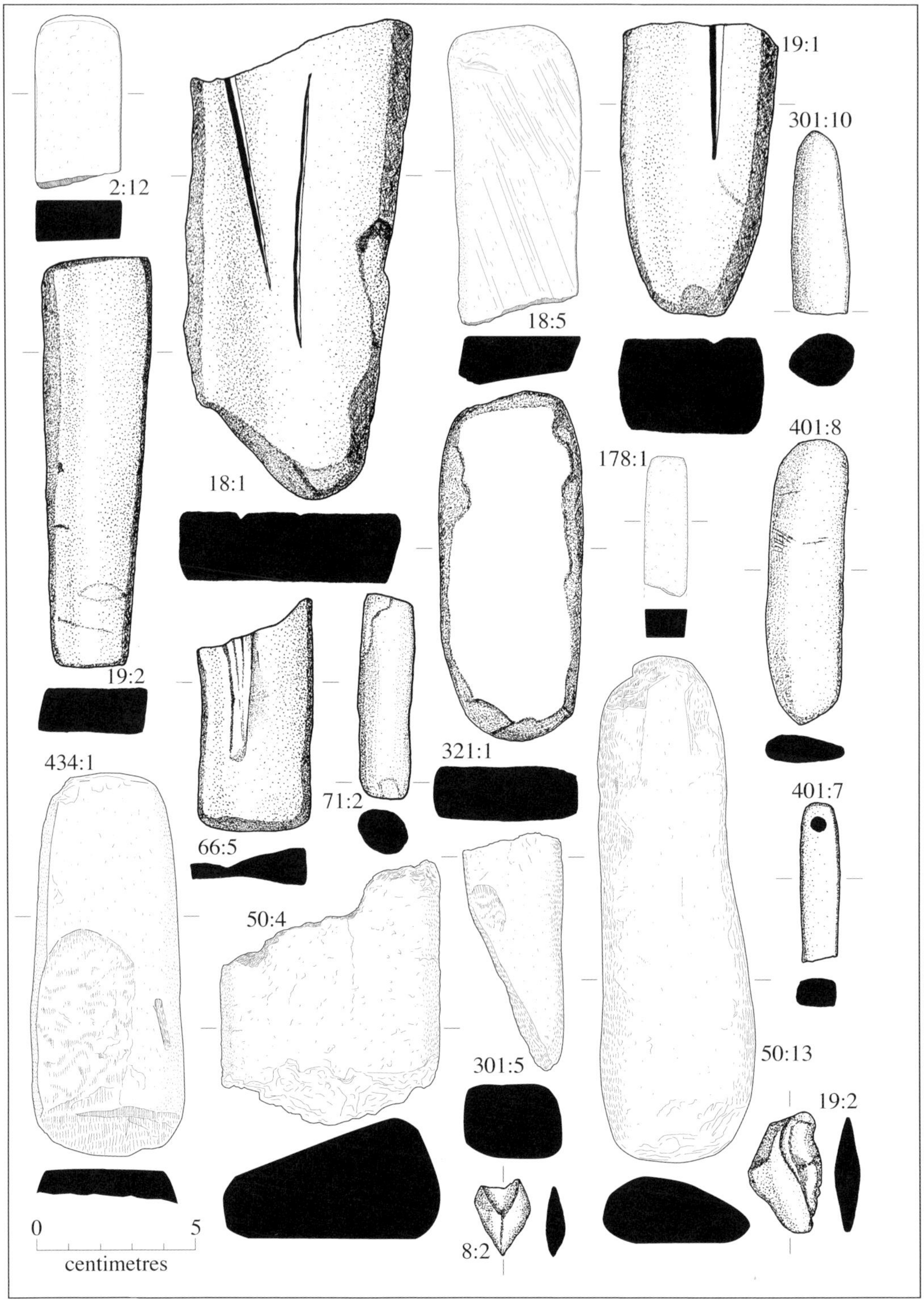

101—Small finds: stone.

Pilgrim crosses
These roughly shaped portable crosses are known from Skellig Michael (Horn *et al.* 1990). They are illustrated in Fig. 5, a–e. None of the Illaunloughan crosses were found in primary contexts.

Flints
Twelve struck flint flakes were recovered from a range of contexts over the site. The flints are of a wide variety of hues, in keeping with their origins as beach pebbles. Some have cortex remaining. None exhibit any secondary working. They were probably used as strike-a-lights. Nos 92E87:19:3 and 92E87:8:2 are illustrated (Fig. 101).

92E87:1:15. Unstratified. Struck face, possibly natural, no secondary working, grey to white in colour. L 27.9mm, W 18.8mm, T 4.3mm.

92E87:88:1. Probable waste flake, no secondary working, light red to brown in colour. L 21.8mm, W 17.3mm, T 5.5mm.

92E87:354:5. Waste flake, struck face, cortex, no secondary working, creamy white to light brown in colour. L 17.1mm, W 10.7mm, T 5.7mm.

92E87:354:6. Waste flake, struck face, no secondary working, grey to light brown with white mottles. L 18.6mm, W 12.3mm, T 7.6mm.

92E87:131:1. Waste flake off beach pebble, no secondary working, brown to white. L 15.4mm, W 10.2mm, T 3.5mm.

92E87:388:1. Waste flake, no secondary working, russet to light yellow-white. L 22.6mm, W 12mm, T 7mm.

92E87:150:1. Struck face, no secondary working, amber colour. L 15.2mm, W 3mm, T 2.7mm.

92E87:301:6. Waste flake, possible cortex, cream colour. L 25.2mm, W 18.5mm, T 8.9mm.

92E87:405:1. Struck edges and face, cortex, no secondary working, cream to very light brown colour. L 22.6mm, W 19.4mm, T 5.9mm.

92E87:301:11. Struck face, no secondary working, dark amber colour with occasional white mottles. L 18.7mm, W 13.8mm, T 5.9mm.

92E87:434:2. Struck face, cortex on one side, brown to cream hue, no secondary working. L 38.5, W 17mm, T 14.5mm.

Shell

Five perforated scallop shells were recovered from beneath the slabs of the reliquary shrine (Fig. 54a). The perforation appears to be deliberate on each shell. The perforations differ from those commonly found on the pilgrim shells from Compostela found in later medieval burials in Ireland at Tuam Cathedral (Clyne 1987–8) and from a medieval burial-ground in Mullingar (on display in the National Museum of Ireland, Medieval Exhibition). These later shells have two small opposing perforations. One of the Illaunloughan shells, however, has two perforations.

Two were found in cist 171 beneath the gable shrine, one came from F169, the upper level within the reliquary shrine, and one from F173, the fill of cist 174.

Ceramics

Pottery

A single sherd of probable Bronze Age pottery was recovered from an unstratified location close to the exterior of hut D (see Appendix 2, report by Rose Cleary). In addition, a single sherd of medieval pottery was recovered, in contrast to Church Island, Valentia Harbour, where several sherds of medieval pottery were recovered (O'Kelly 1958).

92E87:354:4. Sherd from the strap-handle of an unglazed Redcliffe, Bristol, jug. Cliona Papazian suggests a date in the late thirteenth century for this ware. It is the sole sherd of medieval pottery recovered from the site. From the middle level of the midden, trench A.

Metalworking evidence

This comprises decorated and plain mould fragments and crucible fragments. The moulds were recovered from a localised area, in the debris over the timber round house, trench A, level 1. Associated with these artefacts was a bone motif-piece with carved decorative panels (see Fig. 96). Unless otherwise indicated, the finds are all from trench A, level 1.

Small single fragments of crucible were recovered from three locations on the site, but only one crucible fragment was recovered from the concentration of metalworking debris. The metalworking area and furnace have not been uncovered but must have been in a fairly sheltered location. The furnace may have lain a short distance southwards, perhaps sheltered by the walls of the timber round house, and have been lost to erosion.

Very little is known of the layout of a smith's workshop, despite the numbers of sites that have returned evidence for metalworking. At Moynagh Lough, metalworking took place in two discrete areas to either side of a timber round house on the periphery of the crannog (Bradley 1993, 76). One work area was a spread of charcoal that measured 4.2m by 4m and contained mould fragments, crucible sherds, three motif-pieces and an iron tool. The second work area comprised a furnace, two surfaced areas, metalworking debris and charcoal. The furnace was bowl-shaped and small, only 0.35m in diameter and 0.14m in depth. A spread of burnt clay close by had probably been sheltered by a screen, represented by a fairly random scatter of post-holes (*ibid.*, 79). Another pebbled area may have been the stacking area for the moulds as they cooled. The 1968 excavations at Cathedral Hill, Armagh, yielded evidence for a structure and associated hearth used for metalworking (Gaskell Brown and Harper 1984, 157). This was located in a marginal area, very close to the edge of the infilled ditch of the monastic enclosure.

All the mould fragments recovered were from two-piece moulds. The process of production of moulds of this type and of casting by this method is summarised by Craddock (1989, 170).

Crucible fragments (not illustrated)
92E87:302:1. Rim sherd of a crucible, in two parts. Form probably pyramidal. Fabric is sandy, with a bright red oxidised core. Grey adhesion internally and externally indicates that it would have been placed in the metalworking furnace. T of wall 6.5mm, narrows towards rim. Incidental find from a late grave at the north side of trench A.

92E87:208:2. Small body sherd from a crucible, probably pyramidal. It has a sandy grey core, with frequent crushed quartz particles throughout. Mica is present. The interior is reduced and no adhesions are present. The exterior is coated with a grey, crazed glassy accretion. T of wall 6mm, narrows towards rim. From pea-gravel infilling terrace at east end of oratory, trench B, level 4.

92E87:151:1. Small fragment of oxidised clay with frequent crushed particles throughout. Thick accretion of light grey glassy slag on one face, probably internal. The other face has sheared off. Probably a sherd of a crucible. T 9.5mm. Stray find from north side of trench C.

92E87:72:6. Rim sherd of a small pyramidal crucible. The fabric is probably oxidised; quartz particles and fragments of red oxides are present. A thick grey-green lustrous accretion is present on the outside of the vessel, while the inside has a thin coating of red-grey material. The broken edges of the crucible are covered by a grey frothy slag matter, obscuring the fabric. The sherd must have broken in one usage and remained in the hearth. T of wall 9mm, narrowing towards rim. Internal depth 26mm. From trench A, level 1, recovered in association with the mould fragments.

92E87:519:1. Rim sherd of a small crucible, probably pyramidal. Fabric sandy with frequent small particles. A thin light green/grey slaggy accretion is present on the exterior. The interior has a light green accretion; part of one of the broken edges has also been discoloured to the same colour in contrast to the light white colour of the lower broken edge. May have broken and remained in hearth. Base unknown. T of wall 7.8mm, narrowing to 7.1mm at the rim. From incidental fill of a child's grave.

Fired clay (not illustrated)
Several pieces of fired clay were recovered from the site. These have the same fabric type as the mould fragments and may be related to metalworking activity. They may have originated from a metalworking hearth.

The mould fragments: selective catalogue
Over 80 fragments of ceramic two-piece moulds were recovered, many of them very soft and fragmentary. All are made from a similar fabric: on visual inspection this is a soft, porous, sandy, micaceous paste, with crushed quartzite apparent, but otherwise no obvious temper. The fabric of a mould fragment was subjected to detailed inspection (see Appendix 2, Rose Cleary).

The assemblage can be divided into decorated and undecorated pieces, edge fragments, pouring gate, and fragmentary pieces too shattered to identify. The assemblage provides evidence for the manufacture of a minimum of four objects: a penannular brooch; a circular brooch or mount with fret pattern ornamentation; a pin (possibly of the penannular brooch); and a smaller pin with a decorated square head. None of the mould fragments correspond to either the ring-brooch or the penannular brooch found in the overlying midden layers (see above).

92E87:419:1. Four pieces of fired clay, recovered in close proximity. The pieces are formless, but one piece has possible grass impressions. The fabric is a soft, sandy, porous paste, oxidised throughout, with rounded quartz grains and other small crushed pebbles up to 3mm in diameter. The largest piece measures 43mm by 18mm. Found in the mixed rooted soil over the original ground surface, trench D.

92E87:89:1. A triangular mould fragment consisting of a flat slab with a knob of clay at one end that is approximately circular in shape. This seems to have been attached separately to the flat slab rather than to have been pulled up from the main body of clay. The knob may have been part of the internal section of the mould for a decorative object where a boss was required as part of a pattern or motif. The fabric has a gritty texture with small quartz grains visible on the surface. It is uniformly reddish-yellow in colour, while the knob and core are light grey. The clay is lightly stained by iron oxides/hydroxides. L 39.4mm, W 44.5mm, T (of slab) 6.5mm.

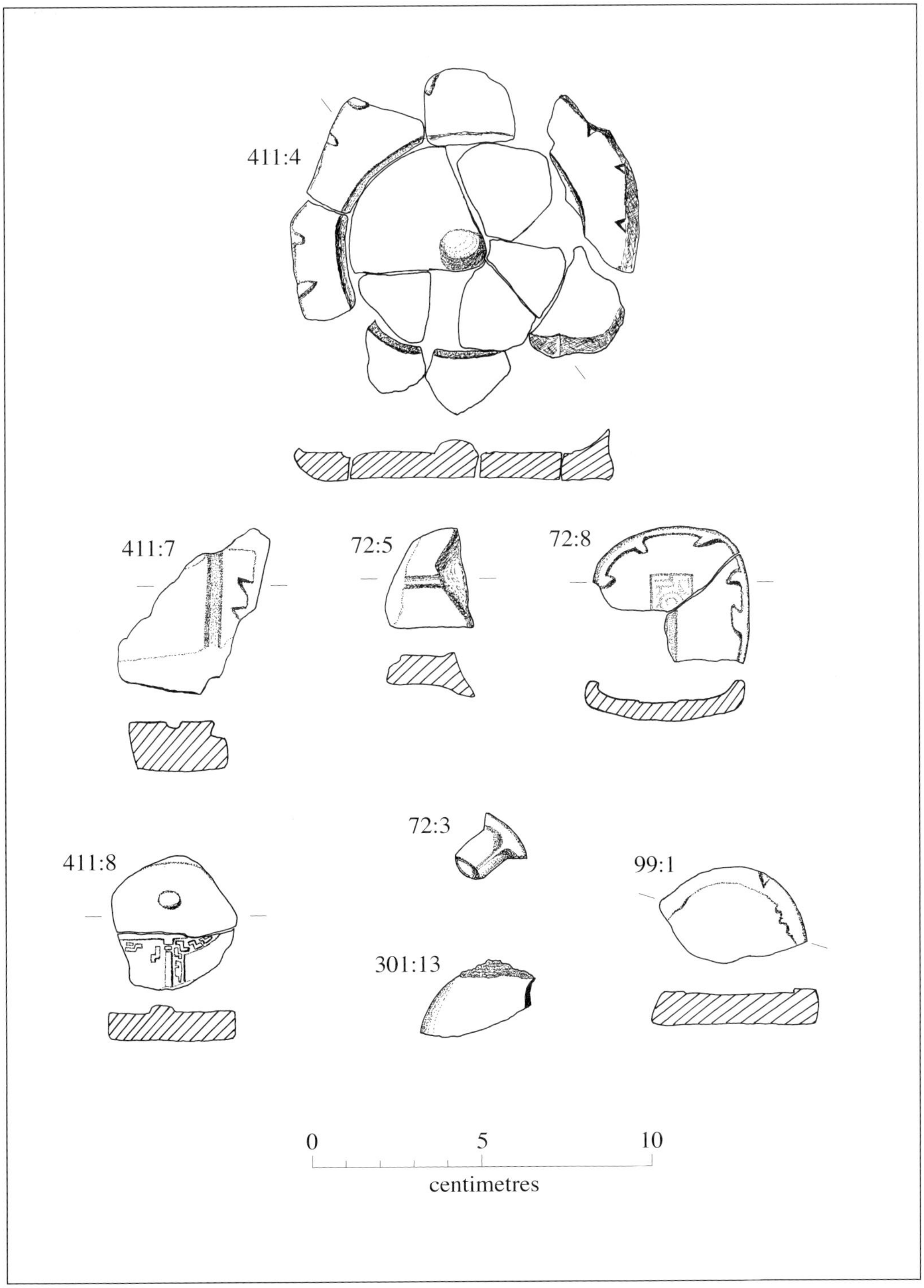

102—Clay casting-moulds.

92E87:411:4 (Fig. 102). Seven pieces of ceramic mould for casting a large circular object, probably a penannular brooch. Three pieces, 92E87:409:1, appear to be part of the same mould, as does another piece from F401, although they are not a perfect fit. The mould is flat, and has broken along the weaker parts where the ring impressions are present. The edges of the mould are incomplete, although several keying devices remain along one side. These consist of small triangular pieces, raised up to 3mm above the face of the mould and irregularly spaced along its edge. There is a large central raised boss, 15mm in diameter, 5mm higher than the flat face of the mould. Part of the pouring gate of the mould is present. The object cast was 7cm in diameter (external), and the ring section was at least 3mm thick. Up to eight other fragments exhibit either the positive or negative elements of this same triangular keying device, e.g. 92E87:411.5, which is negative but has one positive key in place. This piece also has part of a ring impression, of similar diameter to the above, and may be part of the opposite side of mould 411:4. Average T 7mm. Overall size estimated at 10cm.

92E87:411:7 (Fig. 102). Fragment of mould for casting a pin. Diameter of pin 4.5mm. Negative triangular keys present along both sides. L 53.5mm, W 35mm, T 11mm.

92E87:72:5 (Fig. 102). Fragment of a mould for casting a pin. This may be part of mould 411:7 above, although the pieces do not fit. Part of the pouring gate is present. Diameter of pin 4.5mm. L 23mm, D 33mm, T 12mm.

92E87:72:8 (Fig. 102). Two fragments, which fit, of a mould for casting an object of uncertain form. The impression of the object is very light. It may have been a pin (the shaft is fairly well defined) with a squared head, similar to, if more modest in form than, the pin of the ninth-century Killamery brooch (Ryan 1989, 99). This appears to have had a cast decorative motif, but the impression is extremely shallow and too eroded to determine this further. It appears to have a central, probably circular indentation, like the circular head of the pin. The diameter of the pin shaft is 4mm. This mould is smaller and has survived better than the other fragments. There is a grey reduced panel across a confined central, rectangular area of the face of the mould, obviously from its use in casting. A series of positive keys occur around the edges of the mould. Probably a side of mould 411:7. L 45mm, W 47mm, T 9mm.

92E87:411:8 (Fig. 102). Two fragments of mould for casting a circular object. Panelled areas of fret motif occur on the face of the mould, as does a circular boss 7mm in diameter, raised almost 2mm above the face of the mould. The shape of the edge fractures of the mould suggests that the object cast was circular: whether this was a circular mount or a brooch with decorated terminals is unclear, but the latter appears most likely. A brooch with internal diameter of 39mm is suggested. D 34mm, T 8mm.

92E87:72:3 (Fig. 102). This is a complete, stopper-shaped piece of fired clay, fashioned by squeezing the clay into a small column. The fabric is similar to that of the mould fragments and is lightly oxidised. One end is expanded, flat and circular, while the other has a small circular recess. The body of the object retains finger impressions from its shaping. Nessa O'Connor has suggested that the object was used in applying fine ornamentation to moulds. Wax, which could take the impression of fine ornamentation, would be held in the small recess, then pressed into a wet mould. A similar object was recovered from the Clogher excavations (Nessa O'Connor, pers. comm.). L 15.5mm, average T 14mm.

92E87:99:1 (Fig. 102). Fragment of a baked clay object, circular, with an estimated diameter of 4.75cm. Flat-based, abraded rim of clay folded over the body, only 1.5mm higher than the base of the tray. It could have been used as a crucible stand or heating tray, although there is no glaze or vitrification present. For comparisons see Youngs 1989, 181 and 185, although both illustrated examples have more pronounced rims, and internal glazes. A triangular indent on one side suggests that it may be an extremely abraded piece of a circular mould. D 46mm, T 9mm.

92E87:301:13 (Fig. 102) Possible tuyère. Fragment of fired clay, with evident crushed quartz inclusions up to 9mm in diameter. The core is oxidised in the centre and grey (reduced) around the outside, where there is an accreted glaze over one side, and the clay is crazed. This side of the fragment is shaped and rounded, while part of a concave opening is apparent on the other side. It is probably part of a tuyère. Similar pieces were recovered from the metalworking debris at Cathedral Hill, Armagh (Gaskell Brown and Harper 1984, 150, particularly fig. 20, 161). L 38mm, T 19mm. Found in the upper levels of the midden, trench A.

PART 4:
CONSERVATION OF THE ISLAND

Grellan D. Rourke

11

Conservation of Illaunloughan

Introduction

Experience has shown that it is essential at this type of site to integrate the conservation programme into the overall project at the beginning. Ideally, some conservation works need to proceed in tandem with the excavation programme itself. Here that was not possible, as the excavation was an independent initiative and the site was not in State care at the time. After the excavations came to a close in 1995 the site was left untouched until it finally came into State care as a National Monument under a guardianship order in May 2000. During the interval there had been some deterioration, and additional damage had been caused by the winter seas to the north side of the shrine complex. In late 2000 the National Monuments Service set up on the island but the actual preservation works programme did not begin until the following January. There were two seasons of work, from January until May 2001 and from mid-October 2001 to May 2002, with a break in between to continue the major programme of works on Skellig Michael. It was not possible to work on the island each day over the winter season owing to occasional adverse weather and sea conditions. The workforce was very small, comprising one mason and two general operatives, all experienced in the repair and consolidation of drystone structures.[1]

How does one conserve a vulnerable early medieval site such as Illaunloughan, which is not only exposed to adverse weather and sea conditions but which must also stand up to the rigours of unsupervised visitor access? Given the fact that the structural remains are of drystone construction, they are very easily damaged by visitors. In this case there is no presence on the island in the form of guiding or supervising staff. The most important issue is to protect and preserve what remains of the original work. Obviously the top layers of drystone construction are particularly susceptible to damage, and in order to protect these it has been the policy of the National Monuments Service to add some additional layers of stone to provide a sacrificial buffer. When inadvertent or wilful damage does occur, no original work is lost. This is only done where walling would have been higher originally. In the case of orthostats, or stones set vertically into the ground, these have been reset in their vertical positions where they have fallen forward; this makes them much less vulnerable to breaking or cracking when visitors might walk on them and it also makes the presentation of features more intelligible.

The site was backfilled where necessary, using existing spoil. The remainder of the excavated material was subsequently spread out to the south and east of the oratory to provide a protective buffer zone against the encroaching sea. After the excavation the vegetation of the island had been left unchecked and this reverted to a wild state very quickly. The site became unmanageable and very difficult to get around. In order to hold everything together, to allow for ease of regular maintenance and to allow easy access and clear visibility of the structures for visitors, it was decided to re-sod the entire island once the conservation and consolidation works were completed. This turned out to be very effective. However, in the early spring of 2002 there was a bad storm and rough seas came on the south side, causing much damage and lifting some of the newly laid sod. After this event the sods were temporarily secured to allow them to take hold and become established. That was almost three years ago and by now the sod has become firmly established; it has consolidated the ground and allows the site to be easily interpreted by visitors.

Stone to repair the varied structures came, for the most part, from the archaeological spoil. On the west side of the island there is an area of rock that was not quarried. This was probably left *in situ* intentionally to give some protection to the dwelling cells. This rock outcrop gives a good idea of just how easy it must have been to extract stone for construction (Fig. 103). It has close parallel beds that break apart very easily, giving good flat stones, ideal for building drystone structures.

Erosion

The island is now much reduced in size; it has suffered considerable erosion on its north, east and south sides, the west side being protected by rock outcrop. On the north side serious erosion has taken place and the winter seas had caused considerable damage, particularly to the shrine structure, pulling out much of the masonry along its northern side. The only way to combat this erosion and give support to the threatened shoreline was to set up a wall of gabions on this side. The gabions, galvanised metal cages, came in two sizes, 2m x 1m and 1m x 1m, both 1m high.[2] The cages were filled on land with local stone from the Valentia slate quarry and taken out to the island by barge along with a mechanical shovel/digger machine, which was used to position them along the vulnerable north side for a length of almost 30m. Two layers were used along most of its length so that the completed structure was not too high (2m) and is not visible above the ground level of the site. The area between the inside of the gabions and the shoreline was then filled up with some of the excess archaeological spoil, which was consolidated before re-sodding took place. This work was undertaken in the autumn of 2001 and was completed in November of that year. When viewed from the north side, the gabions are now beginning to blend in visually with the exposed rock. (See Fig. 113.)

A different approach was taken on the south and east sides, where the erosion problem was not so acute. A late low revetting wall had been built along a length of the south side to stem erosion, and this required some repair. This walling was continued along the south side to the east and then on the east side to protect the existing structures (oratory, graves, etc.) from the sea. On the east side large stones were placed at the base of this new wall to make it as strong as possible, using drystone construction. The site cannot, in fact, be fully protected from the worst excesses of winter storms; we can only afford some protection in this area. Continual maintenance after bad winter storms will be required in the future and will be essential for the long-term protection of the structures.

The enclosure wall

The original enclosure wall now only exists on the west side, giving some indication of just how much of the island has been lost since the monastic occupation. Excavation revealed the line and width of the wall, but it was not in good condition and falling away to the west as the external face on this side had been undermined somewhat by the sea; the stone construction was not very homogeneous, with a variety of shapes and sizes used. From a structural point of view it was necessary to straighten this wall to stop it from collapsing outwards. The height of the existing wall was raised only a little to protect original work. Larger stones were placed flat on the top to hold it together and protect it from visitor damage. So far it has held well and it has not been necessary to sod it (Fig. 104).

The oratory

The flagstone path leading to the oratory was secured; all the existing original flagstones were intact.

On the exterior the oratory walls were in reasonable condition except for the east end and the south-west corner, where there were structural problems. Repeated tidal erosion had scoured the base on the east side, undermining the bottom of the wall and causing a section of the walling to drop at the north-east corner. In addition, an opening was made on this side in the later medieval period and this further exacerbated structural deterioration. It was necessary to underpin the north-east corner using drystone construction; this corner was then carefully taken down on the exterior under supervision and rebuilt with the existing stone. The south-east corner was in good condition and only needed minor repairs. The later medieval opening was retained and repaired, and new blocking was constructed in drystone set back on the exterior and interior so that the later opening is clearly visible.

103—Natural rock outcrop on the west side of Illaunloughan, showing the natural cleavage of the Devonian sandstone. This made the island stone very easy to quarry and use for building. *(G.D. Rourke)*

The interior of the south wall was in poor condition, with some of the stone quite deteriorated, delaminating and breaking apart, making the upper section of the wall somewhat unstable. Some of this had to be removed and replaced with similar-sized stone. The west wall on the north side of the doorway on the interior had moved and required some stabilisation, as did the door jambs, though not to the same degree. The vertical threshold stone is original. Small stones were sieved out of the archaeological spoil and laid out on the interior to create a serviceable floor surface (Fig. 105).

Generally, the walls were strengthened with the introduction of spalls to tighten loose stonework where loss of such stone had occurred. The walls were raised a few courses to protect original work, and the wall tops were overlaid with sods to consolidate and protect the tops of the drystone walling.

The *leacht*

The *leacht* on the north side of the oratory is a very low solid structure. It was in excellent condition after excavation and required no work. Quartz that came from this feature during excavation was put back on top.

104—The enclosure wall of Illaunloughan from the north after conservation.
(C. Brogan)

105—Oratory on Illaunloughan from the west after conservation work, showing the top of the wall overlaid with sods to consolidate and protect it. *(G.D. Rourke)*

Burials

Two cist graves at the south-west corner of the oratory were substantially intact. The original orthostats were still in position and it was decided to present this feature. Very small stones were sieved out of the archaeological spoil to line the interiors of both graves (Fig. 106).

The dwelling cells

Cell A

This was a circular cell. The remains of the base of the external wall showed both drystone walling and large orthostats, which were secured into the ground with stone wedges (Fig. 107). The construction of the internal face was of drystone masonry although there was not a lot remaining. It is not certain whether the core of the wall was made up of stone or of earth (sods). The remaining wall was conserved and it was possible to present about half the circumference of the cell. The wall was raised a few courses to protect the original work and the top was sodded to consolidate it. The excavation presented two internal features, a drain and a hearth edged with vertical stones. It was necessary to replace a number of these hearth edge stones where they were missing in order to present this feature (see Fig. 84, p. 139); small stones were then placed on the base of the hearth. Very

106—Cist grave on the south-western side of the oratory on Illaunloughan, showing the presentation after conservation. *(G.D. Rourke)*

little of the original paving was still intact. In presenting this cell the entire floor was paved to show its full extent (Fig. 108).

Cell B

It seems most likely that the construction of this cell was post-and-wattle on both the exterior and the interior, with a compacted sod core. It was not practical to present this cell but it is shown on the information panel by the entrance. Its stone-lined hearth was mostly intact; it was repaired and small stones were placed on its base in a similar fashion to cell A.

Cell C

This cell, located to the south-east of the main cell (cell D), had been substantially eroded by the sea and no more than a quarter of the circumference remained. It had been constructed of wattle, using sod as an insulating material on the outside. There was some drystone masonry associated with the exterior of this cell but its exact function is uncertain; it may well have been used to protect the base of the wall sods. This cell was presented using drystone walling (Fig. 109).

107—North side of cell A on Illaunloughan, showing its presentation in stone after conservation work. The three largest upright stones are original. *(G.D. Rourke)*

Cell D

This was the most intact of the cells and the only one visible prior to excavation. The condition of the exterior walling was a little problematic. There had been some collapse on the north side and it was necessary to repair some of the facing along here, particularly above the plinth in the north-west quadrant. Where possible, the original facing was consolidated *in situ*. Only some of the plinth stones were still intact; the remainder had slipped down and had to be repositioned (Fig. 110). The south external wall already had a revetment built against it, presumably to shore up this side of the cell at some later stage and to protect it from erosion by the sea. This revetment had, in turn, become unstable and this was consolidated.

The door opening also needed some attention, and the jambs were built up a little and then sloped back to the existing wall height. This was achieved using large horizontal stones, layered or stepped back to give the sloping wall top sufficient strength to remain intact should visitors climb onto it (Fig. 111). The exterior wall to the north of the door required underpinning and this was achieved by wedging stone under its base.

The interior walling was generally in good condition. It was necessary to insert some fine spalls, matching the existing ones, to tighten some areas that had lost material and so strengthen the wall. At the upper section of the cell at the back it was necessary to rebuild some lost walling in order to consolidate this area. The external walling at this point was higher and unsupported so this was done for

108—Cell A on Illaunloughan from the south, showing the repaired hearth with paving that reveals the full extent of the cell. *(G.D. Rourke)*

109—Cell C on Illaunloughan from the west, presenting the remains of the cell in stone to aid visualisation. *(G.D. Rourke)*

110—Cell D on Illaunloughan from the north-east, showing the repaired plinth and wall on the north side after conservation work. *(G.D. Rourke)*

structural reasons. The base of the wall required some underpinning and this was achieved by wedging stone underneath. Stone, sieved from the archaeological spoil, was spread out in the interior to provide a practical floor surface.

The walls of this cell were raised a little to protect any original masonry; if damage occurs it will only affect the new masonry. To consolidate the top of the wall, once the drystone had been secured, a layer of sod was laid out. In this type of situation this approach is very effective to secure the structure and it allows access to the top of the walls without causing undue damage to the wall top itself.

The later rectangular drystone 'structure' built against the cell by the south jamb was repaired to the height of its highest existing wall face where it abuts the cell. The excavation revealed some original paving to the north-east of this cell; this has been presented.

Shrine and burial complex

This overall structure can be divided up into three elements: drystone and orthostatic walling, areas of paving and the slab-shrine itself.

The access path on the west side, an original feature, was secured. This leads from a paved area uncovered in excavation and is a good representation of what the site paving must have been like. A few paving-stones were missing and these were replaced with similarly shaped stones. The orthostat on the south side at the junction of the pathway with the main structure had fallen forward and this was straightened.

The walling, made of both drystone masonry and orthostatic construction, sets out the terraces. Where the archaeology had indicated missing orthostats, these were replaced. Many of the existing orthostats had fallen outwards, owing to pressure, and these were straightened and secured. This was a slow and delicate process and was undertaken to preserve them. Had they been left at angles, they would have been subjected to greater pressure if visitors walked on them and this might eventually have led to their breaking apart. This work also made the shrine and burial structure much easier to read and understand. In some areas there was some drystone infill walling between orthostats and this was consolidated. Other drystone walling was also consolidated. The walling along the north side was in particularly bad condition and had been lost completely at the north-east corner, where storms had caused severe damage. This walling was repaired where it had fallen away, using whatever stone remained, and the north-east corner was reconstructed once the gabions were in position.

The paving-stones, many of which had been removed during the excavation, were then put back into their original positions using the archaeological drawings. Some additional stones were required to complete the paving. The quartz that had come from this area was then put back onto the structure. It will be difficult to retain this quartz as it is very portable and visitors will undoubtedly take some of the stones away with them. This has been our unfortunate experience at the monastery on Skellig Michael.

The shrine itself, which crowns the construction, was fairly straightforward from a conservation point of view. The fine drystone walling around the base was repaired using the original stone. The two existing sloping side pieces of the reliquary shrine had been carefully removed in the course of excavation and safely stored. These were repositioned and secured in place with small wedge-stones along their bases. It would appear that these two large flagstones (1.3m x 1.35m x 0.12m and 1.28m x 1.38m x 0.12m) came from Valentia Island. Suitable slate was procured from the quarry on Valentia and two new gable ends were cut to shape and positioned to close off either end, presenting this feature as it might have looked when originally constructed (Fig. 112). This also gave support to the edges of the original stones and prevented young visitors from crawling through the space and possibly causing damage to both the original stones and themselves.

The well

The well was generally in excellent condition. It was originally very solidly constructed and only required some attention along the top, where the walling had previously been roughly repaired. The uppermost step was also missing; this was replaced and adjacent walling repaired.

111—Cell D on Illaunloughan from the east, showing the entry jambs stepped back after conservation work using horizontal stones. *(G.D. Rourke)*

Maintenance programme

The preservation of such a site does not end with the completion of conservation, consolidation and presentation works (Fig. 113). It is no use undertaking such work unless there is a maintenance programme in place. Extreme weather conditions, which can occur during the winter months, impinge very much on this vulnerable site. Most of the natural damage here will be caused by the force of the sea. Church Island, off Valentia Island, was conserved and presented in the late 1950s. It did not have a follow-up maintenance programme and it was quite shocking just how much accumulated damage had occurred by the 1990s. It is important that any significant damage is repaired as soon as possible and, in the interim, it may even be necessary to provide temporary support. General maintenance will also keep the grassed areas low and protect all the vulnerable site features. It will also monitor visitor damage and help to keep it in check.

Unfortunately, these sites are very vulnerable. Constructed of drystone masonry, they are easily damaged, often inadvertently, by visitors. It is essential to take precautions to limit numbers should such a site attract too many visitors. One sad note to report is damage that was inflicted on the slab-shrine just as the works were completed. A young visitor to the island over Easter 2002 decided to incise her name onto one of the original sloping sides of this ancient structure. There is a certain irony in the fact that this stone had remained unscathed for over 1300 years only to be damaged once the site had been excavated and conserved.

112— Gable shrine and its mound on Illaunloughan from the south-west, showing the reconstructed shrine. The quartz stone found on the mound has been replaced at random; its original position was unknown. *(G.D. Rourke)*

113— Illaunloughan from the north-west, showing the monastery as it looks now after conservation work. *(C. Brogan)*

Interpretation

The final stage of the project was the provision of interpretation. As there are no guiding or supervisory staff on the island, the provision of an informative interpretive panel is essential to explain the site, particularly its evolution, and to help bring it to life for visitors. This will greatly enhance their understanding of what they are looking at and will help make their visit more meaningful and enjoyable in consequence.

Notes

1 The works team comprised Patrick O'Shea, mason, and Eamonn McCarthy and John Lyne, general operatives.

2 Gabions are metal cages filled with stone. We used Maccaferri woven wire mesh gabions of nominal 80mm x 3.7mm o/d mesh wire and 4.4mm o/d frame wire. British Board of Agrément Certificate 95/3141.

Endnotes

1 Mitchell 1982; Graham 2001, 211–12, 214, 220–1, fig. 9.19.

2 We are grateful to Professor P. Ní Chatháin of University College Dublin and to Nora O'Sullivan, a native of Valentia, for giving us this information. Professor Ní Chatháin also noted that Dinneen was from Kerry and may have had access to the name of the island as it was known to the Irish-speakers of his time. She further commented (pers. comm., 1988) that 'Oileán an Lócháin' poses several problems: 'In the event that Dinneen had the right pronunciation, the English version (Loughan) takes no account in the transliteration of the definite article. Is this just a *Volksetymolgie* for an early "Oileán Lócháin" with an intrusive introduced definite article, which would be felt as necessary for the correct language usage when the word "Lóchán" was no longer understood as a proper name?'

3 We are indebted to Dr Ó Cíobháin for this information (pers. comm., 2004). Dr Ó Cíobháin is presently at work on the Iveragh volume of his series of publications, *Toponomia Hiberniae.*

4 Henry mistook the well for a souterrain; Marshall and Rourke thought that little was left of the eastern end of the oratory.

5 UCLA-2811: AD 960 ± 120. When calibrated at one-sigma deviation the date centred on the eleventh century (calibrated according to Stuiver and Pearson 1986, 980–1021).

6 Two small errors in the written survey were included by O'Sullivan and Sheehan (1996): the well is not spring-fed, and it is not known to be a holy well.

7 The only complete excavation of a major monastery is that of Nendrum, Co. Down, carried out by H.C. Lawlor in 1925. New assessment of this material and new work on the site continue to provide information. Among others see McErlean and Crothers (2001). Important new work has also been done on Clonmacnoise (see King 1991; 1992a; 1992b; 1993; 1994a; 1994b; 1996; 1998; Manning 1994; 1998a; 1998b; Manning and Moore 1991). The excavations at Ardfert by F. Moore are almost complete, and work will finish at Caherlehillan in 2004. Church Island has been revisited by A. Hayden in 2004, with exciting new evidence for a large shrine mound unfolding.

8 The cross stones were recovered from unstratified contexts during conservation works.

9 A rigid distinction between the functions of a local church and that of a monastery may not have existed in rural Ireland, and overlapping functions may have been necessary or convenient in a number of cases. Nevertheless, the logistics of accessibility make an island site more likely to function as a monastery. A simple definition of monastery is difficult because of the constant evolution and development of variant forms. For some idea of the complexity of the situation in Ireland see Etchingham 1999, esp. chap. 8 and 456–7; Bitel 1990, chap. 1.

10 A possibility suggested by John Sheehan before excavation.

11 All radiocarbon dates were calibrated to 2 sigma; a complete list of dates is found in Appendix 6. The charcoal in the hearth for Hut B was UB-4357: 1346±32, 2σ cal. AD 640–751. The human bone in the reliquary consisted of an adult skeleton. Sk. 176 was UB-4104: 1245±18, 2σ cal. AD 686–794. An infant skeleton in the cist with Sk. 176 was OxA-10132: 1308±33, 2σ cal. AD 660–780; and another adult skeleton, Sk. 188, in the second cist was UB-4107: 1290±22, 2σ cal. AD 666–777. For the dating of the metalworking debris see Walsh, Part 2 below.

12 Using OxCal 3.9 of C. Ramsey (1995) with IntCal 98 and Marine98 (Stuiver *et al.* 1998a and 1998b).

13 Mitchell (pers. comm., 1993) identified the stone as slate, possibly from Valentia, but suggested that a small outcrop of slate could have existed on the island.

14 See Craddock 1989, 170–4, for information on the fabrication, design, materials etc. of metalworking.

15 Fanning 1981, app. 7; 1994, app. 1, 1108. For other explanations of their apparent absence see Brinch-Madsen 1984, 95, and O'Meadhra 1987 on the perishable nature of this material.

16 See also O'Meadhra (1979; 1987), who believes that bone motif-pieces were used for a variety of other purposes.

17 Raghnall Ó Floinn (pers. comm., 1999) notes that 'There is a group of late zoomorphic penannulars with hoops of D-shaped cross-section (Kilbride-Jones type D), one of which, from Gransha, Co. Down, comes from levels with E ware. The decoration on the terminals...would be consistent with such a date.'

18 Where clay fragments from metalworking are found, they are generally in disturbed contexts such as graves and structure foundations or in dumps among discarded debris.

19 Kelly (1988, 225) notes that linguistic evidence shows that many of the law tracts were written in the seventh–eighth centuries. *Uraicecht Becc* was translated by MacNeill (1923, 265–311). See also Binchy (1955), who places this text in a Munster *Nemed* collection.

20 Laing (1975, 245) believed that the homogeneity of the style and decoration of pins and brooches throughout the Irish sea province was a strong argument for travelling artisans. See also Mytum 1992, 211; O'Meadhra 1987.

21 Charles envisioned the prefabrication on the ground of the entire roof structure, which was then set on posts. However, in the opinion of skilled carpenters consulted in California it was likely that the ring beam was first fitted to the posts and the roof then added to the ring beam, either in place or on the ground. Several different methods of building the roof were possible. The main point is that it would have been easy and simple.

22 J. Sheehan (pers. comm., 2004); see also O'Sullivan and Sheehan 1992. On thatch see Mogey 1940; Evans 1957, chap. 4.

23 See Gailey 1984, Mogey 1940 and Buchanan 1956–7, 125–42, for good descriptions of the various methods.

24 Gailey (1984, 94–8) mentions alternatives to sod such as underthatch, used in northern Ireland, but sod was the main tradition.

25 Chapelot and Fossier 1985, 257–8. One of the best-preserved examples is at Solvig in South Jutland, Denmark, where a fourteenth-century turf-block wall, 2.8m thick, still

exists in part.

26 Young, as cited by Ó Danachair (1957, 61). These figures cannot be taken literally, as the cost of each type varied from county to county, and over time, but they are indications of relative cost; see also McDonald and Doyle 1997, 8–9. For more discussion of cost estimates see Gailey 1984, 30–2. On late use of sod cabins see Evans 1969; Ó Danachair 1957.

27 *et acclessiam terrenam fecit in eo loco* (Bieler 1979, 144); *et fecit ibi acclessiam terrenam de humo quadratam* (*ibid*., 158–9).

28 The excavators at Tintagel noted 'several phases of ephemeral stone and turf structures' dating from before the seventh century on the lower terrace there (Harry and Morris 1997, 136; see also Thomas and Fowler 1985).

29 Evans (1969) believed that sod houses have a broad temporal context stretching back to the prehistoric period. Evidence of houses of sod construction in the ninth/tenth century exists at Hound Tor in Devon (Minter 1964, as cited in Beresford and Hurst 1971, 91–3 and fig. 14, who add that houses with walls of turf lined on the inside with wattle hurdling were common in south-western England). They are also found on the Isle of Man, of probably pre-Norman date (Gelling 1962–3, 156–72). For similar use of interior wattling over sod walls in eighteenth-century Scottish creel houses see Noble 2000; on Scotland generally see Walker and McGregor 1996.

30 GrN-22547: 1200±80. The date was calibrated to two standard deviations. Several other pieces of charcoal lying on the floor indicate later use of the hut in the eleventh or twelfth century (Walsh 1996).

31 Bones of a third person are more of an enigma and are discussed below.

32 See Edwards 1990, 123, for a more complete list, O'Kelly 1975 and 1958 for Carnsore and Church Island, and Waterman 1959 for White Island.

33 Thomas 1967, 138–40; RCAHMW 1976.

34 Sk. 192 was UB-4108: 1283±22, 1σ cal. AD 677–768, 2σ cal. AD 668–780.

35 O'Kelly 1956. Sheehan *et al.* (2001, 93–119) have proposed a Scandinavian or Hiberno-Scandinavian nature for the Beginish settlement.

36 UCLA-2873E: 315±45, 1σ cal. AD 1486–1642.

37 UB-3860: 1172±34, 2σ cal. AD 777–891.

38 See Taylor 1984, vol. 3, 761–2, for Anglo-Saxon examples of the use of foundations.

39 A. OxA-10133: 698±29 BP.

68.2% probability	95.4% probability
AD 1280 (57.2) 1305	AD 1260 (70.4%) AD 1310
AD 1370 (11.0%) 1380	AD f1350 (@5.0) AD 1390

calibrated using the OxCal program (v3.5) of Ramsey 1995 and atmospheric data from Stuiver *et al.* 1998b.

40 Charcoal in the refuse under the stones blocking the western doorway was UCLA-2873A: 725±30, 1σ cal. AD 1406–1437. Charcoal from F38D was UCLA-2873: 365±55, 1σ cal. AD 1447–1638; the sample had iron residue (McCormick, pers. comm., 1994).

41 A recent study (Ó Carragáin 1998) shows new interest in the topic, and a book on the excavation of four *leachta* on Inishmurray between 1997 and 2000 is being prepared by O'Sullivan and Ó Carragáin (forthcoming).

42 Radford also thought that there were two possible remains, one in the monastery of Birsay, Orkney (Radford 1935, 414), and one at Tintagel, Cornwall (Radford 1959, 18).

43 J. O'Sullivan (pers. comm., 2004) notes that the *leachta* at Inishmurray were constructed in a similar fashion.

44 Professor P. Ní Chatháin (pers. comm., 2002) agrees with Thomas on the origin of the word. Thomas also speculated that *leachta* may relate to altars used on the earliest Christian graves. N. Edwards (1990, 116) briefly notes that they 'may be associated with demarcation of special graves. However, they may also have been open-air altars, and their antiquity is in any case disputed, since they have frequently been renovated in modern times to serve as penitential stations.' Flanagan and Flanagan (1994, 107) note that the word means 'grave' but associate it with wedge tombs and other megalithic tombs.

45 Doubtless some of the confusion in names derives from their recording by outsiders, not all of whom spoke Irish, as well as a tendency to lump all of the stations in the cashel into one or two stations.

46 This is the station known as *Trathá-na-righ fhear*, or Trahanareer, by Wakeman (1893, 128–31). Heraughty (1982, 26) notes that O'Donovan had given it its present name in 1836.

47. O'Sullivan 2000a; 2000b; O'Sullivan and Ó Carragáin 2002; O'Sullivan *et al.* 2002.

48 Heraughty (1982, 14) believes that it was the cemetery for secular people during the active period of the monastery. For a more comphensive discussion of the Inishmurray excavations see O'Sullivan and Ó Carragáin (forthcoming).

49 Taylor 1984, vol. 3, 1066; Hariulphe 1894, 296–306; Lehmann 1965, 376–80; Aethelwold 1953, 31–3.

50 C. Thomas (1971, 143) lists five Kerry shrines, as he counts Caherbarnagh and Kilpecan, for which information he cites Henry. Henry, however, did not mention shrines there, and no gable shrine exists today at either site. At Caherbarnagh there is an enclosure similar to that of the other gable shrines, formed by vertically set stones around a raised mound, and it is possible that it originally demarcated an open-air shrine. Henry mentioned several slabs at Kilpecan that may have formed a gable shrine, but, if so, the shrine had been dismantled. Nevertheless, Marshall and Rourke noted in a field study in 1990 that two slabs of nearly identical size (1.0m by 1.2m) lie on the ground near the enclosure, one with a hole 0.09m in diameter. Their size makes them well suited to having formed the long side of a gable shrine. For another view see O'Sullivan and Sheehan 1996, 250, 263.

51 C. Thomas (1998, 89, 92) somewhat modified this view to see them not as shrines containing translated bones but as shrines erected over burials and that 'the ridged Irish gable-shrine over a burial must be very distantly linked to the continental ridged-lid stone sarcophagus in a church or externally in some *cella memoriae*.'

52 C. Thomas (1971, 72–3) also suggested that there was one at Ardwell Island, off the Kirkcudbright coast in north Britain.

53 Geary 1990; Lucas 1986; Doherty 1984.

54 P.J. Lynch (1902) recorded human bones, including two skulls, in Killoluaig. Today, fragments of bone remain, along with quantities of quartz pebbles and scallop shells (O'Sullivan and Sheehan 1996, 303). The original context and date of this material are uncertain.

55. Sk. 176, UB-4104: 1248±18, 1σ cal. AD 718–82, 2σ cal. AD 686–794. Sk. 188: UB-4107: 1290±22, 1σ cal. AD 675–762, 2σ cal. AD 666–777. Calibrated according to Stuiver and

Pearson 1986. Infant with Sk. 176: OxA-10132, 1308±33, 1σ cal. AD 665–720, 2σ cal. AD 660–780. Calibrated using the Oxcal computer program of Ramsey (1995, 425–30) and using atmospheric data from Stuiver *et al.* 1998b. Oxford accelerator was used because of its high correlation with Queen's University radiocarbon dates (G. F. McCormac, pers. comm., 1997).

56 See T. Ó Carragáin 2003, 143–4, for a more detailed discussion of the sites containing corner-post shrines; he also believes that gable shrines and corner-post shrines were equivalent, alternative forms of shrines.

57 UB-4106: 1508±45, 1σ cal. AD 762–974, 2σ cal. AD 665–1048. Calibrated according to new work done on the correlation of marine and land samples in Reimer *et al.* 2002.

58 See O'Brien 1992 for a discussion of the church's interest in encouraging burial in Christian cemeteries as opposed to the old pagan or familial cemeteries, which generally, but not always, led to burial near the church.

59 H. King (pers. comm., 2004). Fanning (1981, 80, 86) believed that a group of lintel graves at Reask, Co. Kerry, particularly graves 15 and 16, focused on the shrine. It is unfortunate that he was unable to date these graves, because the burial pattern, with the exception of 15 and 16, appears to be too scattered to be focused on the small shrine.

60 UB-4103: 1191±22, 1σ cal. AD 787–884, 2σ cal. AD 777–891.

61 Two of the 33 burials on Church Island associated with the wooden oratory were simple, stone-lined cists; the rest were earth-dug graves (O'Kelly 1958, app. 1). Fanning (1981, 79–84) believed that the cists at Reask dated from the fifth–seventh century. Most of the burials at Caherlehillan were simple, earth-dug shallow graves, but five or six were stone-lined graves in varying states of preservation; two were very well preserved, with lintels, stone sides and paved bases (J. Sheehan, pers. comm., 2004).

62 It was the bishop rather than St Ita who was worried about the supply of milk. For St Brendan see Plummer 1922, 2:44–7; for a less certain reference in Plummer to a king's son sent to Coemgen see the version on p. 159 of *Life of Coemgen*. For a third, more cryptic version of infant adoption see pp 167–8. For an excellent discussion and other examples see Ryan 1986, 207–11.

63 In the mid-twentieth century at Mashanaglass, Co. Cork, local workers referred to them as 'Holy Mary stones' (Fahey 1956). They are also found on gateposts in some parts of rural Ireland.

64 Hill (1997, 473) noted that white stones at Whithorn, though largely associated with graves, also turned up regularly in rubbish heaps. They had, he concluded, been 'collected and deposited somewhat promiscuously', although he still considered them burial talismans. White quartz was found in cairn burials of the seventh–twelfth centuries at St Ethernan's on the Isle of May (Yeoman and James 1999) and, with Class Bii amphorae, in burials at Llanslough, Wales (A. Thomas and N. Holbrook 1996).

65 A translation of this section of *Leabhar Breac* (fol. 54, fol. 44) is given by Petrie (1845, 346); O'Longan 1872-6; Anderson and Anderson 1961, iii:12. See also Marshall and Rourke 2000, 110–11.

66 The shells were examined at Queen's University to determine whether the holes were natural; see Murray and McCormick below, Chapter 4.

67 Fehring 1965, 15. Biddle (1990, vol. 2, 801–3) found a perforated shell and a pendant made to resemble a shell at Winchester and notes that these later medieval, perforated shells all probably related to the Compostela pilgrimage, were worn stitched to the

pilgrim's bag and later to his hat, and had double perforations. Clyne (1987–8; 1990) found a scallop on the left pelvis of a burial.

68 See Wheeler 1957, 48, for an excellent article on the origin and use of scallops in antiquity. On a possibility of transfer of symbolic meaning for Christians, Wheeler notes that 'snails emerging from their shells were used to symbolize the resurrection'.

69 Ousterhout 1990; Goodenough 1958–65, vol. 3, 95–105. Goodenough notes that the scallop symbolised to Jews hope for rebirth and commented that the motif dates back to prehistoric Egypt. Kraeling 1956, pl. 51.

70 See also the scallop done in mosaic on the floors of the sixth-century Beth Shean synagogue near the Sea of Galilee, where it is placed above the Holy of Holies or Torah Shrine, part of a structure inside another structure (Temple of Jerusalem?); also seen above a structure on a fifth-century Syrian–Palestinian limestone plaque meant to be hung as a charm against the Evil Eye (Weitzman 1979, 375–6, 388–9).

71 *Anacreonticon 20*, by Sophronius the Sophist, as quoted by Wilkinson (2002, 157).

72 Biddle 1999, chap. 2, figs 18 and 19; Barag and Wilkinson 1974, 179–84; Kötzsche-Breitenbruch 1984. Wilkinson (2002, 368) believes that the most accurate version of the *aedicule* is on these pewter flasks.

73 See Wilkinson 1972; Biddle 1999, 21–30, 83–4, on the original form of the *aedicule* and the presence of the conch as depicted by the (?)fifth-century model from Narbonne. For the existence of the *aedicule* after the destruction of much of the complex of Christ's Tomb in 1009 by Moslems see Biddle 1999, chap. 4, esp. p. 83. See also Barag and Wilkinson 1974, n. 43.

74 Wheeler 1957, 48; de Maillé 1971, fig. 106.

75 Two late western European exceptions are on the mid-eighth-century cenotaph of Theudechild, first abbess of Jouarre (de Maillé 1971), and on the ivory covers of a ninth-century Carolingian missal, where a bishop instructing a choir of monks is framed by a scallop (Lowrie 1947, pl. 128 and p. 85). In both of these high-status examples, it appears that the artists were looking back to late antique traditions. De Maillé (1971, 236–8) and *l'Archeologue* (Anon. 1997, 10) both believe that the shells on the cenotaph were made by a foreign sculptor and are symbolic of eternal life. The scallop was often associated with baptismal fonts and a scallop is found on the font (twelfth-century?) in St Audoen's in Dublin; many modern baptismal fonts on the Continent are also still shaped like scallop shells.

76 Van Herwaarden's comment (1980, 18–19), however, that the first mention of James's grave in Galicia occurs in the *Martyrologium of Usuard* in *c.* 865 may not be correct, since the *Martyrology of Oengus* (Stokes 1905, 171–2), which dates from around 830, also mentions the translation of his bones to Spain. These are all sources from outside of Spain.

77 Köster (1983; 1985, 88–99) studied several hundred shells mostly found in burials outside Spain. The earliest group, he believed, dated from the eleventh/twelfth century; however, he noted that these burials could only be approximately dated.

78 Whitehill *et al.* 1944, vol. 1, 273–4. On pilgrimage badges see Spencer 1968; Hohler 1957, 56–9. On the origin of the cult of St James see Van Herwaarden 1980. For an annotated bibliography on Santiago see Dunn and Davidson 1994. Hohler believed that the scallop badge at Santiago originated with the ambitious Diego Gelmírez, bishop and later archbishop of Santiago between 1100 and 1140, and was done in imitation of Jerusalem

pilgrimages, possibly because the author of the *Liber Sancti Jacobi* was the former chaplain of a Latin patriarch of Jerusalem.

79 Wixom 1993; Andreescu-Treadgold 1992.

80 For portable reliquaries see Roth 1966; Rollason 1989, 29–31; Ryan 1990, 129–34; 1991, 17; Caillet 1985, 227–8; Ó Floinn 1989–90; Bourke and Warner 1991; Harbison 1989, 37–50.

81 Variants on the tomb/house shrines theme are seen in twelfth-century France and Germany; for example, the late twelfth-century Limoges *chasse* (MMA 1987, 86) and the shrine of St Heribert in Köln-Deutz (Harbison 1999, 15).

82 Richarson (2002) believes that the small stone structures on top of many high crosses relate to Jerusalem, the Heavenly City.

83 Bede 1955, 212. *Est autem locus idem sepulchri tumba ligneas in modum domunculi facta coopertus* (Bede 1896, 212). On Fursey see Fursey 1902, 439.

84 On Early Christian use see Diehl 1925, vol. 1, 1783, 1800, 1833, 1834 among others. On Scotland see Foster 1998, 43; Hudson 1996, 87.

85 Dating derived from preliminary studies by Berger (1992). Until further studies are done, these dates remain tentative.

86 MacCormack 1990; Baratte and Metzger 1985, fig. 116; Coche de la Ferté 1958, 114, pl. 68.

87 For an excellent article on the close continuity of pagan antiquity's devotion to and belief in the active power inherent in both temple and tomb but transformed by Christians into the one structure, the church, see MacCormack 1990; Stambaugh 1988.

88 As in the reference to the tomb-shrines of St Brigid and Bishop Conláeth at Kildare, which may have been coffins. Edwards (1998, 228) suggests that they were of wood but notes that their size is unclear. The clearest evidence of a coffin in Ireland in the early medieval period is the stone shrine at Clones; however, it also resembles a 'church', in that it finishes with finials and a ridge pole.

89 Just as a sarcophagus was used on the baptistery walls in Dura Europos to represent Christ's tomb in *c.* AD 245, as they became popular with Christians, but in total contradiction to biblical information about Christ's tomb. Sarcophagi themselves often imitated secular architectural forms; see Turcan 1986; Goodenough 1958–65, vol. 4.

90 From Bede, as cited in O'Reilly 1994, 360. Farr (1994a, 137–46; 1994b, 447–9) adds important perspective to this argument; see also É. Ó Carragáin 1994, 433. Both Farr and O'Reilly (1994, 382–4) believe that the Temptation scene in the Book of Kells relates to Insular belief in the importance of the priestly and monastic community.

91 Neolithic settlements on the Orkney Islands used corbelled drystone structures that were probably not corbel-vaulted (Ritchie 1985).

92 Stout 1997; O'Flaherty 1986; Ó Ríordáin and Foy 1941; O'Kelly 1956; 1958; Mitchell 1989; Barry 1981; Fanning 1981. It is possible that some of these structures post-date the early medieval period, as do some of the Bray Head huts, but excavation shows that most of them belong to the early medieval period.

93 See Chapelot and Fossier 1985, chap. 6, for a discussion of some of the problems with attributing causation. Similar vernacular use of corbelled drystone dwellings is found in other parts of Europe, such as the oustalets of Gard and the cabordes of Doubs in France, the barracuns of southern Corsica, the barraques found in Valencia, Spain, the casedde of Apulia in Italy and the girnas of Malta. No relationship is evident between the construction of the Irish dwellings, or clocháns, and the ancient megalithic tombs or

the use (contemporaneous?) of this form in other parts of Europe. Complex interrelated hypotheses for their construction are unnecessary, because these simple, attractive structures provide 'a natural and obvious expedient for covering in spaces of moderate dimensions' (Leask 1955, vol. 1, 18).

94 Stones were also outwardly inclined on the corbelled chamber at Newgrange, and capstones were grooved to divert water; the interstices of the chamber roof were further caulked with soil and sea sand (O'Kelly 1982, 22). Keeping out wind and water is the major benefit of mortar and render (Kern *et al.* 1976). There is a natural tendency for rubble fill to slump, causing the walls to drift in any case, which the use of through-stones, blocks of stone that extend from face to face, prevents by connecting the walls. Other causes, of lesser concern for Irish sites, are vibration and alternate freezing and thawing (Heyman 1995, 85).

95 All site numbers taken from O'Sullivan and Sheehan 1996, unless otherwise stated.

96 There are others that are indeterminate, such as the sod-covered remains of the oratory at Shronahiree More (960). Fifteenth-century Papal Letters note that this was a vicarage (O'Sullivan and Sheehan 1996).

97 This is contrary to the evidence from domestic structures, some of which were roofed in organic materials, such as the domestic stone hut at Church Island and at Dunbeg (O'Kelly 1958; Barry 1981).

98 With the sole possible exception being the smaller structure at Labbamolaga (14438).

99 It is possible, although not certain, that the church excavated by Walsh *et al.* on the summit of Croagh Patrick, Co. Mayo, was a corbelled drystone structure (G. Walsh, pers. comm., 13/10/94) and there may be others.

100 There are exceptions, such as Kildreelig, where the window is in the southern wall; occasionally mortared masonry churches have two windows.

101 Finials were used on timber churches and were then translated into stone, as evidenced on St Macdara's church in County Galway. Perhaps the finial became a symbol denoting a church, and the finials on the drystone oratory were used in this manner rather than as an indication that the drystone oratory architecture developed from earlier wooden equivalents.

102 This internal rectilinear shape rises two-thirds of the height of the structure.

103 The drystone oratory on Inishglora, Co. Mayo, may also fall into this category. However, the ground level on the exterior is too high on three sides to establish at what height an offset(s) may occur. The entrance (west) wall is exposed and does not appear to have any offset. It may be no coincidence that it has a dedication to St Brendan. The oratory is reminiscent of the western Kerry structures, and the interior masonry is very similar in style to that of Templecashel. The craftsmanship and expertise involved in building this oratory may well have come from Kerry.

104 See Horn *et al.* 1990, 71–93.

105 Hennessy and MacCarthy 1887–1901, 177. See also Manning 2000, for a general summary; Manning also cites a reference in the annals to a stone church at Armagh, possibly as early as the late eighth century.

106 A solitary radiocarbon date of the charcoal fraction was obtained from the mortar of St Michael's, Phase 1, UCLA-2738D: 1225±25, 1σ cal. AD 688–777. Acceptance of this solitary date, however, requires further research, as it conflicts with the present stratigraphic evidence. See Berger 1992 for a complete list of radiocarbon dates of the

charcoal fraction in mortar.

107 This is in conformity with the allowances that Stout (1998, 85) makes for soil quality and altititude, however, as he found a similar pattern in one area of Offaly, where good soil was limited. Iveragh sites conform in several other ways to Stout's main thesis.

108 The smaller island of Beginish could never have supported more than a few families, and we suspect that the small drystone oratory here was used as a church serving this small community, with both the church and the community, in turn, serving the small monastery of Church Island. Unfortunately, chronological evidence to support this idea is lacking.

109 Indeed, sorting out the essential nature of the early medieval church has provoked much heated debate. For the best summary of old arguments as well as fresh thoughts on this complicated matter see Etchingham 1999.

110 Three dates for adults were obtained by the same laboratory, at Queen's University Belfast. The upper range of the fourth skeleton, F180, is somewhat later than the eighth century. Dates obtained by the Oxford Radiocarbon Accelerator Unit for the set of juvenile bones placed in one of the cists were also in the late seventh to late eighth century.

111 O'Brien (1992, 136) believed that the Irish church was encouraging burial in Christian graveyards by the late seventh century in order to attract patronage and that 'Burial near the bones of the saint became a substitute for burial near the bones of the ancestors'. For relics in Ireland, Doherty 1984 remains requisite.

112 See Augustine 1900. He nevertheless conceded that the prayers of the church and good deeds done in memory of their name would help.

113 For an excellent account of the more complex situation see Treffort 1996, 1-84.

114 Bieler 1963, 136; Connolly and Picard 1987, and Connolly and Picard to Brigid as discussed by Doherty (1984, 93-4).

115 Results of the excavation of the Anglo-Saxon seventh-eighth-century parish of Flixborough, near the Humber estuary and the Trent River in northern England, demonstrated that even a prosperous trading region with substantial domesticated resources vigorously exploited its wild ones. See Loveluck 2001, 78-130.

116 Evidence also exists at other ecclesiastical sites for the eating of meat. Sheehan and Moore (1981) found oyster shells and animal bones at Ballyallaban, Co. Clare; Lawlor's (1925) excavation of Nendrum revealed evidence of animal bones and shells; and bone was recovered during excavation at Kiltiernan, Co. Galway (McCarthy 1995, 192-7). Ervynck (1997b, 67-81) noted that monastic sites in Flanders contained faunal assemblages in all periods. See also discussion in O'Sullivan 2001, 33-53.

117 See Murray, Chapter 4 and Appendix 4. See also McCormick 1998a; 1998b, 49-51.

118 Rynne 1998a, 85. See also Rynne's remarks on the known adaptability of the productive Kerry cow (*ibid*., 14-17). Today, however, there are more sheep than cattle, and farmers are still moving out of the dairy business, according to the South Kerry Local Development Plan 2000-2006.

119 Mitchell (1989) disagreed. The six sites used by Monk *et al.* (1998) for archaeobotanical studies, including the Iveragh cashel, Loher, were all situated on brown podzols. Oats and barley were the primary cereal crops grown, with barley generally more dominant.

120 For a review of the question of the early medieval rising population see Ryan 2000; Rynne 2000, 203-4; 1998a, 87-192.

121 See Fuller 2002 for significant landscape changes due to anthropogenic activity around Mayo Abbey. Mitchell (1989, 13, 20–7) noted, in addition, that the hilly terrain of Valentia Island—which causes water to pool—the naturally acidic soils of sandstone, the high humidity and low evaporation rate of the climate, and human activity had contributed to the formation of peat here for thousands of years before the early medieval period and more recently.

122 Sorrels and Simmons 1992, 115, 116. They note that 'oat requires 300–600 grams extra water per gram of dry matter produced than other small grains', although too much water is detrimental (*ibid.*, 116–17).

123. Kelling and Fixen 1992, 168–73; see also Bentley's comments on nitrogen in Appendix 4.

Bibliography

Aethelwold 1953 *Regularis concordia: the monastic agreement of the monks and nuns of the English nation*, ed. and trans. T. Symons. London. Nelson.

Alexandre-Bidon, D. and Treffort, C. (eds) 1993 *À réveiller les morts: la mort au quotidien dans l'Occident médiéval*. Presses Universitaires de Lyon and Association des Amis des Bibliothèque de Lyon.

Anderson, A.O. and Anderson, M.O. (eds and trans) 1961 *Adomnán's Life of Columba*. London. Nelson. [Revised 1991, M.O. Anderson, Oxford; New York: Oxford University Press.]

Andreescu-Treadgold, I. 1992 The Early Byzantine reliquary discovered at Torcello. *Venezia Arti* **6**, 5–13.

Anon. 1997 *L'Archeologue.* 'Jouarre, le chef-d'oeuvre de la sculpture mérovingien'. *Archéologie Nouvelle* **29** (Avril–Mai 1997), 6–12. Paris. Editions Errance.

Atlas of Ireland 1979 Prepared under the direction of the Irish National Committee for Geography. Dublin. Royal Irish Academy.

Augustine 1900 *De fide et symbolo (et alia opera minora).* Recensuit I. Zycha. Corpus scriptorum ecclesiasticorum Latinorum, v. 41, sect. 5, part 3. Vindobonae. Johnson Reprint Corp., 1979.

Barag, D. and Wilkinson, J. 1974 The Monza–Bobbio flask and the Holy Sepulchre. *Levant* **6**, 179–87.

Baratte, F. and Metzger, C. 1985 *Catalogue des sarcophages en pierre d'époques romaine et paléochrétienne*. Paris. Réunion des Museés Nationaux et la Museé du Louvre.

Barber, J.W. 1981 Excavations on Iona, 1979. *Proceedings of the Society of Antiquaries of Scotland* **111**, 282–380.

Barry, T. 1981 Archaeological excavations at Dunbeg promontory fort, Co. Kerry. *Proceedings of the Royal Irish Academy* **81**C, 295–330.

Bede 1896 *Historia ecclesiastica gentis Anglorum* (2 vols), ed. C. Plummer. Oxford. Clarendon.

Bede 1955 *A history of the English church and people*, ed. and trans. L. Sherley-Price. Penguin. [Revised by R.E. Latham. London: Penguin, 1983.]

Beresford, M.W. and Hurst, J. (ed.) 1971 *Deserted medieval villages*. London. Lutterworth.

Berger, R. 1992 ^{14}C dating mortar in Ireland. *Radiocarbon* **34**, 880–9.

Biddle, M. 1986 Archaeology, architecture, and the cult of saints in Anglo-Saxon England. In L.A.S. Butler and R.K. Morris (eds), *The Anglo-Saxon church: papers on history and architectural archaeology in honour of Dr H.M. Taylor*. Council for British Archaeology Research Report 60. London.

Biddle, M. 1990 *Object and economy in medieval Winchester* (2 vols). Oxford. Clarendon.

Biddle, M. 1999 *The Tomb of Christ*. Stroud, Gloucestershire. Sutton Publishing.

Bieler, L. (ed.) 1963 *The Irish Penitentials*. Scriptores Latini Hiberniae 5. Dublin Institute for Advanced Studies.

Bieler, L. (ed.) 1979 *The Patrician texts in the Book of Armagh*. Scriptores Latini Hiberniae 10. Dublin Institute for Advanced Studies.

Binchy, D.A. 1938 Bretha Crólige. *Ériu* **12**, 1–77.

Binchy, D.A. 1955 Bretha Nemed. *Ériu* **17**, 4–6.

Bitel, L. 1990 *Isle of the saints: monastic settlement and Christian community in early Ireland*. Cork University Press.

Blindheim, M. 1984 A house-shaped Irish-Scots reliquary in Bologna, and its place amongst other reliquaries. *Acta Archaeologica* **55**, 1–54.

Bourke, C. and Warner, R. 1991 A seventh-century reliquary from Co. Armagh. *Archaeology Ireland* **5** (2), 16.

Bradley, J. 1985–6 Excavations at Moynagh Lough 1984, summary report. *Ríocht na Mídhe* **7** (4), 79–92.

Bradley, J. 1989 Moynagh Lough, Co. Meath. In S. Youngs (ed.), *'The Work of Angels'. Masterpieces of Celtic metalwork, 6th–9th centuries AD*, 178–9. London. British Museum.

Bradley, J. 1993 Moynagh Lough Crannog: an Insular workshop of the second quarter of the eighth century AD. In R.M. Spearman and J. Higgitt (eds), *The age of migrating ideas: early medieval art in northern Britain and Ireland. Proceedings of the Second International Conference on Insular Art held in the National Museums of Scotland in Edinburgh, 3–6 January 1991*, 74–81. Edinburgh and Stroud, Gloucestershire. National Museums of Scotland and Sutton Publishing.

Brinch-Madsen, H. 1984 Metalcasting: techniques, production and workshops. In M. Bencard (ed.), *Ribe excavations 1970–1976* (2 vols), vol. 1, 15–195. Erbjerg. Sydjysk Universitetsforlag.

Brown, P. 1982 *The cult of the saints, its rise and function in Latin Christianity*. Chicago. University of Chicago Press.

Buchanan, R.H. 1956–7 Thatch and thatching in north-east Ireland. *Gwerin* **1**, 123–42.

Caillet, J.-P. (ed.) 1985 *L'antiquité classique, le haut Moyen Âge et Byzance au Musée de Cluny*. Paris. Réunion des Musées Nationaux et Ministère de la Culture.

Carey, J. (ed.) 1998 *King of Mysteries: early Irish religious writings*. Dublin. Four Courts.

Chapelot, J. and Fossier, R. 1985 *The village and house in the Middle Ages*, trans. H. Cleere. London. Batsford.

Charles, F.W.B. 1981 Post-construction and the rafter roof. *Vernacular Architecture* **12**, 3–19.

Chase, C. (ed.) 1975 *Two Alcuin letter-books from the British Museum MS Cotton Vespasian A XIV*. Toronto Medieval Latin Texts 5. Center for Medieval Studies, University of Toronto/Pontifical Institute of Mediaeval Studies.

Clyne, M. 1987–8 Excavations at St Mary's Cathedral, Tuam, Co. Galway. *Journal of the Galway Archaeological and Historical Society* **41**, 90–103.

Clyne, M. 1990 A medieval pilgrim from Tuam to Santiago de Compostela. *Archaeology Ireland* **4** (3), 21–2.

Coche de la Ferté, É. 1958 *L'Antiquité chrétienne au Musée du Louvre*. Paris. Éditions de l'Oeil.

Cohen, C. 2002 *The fate of the mammoth: fossils, myth and history*. University of Chicago Press.

Coles, G. and Mills, C.M. 1998 Clinging on for grim life: an introduction to marginality as an archaeological issue. In G. Coles and C.M. Mills (eds), *Life on the edge: human settlement and marginality*, vii–xii. Symposia of the Association for Environmental Archaeology 13. Oxford. Oxbow.

Collins, A.E.P. 1955 Excavations at Lough Faughan Crannog, Co. Down, 1951–1952. *Ulster Journal of Archaeology* **18**, 45–82.

Colvin, H. 1991 *Architecture and the after-life*. New Haven, Connecticut. Yale University Press.

Comber, M. 2002 M.V. Duignan's excavations at the ringfort of Rathgurreen, Co. Galway, 1948–9. *Proceedings of the Royal Irish Academy* **102**C, 137–97.

Connolly, S. and Picard, J.-M. 1987 Cogitosus: Life of Saint Brigit. *Journal of the Royal Society of Antiquaries of Ireland* **117**, 5–27.

Craddock, P.T. 1989 Metalworking techniques. In S. Youngs (ed.), *'The Work of Angels'. Masterpieces of Celtic metalwork, 6th–9th centuries AD*, 170–213. London. British Museum.

Crawford, B.E. 1987 *Scandinavian Scotland*. Leicester University Press.

Crowe, C. 1982 A note on white quartz pebbles found in Early Christian contexts on the Isle of Man. *Proceedings of the Isle of Man Natural History and Antiquarian Society* **7**, 413–15.

Cuppage, J. (ed.) 1986 *Archaeological survey of the Dingle Peninsula*. Ballyferriter, Kerry. Oidhreacht Chorca Dhuibhne.

de Maillé, G.A. 1971 *Les crypts de Jouarre*. Paris. A. and J. Picard.

de Paor, L. 1955 A survey of Sceilg Mhichil. *Journal of the Royal Society of Antiquaries of Ireland* **85**, 147–87.

Dempsey, E. 1993 *The complete guide to Ireland's birds*. Dublin. Gill and Macmillan.

Diehl, E. (ed.) 1925 *Inscriptiones Latinae Christianae veteres* (3 vols). Berlin. Apud Weidmannos.

Dinneen, Rev. P. S. 1904 *An Irish–English dictionary, being a thesaurus of words, phrases and idioms of the modern Irish language with explanation in English.* Dublin. Irish Texts Society.

Doherty, C. 1984 The use of relics in early Ireland. In P. Ní Chatháin and M. Richter (eds), *Irland und Europa: die Kirche im Frühmittelalter*, 89–104. Stuttgart. Klett-Cotta.

Donaghy, C. 1997 Barrel padlocks and their keys. In M. Hurley, O. Scully and S. McCutcheon, *Late Viking Age and medieval Waterford excavations 1986–1992*, 530–6. Waterford. Waterford Corporation.

Doody, M. 2000 Bronze Age houses in Ireland. In A. Desmond, G. Johnson, M. McCarthy, J. Sheehan and E. Twohig (eds), *New agendas in Irish prehistory: papers in commemoration of Liz Anderson*, 135–60. Bray. Wordwell.

Dunlevy, M. 1988 A classification of early Irish combs. *Proceedings of the Royal Irish Academy* **88**C, 341–422.

Dunn, M. and Davidson, L.K. (eds) 1994 *The pilgrimage to Santiago de Compostela: a comprehensive, annotated bibliography*. Garland Medieval Bibliographies 18. New York.

Edwards, N. 1990 *The archaeology of early medieval Ireland*. London. Batsford.

Edwards, N. 1998 The Irish connection. In S. Foster (ed.), *The Saint Andrews sarcophagus: a Pictish masterpiece and its international connections*, 227–39. Dublin. Four Courts Press.

Egan, G. and Pritchard, F. (eds) 1991 *Dress accessories: medieval finds from excavations in London.* London. HMSO.

Ervynck, A. 1997a Possibilities and limitations of the use of archaeozoological data in biogeographical analysis: a review with examples from the Benelux region. *Belgian Journal of Zoology* **129** (1), 125–37.

Ervynck, A. 1997b Following the rule? Fish and meat consumption in monastic communities in Flanders. In G. de Boe and F. Verhaeghe (eds), *Environment and subsistence in medieval Europe. Papers of the 'Medieval Europe Brugge 1997' conference*, 67–81. Zellik. Instituut voor het Archeologisch Patrimonium.

Etchingham, C. 1999 *Church organisation in Ireland, AD 650–1000.* Maynooth. Laigin Publications.

Evans, E. 1957 *Irish folk ways*. London. Routledge and Kegan Paul.

Evans, E. 1969 Sod and turf houses in Ireland. In J.G. Jenkins (ed.), *Studies in folk life. Essays in honour of I.C. Peate*, 80–90. London. Routledge and Kegan Paul.

Fahey, E. 1956 A horizontal mill at Mashanaglass. *Journal of the Cork Historical and Archaeological Society* **59**, 13–57.

Fanning, T. 1981 Excavation of an Early Christian cemetery and settlement at Reask, Co. Kerry. *Proceedings of the Royal Irish Academy* **81**C, 67–172.

Fanning, T. 1994 *Viking Age ringed pins from Dublin*. Medieval Dublin Excavations 1962–81, Series B, vol. 4. Dublin. Royal Irish Academy.

Farr, C. 1994a History and mnemonic in Insular gospel book decoration. In C.

Bourke (ed.), *From the isles of the north: early medieval art in Ireland and Britain*, 137–46. Belfast. HMSO.

Farr, C. 1994b Textual structure, decoration and interpretive images in the Book of Kells. In F. O'Mahoney (ed.), *The Book of Kells. Proceedings of a conference at Trinity College, Dublin, 6–9 September 1992,* 394–7. Aldershot, Hampshire. Scholar.

Fehring, G.P. 1965 Die ausgrabungen in den Stadtkirche St Dionysius zum Neckar. Vorläuftegen Abschlussleicht. *Zeitschrift des Deutschen Vereins für Kunstwissenschaft* **19**, 1–34.

Ferguson, G. 1954 *Signs and symbols in Christian art.* Oxford University Press.

Findlay, W. M. 1956 *Oats: their cultivation and use from ancient times to the present day.* Edinburgh. University of Aberdeen.

Flanagan, D. and Flanagan, L. 1994 *Irish place names*. Dublin. Gill and Macmillan.

Foster, S. 1998 *The St Andrews sarcophagus: a Pictish masterpiece and its international connections*. Dublin. Four Courts.

Fox, H., Earl, B. and Shirley, J. 1910 Numismatic history of the reigns of Edward I, II and III. *British Numismatic Journal* **8**.

Fuller, J.L. 2002 Past vegetation and land-use dynamics in Mayo Abbey, central Mayo. *Archaeology Ireland* **16** (3), 20–3.

Fursey 1902 Vita S. Fursei. In B. Krusch (ed.), *Passiones vitaeque sanctorum aevi Merovingici et antiquiorum aliquot*, 423–9. Monumenta Germaniae Historica, Scriptroum Reurum Merovingicarum 5. Hannover and Leipzig. Impensis Bibliopolii Hahniani.

Gailey, A. 1984 *Rural houses of the north of Ireland*. Edinburgh. John Donald.

Gardiner, M.J. and Radford, T. 1980 *Soil associations of Ireland and their land use potential.* Dublin. National Soil Survey.

Gaskell Brown, C. and Harper, A.E.T. 1984 Excavations on Cathedral Hill, Armagh, 1968. *Ulster Journal of Archaeology* **47**, 109–61.

Geary, P.J. 1990 *Furta sacra: thefts of relics in the central Middle Ages* (rev. edn). Princeton University Press.

Gelling, N. 1962–3 Medieval shielings in the Isle of Man. *Medieval Archaeology* **6–7**, 156–72.

Goodall, I. 1981 The medieval blacksmith and his products. In D. Crossley (ed.), *Medieval industry*, 51–61. Council for British Archaeology Research Report 40. London.

Goodall, I. 1990 Locks and keys. In M. Biddle (ed.), *Objects and economy in medieval Winchester*, 1001–36. Oxford University Press.

Goodenough, E.R. 1958–65 *Jewish symbols in the Greco-Roman period* (10 vols). Bollingen Series 27. New York. Pantheon.

Gosling, P. (ed.) 1993 *Archaeological inventory of County Galway. Volume 1: West Galway (including Connemara and the Aran Islands).* Dublin. Stationery Office.

Gowen, M. 1993 Christchurch Place: stratigraphic report. Unpublished report submitted to the National Monuments Section of the Office of Public Works.

Graham, R. 2001 Devonian. In C.H. Holland (ed.), *The geology of Ireland*, chapter 5. Edinburgh. Dunedin Academic Press.

Gwynn, E.J. and Purton, W.J. 1912 The Monastery of Tallaght. *Proceedings of the Royal Irish Academy* **29**C, 115–80.

Hamlin, A. 1982 Early Irish stone carving: content and context. In S.M. Pearce (ed.), *The early church in western Britain and Ireland*, 283–96. British Archaeological Reports, British Series 102. Oxford.

Hamlin, A. 1984 The archaeology of the Irish church in the eighth century. *Peritia* **4**, 279–99.

Harbison, P. 1970 How old is Gallarus Oratory? A reappraisal of the role of Gallarus Oratory in early Irish architecture. *Medieval Archaeology* **14**, 34–59.

Harbison, P. 1982 Early Irish churches. In H. Löwe (ed.), *Die Iren und Europa im früheren Mittelalter* (2 vols), vol. 1, 618–29. Stuttgart. Klein-Cotta.

Harbison, P. 1984 The study of early Irish churches. In P. Ní Chatháin and M. Richter (eds), *Irland und Europa: die Kirche im Frühmittelalter*, 117–26. Stuttgart. Klein-Cotta.

Harbison, P. 1989 Early Irish reliquary-shrines in bronze and stone. *Würzburger Diözesan-Geschichtsblätter* **51**, 37–50.

Harbison, P. 1991 *Pilgrimage in Ireland: the monuments and the people*. London. Barrie and Jenkins.

Harbison, P. 1994 Early Irish pilgrim archaeology in the Dingle Peninsula. *World Archaeology* **26**, 90–103.

Harbison, P. 1999a The Clones sarcophagus—a unique Romanesque-style monument. *Archaeology Ireland* **13** (3), 12–16.

Harbison, P. 1999b *The golden age of Irish art: the medieval achievement 600–1200*. London. Thames and Hudson.

Hariulphe 1894 *Chronique de l'abbaye de Saint Riquier (Vième siècle–1104)*, ed. F. Lot. Paris.

Harry, R. and Morris, C.D. 1997 Excavations on the lower terrace, Site C, Tintagel Island, 1990–1994. *Antiquaries' Journal* **77**, 1–143.

Hayden, A. 1994 Coarha More, Valentia Island. In I. Bennett (ed.), *Excavations 1993: summary accounts of archaeological excavations in Ireland*, no. 120. Bray. Wordwell.

Hayden, A. 1997 Report on the excavations of early medieval buildings at Bray Head, Valentia Island, Co. Kerry, 1997 (97E278). Unpublished report.

Hayden, A. 1998 Bray Head (Valentia Island). In I. Bennett (ed.), *Excavations 1997: summary accounts of archaeological excavations in Ireland*, no. 231. Bray. Wordwell.

Hencken, H.O'N. 1950 Lagore Crannog: an Irish royal residence of the 7th to 10th centuries AD. *Proceedings of the Royal Irish Academy* **53**C, 1–247.

Hennessy, W.A. 1998 *Annals of Ulster: a chronicle of Irish affairs from AD 431 to AD 1540* (2nd edn), vol. 1. Dublin. Éamonn de Búrca.
Hennessy, W.M. and MacCarthy, B. (eds) 1887–1901 *Annála Uladh: Annals of Ulster* (4 vols). Dublin. HMSO.
Henry, F. 1945 Remains of the Early Christian period on Inishkea North, Co. Mayo. *Journal of the Royal Society of Antiquaries of Ireland* **75**, 127–55.
Henry, F. 1952 A wooden hut on Inishkea North, Co. Mayo. *Journal of the Royal Society of Antiquaries of Ireland* **82**, 163–78.
Henry, F. 1957 Early monasteries, beehive huts and dry-stone houses in the neighbourhood of Caherciveen and Waterville, Co. Kerry. *Proceedings of the Royal Irish Academy* **58**C, 45–166.
Heraughty, P. 1982 *Inishmurray: ancient monastic island.* Island Series 5. Dublin. O'Brien.
Herity, M. 1995 *Studies in the layout, buildings and art in stone of early Irish monasteries.* London. Pindar.
Herrmann-Mascard, N. 1975 *Les reliques des saints: formation coutumière d'un droit.* Société d'Histoire d'un Droit, Collecion d'Histoire Institutionelle et Sociale 6. Paris. Klincksieck.
Heyman, J. 1995 *The stone skeleton: structural engineering of masonry architecture.* Cambridge University Press.
Higgins, J. 1987 *The Early Christian cross slabs, pillar stones and related monuments of County Galway* (2 vols). British Archaeological Reports, International Series 375. Oxford.
Hill, P. 1997 *Whithorn and St Ninian: the excavation of a monastic town, 1984–1991.* Stroud, Gloucestershire. Sutton Publishing.
Hills, C. 1977 *Spong Hill, Norfolk.* East Anglian Archaeology Report 6. Norfolk Archaeological Unit.
Hodkinson, B. 1994 Cormac's Chapel, Cashel. In I. Bennett (ed.), *Excavations 1993: summary accounts of archaeological excavations in Ireland*, no. 203. Bray. Wordwell.
Hohler, C. 1957 The badge of St James. In I. Cox (ed.), *The scallop: studies of a shell and its influences on humankind,* 51–61. London. Shell Transport and Trading Co.
Horn, W., Marshall, J.W. and Rourke, G.D. 1990 *The forgotten hermitage of Skellig Michael.* Berkeley. University of California Press.
Hudson, B.T. 1996 *Prophecy of Berchán: Irish and Scottish high-kings of the early Middle Ages.* Westport, Connecticut. Greenwood.
Hughes, K. and Hamlin, A. 1977 *The modern traveller to the early Irish church.* London. SPCK.
Hunwicke, J.W. 2002 Kerry and Stowe revisited. *Proceedings of the Royal Irish Academy* **102**C, 1–19.
Hurley, V. 1982 The early church in the south-west of Ireland: settlement and

organization. In S.M. Pearce (ed.), *The early church in western Britain and Ireland*, 297-332. British Archaeological Reports, British Series 102. Oxford.

Hurley, M.F., Scully, O.M.B. and McCutcheon, S.W.J. 1997 *Late Viking Age and medieval Waterford excavations 1986–1992.* Waterford. Waterford Corporation.

Hutton, A.W. (ed.) 1970 *Arthur Young's Tour in Ireland (1776–1779)* (2 vols). London.

Ivens, R.J. 1989 Dunmisk Fort, Carrickmore, Co. Tyrone. Excavations 1984–1986. *Ulster Journal of Archaeology* **52**, 17–110.

Kelling, K.A. and Fixen, P.F. 1992 Soil and nutrient requirements for oat production. In H.G. Marshall and M.E. Sorrells (eds), *Oat science and technology*, 165–90. Madison, Wisconsin. American Society of Agronomy and Crop Science Society of America.

Kelly, F. 1988 *A guide to early Irish law.* Early Irish Law Series 3. Dublin Institute for Advanced Studies.

Kelly, F. 1998 *Early Irish farming.* Early Irish Law Series 4. Dublin Institute for Advanced Studies.

Kern, K., Magers, S. and Penfield, L. 1976 *The owner builders guide to stone masonry.* Oakhurst, California. Owner Builder Publications.

King, H.A. 1991 Clonmacnoise New Graveyard, Clonmacnoise. In I. Bennett (ed.), *Excavations 1990: summary accounts of archaeological excavations in Ireland*, no. 97. Bray. Wordwell.

King, H.A. 1992a Excavations at Clonmacnoise. *Archaeology Ireland* **6** (3), 12–14.

King, H.A. 1992b New Graveyard at Clonmacnoise. In I. Bennett (ed.), *Excavations 1991: summary accounts of archaeological excavations in Ireland*, no. 110. Bray. Wordwell.

King, H.A. 1993 New Graveyard, Clonmacnoise. In I. Bennett (ed.), *Excavations 1992: summary accounts of archaeological excavations in Ireland*, no. 157. Bray. Wordwell.

King, H.A. 1994a Clonmacnoise. In I. Bennett (ed.), *Excavations 1993: summary accounts of archaeological excavations in Ireland*, no. 196. Bray. Wordwell.

King, H.A. 1994b New Graveyard, Clonmacnoise. In I. Bennett (ed.), *Excavations 1993: summary accounts of archaeological excavations in Ireland*, no. 187. Bray. Wordwell.

King, H.A. 1996 New Graveyard, Clonmacnoise. In I. Bennett (ed.), *Excavations 1995: summary accounts of archaeological excavations in Ireland*, no. 240. Bray. Wordwell.

King, H.A. (ed.) 1998 *Clomacnoise Studies, volume 1: seminar papers 1994.* Dublin. Dúchas, The Heritage Service.

King, H.A. 2002 Church Island, Lough Key. In I. Bennett (ed.), *Excavations 2000: summary accounts of archaeological excavations in Ireland*, no. 860. Bray. Wordwell.

Köster, K. 1983 *Pilgerzeichen und Pilgermuscheln von mittel alterlichen*

Santiagostrassen: Saint-Léonard, Rocamadour, Saint-Gilles, Santiago de Compostela. Neumünster. Wacholtz.

Köster, K. 1985 Les coquilles et enseignes de pèlerinage de Saint Jacques de Compostelle et des routes de Saint-Jacques en Occident. In P. Caucci von Saucken (ed.), *Santiago de Compostela: 1000 ans de pèlerinage européen. Exposition Europalia 85 España at Centrum voor Kunst en Cultuur, Abbaye Saint-Pierre, Gand,* 80–99. Ghent and Brussels. Crédit Communal.

Kötzsche-Breitenbruch, L. 1984 Pilgerandenken aus dem heiligen Land. *Vivarium: Festschrift Theodor Klauser zum 90 Geburtstag. Jahrbuch für Antike und Christentum* **11**, 229–46. Münster, Westfalen. Aschendorff.

Kraeling, C.K. 1957 *The synagogue. Excavations at Dura-Europos: final report VIII, part I.* New Haven. Yale University Press.

Lacy, B. 1983 *Archaeological survey of County Donegal. A description of the field antiquities of the county from the Mesolithic period to the 17th century AD.* Lifford. Donegal County Council.

Laing, L.R. 1975 *The archaeology of late Celtic Britain and Ireland 400–1200 AD.* London. Methuen.

Lawlor, H. 1925 *The monastery of St Mochaoi of Nendrum*. Belfast Natural History and Philosophical Society.

Leask, H.G. 1955 *Irish churches and monastic buildings* (2 vols). Dundalk. Dundalgan.

LeBlant, E. (ed.) 1856–95 *Inscriptiones chrétiennes de la Gaule antérieures au VIII siècle* (2 vols). Paris.

Lehmann, E. 1965 Die anordnung der altäre in der karolingischen klosterkirche zu Centuala. In W. Braunfel and H. Schnitzler (eds), *Karolingische Kunst*, vol. 2, 373–84. Karl der Grosse: Lebenserk und Nachleben (3 vols). Düsseldorf. Schwann.

Loveluck, C. 2001 Wealth, waste and conspicuous consumption. Flixborough and its importance for mid and late Saxon settlement studies. In H. Hamerow and A. MacGregor (eds), *Image and power in the archaeology of early medieval Britain. Essays in honour of Rosemary Cramp.*Oxford. Oxbow Books.

Lowrie, W. 1947 *Art in the early church*. New York. Pantheon.

Lucas, A.T. 1986 The social role of relics and reliquaries in ancient Ireland. *Journal of the Royal Society of Antiquaries of Ireland* **116**, 5–37.

Lynch, J. (ed.) 1848–51 *Cambrensis eversus*, ed. and trans. with notes by M. Kelly (3 vols). Dublin. The Celtic Society.

Lynch, P.J. 1902 Some of the antiquities around St Finan's Bay, County Kerry. *Journal of the Royal Society of Antiquaries* **32**, 42–63.

McAfee, P. 1977 *Irish stone walls: history, building, conservation*. Dublin. O'Brien.

McCarthy, M. 1995 Archaeozoological studies and early medieval Munster. In M.A. Monk and J. Sheehan (eds), *Early medieval Munster: archaeology, history and society*, 59–64. Cork University Press.

MacCormack, S. 1990 Loca sancta: the organization of sacred topography in late antiquity. In R. Ousterhout (ed.), *The blessings of pilgrimage*, 7–40. Urbana. University of Illinois Press.

McCormick, F. 1993 Excavations at Iona. *Ulster Journal of Archaeology* **56**, 78–107.

McCormick, F. 1997 Iona: the archaeology of the early monastery. In C. Burke (ed.), *Studies in the cult of Saint Columba*, 45–68. Dublin. Four Courts.

McCormick, F. 1998a Calf slaughter as a response to marginality. In G. Coles and C.M. Mills (eds), *Life on the edge: human settlement and marginality*, 49–53. Symposia of the Association for Environmental Archaeology 13. Oxford. Oxbow.

McCormick, F. 1998b Seasonality in a Scottish diet. *Environmental Archaeology* **3**, 55–62.

McCormick, F. and Buckland, P.C. 1997 The vertebrate fauna. In K.J. Edwards and I.B.M. Ralston (eds), *Scotland after the Ice Age: an environmental and archaeological history, 8000 BC–AD 1000*, 63–103. Edinburgh University Press.

McDonald, F. and Doyle, P. 1997 *Ireland's earthen houses*. Dublin. A. and A. Farmar.

McErlean, T. and Crothers, N. 2001 Tidal power in the seventh and eighth centuries AD. *Archaeology Ireland* **15**, 10–14.

MacGregor, A. 1985 *Bone, antler, ivory and horn: the technology of skeletal material since the Roman period*. London. Croom Helm.

MacNeill, E. 1923 Ancient Irish law: the law of status or franchise. *Proceedings of the Royal Irish Academy* **36**C, 265–311.

McNeil, T.E. (forthcoming) Dunsilly rath, Co. Antrim.

Manning, C. 1987 Excavation at Moyne graveyard, Shrule, Co. Mayo. *Proceedings of the Royal Irish Academy* **87**C, 60–8.

Manning, C. 1997 The date of the round tower at Clonmacnoise. *Archaeology Ireland* **11**, 12–13.

Manning, C. 1998a Clonmacnoise Cathedral. In H.A. King (ed.), *Clonmacnoise Studies, volume 1: seminar papers 1994*, 57–86. Dublin. Dúchas, The Heritage Service.

Manning, C. 1998b The very earliest plan of Clonmacnoise. *Archaeology Ireland* **12**, 16–17.

Manning, C. 2000 References to church buildings in the annals. In A.P. Smyth (ed.), *Seanchas: studies in early and medieval Irish archaeology, history and literature in honour of Francis J. Byrne*, 37–52. Dublin. Four Courts.

Manning, C. and Moore, F. 1991 An ogham stone find from Clonmacnoise. *Archaeology Ireland* **5** (4), 10–11.

Marshall, J.W. 1989 The spread of mainland monasticism to the Atlantic Islands. Unpublished PhD thesis, University of California, Los Angeles.

Marshall, J.W. and Rourke, G.D. 2000 *High Island: an Irish monastery in the Atlantic*. Dublin. Town House and Country House.

Mays, S. 1993 Infanticide in Roman Britain. *Antiquity* **67** (257), 883–8.

Mellars, P.A. and Wilkinson, M.R. 1980 Fish otoliths as evidence of seasonality in prehistoric shell middens: the evidence from Oransay. *Proceedings of the Prehistoric Society* **46**, 19–44.

Metzger, C. 1981 *Les ampoules à eulogie du Musée du Louvre.* Paris. Éditions de la Réunion des Musées Nationaux.

Meyer, K. 1974 *The Vision of MacConglinne: a Middle-Irish wonder tale.* New York. Lemma.

Minter, G. 1964 Extracts from the archaeology reports of medieval research groups 1961. *Medieval Archaeology*, 283.

Mitchell, G.F. 1989 *Man and environment in Valencia Island.* Dublin. Royal Irish Academy.

MMA (Metropolitan Museum of Art) 1987 *Europe in the Middle Ages.* New York.

Mogey, J.M. 1940 Thatch. *Ulster Journal of Archaeology* **3**, 134–7.

Monk, M.A. 1991 The archaeobotanical evidence for field crop plants in early historic Ireland. In J.M. Rendrew (ed.), *New light on early farming*, 315–24. Edinburgh University Press.

Monk, M.A. and Sheehan, J. (eds) 1998 *Early medieval Munster: archaeology, history and society.* Cork University Press.

Monk, M.A., Tierney, J. and Hannon, M. 1998 Archaeobotanical studies and early medieval Munster. In M.A. Monk and J. Sheehan (eds), *Early medieval Munster: archaeology, history and society*, 65–75. Cork University Press.

Murray, E.V. 1999 Early evidence for coastal exploitation in Ireland. Unpublished PhD thesis, Queen's University, Belfast.

Murray, E.V., McCormick, F. and Plunkett, G. 2004 The food economies of Atlantic island monasteries: the documentary and archaeo-environmental evidence. *Environmental Archaeology* **9**, 179–88.

Mytum, H. 1992 *The origins of Early Christian Ireland.* London. Routledge.

Noble, R.R. 2000 Creel houses of the Scottish Highlands. In T.M. Owen (ed.), *From Corrib to Cultra: folklife essays in honour of Alan Gailey*, 82–94. Belfast. Institute of Irish Studies, Queen's University Belfast, in association with the Ulster Folk and Transport Museum.

North, J.J. 1975 *English hammered coinage* (2 vols). London. Spink.

O'Brien, E. 1992 Pagan and Christian burial in Ireland during the first millennium AD: continuity and change. In N. Edwards and A. Laine (eds), *The early church in Wales and the west*, 130–7. Oxford. Oxbow.

Ó Carragáin, É. 1994 'Traditio Evangeliorum' and 'Sustentatio': the relevance of liturgical ceremonies to the Book of Kells. In F. O'Mahony (ed.), *The Book of Kells: proceedings of a conference at Trinity College, Dublin, 6–9 September 1992*, 398–436. Aldershot, Hampshire. Scholar.

Ó Carragáin, T. 1998 Leachta as indicators of ritual practice: the evidence of Iveragh and Dingle. Unpublished MA dissertation, University of York.

Ó Carragáin, T. 2003 A landscape converted: archaeology and early church organisation on Iveragh and Dingle, Ireland. In M.O.H. Carver (ed.), *The cross goes north: processes of conversion in northern Europe, AD 300–1300*, 127–52. Woodbridge, Suffolk. York Medieval Press in association with Boydell and Brewer.

O'Connor, L. 1991 Irish Iron Age and Early Christian whetstones. *Journal of the Royal Society of Antiquaries of Ireland* **121**, 45–76.

O'Connor, R. 1841 Ordnance Survey Letters, Kerry (Killemlagh, 55). Dublin. Royal Irish Academy.

Ó Corráin, D. 1972 *Ireland before the Normans.* Gill History of Ireland 2. Dublin. Gill and Macmillan.

Ó Danachair, C. 1957 Material and methods in Irish traditional building. *Proceedings of the Royal Irish Academy* **87**C, 61–74.

Ó Dónaill, N. 1977 *Foclóir Gaeilge–Béarla*. Dublin. Stationery Office.

O'Donovan, J. 1836 'Sligo Letters'. Ordnance Survey Letters 36 (8 July 1836). (Unpublished manuscript in the Royal Irish Academy, Dublin.)

O'Flaherty, B. 1986 Loher cashel. In C. Cotter (ed.), *Excavations 1985: summary accounts of archaeological excavations in Ireland*, no. 34. Dublin. Wordwell.

O'Flaherty, R. 1846 *A choro-graphical description of west or h-iar Connaught*, ed. J. Hardiman. Dublin.

Ó Floinn, R. 1989 Catalogue entries in S. Youngs (ed.), *'The Work of Angels'. Masterpieces of Celtic metalwork, 6th–9th centuries AD*. London. British Museum.

Ó Floinn, R. 1989–90 A fragmentary house-shaped shrine from Clonard, Co. Meath. *Journal of Irish Archaeology* **5**, 49–55.

Ó Floinn, R. 1994 *Irish shrines and reliquaries of the Middle Ages*. Dublin. Town House and Country House and the National Museum of Ireland.

O'Keefe, T. 1994 Omey and the sands of time. *Archaeology Ireland* **28**, 14–17.

O'Keefe, T. 1998 Architectural traditions of the early medieval church in Munster. In M.A. Monk and J. Sheehan (eds), *Early medieval Munster: archaeology, history and society*, 112–24. Cork University Press.

O'Kelly, M.J. 1956 An island settlement at Beginish, Co. Kerry. *Proceedings of the Royal Irish Academy* **57**C, 159–94.

O'Kelly, M.J. 1958 Church Island, near Valencia, Co. Kerry. *Proceedings of the Royal Irish Academy* **59**C, 57–136.

O'Kelly, M.J. 1975 *Archaeological survey and excavation of St Vogue's Church, enclosure and other monuments at Carnsore, Co. Wexford.* Dublin. Electricity Supply Board.

O'Kelly, M.J. 1982 *Newgrange: archaeology, art and legend*. London. Thames and Hudson.

Oliver, P. (ed.) 1997 *Encyclopedia of vernacular architecture of the world* (3 vols). Cambridge University Press.

O'Longan, J. (ed.) 1872-6 *Leabhar Breac/The Speckled Book (otherwise styled Leabhar Mór Dúna Doighre)*. Dublin. Royal Irish Academy.

O'Meadhra, U. 1979 *Early Christian, Viking and Romanesque art: motif-pieces from Ireland* (2 vols). Stockholm. Almqvist and Wiksell.

O'Meadhra, U. 1987 Irish, Insular and Scandinavian elements in the motif-pieces from Ireland. In M. Ryan (ed.), *Ireland and Insular art, AD 500–1200*, 159–65. Dublin. Royal Irish Academy.

O'Reilly, J. 1994 Exegesis and the Book of Kells: the Lucan Genealogy. In F. O'Mahony (ed.), *The Book of Kells: proceedings of a conference at Trinity College Dublin, 6–9 September 1992*, 344–97. Aldershot, Hampshire. Scholar.

Ó Ríordáin, A.B. and Rynne, E. 1961 A settlement in the sandhills at Dooey, Co. Donegal. *Journal of the Royal Society of Antiquaries of Ireland* **91**, 58–64.

Ó Ríordáin, S.P. 1942 The excavation of a large earthern ringfort at Garranes, Co. Cork. *Proceedings of the Royal Irish Academy* **47**C, 17–150.

Ó Ríordáin, S.P. and Foy, J.B. 1941 The excavations of Leacanabuaile stone fort near Caherciveen, Co. Kerry. *Journal of the Cork Archaeological and Historical Society* **46**, 85–99.

O'Sullivan, A. and Sheehan, J. 1992 *Fionnán* enclosures: aspects of traditional land use in south Kerry. *Journal of the Kerry Archaeological and Historical Society* **25**, 5–19.

O'Sullivan, A. and Sheehan, J. 1996 *The Iveragh Peninsula: an archaeological survey of south Kerry*. Cork University Press.

O'Sullivan, D. 2001 Space, silence and shortages on Lindisfarne. The archaeology of asceticism. In F. O'Mahoney (ed.), *Image and power in the archaeology of early medieval Britain. Essays in honour of Rosemary Cramp*, 33–52. Oxford. Oxbow Books.

O'Sullivan, J. 2000a Laghta Patrick, Inishmurray. In I. Bennett (ed.), *Excavations 1999: summary accounts of archaeological excavations in Ireland*, no. 792. Bray. Wordwell.

O'Sullivan, J. 2000b Relickoran, Inishmurray. In I. Bennett (ed.), *Excavations 1999: summary accounts of archaeological excavations in Ireland*, no. 793. Bray. Wordwell.

O'Sullivan, J. and James, H. 1997 *Excavation of an early medieval altar at Trahaun O Riain, Inishmurray, Co. Sligo*. Database of Irish Excavation Reports, no. 468. Bray. Wordwell.

O'Sullivan, J. and Ó Carragáin, T. 2002 Ollamurry, Inishmurray. In I. Bennett (ed.), *Excavations 2000: summary accounts of archaeological excavations in Ireland*, no. 887. Bray. Wordwell.

O'Sullivan, J. and Ó Carragáin, T. (forthcoming) An early ecclesiastical landscape on Inishmurray, Co. Sligo. Vol. 1: survey and excavations 1997–2000.

O'Sullivan, J., Sikora, M. and Lynch, L. 2002 Relickoran, Inishmurray. In I. Bennett (ed.), *Excavations 2000: summary accounts of archaeological excavations in Ireland*, no. 888. Bray. Wordwell.

Ousterhout, R. 1990a Loca sancta souvenirs: sealing the pilgrim's experience. In R.

Ousterhout (ed.), *The blessings of pilgrimage*, 108–24. Urbana. University of Illinois Press.

Ousterhout, R. 1990b The Temple, the Sepulcher and the Martyrium of the Savior. *Gesta* **29**, 45–53.

Petrie, G. 1845 *The ecclesiastical architecture of Ireland* (2 vols). Dublin.

Plummer, C. (ed.) 1922 [reprinted 1997] *Bethada Náem nÉrenn. Lives of Irish Saints* (2 vols). Oxford. Clarendon Press.

Pochin-Mould, D. 1978 *Valentia: portrait of an island*. Dublin. Blackwater.

Power, D., Lane, S., Byrne, E., Egan, U., Sleeman, M., Cotter, E. and Monk, J. (comps) 2000 *Archaeological inventory of County Cork. Volume IV: north Cork*. Dublin. Stationery Office.

Power, P. (ed.) 1914 *Life of St Declan of Ardmore and Life of St Mochuda of Lismore*. London. Irish Texts Society 20.

Radford, C.A.R. 1935 Tintagel: the castle and Celtic monastery. Interim report. *Antiquaries' Journal* **15**, 401–19.

Radford, C.A.R. 1959 *The Early Christian and Norse settlements at Birsay, Orkney*. Edinburgh. HMSO.

Ramsey, C.B. 1995 Proceedings of the 15th international ^{14}C conference. *Radiocarbon* **37**, 425–30.

RCAHMW (Royal Commission on the Ancient and Historical Monuments of Wales) 1976 *Glamorgan. Vol. 1, part III: the Early Christian period*. Cardiff. HMSO.

Reeves-Smyth, T. 1999 *Irish gardens and gardening before Cromwell*. Barryscourt Lectures 4. Carrigtowhill, Co. Cork. Barryscourt Trust.

Reimer, P.J., McCormac, F.G., Moore, J., McCormick, F. and Murray, E.V. 2002 Marine radiocarbon reservoir corrections for the mid- to late Holocene in the eastern subpolar North Atlantic. *Holocene* **12**, 129–35.

Reynolds, N. 1978 Dark Age timber halls and the background to excavation at Balbridie. *Scottish Archaeological Forum* **10**, 40–60.

Richards, J.D. 1991 *Viking Age England*. London. Batsford.

Richarson, H. 2002 Biblical imagery and the heavenly Jerusalem in the Book of Armagh and the Book of Kells. In P. Ní Chatháin and M. Richter (eds), *Ireland and Europe in the early Middle Ages: texts and transmission*, 205–14. Dublin. Four Courts Press.

Ritchie, A. 1971–2 Painted pebbles in early Scotland. *Proceedings of the Society of Antiquaries of Scotland* **104**, 297–301.

Ritchie, A. 1985 The first settlers. In C. Renfrew (ed.), *The prehistory of Orkney*, ch. 3. Edinburgh University Press.

Rollason, D.W. 1989 *Saints and relics in Anglo-Saxon England*. Oxford. Blackwell.

Roth, H. 1966 *Kunst der Völkerwandeungzeit*. Propyläen Kunstgeschichte 4. Berlin. Propyläen Verlag.

Ryan, J. 1986 *Irish monasticism. Origins and early development*. Dublin. Irish Academic Press. [Reprinted 1991.]

Ryan, M. 1989 Church metalwork in the eighth and ninth centuries. In S. Youngs (ed.), *'The Work of Angels'. Masterpieces of Celtic metalwork, 6th–9th centuries AD*, 125–240. London. British Museum.

Ryan, M. 1991 Decorated Irish metalwork in Bobbio, Italy. *Archaeology Ireland* **16**, 17.

Ryan, M. 2000 Furrows and browse: some archaeological thoughts on agriculture and population in early medieval Ireland. In A.P. Smyth (ed.), *Seanchas: studies in early and medieval Irish archaeology, history and literature in honour of Francis J. Byrne*, 30–6. Dublin. Four Courts.

Rynne, C. 1998a *At the sign of the cow. The Cork butter market: 1770–1924*. Cork. Collins.

Rynne, C. 1998b The craft of the millwright. In M.A. Monk and J. Sheehan (eds), *Early medieval Munster: archaeology, history and society*, 87–101. Cork University Press.

Rynne, C. 2000 The early medieval monastic watermill. In J.W. Marshall and G.D. Rourke, *High Island. An Irish monastery in the Atlantic*, 185–214. Dublin. Town House and Country House.

Sexton, R. 1998 Porridges, gruels and breads: the cereal foodstuffs of early medieval Ireland. In M.A. Monk and J. Sheehan (eds), *Early medieval Munster: archaeology, history and society*, 76–86. Cork University Press.

Sharpe, R. (ed.) 1995 *Adomnán of Iona: Life of St Columba*. London. Penguin.

Sheehan, J. 1990 The excavation of a *fulacht fiadh* at Coarhamore, Valentia Island, Co. Kerry. In V. Buckley (ed.), *Burnt offerings: international contributions to burnt mound archaeology*, 27–37. Bray. Wordwell.

Sheehan, J. 1994 Caherlehillan. In I. Bennett (ed.), *Excavations 1993: summary accounts of archaeological excavations in Ireland*, no. 118. Bray. Wordwell.

Sheehan, J. and Moore, F. 1981 An unpublished ecclesiastical enclosure at Ballyallbaban, Co. Clare. *North Munster Antiquarian Journal* **23**, 5–8.

Sheehan, J., Stummann Hansen, S. and Ó Corráin, D. 2001 A Viking Age maritime haven: a reassessment of the island settlement at Beginish, Co. Kerry. *Journal of Irish Archaeology* **10**, 93–119.

Smith, C. 1756 *The ancient and present state of the county of Kerry*. Dublin.

Sorrels, M.E. and Simons, S.R. 1992 Influence of environment on the development and adaptation of oat. In H.G. Marshall and M.E. Sorrells (eds), *Oat science and technology*, chap. 5. Madison, Wisconsin. American Society of Agronomy and Crop Science Society of America.

South Kerry Development Plan, 2000–2006. General Agriculture Review. Online.

Spencer, B.W. 1968 Medieval pilgrim badges. In G.G.N. Renaud (ed.), *Rotterdam papers: a contribution to medieval archaeology*, 137–47. Rotterdam. Coördinatie Commissie van Advies Inzake Archeologisch Onderzoek Binnen het Ressort Rotterdam.

Stambaugh, J.E. 1988 *The ancient Roman city*. Baltimore. Johns Hopkins University Press.

Stokes, W. (ed. and trans.) 1890 *Lives of the saints from the Book of Lismore*. Anecdota Oxoniensia, Mediaeval and Modern Series 5. Oxford.

Stokes, W. (ed.) 1905 *Félire Óengusso Céli Dé: The Martyrology of Oengus the Culdee*. Henry Bradshaw Society 29. London.

Stokes, W. and Strachan, J. (eds and trans) 1901–3 *Thesaurus Palaeohibernicus: a collection of Old-Irish glosses, scholia, prose and verse* (2 vols). Oxford University Press.

Stout, M. 1997 *The Irish ringfort*. Irish Settlement Studies 5. Dublin. Four Courts, in association with the Group for the Study of Irish Historic Settlement.

Stout, M. 1998 Early Christian settlement, society and economy in Offaly. In W. Nolan and T. O'Neill (eds), *Offaly: history and society. Interdisciplinary essays on the history of an Irish county*, 29–92. Dublin. Geography Publications.

Stuiver, M. and Pearson, G.W. 1986 High-precision Decadal calibration of the radiocarbon time scale, AD 1950–500 BC. *Radiocarbon* **28**, 980–1021.

Stuiver, M.P., Reimer, J. and Braziunas, T.J. 1988a High-precision radiocarbon age calibration for terrestrial and marine samples. *Radiocarbon* **40**, 1127–51.

Stuiver, M. *et al.* 1998b 'Intercal 98': radiocarbon age calibration 000–24,000 BP. *Radiocarbon* **40**, 1041–983.

Swan, L. 1983 Enclosed ecclesiastical sites and their relevance to settlement patterns of the first millennium AD. In T. Reeves-Smyth and F. Hamond (eds), *Landscape archaeology in Ireland*, 269–95. British Archaeological Reports, British Series 116. Oxford.

Taylor, H.M. 1965–78 *Anglo-Saxon architecture* (3 vols). Cambridge University Press.

Thomas, A. and Holbrook, N. 1996 Llanslough. *Current Archaeology* **146**, 73–7.

Thomas, C. 1967 An Early Christian cemetery and chapel on Ardwall Isle, Kirkcudbright. *Medieval Archaeology* **11**, 127–88.

Thomas, C. 1971 *The Early Christian archaeology of north Britain*. London. Oxford University Press.

Thomas, C. 1998 Form and function. In S.M. Foster (ed.), *The St Andrews sarcophagus: a Pictish masterpiece and its international connections*, 84–96. Dublin. Four Courts.

Thomas, C. and Fowler, P.J. 1985 Tintagel: a new survey of the island. In *Annual Review of the Royal Commission on the Historical Monuments of England*. London. Royal Commission on the Historical Monuments of England.

Treffort, C. 1996 *L'église Carolingienne et la mort: Christianisme, rites funéraires et pratiques commémoratives*. Collection d'Histoire et d'Archéologie Médiévales 3. Lyon. Presses Universitaires de Lyon and Centre Interuniversitaire d'Histoire et d'Archéologie Médiévales.

Turcan, R. 1986 *Les sarcophages romains à représentations dionysiaques: essai de chronologie et d'histoire religieuse*. BEFAR (Bibliothèque des Écoles Françaises d'Athènes et de Rome) fac. 210. Paris. De Boccard.

Van Dam, R. 1993 *Saints and their miracles in late antique Gaul.* Princeton University Press.

van der Veen, M. 1992 *Crop husbandry regimes: an archaeobotanical study of farming in northern England, 1000 BC–AD 500.* Sheffield Archaeological Monographs 3. Sheffield. Collies.

Van Herwaarden, J. 1980 The origins of the cult of St James of Compostela. *Journal of Medieval History* **6**, 1–36.

Waddell, J. 1976 Kilcholan: an early ecclesiastical site on Inishmore, Aran. *Journal of the Galway Archaeological and Historical Society* **33**, 5–27.

Waddell, J. 1994 The archaeology of the Aran Islands. In J. Waddell, J. W. O'Connell and A. Korff (eds), *The Book of Aran,* 75–135. Newtownlynch, Kinvara, Co. Galway. Tír Eolas.

Waddell, J. and Clyne, M. 1995 M.V. Duignan's excavations at Kiltiernan, Co. Galway, 1950–1953. *Journal of the Galway Archaeological and Historical Society* **47**, 149–203.

Wade-Evans, A.W. 1944 *Vitae sanctorum Britanniae et genealogiae.* Cardiff. University of Wales Press.

Wakeman, W.F. 1893 *A survey of the antiquarian remains on the island of Inishmurray.* London.

Walker, B. and McGregor, C. 1996 *Earth structures and construction in Scotland: a guide to the recognition and conservation of earth technology in Scottish buildings.* Edinburgh. Historic Scotland.

Wallace, P.F. 1982a Carpentry in Ireland AD 900–1300: the Wood Quay evidence. In S. McGrail (ed.), *Woodworking techniques before AD 1500,* 263–99. British Archaeological Reports, International Series 129. Oxford.

Wallace, P.F. 1982b Irish Early Christian 'wooden' oratories—a suggestion. *North Munster Antiquarian Journal* **24**, 19–28.

Wallace, P.F. 1992 *The Viking Age buildings of Dublin.* Medieval Dublin Excavations 1962–81, Series A, vol. 1. Dublin. Royal Irish Academy.

Wallace, P.F. 1998 The use of iron in Viking Dublin. In M. Ryan (ed.), *Irish antiquities: essays in memory of Joseph Raftery,* 210–22. Bray. Wordwell.

Wallace, P.F., Ó Floinn, R. and Butler, V. 1988 *Dublin 1000: discovery and excavation in Dublin, 1842–1981.* Dublin. National Museum of Ireland.

Walsh, C. 1996 Bray, Valentia Island. In I. Bennett (ed.), *Excavations 1995: summary accounts of archaeological excavations in Ireland,* no. 132. Bray. Wordwell.

Waterman, D.M. 1956 The excavation of a house and souterrain at White Fort, Drumaroad, Co. Down. *Ulster Journal of Archaeology* **19**, 73–86.

Waterman, D.M. 1959 White Island church—note on a recent excavation. *Ulster Journal of Archaeology* **22**, 65–6.

Weitzmann, K. 1977 *Late antique and Early Christian book illumination.* New York. Braziller.

Weitzmann, K. (ed.) 1979 *Age of spirituality: later antique and Early Christian art, third to second century*. New York Metropolitan Museum and Princeton University Press.

Westropp, T.J. 1901 Slane. *Journal of the Royal Society of Antiquaries of Ireland* **31**, 405.

Wheeler, M. 1957 A symbol in ancient time. In I. Cox (ed.), *The scallop: studies of a shell and its influences on humankind*, 35–48. London. Shell Transport and Trading Co.

Whitehill, W.M., Prado, S. and García, J.C. 1944 *Liber Sancti Jacobi. Codex Calixtinus* (3 vols). Santiago. CSIC (Consejo Superior de Investigaciones Cientificas) Instituto Padre Sarmiento de Estudios Gallego.

Wilde, W.R. 1870–1 Mémoir of Gabriel Beranger and his labours in the cause of Irish art, literature, and antiquities from 1760–1780. *Journal of the Royal Society of Antiquaries of Ireland* **1,** 32–64, 121–52.

Wilkinson, J. 1972 The tomb of Christ: an outline of its structural history. *Levant* **4**, 83–97.

Wilkinson, J. 2002 *Jerusalem pilgrims before the Crusades* (rev. edn). Warminster. Aris and Phillips.

Williams, J. 1979 *St Peter's, Northampton: excavations 1973–1976*. Archaeological Monograph 2. Northampton Development Corporation.

Wixom, W.P. (ed.) 1999 *Mirror of the medieval world*. New York. Metropolitan Museum of Art.

Yeoman, P. and James, H. 1999 The Isle of May: St Ethernan's revisited. *Current Archaeology* **161**, 192–7.

Youngs, S. (ed.) 1989 *'The Work of Angels'. Masterpieces of Celtic metalwork, 6th–9th centuries AD*. London. British Museum.

A note on specialist reports

The following specialist reports are available on our website at: www.wordwellbooks.com\ftp\illaunloughan.

They may also be obtained in pdf format on CD by contacting Wordwell Ltd at +353-1-2765221, email: illaunloughan@wordwellbooks.com, or by writing to: Sales, Wordwell Ltd, PO Box 69, Bray, Co. Wicklow, Ireland.

Appendix 1
1987 survey
G.D. Rourke and J.W. Marshall

Appendix 2
Clay-mould fragment, Illaunloughan, Co. Kerry
Rose Cleary

Appendix 3
Report on the genetic analysis of skeletal specimens from Illaunloughan, Co. Kerry
Martin Evison

Appendix 4
The environmental archaeology of Illaunloughan, Co. Kerry
Mammal bone by Emily Murray
Mammal palaeopathology by Eileen Murphy
Bird bone by Tanya O'Sullivan
Fish bone by Sheila Hamilton-Dyer
Marine molluscs by Catherine McLoughlin and Emily Murray
Archaeobotanical remains by Brian Bentley, Gill M. Plunkett and Brenda Collins
Wood identification: charcoal by Ellen O'Carroll
Wood identification: coffins by Mary Deevy and Aidan O'Sullivan
The environmental archaeology: discussion by Emily Murray

Appendix 5
Skeletal report
Laureen Buckley

Appendix 6
Master radiocarbon date list